The psychology of
bulimia nervosa

The psychology of bulimia nervosa: a cognitive perspective

Myra Cooper, DPhil.

OXFORD

UNIVERSITY PRESS

Great Clarendon Street, Oxford OX2 6DP

Oxford University Press is a department of the University of Oxford.
It furthers the University's objective of excellence in research, scholarship,
and education by publishing worldwide in

Oxford New York

Auckland Bangkok Buenos Aires Cape Town Chennai
Dar es Salaam Delhi Hong Kong Istanbul Karachi Kolkata
Kuala Lumpur Madrid Melbourne Mexico City Mumbai Nairobi
Sao Paulo Shanghai Taipei Tokyo Toronto

Oxford is a registered trade mark of Oxford University Press
in the UK and in certain other countries

Published in the United States
by Oxford University Press Inc., New York

© Oxford University Press 2003

The moral rights of the author have been asserted

Database right Oxford University Press (maker)

First published 2003

A catalogue record for this title is available from the British Library

Library of Congress Cataloging in Publication Data

(Data available)

ISBN 0 19 263265 5

10 9 8 7 6 5 4 3 2 1

Typeset by Cepha Imaging Private Ltd
Printed in Great Britain
on acid-free paper by
T. J. International Ltd, Padstow

Acknowledgements

I would particularly like to thank Gillian Todd and Hannah Turner for reading and providing detailed feedback on the draft manuscript, and Gillian for her friendship and the many long conversations that we have had in the past three years, and that have contributed greatly to the finished manuscript.

My friends and colleagues on the Oxford Doctoral Course in Clinical Psychology at the Isis Education Centre in Oxford also helped enormously, in many ways, throughout the writing of this book. I suspect they are unaware of just how helpful they have been.

And, as always, I had exceptionally generous amounts of help from Freddie, Humphrey, Oliver, and Bertha.

Contents

Chapter 1

Definition and diagnosis

Bulimia nervosa

Bulimia nervosa (BN) is a distressing and disabling disorder. It consists of recurrent episodes of binge-eating, followed by inappropriate compensatory behaviour (American Psychiatric Association 1994). In the binge episodes, exceptionally large amounts of food are eaten, and a sense of loss of control is experienced, e.g. the individual feels unable to stop eating even if she[1] wanted to.

Compensatory behaviour may include self-induced vomiting, fasting, strict dieting, excessive exercise, or inappropriate use of laxatives and diuretics. These 'compensatory' behaviours aim to stop or prevent weight gain. Great concern and preoccupation with body weight and shape is also usually present. This may involve feeling fat, obsessive weighing or rigid calorie counting. The disorder has many features in common with anorexia nervosa (AN). However, unlike those with AN, those with BN always have a normal or above normal body weight.

Overview of the book

This book will review the major psychological features of bulimia nervosa. It will aim to update the reader on various topics, including key features, associated problems, the relevant psychological theories, and different treatment approaches. The content will be wide-ranging but, reflecting growing interest in cognition in the disorder, there will be a special focus on cognitive factors. Where appropriate, it will also draw on research and theory in non-clinical groups.

A note on related eating disorders

This book focuses primarily on bulimia nervosa. However, as will be seen later, there is some evidence that there are many cases (probably many more than was previously thought) that do not meet full criteria for the disorder, but who have some of its key behavioural features. Many of these would probably fulfill criteria for Eating Disorder Not Otherwise Specified (EDNOS). To date, there has been relatively little research into this group. The clinical impression is that they are often very similar to those who meet full criteria, not only in behaviour, but also in characteristic cognitions. Given the lack

---

[1] The female pronoun will be used throughout, because the majority of patients with BN are female.

Table 1.1 Summary of plan for Chapter 1

The history of bulimia nervosa
Diagnosis in bulimia nervosa
Related eating (and weight/shape) disorders
Other related disorders

of relevant research at present, a cautious approach is in order when drawing parallels between the groups, and in extending cognitive models to this EDNOS subgroup. Nevertheless, it seems very likely that much of the material presented here may well be relevant to this group, as well as to those with a full diagnosis.

Overview of the chapter

The first part of this chapter will provide a brief introduction to the historical background. This will include the emergence of the syndrome bulimia nervosa and its present day identification. The second part will summarize the history of the changing diagnostic criteria. Information on the current diagnostic criteria will also be presented. In the third part, related eating (and other) disorders, and their relationship to BN, will be considered. The plan for the chapter is summarized in Table 1.1.

The history of bulimia nervosa

Historical knowledge helps us to understand how disorders are influenced by social, economic and cultural forces, i.e. how they are 'socially constructed' (Berrios & Porter 1995). This includes the way in which they are affected by the development of medical knowledge and psychological theories (Berrios & Porter 1995). Historical data is likely to be particularly relevant to bulimia nervosa, where societal attitudes to weight and shape, and the development of cognitive theories, have played an important role in shaping the modern day concept (and diagnosis).[2]

Russell (1997) cautions that it is important to avoid jumping to the conclusion that ancient and early accounts correspond directly to modern bulimia nervosa.[3] Nevertheless (as we shall see below), links do seem to exist, although these may be complex, and (at times) unexpected.

---

[2] Naïve historians often look for an historical invariant, when attempting to understand a psychiatric diagnosis. But, as Berrios & Porter (1995) point out, even biological markers evolve. The clear role of social and cultural factors in bulimia nervosa make the chances of finding such a marker—biological or psychological—small.

[3] Rather curiously, Russell (1997) argues that historical accounts are 'probably of no relevance to modern bulimia nervosa'. This is an extreme view, and medical historians (and others) who have written on BN would disagree (see, for example, Parry-Jones & Parry-Jones 1995).

Historians of psychiatry have found it useful to distinguish between terms, behaviours and concepts (Berrios & Porter 1995). Each can have a separate history and a different link to the modern diagnosis. They will be considered below, in turn, to help enrich our understanding of the disorder as it presents today.

Bulimia as a term

The term bulimia is derived from two Greek words. These are the word '*bous*' meaning ox, and the word '*limos*' meaning hunger. The *Oxford English Dictionary* defines bulimia simply as 'morbid hunger'. It suggests having the appetite of an ox, as well as the ability to consume an ox, or as much as an ox (Parry-Jones & Parry-Jones 1995; Tobe & Wolinsky 1986). Excessive consumption, and psychological features, are not mentioned.

'Bulimic' behaviours

There are no early reports of bulimia nervosa as we would recognize it today, but 'bulimic' behaviours have been documented since Antiquity (Parry-Jones & Parry-Jones 1995; Ziolko 1996). These reports are usually of extreme or unbearable hunger, e.g. the reports of 'oxen hunger', which date from the fourth century BC, with no mention of excessive consumption and vomiting, or psychological features. The Ancient Egyptians are known to have practised purging (Crichton 1996), but this seems to be have been independent of excessive consumption.

Bulimia, as a symptom, appears during the Middle Ages, and a few detailed case reports exist (Ziolko 1996). Again, the emphasis is on ravenous hunger, rather than the behaviour and psychological features we associate with modern BN.

Bulimia as a concept

In Antiquity, the concept referred to a syndrome characterized by extreme hunger, weakness or exhaustion, and faintness. Galen (second century AD), for example, noted that bulimia consisted of 'food craving, collapse, paleness, cold extremities, stomach oppression and weak pulse' (Parry-Jones & Parry-Jones 1995, p.146).[4]

However, the concept (or cluster of symptoms associated with it) did not generally include vomiting or purging or any reference to psychological, e.g. weight and shape, concerns.

Kynorexia

Historical research has recently drawn attention to kynorexia (Ziolko 1996). Kynorexia bears some resemblance to modern-day bulimia nervosa. The term was in use throughout

---

[4] Later definitions included reference to a switch between excessive eating and fasting (Paulos of Aegina, seventh century AD) and to patients' experience of loss of control. Excessive wasting and emaciation were also described. It is not clear whether these three sets of features referred to cases of bulimia or kynorexia (see below).

Antiquity and the Middle Ages. It means, literally, 'insatiable hunger like that of dogs' (Ziolko 1996). The concept refers to behaviours in which sufferers lose all control, eat excessive amounts of food, and vomit to stop themselves from coming to physical harm. Given the opportunity, they then repeat the behaviour. Kynorexia refers to excessive consumption and is clearly associated with vomiting. It is not clear whether vomiting was generally self-induced or spontaneous, although Asclepiades (in Ziolko 1996) suggested it was induced to counter the sensation of weight and distention.[5]

Like the modern syndrome, it involves loss of control over-eating, but there is little suggestion of psychological concerns.

Several cases of kynorexia were described in the Middle Ages (Zioklo 1996, reports on two cases in the late sixteenth, and early seventeenth century). The term fell out of use in the late eighteenth century. At that time, a new term appeared, bulimia emetica.

Bulimia emetica

During the eighteenth century, attempts were made to classify eating-related disorders in a scientific way. de Sauvages (1772) distinguished seven different types of bulimia. Cullen's (1780) system, which was very influential, listed three types, including a form in which vomiting followed excessive eating. This was referred to as bulimia emetica.

Following Cullen's classification, a few case reports of bulimia emetica appeared. Parry-Jones & Parry-Jones (1995) identify fifteen cases, most dating from the nineteenth century. Some of these have features or behaviours that seem reminiscent of modern day bulimia nervosa, (e.g. rapid eating, night bingeing, secret eating, normal body weight). Vomiting appeared, on occasion, to be associated with disgust (Ziolko 1996). However, in most of the cases it is usually unclear whether it was self-induced, or spontaneous. There was little reference to a psychological component. Treatment focused largely on somatic aspects. Outcome was mostly unknown, although some cases recovered, some became chronic cases, and some died (one through suicide) (Parry-Jones & Parry-Jones 1995).

Psychological features

Clear reports of psychological features in association with bulimia emetica began to appear in the early eighteenth century. By the late nineteenth and early twentieth century, bulimia was widely accepted as a form of neurosis, i.e. as a psychological disorder. Osler (1892), for example, saw it as an anomaly of the sense of hunger or satiety, in the context of hysteria or neurasthenia. The term emetica was dropped and the disorder became known simply as bulimia.

---

[5] Despite the much publicized Roman habit around this time of self-induced vomiting after banquets, it has been suggested that this was, in fact, relatively uncommon behaviour (Crichton 1996).

Table 1.2 Key features of bulimia nervosa identified by Russell (1979)

An irresistible urge to overeat
Self-induced vomiting or purging
A morbid fear of becoming fat

Emergence of the modern syndrome

Weight and shape concerns began to be mentioned in association with binge-eating (e.g. Janet 1903; Wulff 1932, in Stunkard 1990) in the late nineteenth and early twentieth century (Ziolko 1996). There were also clear reports of self-induced vomiting (Janet 1903; Wulff 1932, in Stunkard 1990). Fear of being overweight was often an issue and vomiting was a way to regulate weight. Preference for sweets and starchy foods, and disgust with the body (Habermas 1989) were noted, as well as depression, shame, and guilt after bingeing. As the twentieth century progressed, more case reports appeared (a well-known and still very readable account is that of Ellen West in Binswanger 1944). A small case series was also published (Nemiah 1950). The patients described were much like those seen with bulimia nervosa today. Treatment changed, there were reports of patients receiving psychotherapy (Lindner 1955), and some detailed accounts of the psychodynamics of the symptoms began to appear (Bruch 1973).

Russell's contribution

Most work in the twentieth century (from 1950 onwards) focused on binge-eating and vomiting in the context of anorexia nervosa. Although case reports of bulimia nervosa-like syndromes increased during the 1960s, it was not until 1979 that bulimia nervosa became separated from anorexia nervosa.

Gerald Russell, of the Royal Free Hospital in London, is responsible for the modern identification of BN. In 1979 he published a description of a series of thirty patients with what he termed 'bulimia nervosa'.[6]

These patients had been seen over a period of six years. They had three features (see Table 1.2): 'an irresistible urge to over-eat', 'self-induced vomiting or purging' and 'a morbid fear of becoming fat'.

Most, but not all, had a history of anorexia nervosa. However, most of them binged and vomited at normal weight. They also had 'overvalued ideas' about body size and fatness. Russell notes (1979, p.438) 'the patients usually remained convinced of the danger and odiousness of fatness'. He saw the disorder as an ominous variant of

---

[6] The word 'nervosa', derived directly from the Latin, and added by Russell, suggests a psychological component. One definition of its derivation 'nervous', cited in the *Oxford English Dictionary*, is 'excitable, highly strung, easily agitated'.

anorexia nervosa, and was pessimistic about its prognosis. Most of his patients had a poor outcome. He noted that they often became severely depressed, and were at risk of suicide. He recommended admission to an in-patient psychiatric unit to interrupt the vicious circle of binge-eating and vomiting, as well as skilled nursing care, anti-depressant therapy, and electro-convulsive therapy (the latter two treatments are not specifically for the eating disorder). He also recommended psychotherapy, including behaviour therapy, believing that the origins of the problem lay in patients' emotional problems. Supervision was often necessary for many months or years. He noted that patients were prone to drop out of treatment.

A variety of terms was invented to describe the new syndrome, including bulimarexia, binge-eating-vomiting, the gorge-purge syndrome (Casper 1983) and the dietary chaos syndrome (Palmer 1979). However, the term bulimia nervosa was eventually adopted as an international term, by clinicians and researchers. It is the term now used by the major classificatory systems (DSM-IV, American Psychiatric Association 1994; ICD-10, World Health Organisation 1992).

A new disorder

Some have argued that bulimia nervosa is a new disorder (e.g. Casper 1983; Habermas 1989, 1992), and two points of discontinuity have been identified in it's history:

(1) between pre-modern bulimia and bulimia nervosa; and

(2) between very early reports of bulimia and bulimia emetica.[7]

Most attention has focused on the first discontinuity. Those who think BN is a new disorder, however, disagree about the date of the first case. Pope *et al.* (1985b) identify four cases of bulimia nervosa among the 236 cases described by Janet (1903). They note that there are 'probably' no reports before this. Habermas (1989), however, suggests that the first clear report occurs rather later, and is that by Wulff (1932, in Stunkard 1990). He argues that Janet's four patients are not true cases of bulimia nervosa.

Recently, it has been argued that BN is not a new disorder (Ziolko 1996). Drawing on new evidence, Ziolko (1996) suggests that self-induced vomiting and psychological features emerged gradually. He also notes a line of continuity (rather than a second discontinuity), from kynorexia through to bulimia emetica. He suggests that historians have confused early accounts of bulimia and kynorexia, and when the term kynorexia fell out of use in the late eighteenth century the disorder it described was subsumed in the concept of bulimia (re-labelled bulimia emetica in Cullen's system). Table 1.3 illustrates the two proposed lines of development, with key features of the historical disorders highlighted.

....

[7] Although others disagree (e.g. Bell 1985; Bemporad 1997; Brumberg 1988), Habermas (1989, 1992) also argues that anorexia nervosa is a new disorder on the grounds that weight and shape concerns were not much in evidence before the mid-nineteenth century.

Table 1.3 The two lines proposed for the development of bulimia nervosa

BN is a new disorder	BN is not a new disorder
Pre-modern bulimia nervosa—extreme hunger	Kynorexia—insatiable hunger, excessive eating, loss of control
Bulimia nervosa	Bulimia emetica—excessive eating, vomiting
	Bulimia nervosa

More historical research is needed to address this question. If weight and shape concerns are continuous, i.e. part of an evolving process, then (to extend Ziolko's argument, and rather as has been argued in anorexia nervosa) one possibility is that the content of the psychopathology has changed over the centuries. Thus, much as has been argued in anorexia nervosa, bulimia nervosa may be a deeper form of self-expression. However, more work is needed to establish whether or not this is likely to be the case.

Diagnosis in bulimia nervosa

Cullen's classification of bulimia was later modified, for example, by Hooper (1811). However, it remained largely unchanged until Russell's paper (Russell 1979) was published. There are now two major classificatory systems for psychiatric disorders. These are the International Classification of Diseases (ICD), developed by the World Health Organisation, and the Diagnostic and Statistical Manual (DSM), developed by the American Psychiatric Association.

Bulimia appeared in early versions of the ICD as a symptom. For example, it was defined in ICD-9 (World Health Organisation 1977) as 'polyphagia, excessive eating or hyperalimentation'. It did not appear in early versions of the DSM (DSM-I, American Psychiatric Association 1952, or DSM-II, American Psychiatric Association 1968). It appears for the first time as a syndrome, or collection of symptoms, in ICD-10 (World Health Organisation 1992) and DSM-III (American Psychiatric Association 1980). ICD-10 is still in use; whereas DSM is now in its fourth edition. The changes that have taken place in its diagnosis criteria in successive DSM editions are discussed below. The key features of the different editions are summarized in Table 1.4.

DSM-III

DSM-III introduced diagnosis based on symptoms and on groupings of symptoms found to have treatment, prognostic and/or familial significance (Singerman 1981). It also took a multi-axial approach—individuals could be rated on five dimensions. Of particular importance was the distinction between Axis 1 and Axis 2 disorders. Axis 1 disorders were the current disturbance; Axis 2 disorders were personality (long-standing) disorders. Eating disorders were listed as Axis 1 disorders.

Table 1.4 Main features of relevant DSM diagnoses

DSM-III:
Recurrent episodes of binge-eating
Excludes anorexia nervosa
DSM-III-R:
Recurrent episodes of binge-eating
Loss of control over eating during a binge
Compensatory behaviour
Over-concern with weight and shape
Frequency and duration criteria for binges
Diagnosis of anorexia nervosa also possible
DSM-IV:
Recurrent episodes of binge-eating
Loss of control over eating during a binge
Compensatory behaviour
Self-evaluation unduly influenced by weight and shape
Frequency and duration criteria
Excludes anorexia nervosa
Two subtypes: purging and non purging

DSM-III defines bulimia as recurrent episodes of binge-eating. Three of five features (e.g. termination of such eating episodes by abdominal pain, sleep, social interruption, or self-induced vomiting) had to be present. There also had to be awareness that the eating pattern was abnormal, fear of not being able to stop eating voluntarily, and depression and self-deprecating thoughts following binges. The diagnosis excluded individuals with anorexia nervosa. Compensatory behaviour was not a necessary feature.

DSM-III-R

The diagnostic criteria in DSM-III-R altered considerably. The name of the syndrome also changed to bulimia nervosa (American Psychiatric Association 1987). As in DSM-III, recurrent episodes of binge-eating were essential for a diagnosis. However, there were also some differences. One important addition was presence of compensatory behaviour following binge-eating. Persistent over-concern with shape and weight also became a necessary feature, as did lack of control over eating during a binge. The frequency and duration (a minimum average of at least two eating binges a week for at least three months) was also specified. An additional diagnosis of anorexia nervosa could also be given. There are a few smaller, less significant alterations. For example, the 2-h time limit on binge-eating episodes was dropped, and vigorous exercising was added to the list of inappropriate compensatory behaviours.

Current DSM diagnostic criteria (DSM-IV)

Work groups, consisting of internationally known experts and representatives of the American Psychiatric Association, were set up to review and revise the DSM-III-R criteria for different disorders. The main issue addressed by the Eating Disorders Work Group, in considering bulimia nervosa, was whether the diagnosis was to be restricted to people who purge, or whether it should identify two subtypes—those who purge and those who do not. It also examined whether an objective criterion should be used to define 'large' in large amount of food, whether the frequency criteria should be revised, and whether over-concern with weight and shape should continue as part of the diagnosis. A summary of the DSM-IV criteria for bulimia nervosa can be seen in Table 1.5.

Two types were identified—a purging subtype and a non-purging subtype, depending on the type of compensatory behaviour engaged in. The size of the amount of food was now more clearly defined, and examples of loss of control were also given.

Table 1.5 Summary of the DSM-IV diagnostic criteria for bulimia nervosa

A Recurrent episodes of binge-eating. An episode of binge-eating is characterized by both of the following:
(1) eating, in a discrete period of time (e.g. within any 2-h period), an amount of food that is definitely larger than most people would eat during a similar period of time and under similar circumstances;
(2) a sense of lack of control over eating during the episode (e.g. a feeling that one cannot stop eating or control what or how much one is eating).
B Recurrent inappropriate compensatory behaviour in order to prevent weight gain, such as self-induced vomiting, misuse of laxatives, diuretics, enemas, or other medications; fasting or excessive exercise.
C The binge-eating and inappropriate compensatory behaviours both occur, on average, at least twice a week for 3 months.
D Self-evaluation is unduly influenced by body shape and weight.
E The disturbance does not occur exclusively during episodes of anorexia nervosa.
Specify type:
Purging type: during the episode of bulimia nervosa, the person has regularly engaged in self-induced vomiting or the misuse of laxatives, diuretics, or enemas.
Non-purging type: during the current episode of bulimia nervosa, the person has used other inappropriate compensatory behaviours, such as fasting or excessive exercise, but has not regularly engaged in self-induced vomiting or the misuse of laxatives, diuretics or enemas.

It was acknowledged that it was difficult to define large, and the guidelines suggested by Fairburn (1987) were adopted. The frequency criterion (two binges a week) was considered somewhat arbitrary but the Work Group found no data suggesting that a change was required. Over-concern with weight and shape was retained, since data suggested that nearly all patients with bulimia nervosa had such concerns. However, the wording was changed to reflect the research. The emphasis was now placed on self-evaluation, which had to be unduly influenced by weight and shape. Finally, In DSM-IV anorexia nervosa 'trumps' bulimia nervosa—both diagnoses cannot be given.

ICD-10

ICD-10 has three criteria for a diagnosis of bulimia nervosa. These are: episodes of overeating in which large amounts of food are consumed in short periods of time; compensatory behaviour—attempts to counteract the fattening effects of food; and a morbid dread of fatness.

The DSM criteria have been widely used, particularly in research. Although ICD-10 includes research criteria, these are less detailed and less frequently used. It is important to note that the two systems may not produce the same diagnosis (First & Pincus 1999), not least because they were developed in very different ways. Whereas DSM is empirically based, ICD-10 relies on expert consensus.

To be most useful, diagnoses must be reliable (consistently produce the same result) and valid (actually measure what they say they measure). This was first widely recognized in DSM-III. One way to increase validity is to identify the cause, instead of relying on a collection of diverse signs and symptoms (the identification of each sign or symptom can be more or less reliable or valid, multiplying the possibility of error). However, as in most psychiatric disorders, we are far from understanding the cause of bulimia nervosa; we know just that both genetic and environmental factors are likely to be involved. This means that bulimia nervosa is still defined by its clinical features or symptoms, and not by its aetiology.[8]

Issues of reliability and validity are, therefore, particularly important.

Reliability

In making a reliable diagnosis it is important to agree on who is to be included in the diagnosis (sensitivity) and who is not to be included (specificity). The most important form of reliability in psychiatric diagnosis is inter-rater reliability. This can be of two types: either a passive observer makes an independent diagnosis; or a second clinician carries out an independent interview.

....

[8] This includes psychological factors, although often in psychiatry, e.g. Robins & Guze (1970), it is assumed that a biological cause will be found.

In the 1950s and 1960s, reliability of psychiatric diagnoses was often very poor. However, in recent years reliability has increased. This is largely due to two factors:

(1) the introduction of operational definitions of disorders in the major classificatory systems;

(2) the use of structured interviews based on these (e.g. the Diagnostic Interview Schedule: Robins *et al.* 1981, 1982; and the Structured Clinical Interview: First *et al.* 1996).

Validity

Diagnostic validity is closely related to the assumption that the concept identified is a discrete entity, and also that a single, possibly biological, cause can ultimately be found. Types of validity relevant to diagnosis include criterion (concurrent and predictive) and construct (convergent and discriminant) validity (Anastasi 1988).

Concurrent validity is the relationship between aspects of the diagnosis itself, and features to which it might reasonably be expected to relate. This type of validity is also known as descriptive validity. Predictive validity is the extent to which outcome, including response to treatment, can be inferred from the diagnosis. Construct validity is the extent to which the diagnosis measures a theoretical construct or trait. (It has convergent validity if it relates to features to which it should theoretically be related, and discriminant validity if it is does not relate to features to which it should not.)

Validity is important for deciding on treatment, determining prognosis, and for prevention. However, it is only relatively recently that empirical studies have begun to ask whether the diagnostic category, bulimia nervosa, is valid. Two main questions have been asked:

1. Can bulimia nervosa be distinguished from other eating disorders?

2. Can it be distinguished from non-clinical bulimic behaviour?[9]

However, as yet there is little relevant empirical evidence. The relevant studies are summarized in Table 1.6, together with the type of validity assessed.

One study has examined the distinction between BN and anorexia nervosa (Keel *et al.* 2000a). This study followed up 177 women diagnosed with DSM-IV bulimia nervosa 11.5 years after initial presentation. At follow-up, bulimic symptoms remained prominent, within both full and sub-threshold DSM-IV eating disorder diagnoses, and few cases of anorexia nervosa had developed. This provides some preliminary support (predictive validity) for the suggestion that the two disorders are distinct syndromes.

---

[9] It is important to remember that, in general, the less reliable a category is, then the less valid it is likely to be. However, there is some recent evidence showing that it is possible to obtain data supporting the validity of a diagnosis yet find its reliability is low (Rice *et al.* 1992).

Table 1.6 Evidence for the validity of bulimia nervosa as a diagnostic category

Distinction	Supported	Not supported
Bulimia nervosa vs. anorexia nervosa	Keel et al. (2000a): predictive validity	
Bulimia nervosa vs. binge-eating disorder	Hay & Fairburn (1998): predictive validity	Hay et al. (1996): descriptive and construct validity
Bulimia nervosa vs. eating disorder—not otherwise specified		Hay & Fairburn (1998): descriptive, construct and predictive validity
Bulimia nervosa vs. non-clinical eating behaviour	Hay et al. (1996): descriptive, construct and predictive validity	Sullivan et al., 1998 – latent class analysis

Two studies have examined the distinction between bulimia nervosa and binge-eating disorder (BED). In a study of 250 young women with recurrent binge-eating, Hay et al. (1996) found no support (descriptive and construct validity) for the distinction. Although groups corresponding to DSM-IV bulimia nervosa were identified, binge-eating disorder did not emerge as a separate cluster. However, in a later study, Hay & Fairburn (1998), using the same group of young women, and looking this time at predictive validity, found support for the distinction.

Some preliminary evidence suggests that Eating Disorder Not Otherwise Specified (EDNOS) may be distinct from bulimia nervosa, with descriptive, construct, and some predictive validity (Hay & Fairburn 1998). Bulimia nervosa may also have greater stability over time than EDNOS. Interestingly, however, there is some evidence (based on phenomenology of the category) that there are different subgroups within the EDNOS category. One subgroup resembles BN patients—differing primarily in frequency of bingeing and compensatory behaviour. Others resemble AN or BED patients (Turner & Bryant-Waugh, submitted).

Hay et al. (1996) provide some evidence that bulimia is distinct from other (non-clinical) bulimic eating behaviour. In an unselected community sample of women with recurrent binge-eating, they found support for four subgroups—including two that resembled bulimia nervosa (one the purging subtype, one the non-purging subtype). However, Sullivan et al. (1998), using a sample of 1897 Caucasian female twins, not selected for bulimic behaviour, and latent class analysis,[10] did not find support for a bulimia nervosa category.

They suggest that there is a continuum of bulimic behaviours, rather than qualitatively different categories, and that DSM-IV does not capture the spectrum of bulimic disorders in the general population.

----

[10] Latent class analysis uses mathematical models to estimate the presence of a 'latent class', i.e. the presence of an underlying disease state; it differs from validity, as used here.

One possible reason for the discrepant findings in these last two studies lies in the sample selection (different in the two studies)—the statistical techniques they used can produce different results, depending on the sampling procedure employed.

While several of these studies confirm the existing (and discrete entity) system of classification, they do not, strictly speaking, rule out the possibility that the different disorders and/or bulimic behaviours actually exist on a continuum (see below). More work is needed, investigating other types of validity, and using more broadly based samples including community groups. This is likely to be difficult to achieve in practice, particularly for studies involving anorexia nervosa, because of its relatively low incidence.

One common feature in the studies is that predictive validity findings support differences between eating disorders, and between bulimic behaviours and eating disorders, whereas other types of validity often do not. It has been argued that predictive validity is the most crucial, and that it is 'perhaps the most important and widely applicable criterion of validity available to the clinician' (Kendell 1989, p.48). This suggests that for clinical purposes it might be most useful to assume that the disorders (and bulimic behaviours) are distinct.

One possibility is that disorders and bulimic behaviour are continuous in terms of symptoms but differ at a more fundamental level. For example, in genetics it is well known that different genes can result in overlapping syndromes (and vice versa). A similar situation may apply to social and environmental causes (and psychological symptoms are usually due to the interaction of biological and social-environmental factors). This may help to explain why two different conclusions have been reached— at different levels both may be valid.

In general, the number of relevant studies is very small, with heavy reliance on one study in particular (Hay *et al.* 1996), and all the studies can be criticised in several ways. Much more work is needed before firm conclusions can be drawn.

Diagnostic issues

A number of other diagnostic issues have been discussed. These are considered below.

Are there distinct subtypes of bulimia nervosa?

DSM-IV identifies two subtypes—a purging subtype and a non-purging subtype. Although clinical experience suggests that the two types have different features, some (relatively unsophisticated) studies find that they do not (Tobin & Griffing 1997). Both categories emerged in a community sample of women with recurrent binge-eating (Hay *et al.* 1996). Hay & Fairburn (1998) also found some support for the two subtypes. However, the two categories did not emerge in Sullivan *et al.*'s 1998a study. Again, sampling differences may explain the discrepant findings. Some of the criteria that have been suggested for subtyping BN are summarized in Table 1.7.

Table 1.7 Criteria suggested for sub-typing bulimia nervosa

Purging vs. non-purging
Frequency of binge-eating and vomiting
Presence of compensatory behaviours
Timing of onset of binge-eating and dieting
History of anorexia nervosa

Are the DSM-IV diagnostic thresholds (e.g. for frequency of binge-eating) appropriate?

DSM IV has a threshold of two binges per week. However, some studies have found no evidence that those who binge once a week are any different from those who binge more often (Garfinkel *et al.* 1995; Wilson & Eldredge 1991). Sullivan *et al.* (1998a) suggested that four objective binges a month and vomiting twice a month may be a more appropriate threshold.

Should some other criteria apart from binge-eating be used to classify the disorder?

Binge-eating has generally been investigated as the core feature of bulimia nervosa. However, it has been suggested that the focus should be on compensatory behaviours— and that these may have greater clinical implications (Garner *et al.* 1991). There is, for example, some evidence that compensatory behaviours, compared to binge-eating, predict greater co-morbid psychopathology.

Subgroups have also been proposed based on the timing of the onset of binge-eating and dieting (Haiman & Devlin 1999). Although many begin dieting before binge-eating, about 15% binge-eat before dieting (Mitchell *et al.* 1986). Bulik *et al.* (1997) found that 17% of their sample began binge-eating before dieting. The two groups (binge first vs. diet first) did not differ on clinical features, lifetime prevalence of other Axis I disorders, or on self-report measures of specific psychopathology. However, they did differ on some sub-scales of the Temperament and Character Inventory (Cloninger *et al.* 1993). The binge-first group had higher novelty seeking and harm-avoidance scores. It was suggested that this combination may lead to an 'approach–approach' style towards food, not initially offset by fears of losing control or gaining weight (Bulik *et al.* 1997). It has also been suggested that those who binge first may resemble those with binge-eating disorder (Mussell *et al.* 1997), who often begin binge-eating before dieting. This fits with the idea of a continuum of eating disorders, in which people move between different diagnoses, and share important key features. However, the suggestion has not been validated using appropriate empirical techniques.

One study has also stratified bulimics by the presence or absence of a past history of anorexia nervosa, and examined differences in the resulting subgroups. However, meaningful subgroups of bulimia nervosa did not emerge (Sullivan *et al.* 1996b).

Implications of historical evidence

Little attention has been given to historical evidence in revising the ICD and DSM systems of classification (Parry-Jones & Parry-Jones 1994). If bulimia is a deeper form of self-expression, for example, then the diagnostic significance of some features may change. This is a relatively new suggestion in BN, although a debate has begun to take place about this issue in anorexia nervosa (particularly in relation to the weight and shape criteria).[11]

The medical model (a category approach)

This model is also known as the disease model (Davison & Neale 1994). It forms the basis for the current diagnostic categories used in eating disorders and, more generally, in abnormal behaviour. It is associated with Emil Kraepelin, and has recently been termed the 'Platonic' approach (Goldberg 2000). Its basic assumption is that abnormal behaviour is similar to physical disease. As in physical disease, symptoms can be grouped into categories or syndromes, on the basis of which a diagnosis can be made. One important assumption of this model is that syndromes are distinct, both from each other and from normal behaviour (this is the basis of the attempt to distinguish bulimia nervosa from other eating disorders, and from bulimic behaviour). Historically, it has also been associated with the assumption that the aetiology of abnormal behaviour is physical, and that diagnoses have an independent existence. Although much criticized, the medical model has facilitated understanding of the factors that cause bulimia nervosa, and helped in the search for effective treatments (Stunkard 1997). The developing definition or diagnosis of bulimia nervosa, as outlined above, has occurred within the framework of this model.

The symptom-based approach (a dimensional approach)

Modern (non-clinical) psychology traditionally takes a rather different view of abnormal behaviour from that taken by medicine and the medical model. Associated with Adolf Meyer, and termed the 'Aristotelian' approach (Goldberg 2000), it is based on the study of personality or individual differences, and the identification of traits in non-clinical groups. It assumes that behaviours (from which traits are inferred) are not either normal or abnormal (as implied by the disease model) but exist on a continuum. Differences between normal and abnormal are one of degree not type. Some have suggested (e.g. Sullivan *et al.* 1998a, above), that this model is the 'best fit' model in eating disorders. While the disease model assumes a physical cause, there has been much

---

[11] Some researchers have recently pointed out that there are cases that meet all but the weight and shape criteria for bulimia nervosa (Goldfein *et al.* 2000). Palmer (1993) has argued strongly for 'over-investment' in eating restraint to replace concerns about weight, in order to extend the range of relevant social factors that may be involved in the disorder. This finding, and Palmer's suggestion, are consistent with the idea that these concerns are culturally dependent, and that bulimia may be a deeper form of self expression. They are also consistent with developments in cognitive theory (see Chapter 8), which place rather less emphasis on dieting as a maintaining factor.

debate over whether genetic or environmental factors are most important in the development of personality. One big advantage of adopting a dimensional perspective is that it facilitates the use of psychological theories, developed in non-clinical populations. Our current understanding of bulimia nervosa has also occurred within this framework.

In writing this book, I have found both approaches useful, and will draw on both throughout. There is no one right approach. Dimensions convey more information—so that finer distinctions are possible. They are flexible, can be converted to categories and back again, and they do not imply unproven qualitative distinctions, or impose boundaries where none may exist. Neither do they distort the perception of people near the boundaries of adjacent categories. Categories, on the other hand, are familiar, easy to understand, remember, and use. They reflect the way we use language, provide a ready guide to treatment, and are often broadly acceptable.

One advantage of the dimensional approach is that it enables us to use psychological theories from non-clinical psychology. These include those that form the basis of psychological treatments, for example, those developed by cognitive psychologists such as Kelly, Bandura, and Rogers. These form a historical link to cognitive behaviour therapy, which has been found to be particularly effective in bulimia nervosa. Importantly, however, it also facilitates the use of theories and research developed, for example, about eating in the normal population. Finally, it has been suggested, even by those trained in the use of the medical model, that, for most purposes, most psychiatric disorders are more usefully represented by dimensions than categories (Kendell 1988, p.376). Much of the research in this book has taken this view, even while working with the constraints of a psychiatric diagnosis.

Related eating (and weight/shape) disorders

Table 1.8 summarizes some of the key similarities and differences between BN and other types of eating disorder.

Anorexia nervosa

In anorexia nervosa there is severe weight loss, or failure to gain weight, as expected during normal growth. As in bulimia nervosa, there is extreme concern with weight and shape, and great fear of gaining weight or becoming fat. Two types are often identified. The binge-eating/purging type is characterized by episodes of binge-eating and inappropriate compensatory behaviour, and resembles bulimia nervosa. In the restricting type, weight loss is achieved and maintained primarily by dieting. The main features of the two disorders have been compared in two ways: by studying case series, and by comparing the two groups directly.

There are several large case series of bulimia nervosa (for examples see: Fairburn & Cooper 1984; Johnson *et al.* 1983; Pyle *et al.* 1981). One of anorexia nervosa (Crisp 1967; Crisp *et al.* 1980) also dates from about the same period. These studies find some

Table 1.8 Similarities and differences between BN and related eating disorders

Bulimia nervosa vs. anorexia nervosa

Differences from AN	Similarities to AN
Older at presentation	Preceded by negative life events
More likely to be married	Similar restraint and eating concern scores on the EDE
Later onset	EAT and EDI scores similar
More likely to be overweight as a child	Family history of depression
Fewer general psychiatric symptoms	
Higher binge-eating and more shape and weight concerns on the EDE	
Earlier menarche	
Family history of physical illness, obesity, alcoholism, drug abuse more likely	
Family history of dieting, criticism related to weight more likely	

Bulimia nervosa vs. binge-eating disorder

Differences from BED
Younger
Weigh less
Lower highest ever weight
Less restrained eating
Later onset of binge-eating (but not dieting)
Binges less like normal meals
More fear of becoming fat
Greater desire to be thinner
More depressed
Score more highly on most EDI sub-scales

demographic similarities but also differences between the two disorders. Bulimia nervosa patients are usually 3–4 years older at presentation. They are also rather more likely to be married. Anorexia tends to start earlier than bulimia. Age at onset of binge-eating was 19.7 years, and age at onset of self-induced vomiting was 20 years for bulimia nervosa in one case series (Fairburn & Cooper 1984), compared with an age at onset of severe dieting/illness of 17.3 years in anorexics (Crisp *et al.* 1980). More of those with bulimia nervosa have been overweight as children. Only about 28% of Crisp's anorexics (Crisp *et al.* 1980), compared with about half of those with bulimia nervosa (Johnson *et al.* 1983; Mitchell *et al.* 1985), had been overweight. In both groups most come from social classes 1 and 2. Bulimia nervosa often seems to follow a change in lifestyle or weight gain. Crisp also noted that many significant life events had occurred prior to weight loss in his anorexic sample.

A small number of studies have compared the two groups directly in the same study, and some have used standardized measures. Herzog (1982), comparing anorexics with bulimics, also found that bulimics were more likely to be married. They were also more likely to have a family history of chronic physical illness or obesity. Using a standardized measure (the Eating Disorders Examination, EDE: Cooper & Fairburn 1987) specific psychopathology was found to differ (Beumont *et al.* 1993). As might be expected, bulimics scored more highly on individual items related to binge-eating, e.g. frequency of objective bulimic episodes. On the sub-scales, they scored more highly on shape and weight concern (the core psychopathology) as well as on bulimia, but did not differ from the anorexics on restraint or eating concern.

Some studies have separated bulimic from restricting anorexics, and compared this group with bulimia nervosa patients. These studies find little difference on measures of eating, e.g. the Eating Attitudes Test (EAT: Garner & Garfinkel 1979) and psychological functioning related to eating disorders, e.g. the Eating Disorder Inventory (EDI: Garner *et al.* 1983a). However, on a measure of general psychopathology (the five sub-scales of the Hopkins Symptom Checklist, HSCL: Derogatis 1977), bulimia nervosa patients scored significantly lower, suggesting fewer general psychiatric symptoms than both restricting and bulimic anorexics (Garner 1991).

Some studies have examined differences in risk factors. A family history of depression and a family and personal history of obesity (Fairburn & Cooper 1982, 1984) are thought to be risk factors for bulimia nervosa. A family history of alcoholism has also been noted (Pyle *et al.* 1981). In anorexia nervosa, a family history of mental illness, particularly depression, seems common (Crisp *et al.* 1980). When risk factors were compared in a single study (e.g. Fairburn *et al.* 1999) few differences were found. However, it did seem that factors that increased the risk of dieting, e.g. a family member dieting, critical comments by family about shape, weight or eating, were more important as risk factors for bulimia nervosa than anorexia nervosa. Parental obesity and early menarche, as well as exposure to more parental psychiatric disorder during childhood (raised rates of parental depression, alcohol, and drug abuse), also seemed relatively more important in bulimia nervosa.

Binge-eating disorder

Like bulimia nervosa, binge-eating disorder (BED)[12] is characterized by recurrent episodes of binge-eating. Indeed, the definition of a binge (in DSM-IV) is the same in the two disorders.

---

[12] Technically, BED is classified as an example of the EDNOS category in DSM-IV. However, draft research criteria for it exist and are in use, so it will be treated separately here whenever possible.

However, a diagnosis is associated with other features (e.g. eating much more rapidly than normal), as well as with marked distress. The frequency criteria for binge-eating is also different. It is defined as the number of days on which bingeing occurs instead of the number of episodes. There is no regular use of inappropriate compensatory behaviours.

There are no large case series of binge-eating disorder. One study has compared binge-eating disorder and bulimia nervosa (Brody et al. 1994) in the context of a study of the reliability and validity of the diagnosis. Those with BED were older, weighed more, and had a greater highest-ever weight. They scored more highly on a measure of dietary restraint, and on a measure of depression. Another study compared obese subjects with BED, with bulimia nervosa patients (Raymond et al. 1995). This found no differences in social class, marital status, employment, and education, although those with BED were more likely to be employed. The patients with bulimia nervosa had a greater fear of becoming fat, and wanted to be much thinner. The BED group had started binge-eating at an earlier age than the BN group (means of 14.3 vs. 19.8 years, respectively), though there were no differences in age at onset of dieting. Only two of those with BED had a history of vomiting. Bulimia nervosa patients scored more highly on all but three sub-scales measuring eating disorder features (on the EDI). They also had higher levels of depression on standardized rating scales.

Early studies were unable to make use of the DSM-IV research criteria for BED, but some investigated apparently similar groups (for example: Fichter et al. 1993; Marcus et al. 1992; Prather & Williamson 1988). These studies also find greater general psychopathology in BN than in those who binge-eat, although the results are not clear-cut. They also find that the nature of binges is different—bulimics eat more carbohydrates and sugar, although they consume an equal number of calories, whereas BED binges are similar in composition to normal meals.

Body dysmorphic disorder

In this disorder, patients are preoccupied with an imagined or exaggerated defect in their physical appearance. This causes clinically significant distress or impairment. It may include aspects of their body shape and size (e.g. their hips) but not disordered eating or inappropriate compensatory behaviour.

Few case series or comparisons with bulimia nervosa on standardized measures exist. One study compared Body Dysmorphic Disorder (BDD) patients with a mixed group of bulimia nervosa and anorexia nervosa patients (almost three-quarters of whom had bulimia nervosa) (Rosen & Ramirez 1998). Using standardized measures, it found that both groups had severe body-image symptoms and low self-esteem. However, the bulimia nervosa group had more widespread general psychological symptoms.[13]

---

[13] Although relevant empirical studies do not yet exist, many clinicians believe Rosen's BDD patients to be atypical, and suggest that BDD is usually more distinct from BN.

Eating disorder not otherwise specified

This can be split into two groups (plus BED, which was discussed above): disorders in which the full criteria for either anorexia nervosa or bulimia nervosa are not met; and disorders that look rather different. Often it is the frequency criteria (an average of two binges over the last three months) that are not met. Alternatively, there may be inappropriate compensatory behaviour after eating small amounts of food, or repeated chewing and spitting out, but not swallowing, of food.

The clinical features of the two Eating Disorder Not Otherwise Specified (EDNOS) categories have not been studied in a case series. Some data comparing bulimia nervosa with EDNOS is available (e.g. Hay & Fairburn 1998). In the course of this study all participants completed the EDE and standardized measures of general psychopathology. The EDNOS patients had a different pattern of binge-eating. Compared to the BN patients, they had fewer objective bulimic episodes and more subjective bulimic episodes. However, they were similar on weight and shape concern, and on restraint, to non-purging bulimia nervosa patients.

Other related disorders

Table 1.9 summarizes disorders that have been thought to be related to BN.

Depression

Bulimia nervosa is associated with depressive symptoms. Sometimes patients may also meet criteria for dysthymic disorder or for major mood disorder. These findings led to suggestions in the 1980s that it was a form of affective disorder (e.g. Hudson *et al.* 1983a; Levy *et al.* 1989). However, research has not confirmed this suggestion. A variety of studies, looking at clinical data, family history, response to anti-depressant therapy, as well as relevant neuro-endrocrine findings, e.g. Levy *et al.* (1989), indicate that depression in bulimia nervosa is usually secondary to the eating disorder.

Table 1.9 Disorders thought to be related to BN

Depression
Dissociative identity disorder
Substance abuse disorder
Obsessive compulsive disorder
Post-traumatic distress disorder
Social phobia
Borderline personality disorder

Dissociative identity disorder[14]

This describes a condition in which two or more distinct identities or personality states recurrently take control of behaviour. Important personal information is also forgotten, beyond that which could be explained by ordinary forgetfulness.

Some preliminary research, using a mixed group of eating disorder patients (mostly with bulimia nervosa), and standardized self-report measures (Bernstein & Putnam 1986), found that nearly a quarter reported symptoms suggestive of multiple personality disorder (Berger *et al.* 1994). Those with dissociative symptoms had more suicide attempts and were more likely to self-mutilate. Others have found that, in a mixed group of eating disorder patients, 29% had a DSM-III-R dissociative disorder diagnosis. This was related to a history of self-harm, and to a history of abuse or trauma (McCallum *et al.* 1992). However, not all studies support a link. One recent study did not find a relationship (also in a mixed eating disorder group) (Gleaves & Eberenz 1995).

Interestingly, there are some case reports of multiple personality disorder, which seem to have initially presented as bulimia nervosa (e.g. Levin *et al.* 1993; Torem 1990).

Substance abuse disorder

Substance abuse was noted to be a feature of bulimia nervosa soon after its modern identification (e.g. Pyle *et al.* 1981; Russell 1979). It was suggested that it signalled problems with impulse control (e.g. Lacey & Evans 1986) and the term 'multi-impulsive' disorder was coined to describe a subgroup of patients who had general problems with impulse control, in addition to binge-eating. Systematic empirical studies have generally identified high rates of alcohol abuse in patients with eating disorders (Goldbloom *et al.* 1992). Community samples, however, have lower rates of alcohol disorder (Bushnell *et al.* 1994; Fairburn & Cooper 1984). It has been suggested that bulimia nervosa is a variant of a substance abuse disorder (e.g. Bushnell *et al.* 1994), but there seems little evidence for this.

Other Axis I disorders

Obsessive compulsive disorder

Obsessive compulsive disorder (OCD) has often been associated with anorexia nervosa. However, one study indicated that only 3% of bulimics met DSM-III-R criteria for obsessive compulsive disorder (Thornton & Russell 1997), compared with 37% of those with anorexia nervosa. Some studies find that DSM-III-R bulimics (and recovered bulimics) have higher scores on OCD symptoms (as assessed by the Yale–Brown Obsessive Compulsive Scale, Y-BOCS: Goodman *et al.* 1989) than normal controls. A recent study found no differences using the Y-BOCS in symptoms in bulimia nervosa

---

[14] Formerly known as multiple personality disorder.

and those in OCD (DSM-III-R) (Matsunaga *et al.* 1999), and another replicated the finding that high Y-BOCS scores persist after recovery (von Ranson *et al.* 1999). Other studies, however, have found no differences in symptoms, using different measures, between mixed eating-disorder groups and those with OCD. It has been asked whether bulimia nervosa is a form of OCD—something often suggested in anorexia nervosa, e.g. Holden (1990). Others, however, (e.g. Thiels 1998b) have argued that OCD is secondary to the eating disorder, just as depression seems to be.

Post-traumatic stress disorder and social phobia

Two other disorders that may overlap with bulimia nervosa are post-traumatic stress disorder (PTSD) and social phobia. The presence of PTSD symptomatology is common (52% of a sample of mixed eating disorders: Gleaves *et al.* 1998). It usually seems to be related to depression, anxiety, and dissociative experiences, and not to the eating disorder. One study found that 64% of bulimics had an anxiety disorder diagnosis. This was mostly social phobia (Bulik *et al.* 1996). A more recent study found that 59% had a diagnosis of social phobia (Godart *et al.* 2000). Other studies report rather lower figures, e.g. in one study, 17% of bulimics had a lifetime diagnosis of social phobia (Brewerton *et al.* 1995). In all studies, the social phobia usually appeared to have developed before the eating disorder.

Borderline personality disorder

Self-report measures find high rates of borderline personality disorder (BPD) in BN. For example, 72% appeared to have a BPD diagnosis when the Borderline Syndrome Index (Conte *et al.* 1980) was used (Kennedy *et al.* 1990). However, only 1.9% of bulimics met diagnostic criteria for borderline personality disorder (Pope *et al.* 1987b). One study, investigating changes in personality and psychiatric features in 50 bulimics over 4 months, found that a decrease in bulimic symptoms was associated with reductions in 'borderline' features, while persistent bulimia was associated with persistently elevated features. This suggests that borderline features are 'secondary elaborations' (Garner *et al.* 1990). It has been argued that self-report measures of personality disorder should be interpreted cautiously in patients with bulimia nervosa, since Axis I disorder may exaggerate personality disorder features or behaviours (Matsunaga *et al.* 2000). However, a specific link with Cluster B disorders, especially with borderline personality disorder, has been proposed by several researchers.

Other Axis II disorders

Some studies find an increased incidence, not only of Cluster B, but also of Cluster C personality disorders in bulimia nervosa (Yates *et al.* 1989). For example, one study found a high frequency of Axis 2 disorders (57% of the eating disorder patients)—including not only borderline personality disorder, but also self-defeating and avoidant personality disorder (Gartner *et al.* 1989). However, another study found no increased incidence for Axis 2 disorder in a bulimic, compared to a depressed, group (Zanarini *et al.* 1990). Another study found that only 21% of bulimics had an Axis 2 disorder— compared to 46% of a control group with major depressive disorder (Herzog *et al.* 1992). As for borderline personality disorder, it has been suggested that these two disorders and features are secondary to the eating disorder. In one study, for example, some patients lost their personality disorder diagnosis following treatment for the eating disorder (Ames-Frankel *et al.* 1992).

State versus trait distinctions

Many of the features associated with bulimia nervosa may be state features, i.e. secondary to the eating disorder (Lehoux *et al.* 2000). Although few studies have been conducted with eating-disorder patients, depression, suicidality, and anxiety often resolve with improvement in the disordered eating of women with bulimic symptoms. Studies often find differences on self-report symptom measures, but fewer differences emerge when patients are interviewed and a DSM diagnosis is obtained. This suggests that, although they may share some of the symptoms associated with personality disorders, particularly when they are acutely ill, they do not necessarily have a diagnosis, and the symptoms are a result of the eating disorder. The exception to this may be social phobia, which usually seems to develop before the eating disorder.

Summary

The first part of this chapter provided a brief introduction to the historical background relevant to bulimia nervosa. It covered reports of 'bulimic' symptoms in early times, the Middle Ages, and the early twentieth century. It noted the importance of distinguishing the separate histories of terms, behaviours, and concepts. The history, role, and importance of kynorexia were also outlined. The emergence of the syndrome 'bulimia nervosa' and its present day identification by Russell in 1979 was discussed. The suggestion that bulimia nervosa may be a deeper form of self expression (i.e. not a new disorder) was considered.

The second part summarized the history of the changing diagnostic criteria, and discussed the current diagnostic criteria (as outlined in ICD-10, World Health Organisation 1992; and DSM-IV, American Psychiatric Association 1994). Issues related to diagnosis were then considered, including the reliability and validity of the disorder bulimia nervosa. Initial findings generally support the existing system of classification although the number of relevant studies is very small. The use of the medical model, and the alternative perspective provided by non-clinical psychology, were discussed, and the advantages of a 'dimensional' approach were outlined. These include the ability to draw on psycological theories from non-clinical psychology.

In the third part of the chapter, related eating disorders (e.g. anorexia nervosa, binge-eating disorder), and the ways in which they differed from bulimia nervosa, were discussed. Anorexia nervosa and binge-eating disorder, in particular, seem to differ in several ways from BN. Other relevant disorders (both Axis I, e.g. depression, and Axis 2, e.g. borderline personality disorder), were also considered and their relationship to bulimia nervosa examined. It was suggested that many (but not all) of the associated features identified here, including of personality disorders, may be state dependent, i.e. secondary to the eating disturbance.

Chapter 2

Key features

Overview

The first part of this chapter will consider key characteristics of binge-eating, both in patients with BN and in general population samples. The relevance of theories of normal and restrained eating will also be explored, together with positive-incentive and settling-point theories. The second part will consider the full range of compensatory behaviours associated with BN, including their frequency in the normal population, and associated theories. The third part will discuss dieting and theories of dieting in some detail, as well as the relationship between dieting and BN. Finally, self-worth linked to weight and shape, including ways in which this has been measured, will be considered. The plan for the chapter is summarized in Table 2.1.

Binge-eating

Many studies have investigated the characteristics of binge-eating. These can be grouped into studies of DSM-IV criteria (concerned with size of eating episode, frequency, and loss of control) and those of associated features (concerned with duration of episode, speed of eating, content, and context of binge-eating). Some studies have used self-report diaries, others have used laboratory methodology (assessing intake in a controlled setting). Binge-eating has been studied in both patients and controls, together with normal eating (i.e. meals and snacks in both groups and, in the case of patients, total non-purged intake). The different characteristics of binge-eating that have been investigated are summarized in Table 2.2.

Size of eating episode

By definition a binge consists of a large amount of food. DSM-IV criteria specify that the amount eaten should be 'definitely larger than most individuals would eat under similar circumstances', (American Psychiatric Association 1994, p.545).

Reviewing diary studies, Guertin (1999) found that, in a typical binge, BN outpatients have mean intakes ranging from 1173 to 2632 calories. A review of laboratory studies produced similar findings (Guertin 1999). Those likely to have more severe symptoms tend to consume more calories in a binge. Thus the mean for a typical binge reported by BN in-patients was 3798 calories (Guertin 1999).

Given instructions to 'binge', such as 'let yourself go and eat as much as you can', control participants typically eat much less than BN patients (e.g. Walsh *et al.* 1989, p.54).

Table 2.1 Summary of plan for Chapter 2

Characteristics of binge-eating
Theories of normal and restrained eating
Compensatory behaviours
Theories linked to compensatory behaviours
Dieting
Theories of dieting
Self-worth linked to weight and shape

Table 2.2 Characteristics of binge-eating that have been investigated by clinical researchers

Size of eating episode
Frequency of eating
Loss of control
Duration of eating
Speed of eating
Content of binges
Context of binge-eating

In one study, a control group consumed a mean of 1412 calories. This compared to a mean of 3352 calories in the patients (Walsh *et al.* 1989).

However, there was no difference between the two groups in this study when they were asked to eat 'as much as they would in a normal meal'. A self-defined meal for the patients consisted of a mean of 464.8 calories. This compared with a mean of 473.7 calories for a meal eaten by the controls. Diary studies produce similar findings (e.g. Davis *et al.* 1988)—calorie intake per snack or meal is similar in the two groups. In both groups binges were larger than the self-defined meal (Walsh *et al.* 1989). The findings of Walsh and colleagues are summarized in Table 2.3.

Overall, the evidence suggests that BN patients consume large amounts of calories in a binge, but meals and snacks are similar in calorie content to those of controls.

Elmore & De Castro (1991) took this research a step further. Instead of looking simply at total calories consumed, they estimated total intake, for both non-binge and binge-eating episodes, when calories lost through vomiting were taken into account. This gave an estimate of number of calories absorbed. Using computer modelling, results indicated that BN subjects and controls did not differ in total number of calories absorbed, in either type of episode.

Elmore & De Castro (1991) also calculated 'deprivation ratios', calories eaten per minute elapsed since the last eating bout, and 'satiety ratios', amount of time waited in minutes per previously eaten number of calories before eating again. Controls and

Table 2.3 Number of calories eaten in binges and normal meals (Walsh *et al.* 1989)

	BN patients	Control participants
Asked to binge	3352	1412
Asked to eat normally	465	474

those with untreated BN did not differ on these two measures for meals, although BN subjects did differ in ratios for binges and meals. Ratios were lower for binges than for meals in the BN group.

These findings suggest that those with BN may not normally be food-deprived, despite engaging in self-induced vomiting, and that binges may not be very clearly related to hunger and satiety. The findings need further investigation. If replicated, they have implications for cognitive theories of bulimia nervosa, which assume that binge-eating is closely linked to dietary restraint.

Loss of control

DSM-IV requires a 'sense of loss of control over eating' (American Psychiatric Association 1994, p.545) during a binge. This has rarely been investigated.

One study (Jansen *et al.* 1990) compared clinical and non-clinical binges, by looking at eating in patients and a community sample who did not meet diagnostic criteria. Sense of loss of control was present in the clinical binges, but was also found in the non-clinical binges.

Frequency of binge-eating

DSM-IV criteria stipulate that bingeing must occur twice a week for three months in order for a diagnosis to be made.

Most clinical samples report much greater frequencies than this. Frequency also seems to increase with likely severity of symptoms. For example, self-identified binge-eaters have, on average, just over four binges a week, BN out-patients have ten and in-patients have thirteen (Guertin 1999).

The high frequency of binge-eating (well above that required for a diagnosis) is probably because many clinics and research centres see only those with the most severe symptoms. The usefulness of 'two binges a week for three months' in the diagnosis of BN is discussed below.

Those with BN do, however, consume fewer meals a day than controls (Davis *et al.* 1988). Since meals and snacks seem similar in calorie content in the two groups, this may explain the lower non-purged intake of those with BN compared to controls (Gendall *et al.* 1997), which is often observed clinically. However, when binges are included in the calculation, number of eating episodes per day is similar in the two groups (Hetherington *et al.* 1994). The frequency of bingeing and normal eating episodes in those with BN and control participants is summarized in Table 2.4.

Table 2.4 Frequency of binge-eating and normal eating in BN and control participants

Bulimia nervosa patients	Control participants
More binges	Fewer (no) binges
Fewer meals	More meals

Duration of binges

In discussing length of binge-eating, DSM-IV refers to a 'discrete period of time' (American Psychiatric Association 1994, p.545). This is usually defined as less than two hours.

Duration of binge-eating, in BN patients, seems to range from 30 minutes to just over an hour (Guertin 1999). In one study (Walsh *et al.* 1989), controls' binges lasted a similar length of time, and both patients' and control's binges were significantly longer than their normal eating episodes (Walsh *et al.* 1989). However, duration of meals was similar in the two groups.

Speed of eating

Patients often describe eating quickly when bingeing (Abraham & Beumont 1982). This is supported by empirical studies.

Jansen *et al.* (1990) found that binges by patients with bulimia nervosa differed from binges reported by a non-clinical binge-eating sample in 'eating rapidity'. Patients ate more quickly during a binge. LaChaussee *et al.* (1992) found that controls, but not most of the patients, slowed their rate of eating when asked to binge. However, when asked not to binge, the two groups did not differ in rate of eating.

Content of binges

Those with BN typically report that their binges are high in carbohydrates (e.g. Abraham & Beumont 1982).

Most research into this has been conducted within the serotonin hypothesis, i.e. the hypothesis that carbohydrates are craved to compensate for low levels of the neurotransmitter, serotonin. However, initial research did not support the suggestion (Walsh *et al.* 1992). Binge meals and normal meals, for both BN patients and controls, consisted of similar amounts of carbohydrate. More recently, studies have found that fat appears to be the most important source of macro-nutrients during bingeing (van der Ster Wallin *et al.* 1994). However, when quantity and patients' stated preferences were examined (as opposed to calories consumed), carbohydrate was indeed the most important ingredient (van der Ster Wallin *et al.* 1994).

One study has examined micro-nutrients (Gendall *et al.* 1997). It found that non-binge-eating was low on iron, zinc, and calcium, compared to RDAs (recommended daily allowances) and, even when binge-eating was included in the calculation, many of those with bulimia nervosa were still low on intake of iron and zinc. However, low levels of these may also be typical of many young women without an eating disorder.

A small number of studies have investigated forbidden foods, i.e. foods that those with BN do not usually allow themselves to eat. Kales (1990), for example, found 69% of binge-eating episodes in BN contained self-defined 'forbidden foods', whereas only 15% of normal eating episodes did. This finding is consistent with the idea, in cognitive theory, that forbidden foods may play a role in binge-eating.

A few studies indicate that the foods eaten and temporal consumption in bulimia nervosa differ from that of normals (and from those with binge-eating disorder) (Cooke *et al.* 1997). Hadigan *et al.* (1989) found that BN patients spent more time eating dessert and snack foods in a binge than did controls. As noted in Chapter 1, those with BED, unlike those with BN, also appear to eat foods normally eaten at a meal when they binge (Fitzgibbon & Blackman 2000).

Context of binge-eating

Anecdotally, binges are more likely to take place in the afternoon or evening (at times when the bulimic is more likely to be alone) than in the morning.

Mitchell *et al.* (1981) found that the usual time for binge-eating was in the afternoon or evening, although three patients (out of 25) preferred to get up during the night and binge. Hetherington *et al.* (1994) also found that a significantly greater number of binges took place in the evening (53.2%) and afternoon (32.6%), than in the morning (14.2%). However, when binges take place seems no different from when non-binges occur, or from when controls' eating takes place (Weltzin *et al.* 1991). One study found a positive correlation between number of people present and total calories eaten in a meal, although the relationship was much weaker in those with BN than controls (Elmore & De Castro 1991).

Other features

One study (Mitchell *et al.* 1999) found that bulimia nervosa patients were less likely than those with BED to say they enjoyed food, including the taste, smell, and texture, while bingeing.

One study found more pathological eating and greater negative affect when bulimics were given a high calorie, as opposed to a low calorie, meal (Hetherington *et al.* 1993). Aberrant eating behaviour included picking at food, food disposal, distaste for food, and abnormal verbalisations. Another study, however, using the same rating scale (Bourne *et al.* 1998), found that BN patient scores did not differ from those of restrained eaters.

Most of the DSM-IV diagnostic criteria for defining a binge (e.g. size) seem to distinguish between binge-eating in patients and controls, and between patients' bingeing and normal eating. An exception is sense of loss of control but, as yet, this has not been investigated in many studies. Other features (e.g. speed of eating) mentioned or observed

Table 2.5 Features that distinguish patients' and controls' binge and normal eating

Binges are larger, and more frequent in BN patients than binges in controls

BN patients eat fewer meals and snacks than controls

BN patients, unlike controls, eat more quickly during a binge than a meal

Patients eat more carbohydrates (by quantity and preference) in a binge than controls, but more fat (by calories)

Patients eat more forbidden foods in a binge than controls

Patients spend more time eating dessert and snack foods in a binge than controls

Patients may show more pathological eating behaviour and negative affect when given a high calorie meal

anecdotally, may also distinguish the binge-eating of patients and controls, and bingeing from normal eating, though others (e.g. time of eating) may not. Characteristics of normal meals are often similar in the two groups, but there may be differences in their frequency. This may explain differences between non-binge intake in patients and total intake in controls (e.g. in number of calories, level of micro-nutrients). However, some studies suggest that, despite these differences, patients and controls may not differ in total number of calories absorbed each day. A summary of the features (including DSM-IV features) that seem to distinguish patients' and controls' bingeing and normal eating can be seen in Table 2.5.

Binge-eating in the general population

Binge-eating is not confined to those with an eating disorder. It is also common in female college students (e.g. Halmi *et al.* 1981; Hawkins & Clement 1980). One early study found that 56% of college women reported binge-eating (Katzman *et al.* 1984), even though most did not have an eating disorder.

Many early studies of binge-eating in the general population were not methodologically rigorous. Very broad criteria, or open-ended questions, were used to identify binge-eating, and often a time frame was not specified. As a result, studies included people who had very different understandings of the term 'binge', and all those who had ever binged, as well as those currently bingeing. Early studies also rarely set a minimum frequency standard.

With tighter methodology, figures tend to be lower. Using a minimum criteria of once a week, and including 'sense of loss of control' in the definition, one study of university and school students found that only 17% had ever experienced binges (Abraham *et al.* 1983).

Focusing on current bingeing and defining 'current' also leads to lower estimates. A study of young women attending a family planning clinic used a narrow definition of binge (Cooper & Fairburn 1983), and looked only at recent behaviour. This found that

20% of the sample had binged once in the last two months, while 6.8% had binged weekly during that time.

Figures are also lower when older women are surveyed. A rate of 3.8% for current binge-eating (defined using DSM-III-R criteria) was found in a sample of women aged 18–75 years (Bruce & Agras 1992).

Recent studies produce much lower estimates of binge-eating in the general population than those of early studies. However, estimates remain high, particularly in adolescents and young women (e.g. Field *et al.* 1997). Some studies also find relatively high rates in diverse samples—as high as, or higher than, in older studies of young women—despite using much more rigorous methodology (e.g. Kinzl *et al.* 1999). These results might, in part, be due to a rise in binge-eating (evidence for an increase in BN will be discussed in Chapter 6).

Theories of normal eating

Most research on the characteristics of binge-eating has been descriptive (see above), and not theory driven. Although theories of binge-eating and BN draw on assumptions historically associated with normal eating, very little attempt has been made to relate binge-eating to recent developments in the field of normal eating. Below, theories of normal (and restrained) eating will be presented and their relevance to bulimia nervosa discussed. The different theories are summarized in Table 2.6.

Early theories of normal eating were based on a set-point assumption. Hunger is triggered by the decline of the body's energy reserves below their set point. We become hungry (and start eating) when blood glucose levels drop below a certain level, and become satiated (and stop eating) when eating brings them back to this point. Normal eating is thus controlled primarily by physiological mechanisms.

This assumption is also made by restraint theory (which forms the basis for early cognitive theories of BN).

Restrained eating

Restraint theory was developed primarily to explain over-eating in non-clinical groups. Herman & Mack (1975) suggested that 'restrained eaters', who attempt to maintain their body weight below its natural (set point) level, are chronically hungry,

Table 2.6 Theories of normal and restrained eating

Set-point theory
Restraint theory
Cognitive theories (e.g. Booth)
Positive incentive theory
Settling point theories

and thus more susceptible to over-eating (initiate episodes of over-eating) in response to external cues, than non-restrained eaters.

Restraint theory evolved into a boundary model with a cognitive component. As well as the two (physiological) hunger and satiety boundaries of normal eating (Herman & Polivy 1984), it identified a third boundary. This is the diet boundary, a cognitive limit on eating, usually set below the satiety boundary. When breached (or perceived to have been breached) over-eating occurs, triggered by dichotomous thinking, sometimes known as the 'what the hell effect'. Eating then takes place until the satiety boundary (which is further from the hunger boundary than in non-dieters)[1] is reached.

In a series of counter-regulation experiments, Herman and colleagues demonstrated that, as would be predicted by the model, restrained eaters over-ate when they consumed a significant pre-load. This work has been extensively replicated and extended by other research groups.[2]

Herman & Polivy extended the theory to incorporate binge-eating. They argued that the binge-eater also has a diet boundary; but, when breached, eating continues to physical capacity. This is because the usual satiety boundary is missing.

Herman & Polivy draw attention to the continuities between bingeing and dieting, noting that 'we should … strive to integrate the various components of the bulimic syndrome into models of normal eating and dieting, rather than regard it as an alien condition' (Herman & Polivy 1988, p.36).[3]

Herman & Polivy (1988) suggest that it is the attempt to bring eating under psychological control that is the cause of dieters' (and BN patients') difficulties. This suggests continuity between dieting and BN. However, it also suggests discontinuity between normal eating and dieting (normal eating, unlike dieting, is assumed to be primarily under physiological control). The latter assumption has been questioned by those interested in normal eating. Recent (and not so recent) evidence suggests that, contrary to what is often thought, psychological factors (in particular, cognitive factors) may play a key role in regulation of normal eating.[4] Some of this evidence will be considered below.[5]

---

[1] Both hunger and satiety boundaries in restrained eaters or dieters are thought to be different from those found in non-dieters—affected to a greater extent by non-physiological cues.

[2] Note that both hunger and cognition are important.

[3] However, they also note that those with BN may differ from dieters in ways that verge on the qualitative. This includes differences in thinking and 'emotional eating'.

[4] Social and environmental factors are also important and will be discussed below—like psychological factors they do not have a clear role in many theories of the regulation of normal eating, especially as discussed in relation to binge-eating and BN.

[5] Some researchers have been arguing for a while that cognition in normal eating deserves more recognition. Booth, for example, notes 'one must hope that the psychology of food can move rapidly now into the mainstream of cognitive psychology' (Booth 1994, p.14).

Normal eating and BN: recent evidence

The factors that determine normal eating are often categorized into amount eaten, initiation of eating (loosely related to frequency of eating), context of eating, and type of food eaten. These categories overlap with most of those studied by those interested in binge-eating (see above), but have not generally been integrated with them. Unlike much clinical writing, explanations rather than descriptions have been presented. Some of these may be relevant to understanding binge-eating in BN. The overlap between the categories used in the two research fields is summarized in Table 2.7.

Amount eaten

This corresponds to clinicians' interest in size or amount eaten. However, rather than describing the phenomena, i.e. amount of calories consumed, researchers have been interested in causes, for example, in what stops eating or increases intake. While physiological factors are important, evidence also suggests that social and environmental factors can significantly influence the amount eaten. In non-clinical samples, palatability, for example, can over-ride physiological signals of satiety. Fat (the main constituent of binges in BN) is particularly palatable. Social factors also affect consumption—although people often eat more when eating with others, the opposite may occur. In bulimia nervosa, patients often eat less in the company of other people. To date, the psychological, particularly cognitive, factors involved in amount eaten in BN have not been investigated.

Initiation of eating

This corresponds (loosely) to clinicians' interest in frequency of bingeing. Initiation of eating can also be influenced by social and environmental factors, e.g. by cultural, family, and work routines. Recently, however, attention has been paid to psychological (cognitive) factors. In particular, it has been suggested that hunger pangs may be preparations for the food that is expected, rather than a response to an energy deficit (Woods 1991; Woods & Strubbe 1994). There is some evidence for this suggestion from animal work (Weingarten 1983). For example, rats for whom meals were paired with a buzzer and light, began to eat when the conditioned stimulus was presented, even though food was continually available and they were never food-deprived.

Table 2.7 Overlap in categories studied by researchers interested in normal eating and binge-eating

Normal eating	Binge-eating
Factors increasing or stopping eating	Size/amount eaten
Initiation of eating	Frequency of bingeing
Socio-cultural factors	Context of bingeing
Learning to eat (new) foods	Content of binges

Such findings form the basis for positive incentive theories (see below) in which cognitive factors play a key role. There has been some preliminary application of these to BN.

Context

This corresponds to interest in time of day and social setting. Social and cultural factors can influence whether or not eating takes place in non-clinical groups. Binges are also influenced by context; they typically take place when the person is on her own. The role of psychological factors in this has not yet been studied, either in a non-clinical or BN group.

Content

We have innate preferences for sweet, fatty, and salty tastes—the kinds of food eaten in a typical binge. However, we learn to eat other foods too, for example, those that contain specific vitamins or minerals. We also learn to eat foods that are initially unpalatable, and that have little nutritional content, but which are culturally valued. Learning can be influenced by psychological, including cognitive, factors although this is also little understood in relation to eating, either in non-clinical or BN groups.

It has been argued that set-point theory is unable to explain the influence of social, environmental, and cultural (including psychological) factors on normal eating (Pinel 2000). Cognition, i.e. what people say about their eating, has often been relatively neglected by those interested in normal and abnormal eating behaviour (Booth 1994), even though it can mediate learning and other processes. Interest in cognition in normal eating has focused primarily on factors that initiate eating. However, cognitive factors may be involved at all points in the regulation of normal (as well as binge) eating, in ways yet to be investigated. One possibility is that a comprehensive cognitive theory of binge-eating, closely linked to theories of normal eating, may be possible. Thus, binge-eating may be conceptualized, in part, as an extension of normal processes.

Positive incentive theories

These have been suggested as an alternative to set-point theory by those interested in normal eating. They assume that we are drawn to eat, not primarily by an internal energy deficit, but by the anticipated pleasure of eating, i.e. by our beliefs. Beliefs are not the only factor—hunger felt at any one time depends on an interaction between internal influences, i.e. gastro-intestinal and metabolic, and dietary and external influences, but beliefs play a more important role than has been thought by those interested in set-point explanations.

There is some preliminary evidence that eating is determined by anticipated pleasure in bulimia nervosa. Using the Eating Expectancy Inventory, Hohlstein et al. (1998) found that two sub-scales—beliefs that eating helps manage negative affect, and belief it alleviates boredom—correlated with bulimic symptoms in a non-clinical sample. In addition, the belief that eating helps manage negative affect distinguished a BN group from anorexics and controls.

If replicated, findings such as these have implications for the understanding and treatment of binge-eating. They shift the focus to a wide range of cognitions and cognitive processes, beyond that of simple dichotomous thinking. As suggested above, they also create a link between normal eating and BN. Thus the challenge in BN may be to work with how the normal process of eating has gone wrong.

Settling point theories

It has often been assumed that the body seeks to maintain weight at a set-point level. This theory, focused on long-term regulation of body weight (defence of levels of body fat), complements the set-point theory of eating regulation. It is also an assumption frequently made in cognitive theories of bulimia nervosa.

However, it has been proposed that it is inconsistent with the facts, e.g. the fact that adults can gain or lose large amounts of weight, and maintain that change. An alternative, the concept of a 'settling point' has thus been proposed. This is a 'point at which various factors that influence the level of some regulated function achieve an equilibrium' (Pinel 2000, p.266). The concept provides a loose homeostatic mechanism without the assumption of a set point. It seems likely, though not yet investigated empirically, that cognitions or beliefs could be one factor that influences an individual's settling point.

Other theories of binge-eating

Many of these are compatible with or extend restraint theory.

Purge opportunity hypothesis

This hypothesis suggests that binge-eating is maintained by the opportunity to purge (Rosen et al. 1985b). Like restraint theory, it is cognitively mediated. In its support, several studies show that bulimic women eat less than control women in test meals composed of 'frightening' foods', when there is little or no opportunity to vomit. The suggestion is that bulimic women both evaluate whether or not there is an opportunity to purge before binge-eating and, in addition, believe that purging will counteract the fattening effects of the food consumed. The model is not elaborated in detail. It is also limited in the types of cognitions specified.

Forbidden foods hypothesis

This model is a version of the abstinence violation effect. It suggests that the finding that women with bulimia typically binge on one or more 'forbidden' foods is mediated by dichotomous attitudes about specific foods. Typically, eating 'forbidden' foods is followed by a perception that a rule has been broken and that all control over eating is lost (Kales 1990). Again, it is limited in its specification of cognitions, but is very compatible with restraint theory—which draws attention to dichotomous thinking (Polivy & Herman 1985).

Escape hypothesis

This theory hypothesizes that binge-eating is motivated by a desire to escape from heightened self-awareness (Heatherton & Baumeister 1991). Focus of attention is narrowed to the present and immediate stimulus environment, thus avoiding any unpleasant thoughts and feelings related to the self. Heatherton & Baumeister (1991) outline six predictions that this model makes, and conclude that existing evidence is broadly compatible with them. Although developed from a social psychology perspective, and phrased in terminology from this area, this model is also compatible with many of the ideas of restraint theory, e.g. the role of cognitions in disinhibited eating. However, it differs in that dieting or restraint is not necessarily a prerequisite for bingeing. In this respect it is more compatible with recent developments in cognitive models of bulimia nervosa (see Chapter 8).

Assessing binge-eating

Two questions have been asked: What is a binge? and Does the size of a binge matter? A 'gold standard' for assessing binge-eating has also been developed.

What is a binge?

The DSM-IV (American Psychiatric Association 1994) definition of a binge emphasizes the amount eaten and sense of loss of control. However, research suggests that there are differences in the use of the term. For example, a community sample of young women emphasized loss of control, while amount eaten was less important (Beglin & Fairburn 1992). A student sample also emphasized loss of control above quantity and amount eaten in a short period of time (Johnson et al. 2000). This suggests that care needs to be taken to make sure that the term is understood in its DSM-IV use, if the aim is to find out about bulimia nervosa (Beglin & Fairburn 1992).

There is also disagreement amongst professionals (when asked about binge-eating disorder) over whether particular eating episodes are binges, as well as between patients, non-clinical binge eaters, and professionals (Johnson et al. 1997).

Does size matter?

One study suggested that a large amount of food might not be a necessary feature (Niego, Pratt & Agras 1997). EDE guidelines were used to rate binges on the daily food records of 101 patients who had received cognitive behaviour therapy. The EDE identifies two types of binge—objective and subjective—with only the objective being large in absolute terms. However, the two types did not correlate differently with measures of psychopathology, though they did change differently with treatment. This suggests that it may not be a clinically useful distinction.

A further study by the same research group found that it was the cumulative number of binges, not size of binge (subjective or objective), that explained most of the variance in Can Do scores on a Self-efficacy measure (Pratt *et al.* 1998). Pratt and colleagues suggest that the emphasis in the diagnostic criteria for a binge may need to change, not least because it determines who has a clinical disorder and helps set an agenda for research. More recently, however, a study found that impulsiveness distinguished objective from subjective binges (Keel *et al.* 2001).

The eating disorder examination

There is considerable agreement among the experts that the 'gold standard' for assessing binge-eating (and other features associated with eating disorders) is the Eating Disorder Examination, a semi-structured interview conducted by a trained researcher (EDE: Fairburn & Cooper 1993). Although several other interviews have been developed to assess the psychopathology of eating disorders, the EDE is reliable (Cooper & Fairburn 1987; Rizvi *et al.* 2000) and valid (Cooper *et al.* 1989; Wilson & Smith 1989) and has generated most research. It defines different types of over-eating—objective and subjective, with or without loss of control. It can also be used to establish a diagnosis. Its big advantage over self-report questionnaires is that it allows the participant to elaborate on the response, and the investigator to clarify the meaning. Unlike some standard structured psychiatric interviews, it does not over-estimate binge-eating (Wade *et al.* 1997).

A self-report version has also been developed (Fairburn & Beglin 1994). Compared with the interview, it appears to be most useful when items are not complex, i.e. for detection of self-induced vomiting, laxative misuse, dietary restraint (see also Luce & Crowther1999). For more complex, less easy to define features, including binge-eating, the self-report questionnaire generates higher figures than the interview. It has been recommended that the interview be used to establish a diagnosis of bulimia nervosa. Once established, and participants have been instructed in the definition of a binge, it can then be used in self-report form for repeated assessment and monitoring progress with treatment (Loeb *et al.* 1994).

Compensatory behaviours

Compensatory behaviours include self-induced vomiting, use of laxatives/diuretics, excessive exercise, fasting, and diet pills. They are not so much studied as binge-eating, perhaps because they are often considered secondary to it, and not thought to need treatment in their own right. Below, the main compensatory behaviours will be discussed in turn and, where these exist (e.g. for dieting), relevant theories developed to explain them will be considered.

Vomiting

Studies of BN patients usually find that they are vomiting more frequently than they are bingeing (although many researchers do not report frequencies separately), and that figures are high. An early study indicated that while 48.6% of patients were binge-eating

Table 2.8 Binge-eating, vomiting, and laxative abuse in clinical and non clinical groups

Bulimia nervosa patients	Non-clinical groups
Vomiting more common than binge-eating	Vomiting less common than binge-eating
Laxative abuse less common than vomiting	Laxative abuse more common than vomiting

at least once daily, 74.3% were vomiting at least once a day (Fairburn & Cooper 1984). Similarly, in the month preceding start of treatment (in a controlled study with rigorous assessment procedures), mean frequency of vomiting was rather higher than bingeing (Fairburn *et al.* 1991b).

However, when binge eaters in the general population are surveyed, figures for self-induced vomiting tend to be lower. In a college sample, only 25% of those who met DSM-III criteria for bulimia had ever vomited to control their weight (Gray & Ford 1985). In more broadly based samples, vomiting to control weight is relatively rare. Cooper & Fairburn (1983) found only 2.9% of a sample recruited through a family planning clinic had ever induced vomiting and only 0.5% were currently engaging in the practice. A replication of this study in a different geographical region produced similar figures (Cooper *et al.* 1987). A recent study of high school girls (aged 12–18 years) found higher rates, 15.4% and 11.4% of two samples, had vomited at least once to lose weight (Phelps *et al.* 1993). However, in all studies (with the exception of Phelps *et al.* 1993, who did not provide the figures), binge-eating was much more common than self-induced vomiting. A summary of the relative frequency of binge-eating and vomiting in BN and non clinical groups can be seen in Table 2.8.

Theories of vomiting

Rosen and Leitenberg (1982) have suggested that vomiting in bulimia nervosa may serve to reduce anxiety, rather as compulsive handwashing serves to reduce anxiety in obsessional disorders. Based on this theory, they developed a response-prevention approach to treatment. Support for the model is, however, limited. While preliminary findings suggested that the treatment was promising (e.g. Rosen & Leitenberg 1982), research has failed to find much support for the hypothesized mechanisms (Leitenberg *et al.* 1984).

Laxatives

In clinical samples, laxative use to control weight, although high, seems less common than self-induced vomiting. Of patients in a case series, 60.6% (Mitchell *et al.* 1985) had a history of abusing laxatives, compared to 88.1% with a history of vomiting. In a community study, following a television documentary about bulimia nervosa, 42.3% of those who fulfilled diagnostic criteria, were abusing laxatives (Fairburn & Cooper 1984). However, in college and community samples, use of laxatives to control weight seems more common than self-induced vomiting. Gray & Ford (1985) found that 36%

of their sample had used laxatives (compared to 25% who had vomited). In a family planning clinic sample, just under 5% used laxatives to control weight (Cooper & Fairburn 1983), compared to 0.5% who currently induced vomiting. A review of 73 studies (Niems *et al.* 1995) found that the lifetime occurrence for laxative abuse in the community was 4.2%. This seems high compared to community figures for vomiting (see above), although it does include reasons for abuse apart from weight loss. A summary of the frequency of laxative abuse, compared to vomiting, in clinical and non clinical groups can also be seen in Table 2.8.

Characteristics of laxative abusers

One study found that laxative abusers with BN (compared to those who did not abuse them) were more likely to take diuretics and diet pills. They were also more likely to chew and spit out food, and to have a history of suicide attempts, self-harm, and prior in-patient treatment for depression (Mitchell *et al.* 1986a). Other studies have found that laxative abuse is associated with greater anxiety (Weltzin *et al.* 1995) and that it predicts perfectionism, and avoidant personality disorder features (Millon 1983). Others have found that laxative abusers are more dissatisfied with their bodies and have a greater drive for thinness (controlling for vomiting). It has also been suggested that they have a fundamental sense of dissatisfaction with themselves, not tied to their weight and shape, which may help to explain a tendency towards other serious self-destructive behaviours (Waller *et al.* 1990).

Diuretics

Data on abuse of diuretics is rarely reported. Thirty percent of those from a clinic sample reported using diuretics at least once a week (Abraham *et al.* 1983). Other studies report lower rates. In an adolescent group, 4.8% of those with a DSM-III diagnosis took diuretics at least weekly (Johnson *et al.* 1984), while 1.7% of the controls also reported this behaviour. Case reports indicate that diuretic abuse is often associated with abuse of laxatives and diet pills, but also with more unusual methods of weight control, including the use of illicit drugs such as amphetamines, and withholding of insulin in diabetes (Pomeroy *et al.* 1988).

Diet pills

There is little information on the use of diet pills. One study (Johnson *et al.* 1984), reported that 24.2% of those with BN in a college sample were taking diet pills at least weekly, compared to 5.3% of controls. A sample of middle and high school children found that 6.1% and 11.9%, respectively, were using diet pills (Phelps *et al.* 1993).

Exercise

Just over a quarter (28.6%) of a patient series (Fairburn & Cooper 1984) used exercise as a weight-control strategy. This was similar in those with bulimia nervosa responding following a television documentary (Fairburn & Cooper 1984). In an unselected community sample the figure was much lower (7.3%: Cooper & Fairburn 1983).

Compulsive exercising seems less common than in anorexia nervosa. Using a detailed structured interview, one study found that a large number (adults and adolescents) with eating disorders were exercising excessively, but that this was more frequent in anorexia nervosa. The authors note that pre-morbid levels of exercising predict exercise in the acute phase, and they also point to some of the adverse effects of strenuous physical activity in those who are malnourished (Davis *et al.* 1997).

There is some suggestion that those with bulimia nervosa who exercise compulsively score more highly on measures of body dissatisfaction and distress following a two pound weight gain, as well as being less likely to vomit or use laxatives. In community samples it has been found that participation in a regular fitness programme is related to weight and shape concerns (Davis *et al.* 1990a). Koslow (1998), also studying exercise, found that 18–30-year-old women rated benefits to aesthetic enhancement (improvements in physical appearance) as more important than other benefits, including health, social and emotional, and improved performance in competitive situations.

Unusual purging techniques

There have been a few case reports of unusual purging techniques in bulimia nervosa. Tiller & Treasure (1992) report four cases in which ipecac and paracetamol were used to induce vomiting. A case in which ipecac abuse led to physical debilitation—muscle weakness, cardiac impairment, and altered levels of serum enzymes—has also been reported (Friedman *et al.* 1987). Aspirin is also used to induce vomiting by some patients (Gordon *et al.* 1997).

Some unusual dehydration techniques have also been reported. Sauna abuse is reported by Mitchell *et al.* (1991a) in 14 patients (who also engaged in diuretic abuse and laxative abuse). Other techniques used to stop or prevent weight gain include the abuse of enemas (Mitchell *et al.* 1991c) and thyroxin (Crow *et al.* 1997).

Dieting

Fairburn & Cooper (1989) identify three types of dieting in those with bulimia nervosa:fasting, or going for long periods of time without eating; attempting to eat very little; and avoiding certain high calorie or forbidden foods.

Dieting is not essential for a DSM-IV diagnosis of bulimia nervosa. Fasting, for example, is only one of a range of possible inappropriate compensatory behaviours.

How common is dieting?

Few studies have evaluated this empirically in bulimia nervosa. In a community sample of restrained eaters, 71.4% of those with a DSM-III diagnosis of bulimia were dieting (Bruce & Agras 1992), while Gray & Ford (1985) found that 89% of DSM-III bulimic college students were dieting. Other studies produce similar findings (e.g. Johnson *et al.* 1984).

Dieting is also very common amongst young women who do not have bulimia nervosa. For example, Abraham *et al.* (1983) found 55% of healthy college students were dieting (defined as dieting strictly for more than two weeks). Nevo (1985) found that 55% of college students tried to lose weight at least once a month. Dieting is also common in pre-adolescent girls (see Hill *et al.* 1990).

Theories of dieting

Knowledge of the factors that lead to the initiation and maintenance of dieting is relatively limited. Recently, two separate theoretical models have been proposed to explain these two processes (Huon & Strong 1998). They bring together many of the factors (from different theoretical perspectives—ranging from attachment theory to social modelling) that have or could be thought to influence dieting in young women.

Initiation of dieting is seen to be the result of social influence (via the media, peers, and parents); individual psychological characteristics (especially autonomous functioning, negotiation skills, and social self-efficacy), together with parental style (care and over protection). Maintenance is seen to be the result of motivational influences, influenced by personality, the social context, self-efficacy beliefs, and diet history. The only cognitive variable considered in these models is self-efficacy.

Preliminary tests of the model (initiation version) suggest that lower perceived parental pressure to diet, perceived parental encouragement of autonomy, and social self confidence were associated with less dieting behaviour, even when BMI was taken into account (Strong & Huon 1998). Another test of the model, as well as confirming the role of parental influence, supports the role of peer influences (Lattimore & Butterworth 1999). A third study, of 1644 adolescent girls, found that social influences, particularly peer influences, were the crucial mediator in initiation of dieting. Differences in social skills, particularly the ability to negotiate and be assertive in social situations, reduced the impact of these pressures (Huon *et al.* 1999). The maintenance model does not yet appear to have been tested. These models include some, but limited, attention to cognitive variables.

Dieting and bulimia nervosa

It is widely accepted that dieting contributes to bulimia nervosa. Nevertheless, exactly how it does so is not yet clear. Two models have been proposed. The continuity model (e.g. Polivy & Herman 1987) suggests that bulimia develops when women have more extreme weight and shape concerns than normal, i.e. bulimia is a more extreme form of dieting. This model also assumes that dieters and restrained eaters are appropriate analogues for bulimia nervosa patients in research studies. The discontinuity model— first proposed by Bruch (1973), for anorexia nervosa—suggests that dieting develops into bulimia only if women also have other predisposing features, e.g. depression or impulse-control problems. This model assumes that dieting is necessary but not sufficient for the development of BN.

If dieting and bulimia are on a 'dieting' continuum, then a graded difference on measures of dietary restraint would be expected. BN patients should have a higher score than restrained eaters who, in turn, should score more highly than non-restrained controls. However, several studies show that BN patients and restrained eaters do not always differ in dietary restraint (e.g. Rossiter *et al.* 1989; Ruderman & Besbas 1992). To account for this finding, it has been suggested that there is a continuum of multiple associated features (features associated with eating disorders) (Dancyger & Garfinkel 1995; Ruderman & Besbas 1992). However, several studies suggest that general psychopathology seems to differ between groups (and is not on a continuum), particularly when clinical groups are studied.

It has been suggested, therefore, that the two-component model can be extended to bulimia nervosa. One component is concern with weight, appearance, shape, and eating, and a tendency to lose control over eating—which is shared with restrained eaters. The other component is general features, e.g. ineffectiveness, distorted interoceptive awareness, that distinguish BN patients from restrained and unrestrained eaters (Laessle *et al.* 1989b). Several findings (using between-group designs) support this general pattern (particularly when clinical groups are included in the study).

More recently, studies have used correlational designs to investigate how the core symptoms (e.g. binge-eating, purging behaviour) relate to associated features, including restraint. One study using this methodology found evidence for both the continuity and discontinuity perspective in a normal group (Lowe *et al.* 1996). Psychological symptoms associated with bulimia nervosa were continuous; for example, restrained eating and current dieting were associated with more symptoms related to bulimia (e.g. concern about weight and shape). But, most importantly, they were not associated with binge-eating itself. Thus continuity exists within normal groups for many symptoms, but does not extend to binge-eating. The findings of this study could help to explain why some studies, using non-clinical groups, have found continuity, but those using patients have not, i.e. findings depend on what features are (or can be) measured.[6]

Recently, it has been argued that the research designs used to date to investigate continuity and discontinuity in bulimia nervosa are not actually capable of distinguishing between the two theories. Meehl (1995), for example, suggests that a better method is to use taxometric analysis.[7]

One study using this method found evidence for a latent taxon or category, with the best indicators of the taxon being bingeing, purging and food preoccupation

---

[6] One recent study found support only for continuity (Stice *et al.* 1998), but this used a sub-clinical group.

[7] Taxometric analysis is based on the assumption that the relationship between indicators for a latent class will be different from the relationship between indicators of a latent dimension. It examines the covariances between all possible indicators of a disorder. Graphs of the distribution of these covariances assume different characteristic shapes according to whether or not the disorder is taxonic or dimensional.

(Gleaves *et al.* 2000). Dieting, except in conjunction with other indicators, did not seem to be important. Thus it seems that bulimia nervosa may not be simply on a continuum with dieting.[8]

Another study (Lowe *et al.* 1998) further suggests that weight-loss dieting may be less important in the maintenance of binge-eating than in its development. In support of their argument they note that not all those with BN are dieting to lose weight (unpublished data in Lowe *et al.* 1996). Moreover, even in the dieters it seems that dieting may not be as important as once thought. For example, patients' food diaries (unpublished data in Lowe *et al.* 1996), showed that the non-purged intake was no different from that of controls. Thus patients, for example, do not appear to be restricting in the way that restraint theory suggests. Contrary to restraint theory, Lowe *et al.* also suggest that attempts to suppress binge-eating may be helpful; without attempts at control, then the psycho-biological pressure created by past weight loss might increase bingeing. In support of this, they note that infrequent dieters who have given up dieting binge more, and that chronic dieting is not related to binge frequency.

Other evidence suggests that dieting may be less important than once thought in the maintenance (though not the development) of BN. For example, Steiger *et al.* (1999) present evidence that, although binge-eating is closely linked to dietary control in most people with bulimia, it is not always—and not in people with marked impulsivity.

A large-scale study has also looked at dieting as a predictor of the development and maintenance of core bulimic symptoms.

Stice & Agras (1998) selected six predictors or risk factors previously found by longitudinal research to be linked to bulimic symptoms (Stice, Nemeroff & Shaw 1996), including dieting. The strongest predictor of onset was dieting, for both binge-eating and compensatory behaviours (few have made this latter link before). However, while lower level of dieting predicted the cessation of vomiting, it did not predict the cessation of binge-eating (i.e. it did not appear to have a role in its maintenance).

For some of those interested in BN, the role of dieting in binge-eating has become less clear than restraint theory would suggest. Further work is required. If these preliminary findings are replicated, they have implications for cognitive theory and therapy, with its (currently) particular strong focus on eliminating dieting. They may also have implications for the use of restrained eaters and dieters as 'analogues' in BN research.

Self-worth linked to weight and shape

Russell (1979) described abnormal attitudes to weight and shape in his bulimia nervosa patients (see also Fairburn *et al.* 1986a). Systematic studies soon began to provide

----

[8] The link hypothesised is between normal eating and binge-eating (see above). It is also possible (and likely) that dieting is linked to normal eating. However, the behaviours do not seem continuous (as previously suggested) with each other. Rather, they seem to have been placed at opposite ends on a false continuum.

empirical data on these observations (Fairburn & Cooper 1984). However, early on (and in DSM editions, not until DSM-IV) these concerns were not closely linked to self-worth. The link with self-worth was implicit rather than explicit. Later, (Fairburn *et al.* 1986a, p.400) the link with self-worth became more apparent, 'by evaluating their self worth in terms of their shape and weight, patients are provided with a simple and immediate measure of their strengths and weaknesses'. These writers also note that weight and shape change may elevate mood and heighten self-confidence. This link has been incorporated into DSM-IV.

The link is also well-established in the general population; for example, weight concern and self-esteem is negatively correlated for 30–49-year-old women, although not for younger or older women (Tiggemann & Stevens 1999).

It is important to note (see Chapter 1) that some present with all the features of bulimia nervosa, except for this criteria (Palmer 1993). It has also been noted that some existing measures of the concept do not distinguish BN patients from restrained eaters (Goldfein *et al.* 2000). This may be because some measures do not tap the cognitive link between the self and evaluation in terms of weight and shape very directly. In addition, studies often fail to separate 'normal' from 'symptomatic' dieters.

Theoretical frameworks

In eating disorders, early studies of self-esteem/self-concept related the link identified above to both depression and body image in the context of socio-cultural factors and male female differences (e.g. McCaulay *et al.* 1988). For example, within a dynamic framework, and drawing upon Winnicott's concept of a 'false self', Striegel-Moore *et al.* (1993) found that body dissatisfaction (in a clinical and non-clinical group) was related to public self-consciousness, social anxiety, and perceived fraudulence—all dimensions of the social self. This suggests (implicitly) a link between weight and shape and the self. In support of this link, Heatherton & Baumeister (1991) found that binge-eaters have a heightened self-awareness of how they are perceived and evaluated by others.

Self-schema theory

A related theoretical framework—relevant both to the early emphasis on a link between weight and shape and self-esteem and, later, to developments in cognitive theory (Cooper *et al.* 1998)—see Chapter 8—is self-schema theory. This theory is taken from social cognitive psychology. Self-schemas are 'cognitive generalisations about the self derived from past experience, that organise and guide the processing of self-related information contained in the individual's social experiences' (Markus 1977, p.64). Markus *et al.* (1987), in an early example of self-schema work, noted that certain schema are more developed in some people than in others. For example, the extent to which weight is important to self-evaluation is more developed in some people. Such people are 'schematic', while those in whom the schema is not important are 'aschematic'.

This concept, Markus and colleagues hypothesized, would be reflected in differences in processing a variety of stimuli, which proved to be the case (although it has not been studied in a clinical sample).

Measures

Measures designed to assess the link between weight and shape and self-esteem are beginning to be developed. Until recently, there were only the two sub-scales of the EDE—weight concern and shape concern. One promising new measure is the Shape and Weight Based Self-Esteem (SAWBS) Inventory (Geller *et al.* 1997) developed on a non-clinical population but used in one study with patients who had eating disorders (Geller *et al.* 1998). It measures the relative contribution of weight and shape to self-esteem—and provides a rank-order score for both weight and shape. Psychometric properties are promising (e.g. Geller *et al.* 2000) and it distinguishes patients from controls. Looking at both positive and negative self-esteem, a recent study (using a specially devised measure) found that eating-disorder patients (a mixed group) involved more domains of self-esteem in negative (but not positive) weight-related self-evaluation than restrained eaters (McFarlane *et al.* 2001).

One problem with all these measures, however, is that they provide relatively indirect measures of the cognitions involved in linking weight and shape to self-esteem, e.g. through 'concern' or relative 'importance'. A measure that attempts to address this issue, is the Eating Disorder Belief Questionnaire (EDBQ: Cooper *et al.* 1997). This will be discussed further in Chapter 9.

Summary

The first part of this chapter examined the characteristics of binge-eating in bulimia nervosa. Empirical support exists for most of the characteristics identified in DSM-IV, and for some of the associated features. Developments in theories of normal eating were described, together with existing theories of binge-eating. The assumptions of existing theories (i.e. those based on restrained eating) were questioned, and the potential usefulness of developments in normal eating was highlighted. A possible link between normal eating and binge-eating, via 'positive expectancies' was discussed. The assessment of binge-eating was also summarized.

In the second part of the chapter, compensatory behaviours, including self-induced vomiting, and abuse of laxatives and diuretics, were discussed, together with related theories. Self-induced vomiting seems more common in clinical samples than binge-eating, but the reverse is true in non-clinical samples. In clinical samples, most other weight control methods, except dieting, also seem less common than vomiting. Vomiting is relatively rare in the general population.

In part three, dieting and its relationship to bulimia nervosa was discussed in detail. Continuum and two factor theories were discussed—it was suggested that the two-factor theory seems more plausible. Recent research also suggests that there may be a distinction between binge-eating/BN and dieting, and is not consistent with the idea that they are ends of a single continuum. There is also some recent evidence (which requires further work) that while dieting may be important in the development of BN, it may be less important than often assumed in its maintenance. Self-worth linked to weight and shape was then discussed. Theoretical frameworks that highlight a cognitive link between these two variables were identified, together with some relevant measures.

Chapter 3

The consequences and dangers of bulimia nervosa

Overview

Part one of this chapter will cover specific physical and physiological sequelae of the key symptoms of BN.

In part two, the dangers of dieting, and the proposal that many features of BN are effects of dieting, will be discussed. Part three and part four will cover effects on social and psychological functioning, and a small number of rare consequences. The plan for the chapter is summarized in Table 3.1.

Physical consequences have often been given a great deal of emphasis in BN. However, while they can be very serious, this outcome is (relatively) unusual. Psychosocial consequences, in contrast, have sometimes been rather neglected. Many of these are also serious, and very damaging for the individual. They may be common, and may have a wider impact (e.g. through direct effects on the family) than physical consequences.

Binge-eating

Clinical impression suggests that repeated and frequent binge-eating is likely to lead to weight gain over time, unless it continues to alternate with lengthy periods of fasting or very low calorie intake.

Bingeing also has other consequences. Its main consequences are summarized in Table 3.2.

It causes gastro-intestinal problems, particularly bloating and abdominal discomfort. It may lead to stomach cramps, wind, constipation, and diarrhoea. If the distended stomach presses against the diaphragm, it may also cause difficulty with breathing. In rare cases it can lead to gastric and duodenal ulcers, bleeding, acute gastric dilation (Mitchell *et al.* 1987b), and necrosis or tissue death (Abdu *et al.* 1987). In very rare cases, the stomach wall can become so stretched that it ruptures (Saul *et al.* 1981).

Frequent binge-eating may also lead to pancreatitis (inflammation of the pancreas), with severe abdominal pain, abdominal distension, fever, and increased heart rate (Gavish *et al.* 1987), although this is also rare.

Elevated cholesterol levels have also been found in binge-eaters (Sullivan *et al.* 1998b). These seem to be linked to chronicity of BN (Vize & Coker 1994) and may increase the risk of coronary heart disease and stroke.

Table 3.1 Summary of plan for Chapter 3

Physical and physiological sequelae
The consequences of dieting
Social and psychological sequelae
Rare consequences

Table 3.2 Physical consequences of binge-eating

Weight gain
Gastro-intestinal problems—bloating, abdominal discomfort
Breathing difficulties
Gastric and duodenal ulcers
Acute gastric dilation
Rupture of stomach wall
Pancreatitis
Increased cholesterol levels

Compensatory behaviour: self-induced vomiting

Vomiting has a number of consequences, some of them potentially very serious and not easy to detect without biochemical assessment. Its main consequences are summarized in Table 3.3.

Pulmonary

Pneumonia can occur (rarely) as the result of aspiration (swallowing into the lungs) of vomitus. There have been several reports of this in bulimic anorexia nervosa, but few in BN (Mitchell *et al.* 1987c).

Teeth

Dental problems, especially erosion, are relatively common in bulimia nervosa. In extreme cases (usually after several years) this may progress to pulp death (rotting of the teeth) and tooth loss. This is often very painful, and may lead to infections and abcesses. The pattern of erosion is atypical (Bouquot & Seime 1997), and can alert dental practitioners to the presence of bulimia nervosa.

Some studies suggest that erosion is related to duration and frequency of vomiting (Altshuler *et al.* 1990; Simmons *et al.* 1986), but others have not found this (Milosevic & Slade 1989; Robb *et al.* 1995). Various factors may be protective, including use of fluoride supplements in childhood or fluoridization of water supply. These differences may explain the conflicting results.

Table 3.3 Physical consequences of vomiting

Aspiration of vomitus—pneumonia

Dental and associated problems—tooth loss, joint (jaw) disorders, increased temperature sensitivity, caries, periodontal disease, gingivitis (gum disease), decreased salivary flow

Swelling of parotid glands

Transient purpura

Xerostomia

Throat injuries, infections, sore throat, blisters, hoarseness

Traumatic petechiae

Sub-mucosal haemorrhages

Loss of gag reflex

Tearing, bleeding, perforations of the oesophagus

Weakening of the oesophageal sphincter

Damaged knuckles

Electrolyte abnormalities—especially low potassium

If many teeth are lost this leads to over-closure of the bite, which can lead to joint disorders affecting the jaw and angular cheilitis (inflammation of the lips and deep fissures at their corners).

The damage to teeth is irreversible, although it will stop once vomiting stops.

Other dental problems may occur. These include increased temperature sensitivity (due to decreased thickness of the tooth between the mouth and the pulp). There may also be an increase in caries. This is probably related to high sugar and high carbohydrate intake during binge-eating. However, these problems are not found in all studies (Touyz *et al.* 1993) and, as with erosion, differences may be due to differences in exposure to fluoride.

Periodontal disease may also occur, and repeated vomiting causes bad breath. Gingivitis and gingival recession (gum disease) appear to be more common (Touyz *et al.* 1993), although most studies have not differentiated gingivitis from the more serious periodontis, where inflammation extends beyond the gums to the root and bone of teeth. Some studies have found reduced salivary flow, which may increase the risk of decay and erosion.

Treatment is possible for some dental consequences, for example, restorative procedures can be performed on severely eroded teeth. However, if vomiting persists this will not stop erosion. Methods to protect tooth surfaces from continued acid exposure may be helpful in some cases. There are also methods to help control increased tooth sensitivity.

Face

The salivary glands, particularly the parotid gland (located near the ear), may swell gradually. The swelling is usually, but not always, painless and the face may take on a round, chubby appearance. It is reversible and will usually gradually diminish as eating habits improve. Its precise cause is unknown.

Other facial problems include transient purpura (purple spots due to haemorrhaging into the skin), and xerostomia (dry mouth), the latter especially in those who are malnourished.

Throat

Vomiting may result in injuries to the back of the throat (e.g. from fingernails), which can then get infected. Recurrent sore throats, blistering (as well as mouth ulcers), and hoarseness are also common. Patients may have traumatic petechiae (red or purple spots caused by leaking blood) or et al.submucosal haemorrhages of the palatal mucosa (bleeding from the connective tissue around the palate).

Stomach

Inducing vomiting may lead to loss of the gag reflex. Although rare, violent vomiting can lead to tearing and bleeding of the wall of the oesophagus (Mallory–Weiss syndrome) or perforation (Boerhaave syndrome) of this tube. Repeated vomiting over several years can also weaken the oesophagal sphincter, the set of muscles at the top of the stomach. The contents of the stomach may then return spontaneously into the mouth, an unpleasant and embarrassing experience.

Fingers

Damage may occur to the knuckles of the hand used to induce vomiting (Russell's sign; Russell 1979). This is relatively common, although it may take many months or years to develop. Abrasions may appear and small lacerations, then callosities or scars will form. It is caused by repeated contact of the incisors to the skin of the hand.

Electrolytes

Body fluids and electrolytes can also be disturbed. The most serious is a low potassium level (hypokalaemia), which can result in cardiac arrythmias and, rarely, in renal failure and cardiac arrest. Symptoms include extreme thirst, dizziness, fluid retention, weakness and lethargy, muscle twitches and spasms. Up to half of those with bulimia nervosa in early studies have some fluid and electrolyte disturbance (e.g. Mitchell *et al.* 1983b). More recently, few and only minor (not clinically significant) abnormalities have been found (Peeters & Meijboom 2000). This may be due to differences in severity of patients—the latter study was conducted in a primary care rather than specialist setting. However, electrolyte abnormalities do not always correlate with vomiting (or other purging behaviour) and their reported frequency (Mitchell *et al.* 1987a). Visible symptoms also do not seem to correlate with abnormalities, and complications often occur unpredictably. If one electrolyte abnormality is found, then others are likely (Hall *et al.* 1988). Some of these may make it difficult to correct hypokalaemia.

Occasionally treatment may be required and/or regular monitoring may be necessary. However, in most cases the disturbance is mild. The effects usually disappear once vomiting (and other purging behaviour—see below) stops.

Vitamins

One study suggested that vomiting (and other methods of purging) decrease vitamin K levels (Mira *et al.* 1989). This is probably because of decreased absorption.

Some of those with BN find it difficult to induce vomiting manually, and use various agents as emetics. These substances can also be dangerous or have negative consequences.

Compensatory behaviour: emetics

Syrup of ipecac is a commonly used emetic (particularly in the USA, where it is relatively easy to obtain). Other agents (e.g. aspirin) are also used. Their dangers are summarized in Table 3.4.

Over a quarter of those with BN report using ipecac at least once (Bulik *et al.* 1992; Pope *et al.* 1986b). However, the rate falls considerably when BN patients are asked about use in the last two months (Greenfield *et al.* 1993). Thus, only a small number use it regularly, or over long periods of time.

It has been suggested that ipecac may have a direct effect on body weight (Salako 1970a, b), although there is no clear evidence for this.

Of its active ingredients, emetine is potentially the most dangerous (Manno & Manno 1977). It is cleared from the body relatively slowly (Gimble *et al.* 1948), and both repeated small doses and a single large dose can be equally dangerous. It can produce severe, even lethal, gastro-intestinal, cardiac, and neuromuscular complications. Most research on ipecac has been on people without eating disorders. Nevertheless, severe complications (and death) from ipecac abuse have been reported in bulimia nervosa (Ferguson 1985). Case reports suggest tolerance may develop (Palmer & Guay 1985), as it does in other groups, so that more is needed to produce vomiting. However, tolerance does not develop to the cardiac effects (Adler *et al.* 1980).

Other emetics used in BN include aspirin (Gordon *et al.* 1997) and paracetamol (Tiller & Treasure 1992). Studies (on groups without eating disorders) indicate that abuse of both can lead to complications. For example, Gordon *et al.* (1997) suggested abuse of aspirin may cause renal failure and coagulation abnormalities. Paracetamol is

Table 3.4 Dangers of emetic agents

Ipecac—gastro-intestintal, cardiac, neuromuscular complications, death
Aspirin—renal problems, coagulation abnormalities
Paracetamol—liver damage

particularly dangerous. Relatively small doses in excess of recommended guidelines can cause complications including, in some cases, fatal liver damage (Proudfoot & Wright 1970). No serious complications were reported, however, in four bulimia nervosa patients who were taking high doses of paracetamol (Tiller & Treasure 1992). There have been case reports of other substances being used as emetics in BN, including heroin (Mitchell 1987).

Compensatory behaviour: laxatives and diuretics

Stimulant laxatives are the type most commonly used by BN patients (Bulik 1992; Mitchell *et al.* 1988). There is little evidence (in non-eating disordered samples), that they reduce the absorption of calories (Bo-Linn *et al.* 1983; Lacey & Gibson 1985). The dangers of laxative abuse are summarized in Table 3.5.

Self-report from BN patients (Bulik *et al.* 1992) suggests tolerance occurs, with increasingly higher doses needed to achieve the same effect. Many continue to use them despite unpleasant side-effects—including diarrhoea, muscle and abdominal cramps, bloating, and dehydration. Stopping often causes constipation, rebound oedema, and craving, and prompts use again. Large amounts can cause electrolyte disturbances, including both hyponatraemia (sodium loss) and hypokalaemia (potassium loss). This may impair renal and cardiac functioning. Those also taking diuretics, and vomiting regularly, are particularly at risk.

A variety of other complications are possible, including gastro-intestinal bleeding, dehydration, and (with some types) unsightly rashes. Stimulant laxatives may also cause permanent damage to the gut wall.

Tolerance also develops to diuretics, and the dose may need to be increased to obtain the same effect. When use is discontinued, reflex fluid retention may occur. In BN this is often perceived as fatness and a cue for further use.

Abuse of diuretics can also lead to electrolyte disturbances, which can affect cardiac functioning. Either hypokalaemia (low levels of potassium) or hyperkalaemia (excess levels of potassium) may occur. Constipation may also result, and prompt abuse of laxatives. Different types of diuretics produce rather different patterns of electrolyte disturbance. Ammonium chloride, and caffeine, present in some preparations, can also cause uncomfortable symptoms.

Table 3.5 Dangers of laxative abuse

Sodium and potassium loss—renal and cardiac effects
Gastro-intestinal bleeding
Dehydration
Rashes
Damage to gut wall

Enemas

Enema abuse in bulimia nervosa (Coovert & Powers 1988) often supplements laxative abuse and, in many cases, these patients are not also vomiting. These patients may have more severe psychopathology, including (possibly) some evidence of thought disorder. The practice is often only elicited in response to direct enquiry. The consequences are similar to those of laxative abuse.

Dieting: diet pills

These include drugs related to amphetamines, which have been increasingly tightly regulated in recent years. Some, including the 'fen-phen' combination, have been banned because they have been associated with valvular heart disease.

Some initial weight loss is usual with these drugs but tolerance tends to develop to the anorectic effects after a few weeks. Dependence may then occur. They have potentially dangerous consequences if abused. In large quantities they can lead to restlessness, tremor, rapid respiration, confusion, hallucinations, and panic states, followed by fatigue and depression. This may result in cardiovascular and gastro-intestinal complications, which can (in extreme cases) lead to circulatory collapse, convulsions, and coma. The potential dangers of diet aids commonly used in BN are summarized in Table 3.6.

Bulk-forming agents do not generally promote weight loss, and may cause abdominal distention and, in extreme cases, intestinal obstruction. In those that reduce fat absorption, some of the weight loss may be due to reduced fat intake (which is usually necessary to avoid unpleasant gastro-intestinal effects). Other possible consequences include menstrual irregularities, headache, anxiety, and fatigue. They may also impair the absorption of fat-soluble vitamins.

Over the counter diet pills contain a wide variety of substances. In the USA many contain phenylpropanolamine (PPA), and are similar to the amphetamine 'look alikes' available on prescription. One study found these to be the commonest type of 'over the counter' diet pills favoured by bulimics (Mitchell *et al.* 1991b). Reports of efficacy in human populations vary, and reviews suggest that any effect is probably small (Blumberg & Morgan 1985; Lasagna 1988). Reports of safety also vary. While some

Table 3.6 Common diet aids and their problems if abused

Bulk-forming agents—abdominal distension, intestinal obstruction
Diet pills—PPAs—cardiac and other effects
Cough and cold pills containing PPA—cardiac effects
Benzocaine—swallowing, biting trauma
Others that may be problematic—caffeine, cascara, chromium picolinate

studies suggest that they are relatively safe (Bulik 1992), others (mostly case reports) have reported adverse effects including cerebral infarction, intracranial haemorrhage, seizures, acute nephritis, and cardiac arrythmias. In many cases they are known to increase heart rate and blood pressure.

Some diet aids contain the PPA-related substances ephedrine and pseudoephedrine. Both can increase blood pressure and heart rate, and both have been associated with heart problems and a number of deaths. Occasionally, patients will report abuse of over the counter medications, such as cold and cough remedies that contain PPA, particularly in the UK where PPA is less easily available in diet aids.

Benzocaine is also used as a diet aid. It decreases taste sensations by numbing the mouth and lining of the stomach. In large doses it can impair swallowing and cause biting trauma.

Other substances used in diet pills include caffeine, and natural fruit and vegetable extracts, such as cascara. None will result in real weight loss. Other substances that have recently become popular include: Chitosan, or animal fibre made from the exoskeletons of crabs, and other marine animals (this is the equivalent of cellulose in plants); Guarana seed extract (which has caffeine in it); Garcinia Cambogia, a form of citric acid; L carnitine, an amino acid; and chromium picolinate, a trace element (which helps in the metabolism of glucose and fat). There is little or no evidence for the efficacy of these substances in promoting weight loss. Some have been associated with adverse consequences, for example chromium has been linked to chronic kidney failure. Most, however, have effects (in the short and long term) that are unknown.

Thyroid hormone

A few case reports of abuse of thyroid hormone to increase basal metabolic rate, help weight loss, and counteract the effects of bingeing exist (Fornari *et al.* 1990; Schmidt & O'Donoghue 1992). Two possible sequelae of abuse include tachycardia and depression.

Dieting: restricting intake

Dieting to lose weight is extremely common. A review notes that about 61% of adults report having ever dieted, 32% report currently trying to lose weight, and 20% report currently dieting to lose weight (French & Jeffery 1994).

It has been suggested that dieting may do more harm than good—both to physical and psychological health. The evidence comes from a variety of sources, and is outlined below. It has also been argued that many of the features of bulimia nervosa may be a consequence of dieting. The sources of evidence that suggest that dieting is dangerous, and some of the problems associated with this evidence, are summarized in Table 3.7.

Table 3.7 Sources of evidence that dieting is dangerous, and its associated problems

Starvation studies	Pre-existing differences may explain the results
	Depression is extreme compared to BN
Obese dieters	Pre-existing differences may explain the results
	Recent evidence suggests the effect is positive, although stressful along the way
Yo-yo dieters	Problems probably predate weight difficulties
Restraint paradigm	Eating not equivalent—in size, loss of control
	Causal link has been questioned recently
Prospective studies	Findings may be due to weight loss or hunger not binge-eating or BN
	Cognitions do not seem comparable
	Pre-existing factors may be important

Psychological consequences

Starvation rations

A much quoted study is Keys *et al.* (1950). The participants (conscientious objectors) were fed starvation rations, so that they lost almost 25% of their body weight. They reported increased focus on food, e.g. they collected recipes, and talked about food and eating a lot. They became upset and irritable, apathetic and lethargic, and less interested in sex. When re-fed, some binged. Some also felt out of control, or became obsessed with food. Many of these features persisted even after weight was restored. Similar findings have been reported in prisoners of war (Polivy *et al.* 1994) and survivors of concentration camps (Favaro *et al.* 2000).

Keys' study is widely quoted in support of the view that dieting can have adverse psychological and behavioural effects, and may be a causal factor in bulimia nervosa. However, other possible explanations for Keys' findings have been suggested, and different conclusions have been reached. One possibility is that pre-existing individual features, and not dieting, best explain the results—there was no control group or relevant baseline. Another is that the very extreme degree of food deprivation and weight loss explains the results, and that this may not be an appropriate paradigm for 'normal' dieting or BN. Neither such extreme physiological deprivation and extreme hunger are typical of dieters or those with BN (see also Chapter 2). Restriction is also self-imposed in dieting and BN, not enforced.[1]

Obese dieters

Early reports on obese dieters suggested that dieting had negative effects, e.g. on self-esteem and depression, and even that it could trigger psychosis (for a review see

---

[1] This may create different psychological (and behavioural) consequences.

Smoller *et al.* 1987). However, more recent studies report positive outcomes when weight is lost, although dieting may be stressful along the way (Smoller *et al.* 1987). Negative outcomes may be due to pre-existing psychological problems. For example, binge-eating after the end of treatment, in obese people on a VLCD (very low calorie diet), was only observed in those who experienced binges during the baseline period (Telch & Agras 1993).

Yo-yo dieters

Yo-yo dieters, like some of those with bulimia nervosa, experience frequent weight fluctuations or 'weight cycling' (Heatherton *et al.* 1991). It has been suggested that this has negative psychological effects. One study (in an obese sample: Bartlett *et al.* 1996), for example, found a possible link between weight cycling, binge-eating, and dietary disinhibition. However, rather than causing eating problems, one possibility is that, as in obese dieters, these may predate weight cycling. Further research is needed to explore this possibility.

Restrained eating

Polivy (1996) argues that restrained eaters are remarkably similar to eating disordered patients. They have heightened affective responsiveness (e.g. Herman & Polivy 1975) and score more highly on personality measures, e.g. anxiety (Herman & Polivy 1975), self-esteem (Polivy *et al.* 1988), narcissism (Ruderman & Grace 1987), and on general measures such as the California Personality Inventory (Edwards & Nagelberg 1986), than non-restrained eaters. Like Keys' subjects they are more distractible and have difficulty concentrating (Herman *et al.* 1978), and tend to be more depressed (Rosen *et al.* 1987), and more anxious (Rosen *et al.* 1987). Importantly, however, restrained eating often leads to over-eating in experimental studies.

These parallels have also been used to argue that restriction of food intake causes many of the features of bulimia nervosa, including binge-eating and other symptoms (see Chapter 2). Most studies use robust experimental designs, so differences are unlikely to be due to pre-existing features. However, the analogy has been questioned. Patients, unlike restrained eaters, often have clinically significant psychological symptoms, and the over-eating of restrained eaters is not usually equivalent to a binge. There is a huge difference in calorie content of eating episodes, as well as in the nature of the over-eating (e.g. in sense of loss of control).

The causal link (that restraint triggers binge-eating) has also been questioned. There is some evidence that, when confounds are controlled, dietary restraint may not lead to over-eating (e.g. Jansen *et al.* 1992b). In a related study, 85% of restrained eaters did not report binge-eating, while over half who did binge were chronic dieters (Rand & Kuldau 1991). This suggests the possibility that dietary restraint may be a consequence of binge-eating, rather than a cause. A recent study found some support for this; tendency towards over-eating was a better predictor of restraint in restraint paradigms, than vice versa (Van Strien *et al.* 2000). Again, more research is needed into this possibility.

Finally, another recent study found that food deprivation of 19 h did not trigger binge-eating, or marked over-eating in bulimics, compared to unrestrained and restrained controls (Hetherington *et al.* 2000).

Prospective studies

These do not find that healthy young women who go on a diet start binge-eating. However, some find changes in psychological features and eating, which have been hypothesized to relate to binge-eating.

A small study (Laessle *et al.* 1996) found that, compared with the unrestrained phase, participants had stronger hunger feelings, and were more preoccupied with thoughts of food and eating, than in the restrained phase. They also experienced a greater sense of loss of control over eating, i.e. drive to eat more than allowed, fear of loss of control, and impulse to over-eat, and had more somatic and negative psychological symptoms.

Warren & Cooper (1988) found increases in preoccupation with thoughts about food and eating, increased ratings of 'felt a strong urge to eat' and 'felt out of control of your eating'.

Participants in these studies are food deprived (possibly unlike BN patients, see Chapter 2) and also usually lose weight. The findings may therefore be the result of hunger and weight loss, and unrelated to binge-eating or BN. There is also no evidence that the cognitions observed in these studies are similar to those found in BN (see Chapters 8 and 9).

Few longitudinal studies exist, but one suggests that pre-existing factors may be more important than dieting. Low self-esteem and psychological symptoms, rather than frequent dieting, were related to increase in psychological symptoms in adolescent girls (French *et al.* 1995). More longitudinal studies are needed to see if such findings are replicated.

Preoccupations

Many studies show that restrained eaters or dieters are more focused on food and eating, and on weight and shape-related information than the non-restrained. As suggested above, both hunger and pre-existing differences may be important in explaining these differences. Moreover, it is unclear whether such preoccupations reflect the key cognitive processes thought to be important in BN.

Cognitive performance

Dieters also do less well on information processing, immediate memory, and simple reaction times (Rogers *et al.* 1992)—again, this could be due to hunger or, in some studies, pre-existing differences.

Physical consequences

Metabolism

Dieting can lead to alterations in metabolic rate (Prentice *et al.* 1991), although this is much less than is popularly believed (Devlin *et al.* 1990). There is no evidence for an altered metabolic rate in bulimia nervosa.

Hormones

Dieting can affect hormonal balance and thus menstruation. One study found that menstrual cycles were disrupted in about 20% of young women for 3–6 months after dieting for 6 weeks (800–1000 kcal/day; Pirke *et al.* 1985). Menstrual disturbances are common in bulimia, but it is not clear whether this is due to dieting or whether it has a psychological basis.

Nutritional deficiencies

Dieters usually have nutritionally sound diets, except for intake of iron and calcium. However, non-dieters also eat less than the RDA for these (Nowalk & Wing 1985). Those with BN seem to have a nutritionally adequate, normal diet too, although early reports suggested that they did not (Kirkley *et al.* 1985a)(see also Chapter 2).

Taste perception

Dieters may show negative alliesthesia, i.e. failure to reject sweet tastes after eating a high-energy intensely sweet pre-load, and some salivary changes (Pliner *et al.* 1990). This has not been investigated in bulimia nervosa.

Serotonin transmission

Serotonin, a neurotransmitter in the brain, which is thought to play a role in normal eating and in food selection, can also be affected by dieting, particularly in women. For example, dieters have reduced levels of plasma tryptophan (the amino acid precursor of serotonin) (Anderson *et al.* 1990). Similar findings have been reported in bulimia nervosa (Jimerson *et al.* 1992). However, serotonin is also involved in mood regulation, and the link with eating in BN is unclear.

Osteoporosis

Dieting can affect bone density, and can contribute to osteoporosis. Preliminary findings suggest that BN may also be related to it (Newton *et al.* 1993). However, none of those in this study had sustained a bony fracture that could be attributed to their eating disorder (Newton *et al.* 1993).

Mortality

Many studies show that dieting, particularly 'yo-yo' dieting, is associated with increased mortality, especially death from cardiovascular disease (Wing 1992). However, there are methodological problems with many of these studies (French & Jeffery 1994). For example, it has not been shown that the weight changes studied are related to intentional dieting, rather than pre-existing illness. Some studies also look only at the overweight. The studies that do focus on intentional weight loss do not usually find excess mortality in dieters (e.g. Lean *et al.* 1990).

An exception is very low calorie diets (VLCDs), i.e. liquid, or meal-replacement diets. These have been associated with sudden death (Seim *et al.* 1995), particularly when protein intake is also low.

In summary, dieting may have fewer adverse effects than was once thought, unless extreme hunger and weight loss is involved.[2] In addition, it is not clear how similar, or significant, the symptoms that normal dieters have are to the understanding of BN.

Fasting

Fasting in BN may last from several hours to several days. One study looking at 24-h fasts, found 32.4% of BN patients fasted at least weekly (Pyle *et al.* 1983). However, little has been written on fasting in bulimia nervosa, and there are few empirical studies.

The closest relevant research is on the effects of short-term fasting in non-clinical volunteers. Much of this has been done with schoolchildren, and focuses on the effects on cognition of missing meals, usually breakfast. There is also some recent work on adults, including a small number of studies on dieters. Some of these investigate effects on mood.

The children's work suggests that missing breakfast interferes with cognition and learning, particularly in less well nourished children (for a review see: Pollitt & Mathews 1998). The evidence in adults is less clear cut (for a review see: Kanarek 1997).

In adults, missing lunch is associated with decreased performance on some cognitive tasks, but improved performance on others (Smith & Miles 1986, 1987). Missing lunch also affects mood. Those who eat lunch experience decreases in alertness and anxiety, and fatigue compared to those who do not eat lunch (Smith *et al.* 1988). However, the effect is mediated by several factors, including usual lunch size, and whether or not lunch is usually eaten. Kanarek (1997) has also suggested that beliefs about food may be important, e.g. the belief that high carbohydrate foods provide a quick burst of energy.

One study found that spontaneous dieters, compared to non-dieters (both groups fasting), showed deficits on a vigilance task, poorer immediate memory, and longer reaction times (Green *et al.* 1994) but that there were no differences between the groups on mood ratings. Another study found that fasting (for 19 h) in BN also did not affect mood, although it did subsequently lead to increased food intake (but not over-eating or bingeing) (Hetherington *et al.* 2000).

Excessive exercise

Excessive exercise can lead to injury and compulsion to exercise may mean that injuries are not given adequate time and rest to heal. Exercise can also increase the risk of stress fractures, e.g. collapse of spinal vertebrae or curvature of the spine, if osteoporosis is present (Rigotti *et al.* 1984).

----

[2] Or, alternatively, unless psychological problems already exist.

Table 3.8 Psychosocial consequences

Poor social adjustment
Lack of social support
?Depression
Lowered fertility
Complications associated with pregnancy
Impaired child rearing

Psychosocial consequences

Although bulimia nervosa can be a severe and disabling disorder, its psychosocial consequences have not been studied in detail. Its effects, however, seem similar to those of having any other chronic mental illness. This can include both psychological and social deterioration, and burden on carers. The main psychosocial consequences that have so far been investigated in relation to BN are summarized in Table 3.8.

Social consequences

Reports of family conflict, negative and rejecting family relationships, financial problems, and impaired work performance are common in clinical practice. These were relatively neglected in many early reports.

Recently, empirical studies have examined social adjustment (role functioning) and social support. This includes social networks and perception of social support. There is some evidence that all are poor in bulimia nervosa.

Social adjustment

Several studies find poorer adjustment in BN than normal community samples. Those with bulimia nervosa scored below community norms on all sub-scales of the Social Adjustment Scale (Weissman *et al.* 1978), including work, social/leisure, extended family, marital, parental, family unit, and overall (Johnson & Berndt 1983). The most frequent problems in those with worse outcome were in heterosexual relationships, job satisfaction, time spent in social activities, and family relationships (Reiss & Johnson-Sabine 1995). Social adjustment was also poorer than in controls, both overall and in work/school, social leisure, and extended family spheres (Herzog *et al.* 1987), and poorer in those with active symptoms, than those who were recovered (Rorty *et al.* 1999).

Early studies suggested that social recovery paralleled improvement in eating disorder symptoms (both in the short term: Keller *et al.* 1992; and in the longer term: Reiss & Johnson-Sabine 1995). However, follow-up studies produce mixed findings. One study found that social problems tended to be greater in those who had not fully recovered (Collings & King 1994). A long-term follow-up of a large sample (*n* = 177) over 10 years also found improvements in social adjustment compared to baseline—including better overall functioning, better work, social/leisure, and extended family relationships. However, it did not find improvements in marital, parental, or family relationships (Keel et al. 2000b). More who had done well with respect to eating disorder symptoms had a better overall adjustment and better work adjustment, but adjustment in other areas did not seem to be related to outcome. Work functioning was at a normal community level (Weissman et al. 1978). Family, as opposed to individual, adjustment seems to be related to client's outcome (Woodside et al. 1996).

Social support

Studies find that less actual and perceived social support are available in bulimia nervosa. For example, one study found that the actively bulimic had fewer relatives available for emotional support, and fewer friends available for needed practical help, though no differences in relatives available to provide practical support. Those with BN were also less satisfied with the emotional support from relatives, though they were no different from controls in satisfaction with emotional support from friends (Rorty et al. 1999). Another study found less actual emotional and social support from family, as well as greater dissatisfaction with this support than in controls (Tiller et al. 1997). Others also find less perceived social support from friends and family (Grissett & Norvell 1992). In addition, there are some reports from recovered BN patients that their parents were more harmful than helpful, or were perceived as not providing sufficient emotional support in the recovery process (Rorty et al. 1993).

Consequence or cause?

It is not clear whether poor social functioning is a consequence or cause of poor outcome. If they do not recover, those with BN generally have a poor social outcome (Johnson-Sabine et al. 1992), especially in relation to marriage or relationship with the opposite sex, and relatives. However, it is not clear whether this is pre-existing or the result of having a long-term eating disorder. Some problems remain when recovered, and it may be that this reflects initial vulnerability factors. Rorty et al. (1999), for example, found recovered BN patients had more kin available to provide emotional support than those actively bulimic, but were still less satisfied with emotional support from kin. Another possibility is that it may simply take some time to build up relationships after recovery.

Poor adjustment and lack of social support may also affect recovery. In other disorders (psychological and physical) there is considerable evidence for this. For example, Brown & Harris (1978) found social support affected outcome in clinical depression. Outcome and support are likely to be interdependent; once the symptoms start to improve, social support may start to improve (and vice versa). Social support has not yet been studied as a predictor of outcome in bulimia nervosa. It was not included in a recent outcome review (Keel & Mitchell 1997). One study found that employment at presentation was not associated with outcome (Collings & King 1994). Another found that there was no relationship between social support and length of illness (Tiller et al. 1997) but this was not a prospective study.

Explanations for poor social functioning

The reasons for poor adjustment and social functioning in bulimia nervosa have not been much investigated. They could be the result of self-imposed isolation, e.g. because of low mood, low self-esteem, shame and embarrassment at symptoms, or poor interpersonal skills (either predating the illness or a consequence of lack of practice). There is some evidence that BN patients have deficits in social skills. For example, they are less socially confident, less likely to seek out social encounters, and are rated as less socially effective than others (Grissett & Norvell 1992).

Negative interactions

Conflict and negative interactions also predict well-being (Abbey *et al.* 1985), and more than positive interactions (Rook 1984) in those without eating disorders. The way in which social support is assessed (received vs. perceived), personality, and coping style may also be important in this relationship (Finch *et al.* 1999). Some studies show that positive support in one domain can protect against conflict in another (Lepore 1992). There is some evidence for more perceived negative interactions and conflict (especially with the family) in bulimia, and it seems these may contribute independently to adjustment/bulimic symptoms (Grissett & Norvell 1992) and may also be involved in hindering outcome (Rorty *et al.* 1993). Importantly, these factors, particularly conflict or unmet needs for support, may be direct triggers of binge-eating (Grissett & Norvell 1992).

There is also some evidence that those with BN set lower ideals for social support (Tiller *et al.* 1997). Other possibilities are that cognitive distortions affect perception of social support, or that, as in depression, behaviour (both in relationship to mood, self-esteem, and eating) may elicit a negative reaction, thus perpetuating lack of support.

Psychological consequences

It is also difficult to separate psychological consequences of bulimia nervosa from causes. Like social consequences, they may or may not correlate with outcome.

It has been suggested that depression (Cooper & Fairburn 1986) is a consequence of bulimia nervosa. This is largely based on two findings: that it seems to resolve when the eating disorder improves, and does not usually need separate treatment; and that depressive (and anxiety: Steere, Butler & Cooper 1990) features primarily focus on eating, weight, and shape. But since treatments sometimes involve a focus on low self-esteem, they may also tackle any depression (the two tend to be highly correlated). Even if the focus of treatment is only on eating, the techniques being taught may generalize to other issues. While patients' most pressing concerns may be related to eating, weight, and shape, especially when the eating disorder is bad, this does not mean that other concerns are not important, or indeed causal.

Focus on depression, both in pharmacological and psychological studies, however, has been largely unproductive. Self-esteem, however, may be a much more important concept, and also more useful clinically (see Chapter 4).

Effects on fertility and pregnancy

Menstrual disturbances are common in bulimia nervosa (Treasure 1988). Nearly half may have amenorrhoea or marked menstrual irregularities; these seem to be related to a history of low body weight, childhood sexual abuse, less benefit from treatment, and greater length of time before seeking help (Glassman *et al.* 1991). Other factors include binge-eating, episodic starvation, weight fluctuations, excessive exercise, stress, and depression (Hudson & Pope 1984). Women with bulimia nervosa appear more likely to be referred to gynaecological clinics. In particular, they are more likely to be investigated for infertility (Abraham 1998) than controls, and this is more likely to occur when their eating disorder is active than when it is not. A recent study found three-quarters of their pregnancies were unplanned. In 75% of cases this was because menstrual irregularities were believed to imply infertility (Morgan *et al.* 1999). Those with BN are also more likely to have terminations than controls (Abraham 1998; Blais *et al.* 2000). Clinically, pregnancy may also occur because women taking the contraceptive pill may not realize that repeated vomiting can make it ineffective.

Many women with bulimia nervosa who become pregnant fear that their eating habits will have an adverse effect on their unborn child. This can result in decreases in binge-eating and vomiting (and other weight-loss strategies), and some stop altogether by the end of pregnancy (Lacey & Smith 1987). However, while some maintain their gains, others resume binge-eating, either late in pregnancy, soon after, or after stopping breastfeeding. Others will continue throughout, especially in later pregnancies (Abraham 1998).

Blais *et al.* (2000) found a reduction in bingeing over pregnancy, and at 9-month follow-up, but no reduction in self-induced vomiting, weight and shape concern, over-exercising, and restraint. Another study found a reduction in bingeing and vomiting as pregnancy progressed, with one-third no longer bingeing in the post-natal period, although the trend was upwards again following the birth (Morgan *et al.* 1999). Overall, although 34% were 'cured', 58% were worse.

During pregnancy, those with BN seem more likely to have hyperemesis gravidarum. They are also more likely to have miscarriages—which may be the result of infertility treatment (a known risk in the induction of ovulation)—but only if they have an active eating disorder. Otherwise the risk is similar to normal. Other possible causes of miscarriage include inadequate weight gain, low pre-pregnancy weight, excessive exercise, and purging (Abraham 1998). Some studies have also found other complications, including maternal hypertension, foetal abnormalities, low birth weight (Franko & Walton 1993), and obstetric complications (Abraham 1998; Lacey & Smith 1987). There is also evidence that low birth weight (small for gestational age, not premature) babies are more likely to have a mother with an eating disorder (including bulimia nervosa), in the three months before pregnancy. However, a past history does not increase the risk (Conti *et al.* 1998). Others find no effect of bulimia nervosa on live births, although one recent study found a trend present (Blais *et al.* 2000), taking into account therapeutic abortions.

Bulimia nervosa patients are more likely to be treated for post-natal depression than controls (Abraham 1998). In one study, one-third developed post-natal depression, and this seemed more likely if they also had a history of anorexia nervosa (Morgan *et al.* 1999). Those with a history of anorexia nervosa were also, in this study, more likely to relapse following the birth.

Effects on children

An early report suggested that some mothers with bulimia nervosa attempted to slim down their babies (Lacey & Smith 1987). A case series found mothers' eating interfered with parenting directly (e.g. the child was ignored for long periods during bingeing). All the mothers had difficulties with breastfeeding, half the children had major feeding problems (including non-organic failure to thrive, and overweight), half had unwarranted concerns about the child's shape and weight, and wanted to keep the child's weight down (Stein & Fairburn 1989), while some restricted food availability. Other reports (most of those that follow are on mixed groups) suggest that mothers with eating problems have difficulties feeding their children in the early months (Evans & le Grange 1995). A recent study found that maternal eating disorder was related to feeding problems such as marked food refusal or food faddiness (Whelan & Cooper 2000).

There is also some evidence of growth faltering in infants of mothers with eating disorders, i.e. smaller weight for length and weight for age. However, there is no evidence that this is related to mothers' psychopathology (Stein *et al.* 1996).

Another study found that conflict at meals, and mothers' weight and shape concerns were related to the infants' weight (Stein *et al.* 1994). Mothers with eating problems were more intrusive and less facilitating, and expressed more negative emotions during meals (negative emotions directed towards the infant). Overall, there was more conflict and infants were less cheerful at meals (and also at play). However, there were no differences in positive expressed emotion (Stein *et al.* 1994). Others have found fewer positive comments during meals (about food, eating), and that mothers do not eat with their children (Waugh & Bulik 1999).

It has been suggested that the antecedents of conflict are failure to acknowledge the infant's cues, inability to put aside concerns about mess, and to put the infant's autonomy first. One study found that eating disordered mothers seemed less likely to respond in a child-centered way (though they could do so). It has been suggested that this may lead to poorer growth, because less food is consumed. It may also have implications for the development of autonomy and pro-social behaviour (Stein *et al.* 1999).

Mothers with more severe eating symptoms also misperceived their infant's shape and preferred smaller infants (Stein *et al.* 1996); although, in general, there is no suggestion that mothers are less satisfied with the child's appearance or shape than controls (Waugh & Bulik 1999).

However, one study found concern about daughters' weight (previous studies had asked about shape and/or appearance), compared to sons' and controls, at 2–5 years, although there were no differences in child's BMI. This was also related to the mothers' eating symptoms. Mothers with eating disorders were also more likely to use food for non-nutritive purposes, and perceive that their children had more negative affect (Agras, Hammer & McNicholas 1999).

Finally, there is some suggestion that there are more emotional difficulties in children whose mothers have an eating disorder (Evans & le Grange 1995).

Other consequences

Bulimia nervosa may be associated with abuse of other substances that pose dangers, or with other potentially dangerous behaviours. These will be considered below. They are summarized in Table 3.9, and are usually relatively rare.

Manipulation of prescribed medication

Binge-eating, frequent dieting, and unhealthy weight loss practices, including use of laxatives and diuretics, seem common among adolescents with chronic physical illness, including diabetes, asthma, attention deficit disorder, physical disabilities, and seizure disorders (Neumark-Sztainer *et al.* 1995). Those with bulimia nervosa and diabetes often have poorly controlled diabetes, a long history of poor glycaemic control (although this may predate the onset of the eating disorder: Steel *et al.* 1987). One possible consequence of a physical illness is that it may be possible to manipulate medication to prevent weight gain or lose weight, e.g. in diabetes, thyroid disorder. Insulin dependent diabetics, for example, without insulin can lose weight even though

Table 3.9 Other (relatively rare) consequences

Abuse of prescribed medication
Abuse of over the counter medication
Complications due to smoking
Alcohol abuse
Caffeine abuse
Use of illicit drugs
Water intoxication
Death
Complications due to cosmetic surgery
Ingestion of foreign bodies, e.g. toothbrushes

over-eating, through urinary losses of glucose and ketones. There have been several case reports and case series (e.g. Hudson *et al.* 1983b; Szmuckler 1984) of patients missing insulin doses for weight control. This often puts them at risk of developing hyperglycaemia and serious physical complications (Steel *et al.* 1987). These can include blindness, and need for dialysis.

Abuse of over the counter preparations

Cough medicines

Patients with BN may abuse cough medicines (see above), because they contain PPA, which is often thought to have a role in weight loss. Some cold remedies (e.g. nasal decongestants) may also contain the related substances ephedrine and pseudoephedrine. Abuse of both these can increase blood pressure and heart rate, and have been associated with heart problems and a number of deaths.

Legal drugs

Cigarettes

The rate of smoking is high in bulimia nervosa—twice the rate of the general female population of a similar age (Bulik *et al.* 1992; Morbidity and Mortality Weekly Report 1989). It is also twice as high as in female psychiatric patients (Welch & Fairburn 1998). A recent study of adolescent bulimics and a non-clinical comparison group, however, found no differences (Wiseman *et al.* 1998). Adolescents with bulimia nervosa are more likely to smoke than those with anorexia nervosa (Wiederman & Pryor 1996).

There is some evidence that smoking in female adolescents correlates with weight concerns. Smoking may also be used to control appetite in bulimia nervosa (Bulik *et al.* 1992). Nearly three-quarters of those with BN had smoked to avoid eating or to control weight, compared with less than 20% in the normal and psychiatric control groups (Welch & Fairburn 1998). It was also, in some of those with BN, a reason for resuming smoking following periods of abstinence.

Alcohol

Alcohol can be used to excess by bulimic women. A large number of BN patients reporting alcohol use also reported alcohol-related black-outs (Bulik *et al.* 1992), although the percentage reporting drinking was lower than that in the general female population of similar age (Wilsnack *et al.* 1984). Many also reported that drinking led to bingeing.

Caffeine

There have been case reports of caffeine being used to help weight control (Fahy & Treasure 1991). It is widely found in tonics, 'pick-me-ups', pain relievers, and preparations to increase energy, as well as in coffee and diet cola. It is not clear how much it constitutes a risk to health, but many heavy users (Fahy & Treasure 1991) report symptoms suggestive of caffeine intoxication, e.g. headaches, anxiety, restlessness, tremulousness, sleep disturbance, and nausea. At high levels, irritability and tonic posturing occur. At very high levels, tachycardia and convulsions have been reported. It acts primarily as a diuretic but there is also some evidence that it influences metabolic rate (i.e. has a thermogenic effect) and that it has an anorectic effect.

Illicit drugs

Those with BN also seem more likely to use illicit drugs including amphetamines, marijuana, and possibly cocaine, than those with anorexia nervosa (Bulik *et al.* 1992), and more often than is found in the general population, although their use relative to other psychiatric groups is unclear. Ecstacy use has also been reported (Fornari *et al.* 1990; Mitchell *et al.* 1985). The extent to which these are used to control weight is not known.

Water intoxication

Excessive fluid intake can affect electrolyte levels, resulting in hyponatraemia (low sodium). It can be very dangerous, as a diagnosis may not be made until it is too late to do much about it. It is associated with a number of non-specific symptoms including tiredness, confusion, excitability, clumsiness, and muscle cramps. A small survey suggests that it may be relatively common in bulimia nervosa (Salkovskis *et al.* 1987). It may be used to induce vomiting, as part of a binge, or as an attempt at self-control (i.e. as a non-calorific binge).

Death

Until relatively recently there was little information on mortality rates in bulimia nervosa. It has been assumed to be less than in anorexia nervosa, where follow-up studies suggest a crude mortality rate (proportion of subjects dead at follow-up) ranging from 0 to 20% or more.

A recent review of follow-up studies, some involving treatment, some not, with a minimum of 6 months follow-up after presentation (Keel & Mitchell 1997), found a crude mortality rate in bulimia nervosa of 0.3% (seven deaths among 2194 women). This may well be an underestimate. Some women could not be contacted or refused to participate, and some of the studies included in this report had relatively short follow-up periods. Studies with a higher percentage followed-up tend to find more deaths. The standardized mortality rate (ratio of number of observed deaths to expected number, adjusted for age and gender) was 9.4% (although statistically insignificant, probably because of the small number of deaths). This is much higher than would be expected, though not as high as for anorexia nervosa. It seems at least equivalent to, or higher than, the rate in female psychiatric in-patients of equivalent age (Zilber *et al.* 1989). Cause of death for the seven cases in Keel & Mitchell's review was accidental in four cases (although one was related to complications of psychiatric drug treatment). Two were suicide and one was due to complications resulting from severe weight loss.

Some groups may have higher death rates. A recent study used a computerized database (Crow *et al.* 1999b) to trace those with BN seen by psychiatric services over a 5-year period in an emergency room. One death was found, giving a crude mortality of 2.4% (5.2% if considering only those over 25 at time of initial visit, i.e. all for whom computerized records could be accessed for deaths). While this may be a group at greater risk, it is also possible that the high ascertainment rate explains the findings.

There is some preliminary evidence that mortality rates decrease with length of follow-up (Nielsen *et al.* 1998). This reflects the pattern in anorexia nervosa, where 20–40-year follow-up produces fewer deaths than 6–12-year follow-up.

Other dangers

Patients may sometimes present for cosmetic surgery—especially surgical fat removal (Willard *et al.* 1996) or for breast augmentation, chin augmentation, or rhinoplasty (Yates *et al.* 1988). They may not tell the surgeon about their eating disorder or, even if they do, the surgeon may still decide to go ahead. They frequently remain dissatisfied with their appearance, even after extensive surgery. It is important to be aware of their history because of the risk from electrolyte imbalance and cardiac arrhythmias during surgery.

Patients may also present to casualty, e.g. after accidental ingestion of a foreign body that has been used to induce vomiting, such as a plastic eating fork (Jones & Luke 1998). While most of these will travel harmlessly through the gastro-intestinal tract, some need active intervention to remove them. Although it is rare, they can perforate the oesophagus or alimentary canal, resulting in severe complications and death. There are several reports of toothbrushes requiring active removal in BN (Riddlesburger *et al.* 1992; Wilcox *et al.* 1994).

Summary

Part one of this chapter covered specific physical and physiological sequelae of the key symptoms of BN. Each key diagnostic feature was discussed in turn. Research on related groups (e.g. chronic laxative abusers) was also considered. It was suggested that some behaviours, particularly self-induced vomiting and laxative abuse, are potentially very dangerous, or can have considerable negative consequences. Fortunately, however, most of those with BN do not experience such outcomes.

In part two the dangers of dieting were discussed in some detail. The abuse of diet aids was considered, and their physical and physiological effects outlined. Restrictive dieting was discussed, together with its psychological (and other) effects. The proposal that many features of BN are effects of dieting was discussed. It was suggested that the dangers of normal dieting (psychological and physical) may have been over-estimated.

There is, as yet, little convincing evidence that the key features of BN are primarily the effect of dieting.

Part three covered the effects of the disorder on selected areas of the patient's life (e.g. on social adjustment, child rearing). It placed particular emphasis on social and psychological functioning. Although there is little research, it was suggested that BN has negative consequences in many important psychosocial domains.

In part four, attention was given to the effects of a set of miscellaneous behaviours (e.g. misuse of prescribed medication), to mortality, and other little researched aspects (e.g. presentation for cosmetic surgery).

Chapter 4

Associated features: internal factors

Overview

This chapter will provide information on important features associated with bulimia nervosa (but which are not key diagnostic symptoms). It will focus primarily on features internal to the individual, including aspects such as personality, rather than those that may be external to the individual, such as abuse, or describe early developmental features.

The first part will cover self-esteem. In part two, body image disturbance, including body size estimation and attitudes, will be considered. Mood disturbance and its characteristics in BN, will then be discussed, including its role in the binge–purge cycle. Part four will present research on personality characteristics. In the last three sections, sexuality, impulsivity, and cognitive impairments will be considered. The plan for the chapter is summarized in Table 4.1.

Low self-esteem

Low self-esteem is not part of the DSM-IV diagnostic criteria for bulimia nervosa (American Psychiatric Association 1994). Despite clinical impressions that it is important (for early emphasis on it see: Bruch 1973), little specific focus has been given to it in eating disorders.

There are many terms for self-esteem, e.g. self-worth, self-acceptance, self-respect, and these are often used interchangeably by psychologists. There is also a huge and very diverse literature, often without a consistent thread, in social psychology. Much of this takes a cognitive perspective.

Self-esteem as a concept

Self-esteem is one aspect of the self, the part of self-consciousness that is evaluative. It asks 'am I good at this?' (Baumeister 1999). It is usually linked to issues that are of personal importance (James 1890/1950).

Initially self-esteem was thought of as a global, uni-dimensional concept, but different ways to categorize or conceptualize it now exist. Two distinctions are particularly relevant to bulimia nervosa: global vs. specific self-evaluations, and affective vs. cognitive aspects.

Table 4.1 Summary of plan for Chapter 4

Self-esteem
Body image disturbance
Mood disturbance
Personality features
Sexuality, impulsivity, cognitive impairment

Global vs. specific self-evaluations

Some have suggested that we should equate self-esteem with the sum of specific evaluations. Others have argued that global self-worth affects specific self-evaluations. In bulimia, the distinction is relevant to the relationship between global self-worth and two specific domains, weight and shape. In non-clinical studies of adolescents, both pathways mentioned above have been proposed. For example, some suggest assessment of physical attractiveness affects global self-esteem, while some say it is the other way round (Zumpf & Harter 1989). As yet, this has not been investigated in BN.

Affective vs. cognitive

Self-esteem is now also often thought of as having two parts. One is the affective part, i.e. the feelings that we have towards ourselves, including feelings of value, worth, liking, and acceptance (Hoyle *et al.* 1999). The other is the cognitive part, i.e. what we think or believe about ourselves, including beliefs that we can achieve or complete things. The former is sometimes known as self-acceptance, self-respect, and self-worth; the latter may be known as self-confidence or self-efficacy. The distinction has also been called one of subjective vs. objective self-esteem.

Both aspects have been studied in a small group of eating disorder patients (mostly with bulimia) and an 'at risk' group. The study found evidence for a strong relationship between self-liking, but not self-competence, and eating related cognitions in the at-risk population (Silvera *et al.* 1998). In addition, diagnosis was also associated with self-liking but not self-competence. This suggests that treatment (at the level of self-esteem) may need to focus on subjective experience, rather than personal competence and ability to achieve.[1]

Cognition and self-esteem

Self-schemas, i.e. how people represent and store information about themselves, are much studied by cognitive psychologists, and are also relevant to self-esteem, although

---

[1] This may seem contrary to the emphasis on cognition in cognitive models, but the distinction may map onto the identification of rational and emotional self-beliefs in cognitive theory (see Chapter 13). Clinically, it reflects the experience that shifting an 'emotional' belief is often a crucial factor in progress in treatment.

they have not been widely studied in eating disorders. Schemas influence the way we perceive, understand, make sense of, and recall the information presented to us (Eysenck 1993), i.e. they have schematic properties. Most people have a self-concept with a large number of self-schemas. These schemas vary in complexity and type; we also tend to have self-schemas on some dimensions but not others. Negative self-beliefs (see Chapter 8) are one possible content of self-schemas—and may be the location of low self-esteem. Of particular interest in BN is the 'weight and shape schema'. This has been studied in a non-clinical population but not in patients with BN. It links to the clinical idea of self-worth tied to weight and shape, and the concept of underlying assumptions (see Chapter 8).

Some cognitive theorists have attempted to explain how the negative emotion in low self-esteem arises. Higgins (1987), for example, identifies three types of self: actual, ideal, and ought. He suggests that failure to resolve discrepancies between them is the source of negative emotion. Others also identify several possible selves (Markus & Nurius 1986), although discrepancies between them are not explicitly linked to emotion (except in relation to cultural differences, see below).

Cultural selfways

Recently, cultural selfways, characteristic ways of engaging in the world (an extension of self-schemas), have been identified. In the West, this is reflected in a drive to be distinct and unique (Markus *et al.* 1997). It has been suggested that this tendency may help to explain why negative affect gets linked to low self-esteem in the West, but not in other cultures. The mismatch between cultural drive in the West and individual experience (especially for women) leads to negative affect. This may then help to explain why eating disorders are more common in the West, and in women (Cooper 2001).

Other cognitive psychologists have also suggested how self-schemas might differ in ways that may be relevant to bulimia. Linville (1987), for example, notes that having a wide variety of schemas buffers against negative life events—there is always something one can get a sense of satisfaction from. One possibility is that bulimics have a restricted number of schemas. Another is that they value one more than others, i.e. they are more 'schematic' for that trait in Markus's terms (Markus *et al.* 1987).

Measurement

Little attention has been paid to the measurement problems in self-esteem (Demo 1985), and the development of measures has not evolved at the same pace as the development of concepts. This is particularly true in BN. One detailed study suggested two questionnaires, the Rosenberg Self-Esteem Scale (Rosenberg 1965) and the Self-Esteem Inventory (Coopersmith Self-Esteem Inventory: Coopersmith 1959), are both valid measures in eating disorders (Demo 1985). However, a recent study (Griffiths *et al.* 1999) compared the usefulness of both measures in a mixed group of eating disorder patients—and recommended the Rosenberg Self-Esteem Scale (Rosenberg 1965).

Both are global measures and do not break self-esteem into its theoretical parts, e.g. affective vs. cognitive or global vs. dimensional. The different aspects of self-esteem have not generally been assessed separately in eating disorders.

The role and importance of self-esteem

A small number of studies find that self-esteem predicts outcome in BN (Baell & Wertheim 1992; Fairburn, Kirk, O'Connor, Anastasiades & Cooper 1987), both at the end of treatment and at 3 and 12 months follow-up. These findings support its role in the maintenance of the disorder.

It has also been suggested that self-esteem has a role in the development of BN. It has been argued, for example, that it is the cause of eating disorders (Silverstone 1992); the final common pathway through which various aetiological factors act; and, also, that it is a pre-requisite as opposed to a vulnerability factor (Silverstone 1992). In support of this, there is some evidence for low self-esteem in BN, even in the absence of depression (Silverstone 1990). There are also some prospective studies on non-clinical populations showing, for example, that low self-esteem at age 11–12 predicts eating disorder symptoms at age 15–16, including self-induced vomiting, laxative, and diuretic abuse (Button *et al.* 1996).

Self-esteem has been relatively neglected in BN, despite evidence that it plays a role in the maintenance and development of the disorder. This is beginning to change, however; recently it has been given a key role in developments in cognitive theory of the disorder (see Chapter 8).

Self-esteem has been extensively studied in social and cognitive psychology but, as yet, this work has not often been applied to improve our understanding of BN. Some ways in which it may enhance theoretical understanding and theory development in BN have been identified here.

Body image disturbance

Body image disturbance is not a diagnostic criterion for bulimia nervosa, as it is for anorexia nervosa (DSM-IV: American Psychiatric Association 1994). It was first identified as an important feature of eating disorders by Bruch (e.g. Bruch 1962). After initial interest, however, it fell out of favour in the early 1990s. Recently, there has been renewed interest. It has been described as an important area of study (Cash & Deagle 1997) and a problem for which patients with BN may well need treatment (Rosen 1996).

Psychological aspects of body image were first investigated by Schilder in the 1920s. Most early studies focused on attitude towards the body. Since then, however, the term has broadened. A recent definition is 'a person's perceptions, thoughts and feelings about his or her body' (Grogan 1999, p.1).

In eating disorders, body image is used to mean two things: body size estimation (perceptual aspects) and body dissatisfaction (cognitive and emotional aspects, i.e. thoughts and feelings about size and shape). The latter is usually measured as

Table 4.2 Dimensions of body image investigated in BN

Body size estimation
Body dissatisfaction—feeling fat
Body dissatisfaction—shame
Body avoidance
Investment in weight and shape

a single construct. There has also been a limited amount of work on other dimensions, including some on avoidance (behavioural aspects), and some on feelings of heaviness or fatness.[2] Bodily shame (an affective aspect) has also been considered. The dimensions of body image investigated in BN are summarized in Table 4.2.

Body size estimation

This has been assessed in two ways: judgements of current/actual body size and ideal body size preference. The difference between actual and ideal has then sometimes been taken as a measure of dissatisfaction (see below). There is some support for the validity of this as a measure in bulimia nervosa (Williamson *et al.* 1993b).

Methods to assess body size are of two main types (Cash & Deagle 1997). In body part size estimation procedures, individuals estimate body width and/or depth at several discrete sites. In whole body or distorting image techniques, adjustable mirrors or videographic techniques are used to estimate body size as a whole. Both methods generate an index of the direction and size of distortion, taking into account actual body size. Alternatively, a small number of studies have used silhouettes (Cash & Brown 1987).

Within the two categories, a wide variety of methods have been used, making studies difficult to compare. The literature also has a lot of methodological and sampling faults (Cash & Deagle 1997). It has been suggested that variations in subject characteristics, measurement techniques (e.g. failing to control for actual body size when comparing anorexics with bulimics: Williamson *et al.* 1993a), and setting can influence the results (Cash & Brown 1987). Reliability data are limited, and may also vary depending on the method used and sampling characteristics (Cash & Brown 1987). Validity is little studied, and it is still not clear what body size estimation tasks are actually measuring. Some studies have looked at correlations with other measures, e.g. with the EDI Drive for Thinness scale (Willmuth *et al.* 1985). It has also been suggested that it may be a form of communication, e.g. a signal of the extent to which a patient feels fat (Cash & Brown 1987).

---

[2] This was included in Schilder's (1950) definition as an example of feelings. More recently, however, it has been suggested that it may include cognitive aspects (e.g. feeling fat can be a cognition, distressing because of what it means, or a metaphor for negative emotions and cognitions: Cooper *et al.* 2000). Feeling fat is discussed further in Chapter 13.

Body attitudes

Measurement of these has largely focused on satisfaction with a range of body parts (e.g. the Body Dissatisfaction Scale: Slade *et al.* 1990) or on overall body satisfaction. Some measures have assessed specific aspects, e.g. satisfaction with weight and shape (see the Body Shape Questionnaire: Cooper *et al.* 1987). Many of these are self-report questionnaire measures. A semi-structured interview, the Body Dysmorphic Disorder Examination (BDDE)(Rosen *et al.* 1995) also asseses attitudes, including dissatisfaction, as well as investment in body weight and shape (and in more detail than the EDE). It has promising psychometric properties in bulimia nervosa. The BDDE also assesses behaviours, e.g. body image avoidance. In addition, there are some self-report questionnaire measures of behavioural avoidance (Rosen *et al.* 1991).

Evidence for body image disturbance

All relevant studies show high levels of body dissatisfaction in bulimia nervosa, but have disagreed on whether or not there is also perceptual distortion. However, a recent meta-analysis (of 66 studies) found support for perceptual distortion in bulimics (and anorexics) compared to controls, in both whole body and part body measures (Cash & Deagle 1997). There were also no differences in estimation of neutral objects between bulimics and controls—suggesting that the deficit is not a general one. Despite this, there are much larger effect sizes for attitudes than perceptual aspects (Cash & Deagle 1997), and it has been suggested that perceptual body image may be less important than attitudinal body image.

Explanations for body size over-estimation

Early studies favoured a perceptual explanation for body size over-estimation in BN. Recently, however, it has been suggested that it is influenced more by attitudinal (cognitive and emotional) factors. Cash & Deagle (1997), for example, suggest that image exposure may prime appearance-related cognitions and result in negative body image-related affect. This might explain why there is usually a smaller effect in body part studies; unlike body whole studies, these do not involve exposure to the body using mirrors or video feedback. More recently, signal detection theory has been successfully employed in BN to separate cognitive/affective from sensory/perceptual biases. The results suggest that over-estimation is consistent with cognitive affective biases rather than sensory perceptual biases (Szymanski & Seime 1997). In other words, bulimics do not see a fat person in the mirror but respond to the image as though it were a fat person. This suggests that the focus should be on changing attitudes, not perceptions. This might increase satisfaction with body image (cognitive and emotional), as well as reduce over-estimation.

Attitudes: affective vs. cognitive aspects

There is some evidence that affective aspects of attitudes are more closely related to eating pathology than cognitive aspects, i.e. how they feel vs. how they think they look

(Slade 1994). An affective judgement was also fatter than a cognitively based estimate in a normal sample (Beebe *et al.* 1999), and in bulimia nervosa (Bowden *et al.* 1989). These findings have been related to Arkes (1991) idea of judgement under uncertainty, i.e. body image disturbances are forms of judgemental biases (Williamson *et al.* 1993a). This highlights the possible role of information processing errors influenced, for example, by activation of associative memories related to weight gain. In addition, although both may be disturbed, there also seems little relationship between body size estimation and body satisfaction in many studies (Cash & Deagle 1997). The importance of the affective component of body image has implications for theory development and for its treatment using cognitive therapy (see below).

Bodily shame

Bodily shame has been investigated in a very small number of studies in BN. An important aspect is how the individual appears in the eyes of others. It can be related to feelings of inferiority, submissiveness, hiding, concealment, increased self-focus and self-consciousness (Wicker *et al.* 1983). It has been suggested that bodily shame mediates between early abuse and bulimia, and is not explained by body dissatisfaction (Andrews 1997).

Behavioural aspects

These are rarely studied. One study found that avoidance of situations that trigger concern about physical appearance (Rosen *et al.* 1991) was greater in bulimics than controls, and changed with treatment for body image dissatisfaction. Eating disordered patients (a mixed group) also seem to show less avoidance than body dysmorphic disorder patients (Rosen & Ramirez 1998). It may be that behavioural aspects also reflect attitudinal disturbance in BN (Rosen 1990), but this has not yet been investigated.

Investment aspects

This refers to the importance placed on weight and shape. It is assessed by the Weight and Shape Concern sub-scales of the Eating Disorder examination (Cooper & Fairburn 1987), and also by the Shape and Weight Based Self-esteem Inventory (Geller *et al.* 1997). It is assessed more directly in cognitive terms by the two assumption sub-scales of the Eating Disorder Belief Questionnaire (Cooper *et al.* 1997). The concept overlaps with that of self-esteem (see above). Those with BN invariably score more highly on these measures than healthy controls.

The role and importance of body image

Both perceptual and attitudinal aspects have been related to overall adjustment in bulimia nervosa (Cash & Brown 1987). But there seems no relationship of perceptual aspects to frequency of bingeing or vomiting (Birtchnell *et al.* 1985). There is also no relationship to clinical variables, including both scores on the EDI and measures of general psychopathology (Probst *et al.* 1998). Body size estimation also does not predict response to treatment (including when treatment included body-work sessions: Fernandez-Aranda *et al.* 1999).

Body image, however, assessed using an attitudinal measure, does predict relapse (Fairburn *et al.* 1993c; Freeman *et al.* 1985).

Reactive body image

It has been suggested that body image disturbances helps to maintain BN, and that dieting and vomiting may decline when body size distortion is reduced (Williamson 1990). This suggestion has some empirical support (McKenzie *et al.* 1993), with studies finding that body size estimates increased after eating a candy bar and soft drink, and after exposure to food (and mood) cues, (Carter *et al.* 1996; Kulbartz-Klatt *et al.* 1999). The effect is not typically found in anorexia nervosa (Freeman *et al.* 1983). This may be related to use of different methods—body part techniques often find the effect, whereas whole body techniques do not (Slade 1988). Alternatively, it has been suggested that body image is not a stable feature, and may be affected by other variables. One study, for example, found a bulimic and anorexic sample over-estimated body size more when an easy task was perceived as difficult, than when they perceived it as easy (Waller & Hodgson 1996). Body size estimation also varies in response to media information, e.g. female bodies in women's fashion magazines (Hamilton & Waller 1993), and when patients have recently been abused (Waller *et al.* 1993). Given that body size estimation is primarily a cognitive/affective bias, it seems likely that the effect is affectively mediated— although the relevant studies have not yet been conducted. The notion of reactive body image makes clinical sense—many patients report an increased sense of feeling (as well as thinking) that they are fat after eating relatively small amounts of food.

Treatment

It has been suggested that both perceptual and attitudinal aspects of body image disturbance need to be addressed for eating disorders to be effectively treated (Bruch 1962, 1973). However, body image may be one of the most difficult things for patients to change (Rorty *et al.* 1993), and dissatisfaction with body image, including 'feeling fat', often persists after recovery in many other areas.

Attitudinal

A recent review (Rosen 1996) found that treatment of body image disturbance typically focuses on changing attitudinal features. This is often in the context of CBT, but although helpful, change is modest on assessment measures, and less than found in CBT programmes for body image in other groups, including body dysmorphic disorder (Rosen 1996). This may be because relatively less time is devoted to it in bulimic programmes. However, studies that do not address it, including pharmacological studies, also obtain improvements—suggesting change may not be due to the use of standard CBT techniques.

Perceptual

There is some evidence that patients estimate body size more accurately after treatment (Birtchell *et al.* 1985), although this has not often been measured. There do not seem to be any studies of direct work on perceptual over-estimation in bulimia, although it has been suggested that this might be helpful (e.g. Weiss *et al.* 1985; Wooley & Wooley 1984). If it is mediated by attitude change, then change in this might also be achieved by focusing on attitude change.

Origins of body image disturbance

It has been suggested that deprivation of touch and/or tactile nurturing during childhood and in the present may help explain body image disturbance (Gupta *et al.* 1995). This suggestion is supported by the developmental literature (e.g. Winnicott 1965), which suggests that physical types of nurturing are important for the development and maintenance of a healthy sense of the physical self and a healthy body image. This is sometimes thought to be especially important among women.

Recent evidence suggests size estimation may be an attitudinal disturbance rather than a perceptual one. This is important because attitudes seem to be related to the development and outcome of BN. The affective aspects of these attitudes may also be more important than cognitive aspects. Standard cognitive therapy may not be terribly effective at changing body image; it may be that to change the affective component non-standard techniques, including imagery strategies, are needed.[3] However, it is important to remember that there has been relatively little empirical research, as yet, in this area.

Mood disturbance

Those with BN often have a DSM-IV diagnosis of depression, or anxiety. However, the focus in this section will be on symptoms, not diagnosis.

Mood disturbance in bulimia nervosa has rarely been the main focus of research. With the exception of the view that bulimia is a variant of depression, it also does not feature much in theories. This may seem surprising; not only are patients distressed about their behaviour but they often feel depressed and generally anxious.

One reason for this may be that psychological disturbances, including depression, are often seen as secondary to the eating disorder (Garner *et al.* 1990). Usually (but not always) they resolve when the eating disorder improves (Fairburn *et al.* 1986b).

---

[3] It is important to remember that body image is a complex concept and little is known about how it fits into cognitive theory, or therapy.

Depression

Levels of depression are usually moderate in bulimia nervosa.[4] They are also often comparable to those with a diagnosis of major depressive disorder. However, it has been suggested that qualitative differences exist between depressive symptoms in bulimia nervosa and major depressive disorder (Cooper & Fairburn 1986).

Cooper & Fairburn (1986) found some differences, although there were methodological problems with their study; a large number of correlations were carried out (some might be significant by chance alone), and the depressed patients were older than the bulimics. Key distinguishing features were obsessional ideas (specific to bulimics' eating concerns) and ruminations, and depressed mood (not typical of bulimics). However, in another study, no differences were found between bulimic and depressed subjects (Pope *et al.* 1989).

One study has looked at depressed and non-depressed bulimics. It found that the two groups were distinguished by items reflecting loss of satisfaction, discouragement, expectation of punishment, and decision-making (Kennedy *et al.* 1994). Depressed bulimics, compared to the non-depressed, seemed to have primarily cognitive symptoms of depression.

In Chapter 3 it was suggested that dieting can cause depressive symptoms, and that this might explain some BN symptoms. However, it seems that the relationship of depression to dieting and BN may differ depending on what symptoms are measured. Bulimia nervosa (see above) seems to be primarily related to cognitive symptoms, whereas studies have shown that starvation (measured by weight and biochemical variables) relates primarily to depressed mood and psycho-vegative symptoms (Laessle *et al.* 1988).

The role of mood, specifically of depression, in the binge–purge cycle has also been considered (Beebe 1994). For example, mood has been included as a disinhibitor of eating, and as a triggering factor in the escape from aversive self-awareness hypothesis.

Anxiety

Anxiety symptoms have been little studied in bulimia nervosa. One study, comparing bulimics with generalized anxiety disordered patients found that the bulimics had more depressive symptoms, whereas the GAD patients had more specific anxiety symptoms (Steere *et al.* 1990). The groups were equivalent in overall psychopathology, and the anxiety symptoms in bulimia seemed to be related to concerns with food, weight, and shape. Anxiety is given a specific role in the binge–purge cycle by those interested in exposure and response-prevention treatment (Leitenberg *et al.* 1984; Rosen & Leitenberg 1982). It may also be a disinhibitor or trigger in the restraint and aversive self-awareness models.

---

[4] As opposed to anorexia, where levels are often very high.

Personality characteristics

Based on factor analysis, several research groups have identified five personality traits that seem to recur in the general population: extraversion, agreeableness, conscientiousness, neuroticism, and openness (e.g. McCrae & Costa 1985). Others give the fifth a different label, e.g. tough-mindedness (Eysenck & Eyssenck 1976).

However, factor analytic work in the general population may not capture all the domains of personality that are relevant to clinical disorders or disorders of personality. Clinicians have thus drawn on approaches developed within a clinical framework—especially those that emphasize cognitive factors, e.g. those of Kelly, Rogers & Bandura, and those that attempt to explain how personality develops.

Two fundamental processes have been identified in this work: the development of satisfying interpersonal relationships, and a well-differentiated sense of self (Blatt 1995). This theme is echoed in cognitive theory (e.g. Beck & Freeman 1990), in notions of sociotropy and autonomy. It has also been linked to themes in perfectionism, with two dimensions—self-oriented and socially prescribed perfectionism—being particularly important in eating disorders (e.g. Hewitt & Flett 1990).

There are few descriptions of personality in BN. One review suggests that it is characterized by compulsiveness, impulsivity, and affective instability, and that the binge–purge cycle plays a role in dealing with trait variables; the latter being evident in bingeing as a form of affect regulation (Vitousek & Manke 1994). However, in general, an inconsistent picture emerges.

Much of the work has investigated differences between eating disorders, often with a particular interest in anorexia nervosa. There are few studies specifically on bulimia. Most of these study the acute disorder, and very little is known about bulimics' pre-treatment or post-treatment personality.

A summary of the personality characteristics and models, including some specific aspects, is presented in Table 4.3.

Differences between types of eating disorder

Clinical measures

These studies have largely used measures based on psychodynamic conceptualizations of personality. For example, a study in adolescents, using the Millon Adolescent

Table 4.3 Aspects of personality investigated in BN

Psychodynamic conceptualizations
Biological features/models
Temperament
Five factor model
Specific aspects: perfectionism, sociotrophy and autonomy, impulsivity

Personality Inventory (Millon *et al.* 1982), suggested that bulimics had an inhibited personality style—they were shy, fearful of rejection, and did not think it safe to trust others (Pryor & Wiederman 1998). However, they were not high on impulsive characteristics. Weiderman & Pryor (1997), also using the Millon Inventory (adult version), found that bulimics were characterized as more social, impulsive, and affectively labile than anorexics, although they were not different from controls.

Some studies have used measures based more directly on psycho-analytical concepts of personality, e.g. the Ego Function Assessment (Bellak, Hurvich & Gediman 1973). In one study, severely disturbed ego functioning was associated with more problems at follow-up—one and two years later (Sohlberg 1990).

Non-clinical measures

Some studies have used personality instruments developed in non-clinical groups; these often draw on biological models of personality, e.g. as developed by Cloninger (1986).

Several studies have used the Multidimensional Personality Questionnaire (Tellegen 1982, 1985). Compared to norms, bulimics appeared to experience little joy or excitement, and were seldom happy; they showed excessive worry, irritability, and emotional lability (Pryor & Wiederman 1996). They also had a sense of mistrust, and of social isolation, feeling mistreated by others, and had a preference for working out problems alone. Anorexics were not dissimilar but had a greater need for control, both behaviourally and emotionally.

Another study, also using the MPQ, found that both bulimics and anorexics had reduced well-being, more stress, more irritability, and, compared to controls but not bulimic anorexics, preferred to be alone more. They were not higher than normal on impulsivity. They had more intense negative affect, including tension, self-dissatisfaction, guilt, and little positive affect or feelings of contentment or happiness compared to controls (Casper *et al.* 1992).

Other studies have used the Tridemensional Personality Questionnaire (Cloninger 1987), which measures novelty seeking, harm avoidance, and reward dependence (e.g. Brewerton *et al.* 1993; Garner, Olmsted, Davis, Rockert, Goldblum & Eagle 1990). Results here have also been conflicting.

A small number of studies have investigated temperament. In one study, Shaw & Steiner (1997) found that bulimics differed from anorexics in general rhythmicity (less regular pattern of diurnal activities, including sleep and eating) and attentional focus (less ability to concentrate and persist with activities), but did not differ from a depressed group.

One study has used the five-factor model and measure of personality (Costa & McCrae 1988). In a mixed eating disorder group, patients were lower on Openness to Experience (blunted in affect, disregard the importance of emotional life, accept authority, and tend to be conservative) and Conscientiousness (not learned to manage their desires, cannot resist impulses and temptations, lack self-control, not able to plan and organize tasks). The only difference between the bulimics and anorexics was on Impulsiveness, e.g. on Excitement Seeking scores (Podar *et al.* 1999).

A small number of studies have investigated the contribution of current mood to personality. One study found that some differences between groups disappeared after current depressive symptoms were controlled, e.g. in social closeness (Pryor & Wiederman 1996). Consistent with this, the Big Five study found that personality dimensions made a bigger contribution to eating symptoms (EDI-2: Garner 1991) than emotional experience (Podar *et al.* 1999).

The relationship between personality, binge eating, and mood has been investigated in a preliminary study. Those high on trait hostility were more likely to binge after hostile and anxious affect than those low on it. Those high on external locus of control were more likely to binge in relation to state anxiety, depression, and hostility (Rebert *et al.* 1991). These findings fit with the suggestion that negative affect leads to binge eating (Rebert *et al.* 1991). They also suggest individual variation in specific emotions and personality traits linked to bingeing.

Studies also find that MPQ dimensions are associated with greater risk of developing an eating disorder (Leon *et al.* 1993), and that personality factors are significant predictors of severity (Sullivan *et al.* 1996b).

It seems likely that personality will affect how bulimics deal with their weight and shape concerns, and depressive symptoms; it may also affect manifestation of the disorder: thus, it may have important treatment implications. However, at present, little is known about these issues. Similarly, little is known about how personality might be affected by treatment or recovery, or by symptom severity. Of particular interest is how it may be related to the development of the disorder and whether it predicts outcome. Many current studies do not separate stable (personality) traits from the effects of acute disturbance. Some of the findings also produce conflicting results, i.e. some find differences between patients with BN and controls (or anorexics), and others do not. One possibility is that the characteristic profile depends on the precise nature of the trait being measured, and that the detail varies by theory and measure. Much more research is needed on the role of personality in BN.

Perfectionism

Slade (1982) suggested that (neurotic or maladaptive) perfectionism was one of the setting conditions for eating disorders, i.e. that it was important in its development. It has been much less studied in bulimia than in anorexia. Studies have also tended to focus on its relationship to bulimic symptoms in non-clinical samples.

One study, for example, found that perfectionism (assessed by the EDI) is a long-term predictor of bulimic symptoms (using a DSM-III based measure), and a better predictor than the EDI bulimia sub-scale, 10 years later (Joiner *et al.* 1997a).

Nevertheless, perfectionism is generally only a relatively weak predictor of bulimic symptoms. This could be because perfectionism is multifaceted (Hewitt & Flett 1991).

However, the link is often still unclear when multidimensional models are used (Pliner & Haddock 1996). A theoretical explanation for its role is also often lacking. Recently this has been partly addressed with the development of a diathesis stress model, to explain how it relates to the development of the disorder. This suggests that perfectionism is a risk factor only for those who also perceive themselves to be overweight (Joiner *et al.* 1997b). However, it has been noted that many questions remain, e.g. it is not clear why the interaction with body esteem triggers bingeing and vomiting.

One recent suggestion is that self-esteem acts as a moderator. This has some empirical support. A study, using perfectionism, body esteem, and self-esteem, found that it was possible to predict change in bulimic symptoms 9 months later (Vohs *et al.* 1999). The researchers propose that the link is not straightforward; self awareness is aversive when bulimics are aware of the discrepancy between desired and current state—this then makes escape more likely. Failure to lose weight in the context of low self-esteem, leads to reduced self-esteem (because pre-existing beliefs guide situation-specific expectancies: Carver & Scheier 1990). This then increases actions that are counter to the desired state, including binge eating (Vohs *et al.* 1999). More research is needed into this idea.

Sociotrophy and autonomy

Sociotropy (need for approval from others, stong investment in attachments, avoidance of social rejection) and autonomy (exaggerated concern with performance evaluation, strong investment in personal independence, control, and achievement) have been identified as cognitive personality variables (Beck 1983). Neither have been much investigated in bulimia. There is some evidence that both are related to eating disorder symptom scores (in a non-clinical group), though only sociotropy was still related once depression was controlled (Friedman & Whisman 1998).

Sexuality

Bulimics are sometimes said to be prone to sexual excesses, often as part of a multi-impulsive disorder. However, there have been relatively few studies of sexuality in bulimia.

Studies tend to look either at attitude or behaviour or both. Many have also compared bulimics to anorexics. One early study (Allerdissen *et al.* 1981), found that bulimics were less able to enjoy sexual relationships. Another found that there appeared to be few psychosexual triggers for the disorder, and that sexual interest decreased with onset of the eating problem (Pyle *et al.* 1981).

A large study (Wiederman *et al.* 1996) found that bulimics were more likely to have had sexual intercourse than anorexics, even when possible confounds were controlled (e.g. weight, age, symptom severity). They also had an earlier median age of first sexual intercourse, and greater pre-morbid sexual interest, but were generally and currently less satisfied with their sexual relationships, including when confounds were controlled.

Sexual development has also been studied (Schmidt *et al.* 1995). Compared to normals, bulimics did not have delayed psychosexual development; apart from age at first intercourse, all other milestones were similar. The authors thus suggest that there is no evidence that psychosexual delays occur before onset of the disorder in bulimics—and any differences observed in attitudes and behaviour may be secondary to the eating disorder.

The same study also found that bulimics had fewer sexual partners than normal controls. They also evaluated sexual relationships less positively, but other attitudes, to masturbation, marriage, children, and pregnancy, were no different (Schmidt *et al.* 1995).

A study following up bulimics (Morgan *et al.* 1995), however, found no difference, compared to normals, in age of first sexual intercourse, and similar erotophobia/erotophilia scores—propensity to respond to sexual cues and situations along a positive–negative dimension of affect and evaluation—as well as similar sexual esteem. However, compared to normals they reported less sexual interest and responsivity, more negative affect, and were much more likely to have clinically significant levels of sexual discord in their current relationship.

Many variables may mediate between sexuality and bulimia. Those proposed include personality characteristics (e.g. borderline personality features seem to be related to earlier onset of sexual activity, and greater number of sexual partners, but greater sexual dissatisfaction). Others include impulsivity, family history (of less tactile and more use of food as nurturance), body image and sexual trauma (Rorty *et al.* 1993). However, most of these variables have yet to be investigated. Preliminary work suggests that body dissatisfaction is unrelated to experience or age of first sexual intercourse, but related to masturbation, lower incidence, and later onset. There also seems to be a trend for it to be related to current satisfaction with sexual life (Wiederman & Pryor 1997a).

Ever married vs. never married

There is very little research on marriage and bulimia nervosa. Most of what we know is based on clinical observation, and a few isolated case reports (e.g. Van den Broucke & Vandereycken 1988).

In bulimia, onset is often before or at the start of a relationship/marriage—thus it may influence the development or course of the disorder (and vice versa). It has been suggested that interaction is more hostile and chaotic, but that while the eating disorder remains hidden from the partner, bulimics may appear well-adjusted. However, it can precipitate a power struggle once revealed. It does seem to interfere with relationship quality—tension can be high, this may be due to lack of intimacy—and the relationship may be co-operative and satisfactory, but only for superficial and routine matters. Patients may see the cause of their eating disorder as separate from their marital difficulties, but it does seem that eating problems (in a mixed group) may also be triggered by marital problems, separation, or divorce (in 69% of those with post marital onset: Kiriike *et al.* 1998).

Specific aspects of marital relationship have also been studied, particularly intimacy. A mixed eating disorder group (Van den Broucke *et al.* 1995), for example, were low on intimacy, especially openness, (controlling for satisfaction), compared to controls and a marital distressed group.

There are methodological problems with most of the studies comparing married and not married patients. The married group is often much older and, in one study, after controlling for age, the married were younger at menarche, and more likely to have experienced sexual intercourse, but there was no difference in eating disorder symptoms (Wiederman & Pryor 1997b). As has been pointed out, this does not mean that marriage is unrelated to eating disorder—there are many suggestions of dysfunctional communication that may link to the symptoms (Van den Broucke *et al.* 1994, 1995), and that are yet to be studied.

Sexual orientation

One preliminary study (Heffernan 1996) in lesbians found that the risk for bulimia nervosa was no greater than in the general female population, although there was a higher rate of binge-eating disorder. Binge-eating was also predicted by negative affect regulation rather than by body dissatisfaction and dieting.

Impulsive behaviour

The concept of multi-impulsive bulimia has been proposed (Lacey & Evans 1986) to describe bulimia with one or more of the following features: gross alcohol abuse, street drug abuse, multiple overdoses, recurrent self-harm, sexual disinhibition, or shoplifting. It is characterized by a 'failure to consider risks and consequences with a lack of deliberation' (Lacey 1993). Lacey (1993) identified high rates, in 40% of 112 women, referred by GPs: 80% reported at least three self-damaging behaviours. Each behaviour was associated with a similar sense of being out of control, and seemed to have a similar function—to reduce, or block unpleasant or distressing feelings.

Some studies, however, have not found such high levels (e.g. Fairburn & Cooper 1984). This may be due to sampling differences, many in the latter study were students. However, a carefully controlled study (Welch & Fairburn 1996), using a community sample, yielded similar findings.[5] Bulimics were not different from controls on alcohol consumption; they were not more likely to have used drugs regularly, including cannabis, amphetamines (for weight control), cocaine/crack, than healthy or psychiatric

---

[5] As Welch & Fairburn note, a problem with clinic samples is Berkson's bias (Berkson 1946). With two disorders, or co-morbidity, patients are more likely to seek treatment—the probability is greater than it is for one disorder.

Table 4.4 'Impulsive' characteristics studied in BN

Binge-eating
Self-injurious behaviour
Suicide attempts
Stealing
Self-mutilation

controls, although any illicit drug use was more common. Self-harm, overdose, cutting, and burning were all more common in bulimia than normals and psychiatric controls, but there were few (7%) with more than one 'impulsive' behaviour. The characteristics of 'impulsivity', including binge-eating, which have been investigated in BN, are summarized in Table 4.4.

The psychometric concept of impulsiveness differs from the clinical concept of impulsive disorders. It includes several factors, i.e. tendency to make rapid decisions, act without thinking, and tendency to indulge in risky behaviour.

Working within this framework, Fahy & Eisler (1993), found that bulimics have higher impulsivity scores than anorexics, but not higher than controls. There were also no differences in impulsivity scores (using the Impulsiveness Questionnaire: Eysenck *et al.* 1985) between the multi-impulsive group and the other two groups. High and low impulsive scorers did not differ in binge frequency, and there were no significant correlations with symptom severity.

Impulsivity, however, correlates with sensation seeking (Zuckerman 1971), and it has been suggested that bingeing and purging satisfies sensation-seeking needs, i.e. exaggerated need for stimulation from the environment (Schumaker *et al.* 1986). However, there was no evidence for higher scores in bulimics on the Zuckerman Sensation Seeking Scale (Zuckerman 1977). One possible explanation suggested by the researchers is that bingeing and purging effectively reduce any exaggerated need for arousal.

There are many problems with the idea of multi-impulsivity in bulimia. For example, it has been defined in many different ways (Fahy & Eisler 1993; Fichter *et al.* 1994). Definitions do not always include the same behaviours. The number of behaviours needed for a diagnosis also differs. Wiederman & Pryor (1996) stipulated three of four behaviours, but others often specify fewer behaviours.

Studies have not always found differences in the current symptoms of impusive and non-impulsive bulimics, but it has been suggested that the multi-impulsive may have more extensive histories, e.g. a longer duration, earlier onset, and that the pathway to it—through CSA, temperament, personality disorder, or substance abuse—may be different. Fichter *et al.* (1994), for example, found differences in personality and early attachment. Consistent with this, there is some evidence that impulsivity predicts poor outcome (Sohlberg *et al.* 1989) at 2–3 and 4–6 years follow-up.

Self-injurious behaviour

One recent study of 125 consecutive referrals found that 72% reported at least one form of self-injurious behaviour (SIB), and of the 52 who reported at least one impulsive behaviour, 13 (25%) reported two or more (Favaro & Santonastaso 1998). Factor analysis distinguished impulsive from compulsive behaviour. Compulsive included vomiting, severe nail biting, and hair pulling; impulsive included suicide attempts, alcohol/drug abuse, laxative abuse, and skin cutting and burning. Few studies have looked at compulsive SIB.

Impulsive SIB seems to provoke little resistance, unlike compulsive behaviours, and is often triggered by events. Compulsive was predicted by short duration of illness, and greater lack of interoceptive awareness. Impulsive was predicted by a history of sexual abuse and greater depression. The two seem to be different dimensions—and not related to severity of eating symptoms (Favaro & Santonastaso 1999).

The idea of impulsive and over-controlled regulation of behaviour as a feature of bulimia nervosa fits with the suggestion (Vitousek & Hollon 1990), that a single-minded focus on dieting is an easy way to simplify life. This may be particularly important for someone who lacks ability to self-regulate (Sohlberg 1991).

Suicide attempts

The prevalence and severity of suicide attempts is similar in bulimia and major depression. Studies have also found certain personality characteristics are associated with suicide attempts in BN, e.g. high neuroticism, mood and anxiety dysregulation, impulsivity, autonomic lability, and aggression. There is also a trend for bulimics to have less serious intention to die, although medical threat is similar (Bulik *et al.* 1999b). Attempts are more common if patients have a history of depression (this is not so for AN). Suicide attempts and depression are important—suicide is a frequent cause of death in bulimia (Keel & Mitchell 1997). About 25% report more than one attempt (Favaro & Santonastaso 1997) and research in other disorders suggests that overall, repeaters are more likely to die than non-repeaters (Kotila & Lonnqvist 1987).

Stealing

This is common in bulimia nervosa (e.g. Pyle *et al.* 1981; Krahn *et al.* 1991), and seems to be associated with more severe psychopathology. It also tends to occur after the onset of BN. Of 312 BN patients (Rowston & Lacey 1992), 42% had a history of stealing and items stolen were: food (53%), money (19%), clothes (12%), and cosmetics (5%).

Self-mutilation

Few studies have examined self-mutilation in BN, although one or two studies suggest that it is related to eating disorders. One study defined it as 'deliberate self-injury to body tissue without the conscious intent to die' (Dulit *et al.* 1994). It found that those who were frequent self-mutilators were more likely to receive a diagnosis of BN than those who were not, and that BN was associated with a four times risk of being a frequent mutilator. Explanations related to serotonin dysfunction, as well as psychoanalytic explanations, e.g. tension relief and the formation of ego boundaries have been proposed (Favazza 1989).

Cognitive impairments

There are also very few studies of cognitive impairment in bulimia nervosa (unlike anorexia nervosa, where it has been more extensively studied). However, the topic is important because it has been suggested that those with a psychiatric disorder, plus specific cognitive impairments, have a relatively poor outcome (Keefe 1995).

An early study found no differences in bulimics from theoretical norms, or from anorexics, on cognitive tasks, i.e. the Benton Visual Retention Test (Benton 1974)—recall of visual material—and the Trail Making Test (Reitan 1958)—assessing planning ability. There were, however, impairments on a vigilance task (Laessle *et al.* 1989a), similar to that found in underweight anorexics.

A more recent study looked at attention, memory (short-term), and problem solving. This found that bulimics did not differ from anorexics pre-treatment. There were some mild to moderate deficits on attention and problem-solving tasks—but scores all improved with treatment, and no significant predictors of outcome could be found. At an individual level, over half seem to have well-preserved cognitive skills, but only a few of those with deficits returned to normal levels. Cognitive and clinical deficits did not seem to be directly related—suggesting that a third factor may mediate the relationship. In this respect, neither hospital admission or depression seemed to be important. The authors of this study suggested that metabolic turnover in certain brain areas, as well as level of steroid hormones, may be a modulating factor (Lauer *et al.* 1999).

There is no evidence that cognitive deficits are related to crude morphological measures, i.e. ventricular size (Laessle *et al.* 1989a). In addition, although 40% of bulimics had enlarged cortical sulci and ventricles, this was not related to duration of illness, vomiting, or past history of anorexia (Krieg 1991).

Summary

This chapter has discussed important features of BN that are not diagnostic items, focusing on features internal to the individual. In the first part, self-esteem was considered. Both conceptualization of the concept and its measurement were discussed—with an emphasis on cognitive aspects. Implications of the evidence (and theories) presented for the development of cognitive theory and therapy were briefly outlined. Much relevant work in social and cognitive psychology has not yet been applied to BN, but has considerable potential to enhance the understanding of cognition and the development of cognitive theory in BN.

Body image disturbance was considered in part two. This covered body size estimation and attitudes. The importance of attitudinal aspects was highlighted, together with the suggestion that affective aspects may be relatively more important than cognitive aspects. Ways in which this suggestion (seemingly at odds with an emphasis on cognition) might affect cognitive theory and treatment were briefly considered. In particular, it was suggested that to change the affective component of body image non standard techniques, including imagery strategies, may be relevant.

Research on mood disturbance and its characteristics in BN was discussed in part three. This provides further evidence relevant to the link hypothesized to exist between dieting and mood. It also suggests that both anxiety and depression may play an important (and often neglected) role in the moment to moment experience of bingeing and purging.

Personality was discussed in part four, followed by sexuality, impulsivity, and cognitive impairment in BN. Relatively little reseach has been conducted here, and some preliminary findings were presented. Some of these are contradictory, especially in the area of personality.

Chapter 5

Associated features: external and developmental factors

Overview

This chapter will provide information on important features associated with bulimia nervosa (but which are not key diagnostic symptoms). It will focus on factors external to the individual, such as abuse, and factors that have been considered primarily in an external context. Early developmental factors relevant to the disorder will also be covered.

The first part will discuss abuse, sexual, physical, and emotional, in bulimia nervosa. Part two will consider the developmental history of BN, focusing on tasks particularly relevant to the disorder. This will include the development of hunger and satiety, and emotional development. The development of self-concept, self-esteem, and gender identity will then be considered. Part three considers the role of the family. Both general and specific family climate variables, which may have a role in BN, are outlined. In part four, the role of life events, appraisal, coping, and social support is considered. The plan for the chapter is summarized in Table 5.1.

Abuse

Women with a history of sexual abuse have considerable psychopathology in later life (Browne & Finkelhor 1986), including a high prevalence of bulimia (Pribor & Dinwiddie 1992). It has been suggested that, in bulimia, this has implications for understanding its development and the application of treatment strategies (Pope & Hudson 1992). It may also affect outcome and prognosis. This section will consider some of the key issues associated with this link. It will focus primarily on childhood sexual abuse (CSA).[1]

Sexual abuse

One problem in the field is that definitions of CSA vary. It is also very difficult to assess. The nature of the questions asked, for example, may affect both the response rate and the identification of 'cases' (Connors & Morse 1993). Further, there is some evidence that those with a history of CSA, including those with eating disorders, are

---

[1] There are very few studies on physical and emotional abuse in BN.

Table 5.1 Summary of plan for Chapter 5

Abuse—sexual, physical and emotional
Developmental history—hunger and satiety, emotional
Role of family—general and specific family climate
Life events—appraisal, coping, social support

more likely to be in a current abusive relationship, making the link with early abuse difficult to elucidate. Some studies have not set a cut-off age when considering abuse (e.g. occurred before age 16). These points should be borne in mind when assessing the literature.

The link between CSA and BN

Case reports describe a history of sexual abuse in some patients with BN (e.g. Goldfarb 1987). Uncontrolled studies (e.g. Oppenheimer *et al.* 1985) estimate rates of abuse ranging from 7% (Lacey 1990) to 67% (Oppenheimer *et al.* 1985).[2]

Controlled studies also report high rates, from 28% (Root & Fallon 1988) to nearly 50% (Tice *et al.* 1989). Rates in non-clinical groups are lower, from 9% (Steiger & Zanko 1990) to 28% (Stuart *et al.* 1990). Most studies also report higher rates in bulimics than in controls.

However, an influential early review argued that most of the control groups in these studies were highly selected (Pope & Hudson 1992) and that, when patient rates were compared with general population rates, they were similar, ranging from 28% (Bagley & Ramsey 1986) to 67% (Wyatt 1985).

More recently views have changed. Studies using tighter methodologies (reviewed in Wonderlich *et al.* 1997), now indicate a positive relationship. They include studies comparing the presence of bulimic symptoms, or diagnoses, in victims of CSA and controls (e.g. Wonderlich *et al.* 1997) and in non-clinical or community samples (e.g. Dansky *et al.* 1997). Wonderlich *et al.* (1996b), for example, found that those women who had been sexually abused in childhood were more likely than those not abused to report binge-eating and purging.

Comparison with anorexia nervosa

Studies of rates of CSA in eating disorder patients are currently inconclusive about differences between disorders (Wonderlich *et al.* 1997). For example, Waller (1991), found higher rates of unwanted sexual experiences in bulimics than restrictive anorexics (as did Steiger & Zanko 1990), while Palmer *et al.* (1990) appeared to find no differences.

---

[2] See, for example, a review (Pope & Hudson 1992), including only studies with 10 or more participants.

Comparison with other psychiatric groups

The association between CSA and bulimia nervosa does not seem to be specific to the disorder. For example, rates of CSA in bulimics are similar to those of depressed patients, e.g. Vize & Cooper (1995). In addition, in CSA victims, rates of symptoms of other disorders, apart from eating disorders, are also elevated. Bushnell *et al.* (1992), for example, found increased risk for depressive, manic, generalized anxiety, somatization, and conduct disorder symptoms.

The nature of the relationship

The precise nature of the relationship between CSA and bulimia is unclear. It could be causal (e.g. CSA may be a risk factor for bulimia nervosa, although clearly not a specific risk factor). It could be that a third factor explains the development of both. Or the presence of the two could simply be coincidental, i.e. due to the fact that both are common in young women. The three possible links are summarized in Table 5.2.

The third factor hypothesis

One study suggests that part of the association between CSA and bulimic symptoms may be due to co-morbid personality disorder or pathology (Steiger *et al.* 1996). In other words, the relationship of each to a third variable (i.e. personality disorder) and possibly a common background, e.g. the 'matrix of disadvantage' of Mullen *et al.* (1993), may explain the link.

The coincidental hypothesis

One study (Sullivan *et al.* 1995) has suggested that CSA and BN are not linked, except by chance. This is based on the finding that bulimics with a CSA history did not have more severe eating disorder symptoms, but did have more Axis I disorders, worse global functioning, and more severe depressive symptoms.

The causal hypothesis

A lot of research has been conducted based on the assumption that CSA is causally linked to bulimia. However, there does not seem to be a specific link. A small number of studies have looked at possible mediators or moderators of the relationship. One study, for example, found that shame about physical appearance is a mediator between abuse and bulimia (Andrews 1997). Another study found that adult psychological functioning (symptoms of depression, suicidality, and impulsive behaviours) mediated

Table 5.2 Sexual abuse and BN: possible practical links

Possible practical links
Causal—CSA is a risk factor for BN
A third factor explains both CSA and BN
CSA and BN are coincidental

the impact of CSA (Casper & Lyubomirsky 1997). In addition, family environment has been suggested as a moderator (Hastings & Kern 1994), i.e. CSA is only associated with bulimia in chaotic families.

A dimensional perspective

In an attempt to explore the causal nature of the link in more detail, some studies have investigated whether CSA is associated with specific symptoms or severity of eating disorder symptoms. There seems little evidence for this, however, particularly when the relationship to binge frequency is examined. One study, for example, found no relationship between severity of eating disorder symptoms and history of abuse (Folsom *et al.* 1993). Another study found higher scores on symptoms (and on symptoms of depression and anxiety), but not on actual eating behaviours, in those who had been abused (Anderson *et al.* 1997).

More recently, studies have examined whether or not specific aspects of abuse are related to specific eating disorder symptoms. One study, for example, found that severity of CSA (Hastings & Kern 1994) appears to be related to severity of bulimic symptoms. A series of studies by Waller and colleagues has investigated this in some detail. Waller & Ruddock (1993), for example, found that perceived negative response to disclosure of the CSA was associated with increased frequency of vomiting. It was also associated with bingeing frequency (and vomiting) when abuse was intra-familial, involved force, or occurred before the victim was 14 years old (Waller 1992). EAT scores and BMI, however, were not different between those abused and those not abused. Other studies also suggest purging is strongly related to abuse (e.g. Tobin & Griffing 1996), while a study of college women also found that relationship of perpetrator was important. Those whose abuse was intra-familial were more likely to develop a serious eating problem (47%) than a no-abuse group (21%), and than those whose abuse was extra-familial (36%).

Work has also sought to identify the factors that mediate these specific links. There is currently evidence that a variety of symptoms, including dissociation, self-denigration, borderline personality disorder, and disclosure experiences, as well as family factors and developmental level, are important. Cognitive processes, schemas, and information processing also seem to be important (Everill & Waller 1995). The latter suggest that a cognitive framework might provide a useful conceptual basis for the link between CSA and bulimia. CSA, for example, may lead to the development of cognitions and processes that increase vulnerability to bulimia. This might include self-denigratory beliefs.

Co-morbidity

There are lots of evidence that CSA in bulimia is associated with greater co-morbidity, including more DSM-III Axis I disorders (Rorty *et al.* 1994), more depression, alcohol problems, shoplifting, and suicide attempts (Fullerton *et al.* 1995), and more personality disorders (McClelland *et al.* 1991).

It has been suggested that those with multi-impulsive behaviours may be more likely to have experienced CSA (Lacey 1993). In one study, for example, women with BN who also had substance abuse disorder had the highest and most severe rates of abuse (Deep *et al.* 1999). However, the nature of the link is not clear. One possibility is that poor impulse control contributes to both abuse and bulimia, another is that poor impulse control is the result of abuse (Briere 1992; van der Kolk 1987).

Impact of CSA on outcome

There is limited work on the impact of CSA on response to treatment or outcome in bulimia nervosa. However, many features co-morbid with CSA have been associated with poor prognosis. It has also been associated with symptoms that might make poor prognosis more likely, e.g. hospitalization, self-injury, drug or alcohol problems (Gleaves & Eberenz 1994). Personality disorders, especially the borderline type, for example, may lead to poorer outcome (Rossiter *et al.* 1993; Wonderlich *et al.* 1994a). One study has also found that severity of abuse tends to be associated with outcome (Anderson *et al.* 1997). However, there seems to be no relationship found in other studies (Fallon *et al.* 1994).

A conceptual link

It has been suggested that CSA may relate conceptually to bulimia nervosa in two ways. Rorty & Yager (1996) suggest that the relationship is one facet of a complex post-traumatic disorder. Binge-eating, purging, and starving are all attempts to regulate intolerable internal states, which are heightened in those who have been abused. It may also facilitate escape from physiological arousal (Rorty & Yager 1996) precipitated by CSA. In a not dissimilar explanation, Heatherton & Baumeister (1991) suggest that cognitive narrowing of attention precedes binge-eating, which facilitates avoidance of or escape from negative emotions and thoughts, all of which are likely to be present in those with a history of abuse. Both these suggestions are compatible with recent developments in the cognitive theory of bulimia nervosa (see Chapter 8). These three possibilities are summarized in Table 5.3.

Physical and emotional abuse

There are very few studies of physical and emotional abuse in bulimia nervosa. Findings suggest that there are high rates of parental physical abuse that is perceived as harsh

Table 5.3 Sexual abuse and BN: possible conceptual links

Possible conceptual links
Cognitive, e.g. via self-denigratory beliefs (see Everill & Waller 1995)
Through PTSD, e.g. as one facet of a complex post-traumatic disorder (see Rorty & Yager 1996)
The escape hypothesis, e.g. as facilitating escape from physiological arousal (see Heatherton & Baumeister 1991)

and capricious, and that this is associated with greater global family pathology (Rorty *et al.* 1994). Physical abuse was also a risk factor in one study of bulimia nervosa (Welch & Fairburn 1994) but, like CSA, it was not specific to bulimia. There is some evidence that physical abuse is associated with poor outcome, (together with disturbed family environment, i.e. low cohesion and high control) (Fallon *et al.* 1994).

There is also some evidence that psychological, and also sexual and multiple abuse, are associated with more Axis I co-morbidity. Psychological and multiple abuse are also associated with more personality disorder diagnoses. Again, however, the relationship does not seem to be specific to bulimia (Rorty *et al.* 1994).

More research is needed on the nature of this relationship. As has been done for CSA, it is important to examine whether or not the relationship is causal, and what the mediators might be. Again, it is possible that a cognitive link will provide an explanation.

Developmental history

Certain developmental tasks and events have been thought to be particularly important in eating disorders. They are summarized in Table 5.4. They include the development of hunger and satiety, emotions, self-concept, self-esteem, and gender or sex role identity.

Hunger and satiety

Bruch first drew attention to 'disturbance in the accuracy of the perception or cognitive interpretation of stimuli arising in the body' (1973, p.252), as a key issue in anorexia nervosa. This disturbance referred particularly to hunger and satiety, but also to emotional states (see below).

Some relevant research exists for anorexia but focused work has not been conducted in bulimia. However, there is some relevant (indirect) evidence. The interoceptive awareness sub-scale of the EDI, for example, includes questions on confidence in recognizing and accurately labelling sensations of hunger and satiety. Many studies using this measure show that bulimics, like anorexics, score highly on this sub-scale, and higher than many comparison groups. However, it is not clear what is disturbed here—perception, interpretation, or indeed expression. For example, patients may be able to perceive and label internal sensations accurately, but deny the experience of hunger.

Table 5.4 Developmental tasks and events important in BN

Hunger and satiety
Emotions—expression and regulation of emotions
Self-concept
Self-esteem
Gender or sex role identity

Emotional states

There has also been very little focused or direct work on the perception or interpretation of emotional states in bulimia. Elevated scores on the EDI interoceptive awareness sub-scale, provide some evidence for disturbance but, as with hunger and satiety, it is not clear precisely which aspect is disturbed.

Normal development

Research in child development suggests that emotions, particularly negative ones, are not well differentiated from one another in infancy (in so far as they can be inferred from facial expression and behaviour). Neither are they expressed in consistent, recognizable ways (there seem to be few discrete states, also no one to one link between state and expression early on). It is only with time that internal emotions become discrete and more organized, and expressed in characteristically individual and cultural ways, i.e. all develop and change.

A theoretical framework

One possibility is that this development is maturational. But environmental influences are also believed to play an important part—both in shaping the nature of the internal experiences (perception) and the way in which these are interpreted and expressed (Oatley & Jenkins 1996), and environmental influences have a role in many theories (e.g. Cassidy 1994). Attachment theory has been particularly influential in the field.

Attachment theory and emotional development

In attachment theory, various processes are thought to be important in the development of emotional states (and also hunger and satiety). These include maternal sensitivity, such as synchronization or affect attunement (Stern 1985), i.e. accurate response to the child's inner affective state. Although not expanded on in detail, this might serve several functions, including accurate discrimination (perception) of internal states, appropriate interpretation/labelling of internal states, and appropriate expression, including sending the message that different states can be communicated/shared. Such experience and development might help build up an internal working model of relationships, which is important for the development of relationships later in life. Bruch also notes that direct mislabelling of the child's interoceptive and emotional state may occur. The implications of such experiences, in attachment theory terms, are far reaching. Generally, they may lead to a poor sense of self/individuation, including a sense of ineffectiveness (finding it difficult to use feelings, thoughts, body sensations to guide behaviour, and mistrust of these), as well as specific difficulties with hunger, satiety and some emotional states.

Expression of emotion

Emotional expression also develops with age. For example, an angry child learns to yell instead of hitting out. Children also learn to talk about emotions as they grow up.

Clinically, it has been observed that patients with eating disorders often have problems with expressing how they feel. This could be due to several factors. For example, if internal states are not clearly differentiated (perceptually and cognitively), talking about them will be difficult. This might also be difficult if there has not been much opportunity to discuss internal states, or if discussion has led to negative consequences. Abused children, for example, (hypothesized to have fewer opportunities to discuss internal states, and whose attempts to do so may meet with negative consequences) use fewer words for negative emotions, such as hatred, anger, and disgust, and interestingly also for bodily states, such as hunger (Cicchetti & Beeghly 1987).

Emotional regulation

The term emotional regulation has been used in three main ways. It can refer to emotionality, e.g. high levels of anger or other specific emotions. It can refer to the processes that affect the expression of emotion, e.g. trying to distract oneself. In the developmental literature, it has also been used to refer to the fact that some individuals, for genetic or environmental reasons, or both, come to have a bias towards experiencing and expressing certain sorts of emotions.

The term dysregulation has also been used. This describes an inability to regulate or control emotions. It is the basis of theories that argue that bulimia is a disorder of self-regulation and affect regulation. This includes those suggested by self-psychologists (see Chapter 7). However, the precise nature of the dysregulation is not clear. It is not known whether bulimia is associated with more intense emotions or affect than is usual, inability to modulate these, inability to modulate normal levels of emotion, or use of binge-eating, instead of more usual methods, to modulate either normal or more intense levels of affect. Some have also argued that the concept is fundamentally flawed and not useful (Oatley & Jenkins 1996). As often used it implies that everyone has certain emotions, and that there is an optimal level at which these should be experienced and expressed (Oatley & Jenkins 1996). Instead it has been suggested that it may be better to conceptualize emotions rather differently, namely as becoming organized in relation to the self and the environment, including interpersonal relationships.

Emotional regulation (or organization) also develops in childhood, and is the result of developmental changes in neurophysiology (Thompson 1994), as well as the environment. It goes through a series of stages (Cicchetti *et al.* 1991) similar to those involved in the development of emotions, i.e. perception, interpretation, and expression. Like the development of emotion it has also been conceptualized within an attachment framework. Again, maternal sensitivity, synchronization, and learning to speak about feelings, as well as modelling, are thought to be important. There is some preliminary evidence that certain responses may increase the expression of negative emotions (e.g. anger/aggression) on future occasions. The child's temperament may also play a role.[3]

---

[3] It is important to remember that the presence of supportive relationships continues to be crucial to emotional life throughout the lifespan.

Empirical evidence

In addition to indirect evidence, evidence for difficulties in perception, interpretation, and expression of emotional states in bulimia nervosa, comes from a small but growing number of studies conducted within the framework of alexithymia. There is very little empirical work, however, on emotional regulation or organization in BN.

Alexithymia

Alexithymia is usually thought of as having three components (Taylor *et al.* 1997). It includes difficulty in identifying feelings, distinguishing between feelings and the bodily sensations of emotional arousal, and difficulty describing feelings to other people. Those with alexithymia also often have constricted imaginal processes; they tend to be stimulus bound, literal, and to have an externally oriented cognitive style. Definitions imply that both perceptual and cognitive aspects are important, but in research studies it is usually operationalized primarily in terms of cognitive characteristics.

Several tools have been developed to measure alexithymia. A popular tool in eating disorders is the Toronto Alexithymia Scale (TAS: Taylor *et al.* 1985). High rates of alexithymia have been found in bulimics, with 56% classified as alexithymic, in one study (Cochrane *et al.* 1993). Alexithymia was also related to depression in this study, and not to eating behaviours, although a more recent study has found a relationship to eating, even when depression is controlled (de Groot *et al.* 1995).

Some studies have also found that bulimics, compared to controls, score highly on two factors of the TAS in particular: difficulty identifying feelings and bodily sensations, and difficulty expressing feelings (e.g. Cochrane *et al.* 1993; Troop *et al.* 1995). A study using bulimics who were not depressed also found differences on these two factors (Jimerson *et al.* 1994). One study found that ability to identify feelings does not improve with reduction of bingeing and vomiting (Schmidt *et al.* 1993a), although another found evidence of change with treatment (de Groot *et al.* 1995). A recent study (Bagby *et al.* 1994) used a revised version, the TAS-20, to confirm some of the earlier findings (Corcos *et al.* 2000).

Self-soothing

One study is relevant to affect regulation or organization. On a measure of self-soothing (the Soothing Receptiveness Scale: Glassman 1988), bulimics had decreased capacity or openness to achieve a psychological state of calmness or to be comforted. A lower level of soothing is generally associated with decreased capacity for evocative memory, and both are associated with greater aloneness (Esplen *et al.* 2000).

Treatment implications

It has been suggested that impaired ability to talk about feelings makes BN patients unsuitable for psychodynamic treatments. Recently, however, psychodynamic treatments that focus specifically on emotional identification and affect regulation have been described (Taylor *et al.* 1997). These aim to elevate emotions from a perceptually bound experience (sensation and action) to a conceptual representational level (feelings and thoughts). This may include learning accurate labels for perceptual experiences, and discriminating between different feelings. In eating disorders, therapy may also be needed to deal with cognitive mislabelling and emotional expression. The modifications suggested by Taylor *et al.* (1997), overlap a little with recent developments in cognitive therapy. However, it is still unclear whether perception, the foundation of cognition, is also disturbed in bulimia. It is also unclear whether other aspects of alexithymia are disturbed, e.g. whether bulimics confuse sensation and action with feelings and cognition, how this might happen, and how this relates to what we know of normal development.

The self

It has been argued that fear of abandonment, the development of self-identity/self-concept (including a sense of agency or self efficacy), self-worth, and autonomy are all important developmental issues in bulimia. Self-worth has been considered briefly in Chapter 4. The others will be considered here, together with evidence for disruption in the associated developmental processes. These have usually been conceptualized in terms of attachment theory, i.e. it has been proposed that problems in the relationship with the primary caregiver explain many later 'self-related' difficulties.

Attachment theory and the development of the self

Attachment theory is about the relationship between an individual and her caregivers (Ainsworth *et al.* 1978; Bowlby 1969, 1973, 1980). The main function of the attachment relationship with the primary caregiver is protection (which makes it different from other relationships). The outcome is behavioural and/or psychological proximity, and the goal of the attachment relationship is a sense of subjective 'felt security' (Cicchetti *et al.* 1990). A 'secure' attachment provides the basis for exploration and psychological development, including emotional development, through the mechanisms, such as maternal sensitivity, discussed above. Insecure attachments create risk of significant impairments in these areas of functioning, and also may be a risk for disruption or delay in psychological development through 'sensitive periods' (Cicchetti 1993). This may be particularly likely if these involve changes in important attachment relationships, e.g. at adolescence with its emphasis on separation from parents and increased independence.

Self, attachment, and bulimia

It has often been assumed that a baby has no sense of separateness or self. Freud and Piaget, both influential in this area, believed this. However, it is now generally agreed that the infant does have a sense of separateness (Harter 1998), albeit a primitive sense, from the beginning. As many have assumed, this also develops with maturation and experience. Attachment is generally thought to be important in this development, and to have implications for the development of identity and autonomy.

Fear of abandonment has been described as an important feature of eating disorders, particularly anorexia (Masterson 1977), but also bulimia (O'Kearney 1996). Typically, it has been argued, bulimics develop insecure or anxious attachments (although the theory is not specific about which type of anxious attachment) in which expectation of parental availability (and personal self-worth) fails to develop. This is usually thought to be the result of perceived inaccessibility and/or inappropriate responsiveness of caregivers, e.g. intrusiveness, overcontrol, and unresponsiveness. These factors may then interact with characteristics of the infant, such as temperament, and result in self-deficits, e.g. fear of abandonment. However, fear of abandonment has not been measured directly in BN.

The roots of self-efficacy and control with inanimate objects, and with people, may also lie in the early attachment relationship. For example, when a baby smiles, the mother typically smiles back, and these connections between behaviours are vital in building up a sense of agency. Self-worth and autonomy have similar roots, i.e. in the perceived inaccessibility or inappropriate responsiveness of the mother. However, as for self-worth, the links proposed are primarily theoretical and not empirically established. There are no longitudinal prospective studies, and few retrospective studies, to see if these early experiences actually affect the development of self-efficacy and self-control in practice. There are also no direct measures of most of the important aspects, e.g. responsiveness, inaccessibility.

Evidence for disturbed attachment

A few preliminary studies have used self-report questionnaires in retrospective studies to see if attachment is disturbed in BN. The results of this research are summarized in Table 5.5.

Most research has used the Parental Bonding Instrument (PBI: Parker *et al.* 1979), which assesses perceptions of maternal and paternal care and protection in childhood. Typically it finds that parents are over-protective and controlling (although there is some evidence for differences between mothers and fathers in this: Leung *et al.* 2000a). In one study, parents of bulimics were found to be caring but overwhelming (Sordelli *et al.* 1996). A few studies have used the Parental Attachment Questionnaire (Kenny 1990), an adaptation of Ainsworth *et al.*'s (1978) conceptualization of attachment.

Table 5.5 Evidence for disturbed attachment in BN: a summary

Parental bonding instrument studies: parents are over-protective and controlling
Parental attachment questionnaire studies: patients are less securely attached; parents are less supportive of independence
Parental intrusiveness scale studies: both maternal and paternal attachment is disturbed

One study found a mixed eating disorder group (74% bulimics) were less securely attached than college women, and that their parents were affectively more negative and less supportive of independence (Kenny & Hart 1992). Some researchers have also attempted to link attachment theory to specific eating disorder symptoms (Armstrong & Roth 1989), and a few preliminary studies have investigated possible links with no definite conclusions (e.g. Heesacker & Neimeyer 1990; Kenny & Hart 1992), but this has not been much developed. Recently, a measure of attachment has been designed specifically for bulimia—the Parental Intrusiveness Rating Scale (Rorty *et al.* 2000a). An initial study suggests that both mothers' and fathers' attachment may be disturbed (Rorty *et al.* 2000b).

Problems with attachment research

O'Kearney (1996) provides a summary of the main problems with attachment research in eating disorders, including BN. He notes that there are methodological weaknesses in most studies, in particular there are no psychologically disturbed control groups, e.g. depressed women, or dieters. The measures used have variable validity, and studies disregard current attachment relationships, which may influence the findings. Studies are also invariably retrospective and as such rely on memory. The arguments linking the PBI to eating disorder symptoms are often unclear, and not always based on key issues. Finally, the work is not often translated into empirical studies. Theoretically, a single pathway model is also often used. Rutter (1972) expressed concern about this with respect to maternal deprivation, and similar concerns apply to attachment. Attachment is likely to be the basis of many later problems, and it is unlikely to provide a sufficient explanation of the development of eating disorders. Importantly, studies in eating disorders do not assess the full range of beliefs, expectations, goals, and strategies in the cognitive domain of an individual's working model of attachment. Studies in other disorders have, for example, looked at attention and memory (from a cognitive perspective) for attachment related information (Kirsh & Cassidy 1997). A few studies, mainly in aggression, have also investigated the relationship between parental support and control, and social information processing (e.g. Gomez *et al.* 2001). The framework for these studies is not dissimilar to that of attachment-based studies. Their emphasis on relational schemas and attributional processes parallels the emphasis of attachment on internal working models. To date, however, no detailed attempt has been made to link cognitive theories of eating disorders with the developmental literature, either in relation to information processing (including social information processing) or attachment. Some of the problems with attachment research (based on O'Kearney 1996) are summarized in Table 5.6.

Recently, shame has been suggested as a mediator in the relationship between perceived parental style in childhood and bulimic symptoms, i.e under-protection has a direct influence on internalized shame, but over-protection leads to higher levels of internal shame only if one is already predisposed to be shame-prone. Both these

Table 5.6 Problems with attachment research in BN (based on O'Kearney 1996)

Many methodological weaknesses
Links between attachment and eating disorder symptoms are not clear
Lack of empirical studies
No links between cognitive theories of eating disorders and developmental literature—either information processing or attachment based
Tend to prefer single-pathway models
Do not assess the full range of factors in individual working models of attachment

aspects of shame have been linked empirically to bulimic symptoms (Sanftner *et al.* 1995). Both are also thought to originate in interpersonal relationships. It has been suggested, for example, that internalized shame is seeing the self as worthless, rejected by others, while shame-proneness is oversensitivity to experience shame in social situations. The concept has been extended to the family environment, which can be 'shame-bound' (Murray *et al.* 2000). The concept, and its content overlaps with the idea of negative self-beliefs in recent developments in cognitive theory (see Chapter 8).

Gender concept/sex role development

This is part of the self-concept, and it has been suggested that its development poses a particular difficulty for those with eating disorders. Three main theories exist. It has been suggested, for example, that bulimics are trying to reject the traditional feminine, maternal role (Silverstein *et al.* 1988). Others, however, have suggest that eating disordered women are particularly high on characteristics typically associated with high scores on femininity measures, i.e. passivity, dependence, and need for approval from others (Boskind-Lodahl 1976). Yet others suggest that aspiration to the masculine role is important (e.g. Steiner-Adair 1986). The different theories have led to different questions, and use of different measures and samples. The data obtained are so variable in their findings, that it has been concluded by some that there is no relationship between gender role endorsement and eating disorders (e.g. Lancelot & Kaslow 1994).

A recent meta-analysis, including examination of evidence for the three main theoretical links proposed, appears to support this conclusion. Studies could not usually distinguish anorexics from bulimics and, although there were higher levels of femininity and lower masculinity in the eating disordered, the effect sizes were generally too small to draw firm conclusions (Lancelot & Kaslow 1994).

Interest in gender concept in eating disorders has declined in recent years. Many books now do not include a chapter on gender role when discussing aetiology. One possible reason for this lack of interest is that the measures need revising, e.g. modern ideals of the 'superwoman' (Steiner-Adair 1986, 1989) are more important than the qualities assessed on traditional measures. In one study, for example, those endorsing this image had greater eating disorder pathology. Another possibility is that individual gender role adoption is not necessarily the key aspect, e.g. it could be a mismatch with parental expectations that is important (see Silverstein & Perlick 1995). In other words, we may need to reconceptualize the way in which it is relevant. It has also been suggested that being female means certain other experiences may become more likely, e.g. sexual harassment, rape, and sexual abuse, and these may interact in crucial ways with gender concept to determine the development and expression of BN.

Early adolescence is a particularly important time for gender role shifts and gender intensification (e.g. Brown & Gilligan 1992)—just when eating problems start to be a problem. Parent, peer, and teacher expectations in the social and cultural context are all known to influence these shifts. However, they have not been studied in bulimia, or linked with existing findings. One important aspect might be how the development of relevant cognitions occurs, in the context of an updated view of gender and sex role development.

Beyond early attachment

Peer relationships are likely to be important in the development of BN. Anecdotally, there are reports of teasing by peers about weight, as well as bullying or general teasing related to being different in some way (Cooper *et al.* 1998). Peer relationships develop and change, and friends become more important in support networks in adolescence (Berndt & Savin-Williams 1993). Intimacy increases and friendships become increasingly based on sharing thoughts and feelings with others. Loyalty also becomes important (Berndt & Perry 1990). However, little is known about the harmful or protective aspects of peer (and parental) support on the child's general psychological development and adjustment in adolescence; even less is known in relation to the concerns specific to bulimia. In other mental health problems there seems some relation of parental support to adjustment in children/adolescents (e.g. Windle 1992). For example, girls reporting less family support had increased depression, alcohol problems, and delinquent activity (Windle 1992). It also seems likely that such support is affected by the child's behaviour. A recent study, for example, found that friendship cliques predicted individual body image concerns and eating behaviours, although not binge-eating (Paxton *et al.* 1999). Again, links have not been made between developmental issues and cognition, or how these may both relate to the development of BN. Both general and specific beliefs may be important (see Chapter 8).

Family characteristics/history

Support from parents is also likely to be important in the development of BN. This has usually been considered within the broader context of the family. Two topics have been considered: whether early food fussiness, influenced by family factors, develops into an eating disorder; and whether the family is involved in the development of control issues (both around food and more generally). Some studies have investigated demographic features, e.g. parental psychiatric history, birth order, sibships, etc. These are

Table 5.7 Family characteristics investigated in BN

Early food fussiness
Control issues—related to food and also to more general control issues
General features—poor communication and problem-solving skills, conflict, cohesiveness of family
Specific features—family concern with weight and shape, and with achievement

likely to be a relatively crude way of assessing the influence of specific family factors and will not be discussed here. General family climate studies, however, will be considered. The factors discussed in this section are summarized in more detail in Table 5.7.

Early food fussiness

It is not entirely clear whether the family influences food preferences or fussiness. Early on, maternal mood may be linked to perception of the infant as fussy and demanding over food (Hellin & Waller 1992), rather than to actual fussiness. When the child gets older, there is some evidence that modelling may influence food preferences (e.g. Birch 1987), although the evidence does not fully support this. However, although it seems likely that they may operate through parental influence, many other factors affect food preference and food refusal in children and adolescents. More importantly, there is no evidence for a link between a child's early fussiness and refusal, or food preferences, and later bulimia. As Waller & Calam (1994) point out, a good epidemiological study would be very difficult to conduct. However, food fussiness and refusal in young children are common (Eppright *et al.* 1969), while the prevelance of bulimia is relatively low, suggesting that it is unlikely to be a major factor by itself.

Control issues

Food and control

Bruch (1969) suggested that difficult interactions during meal times could have a long-term effect on behaviour, and that early battles with feeding could make food a focus for control in later years. However, there is very little research on this. There is some evidence for more negative experiences around family meals in bulimics, compared to dieters and controls (Miller, McCluskey-Fawcett & Irving 1993). Negative experiences included conflictual conversations during meals dominated by parents, as well as greater parental control over eating, e.g. to finish all their food. Food was also used as punishment and reward, or as a treat when the child was hurt or upset.

General control

This has not often been studied directly. One study that separated it from other issues (e.g. low tolerance of independence) found no differences between the families of those with and without bulimia (Johnson & Flach 1985).

Family climate variables

Several studies confirm that bulimics perceive their families to have a poor family climate. For example, families are perceived as having poor communication and poor problem-solving skills (McNamara & Loveman 1990). They are also less cohesive and nurturing (Johnson & Flach 1985), and experience more conflict (McNamara & Loveman 1990). Several researchers have argued that this is important in the development of bulimia (e.g. Humphrey & Stern 1988). A small number of studies have attempted to link family climate variables to specific symptoms or severity of symptoms. For example, bingeing appears to be more frequent if patients perceive their family as having poor problem-solving skills, and being less cohesive (Waller 1994).

However, this relationship may well be non-specific. A similar family pattern has also been associated with other problems, e.g. depression, and not with diagnosis of eating disorder *per se* (Thienemann & Steiner 1993). Thus it may just create a general vulnerability, e.g. to low self-esteem (Strober & Humphrey 1987), or to poor attachment. In addition it does not seem to be associated only with severity or specific eating disorder symptoms. For example, family functioning was not found to be uniquely related to bulimic symptoms, when compared with those who had CSA-related symptoms— apart from a specific link between bulimia and family emphasis on achievement (Kern & Hastings 1995).

Specific family climate variables

More recently, specific family climate variables, e.g. family concern with weight and shape, and achievement, have been investigated. One study found that these variables predicted disturbed eating better than general family climate variables (e.g. conflict, cohesiveness, expressiveness), although this was in a non-clinical sample. These variables also distinguished bulimics from depressed and control patients, while general variables did not (when depression was controlled) (Laliberte *et al.* 1999). Other studies, mostly also on non-clinical groups, support general family dysfunction as a non-specific vulnerability factor. It seems, for example, that it may have a direct effect on self-esteem, and then indirect effects on eating and psychiatric symptoms through self-esteem. Weight and shape, and other more specific family climate factors, however, seem to have a more direct effect on body dissatisfaction and eating symptoms (Leung *et al.* 1996).

Some findings are inconsistent with the suggestion that family variables have an important causal role. This evidence is summarized in Table 5.8.

For example, perception of functioning often improves with treatment, which would not necessarily be expected if family variables were causal. Indeed, some family theorists would predict that it should get worse because the presence of the problem may stabilize family functioning (Woodside *et al.* 1995b). Much of the poor functioning is also reported by patients rather than parents, so only one side of the story is obtained

Table 5.8 Problems with family studies

Family problems often seem to improve with treatment, i.e. may not be causal
Most rely on patient report only, and not parent report
Most are conducted with adults, often no longer living with their families
They usually ask about current functioning, or for a (very) retrospective report
Problems may result from having a child with BN

(Woodside *et al.* 1995a). However, it is important to recognize that patient perception alone may be very important (Wonderlich *et al.* 1994b), even if parental relationships are seen very differently by the patient and other family members (Dunn & Plomin 1990).

There are also methodological problems with many of the family climate studies. A lot of the research is on adults, and it often asks about current functioning—which does not rule out the possibility that family problems did exist and/or were severe in the past. Studies on adolescents are needed to address this question. In addition, patients are often no longer living with parents, report of early experiences is retrospective, and the relation between current relationship and functioning is unclear if patients are not in frequent contact with parents. As suggested above, while bulimia may be a consequence of family factors or patterns of interaction, family factors may also, or instead, be the result of having a child with bulimia. Current research does not allow us to decide which of these is most likely.

Recent developments

Recently, including within a cognitive framework, there has been some research on the direct effect of modelling, teaching, and direct criticism on a child's behaviour and attitude to food and eating (including the development of eating disorder behaviours and attitudes). Most of this work has been conducted in non-clinical samples. Specifically, attempts have been made to link eating disorder-related symptoms and/or features to specific members' functioning, usually the mother. Kanakis & Thelen (1995), for example, found that specific pressure to lose weight from mothers was linked to bulimic symptoms in daughters. Some also try to elucidate the mechanism of transmission. These studies investigate two types of factors: those that are thought to place the child at general risk (e.g. perfectionism in parents and child); and those that are specifically associated with bulimia. The former may also be conveyed through modelling, teaching, and direct criticism. Positive relationships are generally found in non-clinical samples. However, only a very small number of these studies have been conducted with patients, and none with bulimia nervosa patients. Most have also been on shared concerns (i.e. they assume modelling), and not direct criticism or teaching. To date, most of the studies in patients do not find a relationship between mother and child concerns (e.g. Cooper *et al.* 2001), or find a similar relationship in controls (e.g. Steiger *et al.* 1995), suggesting that the relationship in those with a diagnosable eating disorder is complex. One possibility is that it may not be easily captured by social learning explanations. A more sophisticated cognitive theory, e.g. social information processing, might provide a better explanation.

Life events, appraisal, coping, and social support

It has been suggested that certain life events may be important precipitating factors in bulimia nervosa. In other disorders these are often considered together with cognitive appraisal, coping, and social support (the latter thought to mediate life events and coping). The term is also often used together with the term stress. Stress (a biological and behavioural response) is the result of, or response to, the environment—including life events, which are more properly called the stressor. In itself stress is not a stimulus or a cause.

Life events

There is considerable evidence that depressed people experience more life events than non-depressed people (Paykel 1979). This finding has usually been conceptualized within a model that hypothesizes underlying vulnerability factors and precipitating life events (Brown & Harris 1978). Life events have also been studied in anorexia nervosa, but less often in bulimia. Nevertheless, there is some anecdotal evidence for their importance (Pyle *et al.* 1981). One study, for example, found that rates of life events were high, (evident in 77% of bulimics), in the year before onset of the disorder (Troop & Treasure 1997). Another study found more life events, including abuse, in the year before onset of bulimia than in controls in an equivalent year (71% vs. 47%). The risk of bulimia also increased with number of life events (Welch *et al.* 1997). Important types of event were disruption of family or social relationships, and threat to physical safety. Life events can also affect the course of recovery during the first year of illness, but there is some preliminary evidence that they do not seem to have a great effect on its overall course (Sohlberg & Norring 1992).

Appraisal and coping

Exposure to life events may only be part of the story. It has been pointed out that life events cannot be objectively defined (e.g. Lazarus 1966), and that the way we appraise the event is also important. Stress is experienced when a situation is appraised as exceeding the person's adaptive resources and endangering his/her well-being (Lazarus & Folkman 1984). This includes (which may be particularly important for bulimia) perception of control. Appraisal is in two parts. Primary appraisal evaluates the significance or meaning of the event, i.e. as irrelevant, benign-positive, or stressful (harmful, threatening, challenging). Secondary appraisal evaluates options for coping with the event. Coping is usually conceptualized along two dimensions: problem-focused coping, taking action to solve the problem or find information to solve it;

and emotion-focused coping, attempts to reduce the negative emotions that form part of the stress reaction, e.g. distraction from the problem. The most effective way of coping will depend on the situation, although some strategies are likely to be more effective than others, e.g. for managing emotional demands, reappraisal and cognitive restructuring may be useful, while avoidance or escape, e.g. binge-eating, is less likely to be useful. There have been one or two attempts to apply this model to bulimia (Cattanach & Rodin 1988; Christiano & Mizes 1997), the latter focusing mostly on appraisal and coping.

Evidence for its key constructs in bulimia has largely focused on existence of life events (see above), coping strategies, and social support (see below). Less research has been done on appraisal, although in their review, Christiano & Mizes (1997) found evidence for deficits in primary appraisal, i.e. that bulimics evaluate events as potentially stressful, particularly as threatening. In other words, they report that they are experiencing higher levels of daily stress than controls (Soukup *et al.* 1990). This research has the potential to contribute to a cognitive theory of the disorder.

Coping

Studies in BN have usually looked at current or very recent coping. These may assess trait coping (which could include how they cope in general, including with daily hassles as well as more severe stressors), or may assess coping in relation to a specific, relatively severe, current stressor. Research has not usually investigated an apparent causal event, even though the theory states that it is how the person copes at the time of the key crisis that predicts later psychopathology, e.g. depression (Lazarus & Folkman 1984).

Active or problem-focused strategies are generally associated with lower levels of psychological distress, and emotion or avoidant-focused strategies are associated with higher distress. Patients with bulimia tend to use more emotion-focused and fewer problem-focused coping strategies than controls. This includes more wishful thinking, less social support, and more avoidance (Troop *et al.* 1994). Cognitive strategies seem particularly important, including more cognitive avoidance (information consciously pushed out of mind), cognitive rumination (thought, worried or obsessed about the problem), and less downplaying (de-emphasizing the negative implications and appraising the situation positively) (Troop *et al.* 1998). A more recent study also found emotion-oriented coping (emotional responses, self-preoccupation, fantasizing reactions) may be greater than in controls (and particularly high in impulsive bulimics) (Nagata *et al.* 2000).

One study attempted to link coping to symptoms, and found that avoidant coping may be related more to symptoms of depression than to bulimia (Tobin & Griffing 1995). Social support seeking also seemed to be related to depression—there was more at mild and moderate levels of depression than at non-depressed or severely depressed levels.

One study (Troop & Treasure 1997) found that cognitive rumination (thinking or worrying about the problem) was related to the onset of bulimic symptoms. Patients also tend to be more helpless and less masterful in response to the crisis, which is consistent with the finding that various dimensions of coping, apart from presence or absence of particular strategies, may be important.

Another study suggests that additional dimensions of problem solving may also be relevant. Bulimics, for example, may have lower levels of confidence in their ability to solve problems, avoid problems more often, and are reluctant to share personal problems with others (Soukup *et al.* 1990).

It is not clear why differences develop in coping strategies in bulimia nervosa. One suggestion is that bulimics are socially anxious (Striegel-Moore *et al.* 1993), and this may reduce their reliance on social support as a coping strategy. Others suggest that past failures may reduce active coping (Troop *et al.* 1994).

It is difficult to determine whether bulimics differ from controls in response to daily hassles. These have not been investigated separately or systematically.

Social support

Two types of social support (Cohen & Wills 1985) have been identified. Structural refers to a person's network of social relationships, e.g. number of friends. Functional refers to the quality of a person's relationships, e.g. does she have friends to call on if need be. Social support has mainly been investigated and applied to depression (as well as physical illness). Quality has been found to relate to depression (Brown & Harris 1978), and to other psychiatric disorders. In particular, it is the perceived adequacy of the available social support that is thought to influence vulnerability to psychiatric disorder (Henderson *et al.* 1981). Quality is often used to refer to emotional support, but practical support is also important (Cohen & Wills 1985).

Structurally, studies have found that bulimics have smaller social networks than controls. Functionally, they report lower levels of support from six potentially important relationships—both emotional (e.g. having someone to confide in) and practical (e.g. help giving) than controls, and also set lower ideals for support. They are also more dissatisfied with their support (Tiller *et al.* 1997).

One study separated support from friends and kin. Bulimics had fewer friends and kin to provide emotional support, but were no different from controls on practical support (for both friends and kin). They were as satisfied as the controls on practical support from both friends and kin, and with emotional support from friends, but less satisfied with emotional support from kin. Number of supports (friends and kin) and satisfaction, correlated with social adjustment. A recovered group seemed to have made improvements in relation to friends, but not kin (Rorty *et al.* 1999).

Lack of a close supportive relationship may affect outcome of bulimia nervosa, and was associated with psychiatric problems (Collings & King 1994). These factors are important in the light of evidence that interpersonal psychotherapy (IPT) may be an effective treatment for bulimia nervosa. This treatment addresses social support explicitly. However, it is not yet very clear where the deficit is in bulimia, and what precisely should be the focus of treatment. For example, it may be beneficial to broaden the social network, or develop more effective methods for eliciting social support, or both.

In other areas, it has been found that social support from parents and peers reduces the impact of negative life events. For example, in older adolescents, it reduces psychological distress. This relationship has not yet been investigated in bulimia nervosa. Cumulative levels of ongoing everyday problems or hassles seem to be related to adjustment in adults (Kanner *et al.* 1981). Indeed, in some studies everyday problems have been found to be a better predictor of mental health problems than acute events (Burks & Martin 1985). These have yet to be investigated in bulimia nervosa.

Summary

This chapter has discussed important features of BN that are not diagnostic items, focusing on features that have been considered primarily in an external context. In the first part, sexual and other forms of abuse were highlighted. A cognitive link between BN and abuse was considered.

The development of hunger, satiety, and emotions was then discussed, together with the development of self-concept, self-esteem, and gender identity. Attachment theory was proposed as a framework for understanding these. Links, including cognitive links, remain to be made between attachment and these features of BN. The relevance of alexithymia in BN was also considered.

General and specific family climate variables were discussed in part three. There is some evidence that specific family climate variables are related to patient's symptoms. There are many methodological problems with these studies. Recently, there has been interest in links between maternal and child behaviour, and general and eating disorder specific attitudes—although most of this research has been conducted on non-clinical populations. It seems likely that relationships between mother and child concerns are complex, and may not be explained by the social learning theories usually employed in related areas.

Life events, appraisal, coping, and social support were considered in part four. Most research has focused on life events, coping, and social support, all of which seem disturbed in BN. Appraisals have yet to be studied in detail, despite their potential importance in a cognitive theory, although some preliminary evidence suggests that there are deficits in primary appraisal. The influence of daily hassles has also been relatively neglected.

Chapter 6

Epidemiology

Overview

This chapter will summarize the epidemiology of bulimia nervosa. Part one will provide a brief outline of ways in which epidemiological research can be helpful. Part two will summarize information about the prevalence and incidence of bulimia nervosa in the general population. It will also discuss the risk factors that have been identified. Part three will cover the presence of the disorder in certain 'at risk' populations. Part four will consider evidence for bulimia nervosa in older women and men. Part five will examine cultural differences in the presence of the disorder, both between and within countries. Finally, in part six, evidence relevant to an apparent increase in its frequency (particularly in the West) will be discussed. The plan for the chapter is summarized in Table 6.1.

Epidemiological research

Epidemiology is usually concerned with three things. These are:

(1) prevalence—the proportion of the population that has the disorder at a given point or period in time;

(2) incidence—the number of new cases of the disorder that occurs in a given period (often one year, and often expressed as the rate per 100 000 of the population); and

(3) risk factors—conditions or variables that, if present, increase the likelihood of having, or developing, the disorder.

Risk factors may, of course, include psychological variables.

Epidemiological research can be helpful in at least four ways.

1. It can help decide how much demand there will be for psychological (and other) help in a given geographical area, or in certain populations (e.g. in those who have diabetes). Historical analysis (examination of trends over time) is important in this, particularly in planning demand for services several years' hence.

2. Epidemiological research can contribute to understanding the aetiology of the illness. For example, finding that a disorder is more common in certain groups of people can play a role in developing ideas about its possible causes.

3. It can help determine individual and group risk, by isolating factors that predict the development of the disorder. Importantly, if we know what the risk factors are then we can start to design prevention programmes.

Table 6.1 Summary of plan for Chapter 6

The usefulness of epidemiological research
The prevalence and incidence of BN
Risk factors
'At-risk' groups and features
Older women
Men
Cultural differences
Evidence for an increase in the frequency of BN

4. Both knowledge about possible causes, and the identification of specific risk factors, can aid theory building.

Although there is no example of epidemiological research providing a convincing aetiological theory of a psychiatric disorder, useful clues can often be obtained (Davison & Neale 1994), particularly where there are distinct patterns in the distribution of the disorder (as there are in BN).

The social, economic, and political context

Epidemiological studies (including in BN) are often confined to mere counting of cases, and reporting of figures and statistics, with little detailed analysis of possible explanations for the figures that have been obtained. Studies of associated risk factors go some way towards addressing this issue (although very few have been conducted in BN), but it can also be helpful to examine the social, economic, and political context of a disorder in more detail. This is particularly important if epidemiological studies are to contribute to prevention, but also if we are to link individual risk factors to the broader context, and develop a comprehensive theory of the disorder, and one that operates at different levels. A cognitive analysis may make a particularly useful contribution to this in BN (Cooper 2001), and will be elaborated briefly below, where relevant.

Special problems in BN

For many purposes (e.g. service planning) it is important to estimate the rates of a disorder accurately. This means that researchers need to attend carefully to issues of diagnosis (criteria for case-finding: Wing 1975), and sampling. However, there are some special problems that may affect this in BN.

Case definition in BN has varied greatly over the years, and can be more or less strict (e.g. in specifying binge frequency). This leads to different estimates. Hsu (1996) notes that the definition used (or required) may depend on the purpose of the study. It is likely to be strict if the aim is to plan number of in-patient beds, but less strict if the aim is to investigate the possible causes of the disorder (Hsu 1996).

Formal diagnostic criteria have also changed over time (see Chapter 1) and, in addition, may identify different cases. One study, for example, confirmed the impression that the DSM-III criteria are broader than the DSM-III-R draft criteria. Whereas 12.7% of women in a community sample could be diagnosed as bulimic with DSM-III, only 1.7% fulfilled the draft DSM-III-R criteria (Ben-Tovim 1988). These points need to be taken into account when assessing studies in BN.

Prevalence

Four main types of prevalence study can be identified in BN. These are:

(1) studies using self-report questionnaires;

(2) interviews of whole population samples;

(3) interview-based studies using either a two-stage design (screening by self-report then interview to check if the person definitely had a diagnosis); and

(4) interview studies that also test the performance of the screening instrument.

Most have focused on estimating prevalence in young women, where evidence suggests that the disorder is most common. Figures based on these sources of evidence will be discussed below. An overall summary, with typical figures obtained using the various different methods, is presented in Table 6.2

Self-report questionnaires

Most of the self-report questionnaire studies are on college students, although some are on adolescents still at school. A small number have a rather broader sample base

Table 6.2 Summary of typical prevalence figures using different sources of evidence in different populations

Self-report questionnaire studies
College students: 4–10%
School students: 1.2–8.5%
General populations: 1.62–2.99%
Whole-population studies
Northern Florida Study: 0.7–1.3%
Ontario Health Survey: 1.1–2.4%
Two-stage studies—not evaluating screen
College students: 6–14%
General practice: 1.5–1.7%
Two-stage studies—evaluating screen
School students: 0.99%
General practice: 1.1%

and include, for example, older women. Most of these studies find high rates of BN, especially in younger women.

College students

An early study using broad criteria (DSM-III), found rates of 13% in college women from a liberal arts campus of the State University of New York (Halmi *et al.* 1981). Another found that 4% of female college students met DSM-III criteria (Katzman *et al.* 1984).

School students

A study of school students found that 4.9% met criteria for bulimia, using narrow criteria, i.e. weekly or greater binge-eating, while 8.5% met criteria using DSM-III (Johnson *et al.* 1984). A large study of a high school population in one county, however, estimated the prevalence of DSM-III BN to be 1.2% (Whitaker *et al.* 1989).

General population studies

Studies with a broader sample base include those conducted in family or GP practice settings, and those that survey older as well as younger women.

One large study—2500 women from the Norwegian population, aged up to 60— found a lifetime prevalence[1] of DSM-III-R bulimia nervosa of 1.62%, and a point prevalence[2] of 0.7%. As expected, prevalence was higher in the younger group (for those aged 18–29, lifetime prevalence was 2.99%, and point prevalence was 1.76%) (Gotestam & Agras 1995).

Overall, prevalence rates in self-report questionnaire studies suggest between 0.7 and 10% of the (usually young female) population may have BN.

Problems with questionnaire studies

There are several problems with studies that rely only on self-report questionnaires. Most of these studies are on college and school students, and have used the broad DSM-III criteria. Response rates are often (but not always) low; thus those who respond may not be representative of the total population. They may, for example, be more likely to have disturbed eating. In studies where the response rate is high and diagnostic criteria narrower, then prevalence estimates tend to be lower (e.g. Whitaker *et al.* 1989).

There are also some problems with the measures used. Most of the questionnaires used to estimate prevalence are of unknown sensitivity (agreement on the presence of a specific diagnosis) and specificity (agreement on the absence of a diagnosis). This means, for example, that because of the low prevalence of bulimia, a case identified may not actually be a case. Moreover, questionnaires may not produce the same findings in

---

[1] Lifetime prevalence refers to all those who have had the disorder.

[2] Point prevalence refers to those who had the disorder at the time of the study.

different populations. For example, people from different backgrounds may interpret items or respond differently. Some features, e.g. binge-eating, may also be difficult to detect using self-report.

Several studies have used the Eating Attitudes Test (EAT: Garner & Garfinkel 1979), a measure of the symptoms of eating disorders, to detect cases. However, research suggests that this has a very high false-positive rate, i.e. it categorizes as eating disordered many who do not actually have a diagnosis when interviewed (Carter & Moss 1985). In particular, items on binge-eating tend to lead to inclusion of binges that do not meet DSM-III criteria (Carter & Moss 1985). Little is known about the psychometric properties of most of the other measures used.

Interviews: samples of the whole population

Two whole-population studies have been conducted that are relevant to BN. Both are methodologically sophisticated, large-scale, and carefully designed.

The first study used data collected from a survey of health and family life in northern Florida. The sample was selected using stratified, multi-staged probability procedures. Persons over 60 and blacks were over-sampled, to fit in with some of the aims of the research. Trained interviewers used the Diagnostic Interview Schedule (the field survey version of DSM-III), which has been tested extensively and shown to produce reliable and valid diagnoses in field settings. The response rate was 80%. The prevalence of bulimia nervosa was 0.7% for females (1.3% for 18–29-year-olds), (Warheit *et al.* 1993).

The second study used data from the Mental Health Supplement to the Ontario Health Survey. This was also a multi-stage study, with a stratified sampling design. The probability of sampling 15–24-year-olds was triple that of all other age groups, because the study was particularly interested in young adults. Altogether, 4285 females were interviewed using DSM-III-R criteria and standardized assessment measures: 2.4% had bulimia nervosa currently, while the lifetime prevalence was 1.1% (Garfinkel *et al.* 1995).

Taken together the two major whole-population studies suggest prevalence rates of 0.7–1.3% for young women.

Two-stage studies—part 1

Two-stage studies first identify an at-risk group—usually those who score above a predetermined cut-off, then they interview these people.

College students

An early two-stage study of college women found 6–14% were defined as bulimic (Nevo 1985).

General population

A general practice study, using DSM-III-R criteria, found a point prevalence for bulimia nervosa of 1.5% (Whitehouse *et al.* 1992). Importantly, in this study half of the cases identified were not known to the GP, and some had been referred to specialist care (usually for a problem linked to their eating), without disclosing their eating disorder.

A recent study improved upon the basic two-stage design by conducting two interviews. It involved 1498 women aged 18–44 years, and used probability sampling and trained lay interviewers. Questions enabled a DSM-III and a draft DSM-III-R diagnosis to be made. Those who had symptoms of interest in a preliminary interview were then re-interviewed by a clinician, blind to the original findings, to check the DSM criteria. Overall there was a response rate of 70%. The DSM-III lifetime prevalence was 1.7%, and for DSM-III-R it was 1.6%. The recent disorder prevalence was 0.2% for DSM-III, and 0.5% for draft DSM-III-R (Bushnell *et al.* 1990).

Overall, these studies suggest rates of BN in young women of between 1.5 and 14%.

Two-stage studies—part 2

These studies improve upon the basic two-stage method by evaluating their screening instruments, i.e. by calculating the efficiency of the screening measure in identifying cases.

School students

One study, using the EAT as a screen, surveyed 1010 schoolgirls, aged 14–16 years. Four cases of bulimia nervosa, a point prevalence of 0.99%, were detected (Johnson-Sabine *et al.* 1988).

General practice

One general practice survey of 16–35-year-olds identified 1.1% as having bulimia nervosa (using Russell's criteria). A total of 96% agreed or completed the screening questionnaire (the EAT) fully. However, the EAT produced rather a high number of false-positives (King 1986).

Overall, these two studies suggest prevalence rates of 0.99–1.1% in young women.

Problems

Most of these studies have been conducted in general practice—a sensible strategy in the UK, where most of the population is registered with a GP. However, in some cases the number interviewed was low, and may not give an accurate estimate of the number of missed cases.

Several studies have used the EAT as a screening tool. However, there is evidence that it has low positive predictive power, i.e. low certainty that a screened positive respondent actually is a case (Williams *et al.* 1982). Even when sensitivity and specificity (false-negative and false-positives) are high, as they are in some studies, positive predictive power can be low, particularly when the prevalence of a disorder (e.g. bulimia nervosa) is less than 20% (Williams *et al.* 1982).

Conclusion

Studies suggest that the prevalence of BN ranges from 0.7 to 14%. Most, but not all of these studies have been conducted on young women. Many have methodological problems, but those with more rigorous methodologies (particularly the two whole population surveys) produce estimates of BN for young women that seem slightly higher than that (1–2%) suggested by Fairburn & Beglin (1990).

Incidence

Case register studies[3] are usually used to estimate incidence in BN, and several have been conducted in recent years.

One Dutch study consulted the register of diseases in 58 general practices (1.05% of the Dutch population). The study found an incidence of 9.9 per year per 100 000, in 1985 and 1986, and a point prevalence of 20.4 per 100 000 (Hoek 1991).

A study in Rochester, Minnesota, USA, used a population-based data resource (the Rochester Epidemiology Project), over 10 years, from 1980 to 1990. Using DSM-III-R criteria, the estimated incidence (age-adjusted) was 26.5 per 100 000 for females. The overall age and sex adjusted rate was 13.5 per 100 000 (Soundy *et al.* 1995).

Perhaps surprisingly, some studies have found lower incidence rates for BN than for anorexia (e.g. a study in Fyn County, Denmark, conducted between 1977 and 1986: Joergensen 1992). Hsu (1996) suggests this may be because the onset of bulimia is usually later than anorexia, and studies of a relatively young group may find a higher prevalence of anorexia.

It is important to remember that these studies only pick up diagnosed cases, i.e. cases that have come to the attention of services, and not those who have not sought help. Comparison of figures across studies can also be difficult. They often cover different age and sex ranges, and few report figures that are standardized, i.e. adjusted for age and sex. Again, diagnostic criteria used may also vary (both between and within studies) thus producing different estimates that may not be comparable.

Risk factors

Little systematic research has been conducted on individual risk factors in bulimia nervosa. Such studies are important for targeting prevention programmes.

Many factors have been identified as possible risk factors for later eating disorders. However, most of this work has focused primarily on anorexia nervosa, and few studies have investigated BN. Additionally, few researchers have assessed risk factors in a systematic way, although there are some reviews of potential factors (e.g. Striegel-Moore *et al.* 1986). Two well-conducted empirical studies have produced relevant results.

---

[3] These are cases that have already been identified by medical or psychiatric services.

One investigated predictors of risk in an adolescent group, with a particular emphasis on personality variables (Leon *et al.* 1993). It found that negative emotionality, low interoceptive awareness, and body dissatisfaction were good predictors of later risk. The second study used a case control design to investigate predictors in those with BN, compared to healthy controls and those with other psychiatric disorders (Fairburn *et al.* 1997). Important factors identified were exposure to dieting, negative self-evaluation, and certain parental problems, including alcohol misuse.[4] In addition, those with BN were more likely to have experienced parental obesity, an early menarche, and parental psychiatric disorder, than those with AN (Fairburn *et al.* 1999).

Comparability of samples

While some epidemiological studies focus on identifying clinical cases, others focus primarily on community cases. However, it is possible that the community cases are not comparable to the clinical cases. They may differ, for example, in severity of symptoms, associated psychopathology, or in likelihood of spontaneous recovery. Moreover, in the two settings, different factors may increase the risk or lead to the development of the disorder. These are important issues when planning and predicting need for services, including preventive interventions.

Some initial findings suggest clinical and community populations may differ in type of compensatory behaviour (Fairburn & Beglin 1990). One study found that vigorous exercise, strict dieting, and diet pills were more common in a community sample than self-induced vomiting or laxative use (Garfinkel *et al.* 1995). The disorder was also more severe in the clinical group, i.e. individuals had more objective binges and higher scores on measures of specific psychopathology. However, on some variables the community sample scored more highly than the clinical sample—including self-harm and physical abuse in childhood (Fairburn *et al.* 1996).

Bulimia nervosa remains relatively rare in absolute terms, but is particularly common in young women. It has also been identified as one of the most common psychiatric disorders in young women (Kendler *et al.* 1991; Whitaker *et al.* 1990). As noted earlier, Fairburn & Beglin's (1990) conclusion that between 1 and 2% of young women have the disorder generally remains valid, although more recent methodologically sophisticated studies suggest a slight increase. Evidence for an increase will be considered later in the chapter.

Why young women? A cognitive analysis

Developments in cognitive theory of BN focus on three key constructs—beliefs about weight and shape; beliefs about the self; and beliefs that unite the two (see Chapter 8).

---

[4] Studies that identify risk factors for bulimic symptoms (as opposed to diagnosis) are discussed in Chapters 2 and 3.

Table 6.3 Reasons why young women are vulnerable to BN: a cognitive analysis

Beliefs about weight and shape (e.g. fat = bad, thin = good) have a greater impact on young women than older women
Women tend to have lower self-esteem than young men
Self-esteem in women is tied to interpersonal approval
Female puberty is particularly stressful

The presence of these constructs is thought to increase vulnerability to BN. A summary of the key (cognitive) reasons why women might be more vulnerable is presented in Table 6.3.

It has been suggested that beliefs about weight and shape, i.e. that fat is bad and thin is good, are commonly held but tend to have a greater impact on women than men (Wooley & Wooley 1980), and a greater impact on younger women than on older women. This has been linked to cultural forces that act selectively on (younger) women. These include sexual liberation (Bennett & Gurin 1982), recent changes in the role of women in some societies, and in the cultural demands and expectations for women. Being thin has acquired a multiplicity of (positive) new meanings for young women, including independence and rejection of the female stereotype (Szrynski 1973). It has also become symbolic of female sexual liberation (Bennett & Gurin 1982). These pressures act particularly on young women, and mean that they are more likely to endorse 'thin is good' and 'fat is bad'.

Cultural factors may also affect the development of identity formation, including general self-concept (Chodorow 1971), and may affect self-worth and self-esteem in women. Women typically have lower self-esteem than men, and young women, in particular, may be very aware of differences in status between women and men at a time of increased expectations that women will succeed in traditionally male-dominated spheres. This awareness may contribute to low self-esteem in young women.

Self-esteem also tends to be tied more to interpersonal approval in women than men (Bardwick 1971)—this may be reflected in one of the ways in which BN is expressed. One aspect, for example, seems to be the belief that weight and shape is tied to acceptance by others (Cooper, Todd & Wells 1998), so that women may believe, for example, 'if I'm thin people will like me more'.

Many of these factors are likely to cause particular stress around adolescence, when the arrival of puberty brings certain adult female expectations. This may help explain why young women are particularly vulnerable to BN.

In general, it seems to be the case that BN occurs most often where all these forces acting on women are evident, i.e. in highly developed cultures or ones that are rapidly adopting similar values (Gordon 2001). These are often (but not necessarily) Western cultures.

'At-risk' populations

Rates of bulimia nervosa also seem higher that might be expected in some disorders and in some groups of people.

Physical illness

The disorders thought to increase the risk of BN are summarized in Table 6.4.

Insulin-dependent diabetes mellitus

It has been suggested that insulin-dependent diabetes mellitus (IDDM) may trigger BN by the focus on food and eating that managing diabetes effectively involves. One early report in 264 young diabetic women found that 35% reported a history of bulimia. While this study had a low response rate, including all those who could have responded, it still gave rates of 15% and 7.9% in the two samples studied (Hudson *et al.* 1985).

A recent two-stage study of IDDM, including 340 people, assessed DSM-IV diagnosis. The study also took into account behaviours and symptoms that might result from IDDM. It found a point prevalence of 2.1% and a lifetime prevalence of 5.3% in 187 females. It also validated the screening instrument. No cases were found in non-insulin-dependent diabetes mellitus (NIDDM), but the mean age of this group was considerably older (Herpertz *et al.* 1998).

A study of 14–18-year-old girls with Type 1 diabetes (89 girls), also two-stage and using DSM-IV diagnosis, found no cases of bulimia nervosa, but six met EDNOS, usually binge-eating and purging, criteria (Engstrom *et al.* 1999).

As in the studies discussed earlier, the rates obtained may vary depending on diagnostic criteria and specific methodology. Rates tend to be lower if narrow criteria and more sophisticated methodologies are used. There are also some additional issues that might affect the rates in diabetes. Many studies incorporate measures of dietary concern; this is typically prescribed as part of the management of diabetes, and may lead to over-estimation of rates of BN, particularly in questionnaire studies. One study, for example, found that although EAT scores were higher in IDDM females compared to controls, eating disorder rates were equivalent when a structured interview (the EDE) was used (Fairburn *et al.* 1991c).

Table 6.4 Disorders thought to increase risk of BN

Suggested at risk disorders
Insulin-dependent diabetes mellitus
Cystic fibrosis
Thyroid disease
Migraine

Another study, also using the EDE, found that when concerns about weight and shape were isolated from dietary concerns, prevalence or severity of eating disorders was similar to that in those without diabetes (Striegel-Moore *et al.* 1992).

It has been suggested that some studies may miss cases, since they often study young adolescents below the age at which bulimia typically develops. Some of those finding low rates also have quite small sample sizes—thus less power to detect differences.

Interestingly, one study found that in 30% of Type 1 cases (and in 90% of Type 2) the eating disorder preceded the diabetes (Herpertz *et al.* 1998). If replicated, it calls the proposed mechanism, i.e. that focus on eating is causal in the development of the eating disorder, into question. Currently it seems that any evidence for an increased prevalence of BN in IDDM is unclear.

Cystic fibrosis

It has also been suggested that chronic childhood illness, e.g. cystic fibrosis, may increase vulnerability to eating disorders. Several factors may make a child with cystic fibrosis vulnerable. These include the cognitive and emotional changes of adolescence, e.g. increasing pressure for autonomy, separation conflicts with dependency due to illness, and shortened lifespan. Delays in physiological maturation may also heighten body awareness. Finally, the illness also causes delayed sexual maturation and nutritional complications.

One early study of adolescents with cystic fibrosis, found several showed many of the symptoms of an eating disorder. However, none appeared to have BN—there was no self-induced vomiting or binge-eating (Pumariega *et al.* 1986).

It is possible that other illnesses in childhood (e.g. coeliac's disease), which may produce similar conflicts and emphasis on food and eating, might increase vulnerability to bulimia nervosa. These have not yet been studied in detail.

Thyroid disease

It has been suggested that thyroid disease might predispose to eating disorder. It often leads to focus on weight, particularly as treatment frequently causes weight gain. It can also lead to distressing changes in physical appearance, e.g. exopthalamus, goitre, and allopecia.

A two-stage study, using DSM-III-R criteria, found three patients met bulimia nervosa criteria (4%)—two of these also reported misusing their thyroxine to lose weight (Tiller *et al.* 1994).

Other disorders

There has been some suggestion that BN is associated with migraine. A small pilot study, using a self-report questionnaire, identified 19% (6 of 32) as having a diagnosis, using DSM-III-R criteria (George *et al.* 1993). It is not clear what the psychological mechanism might be.

Career and sport interests

The career and sporting interests thought to increase the risk of BN are summarized in Table 6.5.

As result of career or sporting interests, eating, weight, and shape, and physical appearance may become a focus of attention and could encourage BN. Some careers or interests may also promote the development of other risk factors.

Ballet and fashion students are often thought to be at risk of eating disorders (Garner & Garfinkel 1980). One case of bulimia nervosa (2.8%) was found when 35 ballet students were tested and at-risk subjects were interviewed (Garner *et al.* 1987).

No studies have assessed BN in fashion students.

Athletes

It has been noted that sport is a subculture that may amplify socio-cultural pressures to be thin (Striegel-Moore *et al.* 1986). As a result, athletes may be more likely to develop eating disorders, particularly in sports where leanness and/or a specific weight are thought to be important for performance or appearance (Powers & Johnson 1996).

A rigorous two-stage study, which also evaluated the screening instrument, was conducted on elite female athletes aged 12–35 years in Norway. Complete responses were obtained from 522 (86%), 93% of those eligible. Four refused to take part because they were receiving treatment for an eating disorder. Using DSM-III-R criteria, 42 (8%) had bulimia nervosa. Those in aesthetic (e.g. figure skating, gymnastics) and weight-dependent sports (e.g. judo, karate) were more likely to have BN than those in other sports (e.g. technical, ball-games, and power) (Sundgot-Borgen 1994).

Some, however, suggest athletes may be protected from eating disorders. For example, they often have a more positive body image, better psychological well-being, and diet less (Wilkins *et al.* 1991). However, evidence from the methodologically stronger studies does seem to suggest that those who participate in some (though not all) sports may be more at risk.

Table 6.5 Careers and sporting interests thought to increase risk of developing BN

Suggested at risk groups – sports and careers
Ballet
Fashion
Athletics
Wrestling
Military life

Wrestling

Extreme weight control practices, to fit into a lower weight class and gain an advantage over a smaller opponent, are common amongst wrestlers. These include vomiting, and abuse of laxatives and diuretics.

One study, using DSM-III-R criteria, found that 1.7% of high school wrestlers met criteria for bulimia nervosa (Oppliger *et al.* 1993).

A two-stage study, however, found no cases of DSM-IV bulimia nervosa, either when the wrestlers were interviewed in season or off season. Some of the eating disorder-related behaviours were transient—present during but not after the wrestling season. Most of the wrestlers were concerned about weight to 'make weight', i.e. concerns were related primarily to the demands of wrestling (Dale & Landers 1999). Unlike many early questionnaire studies, this study asked specifically about psychological and emotional factors, as well as behaviour.

One problem with several studies here is that the competitive level is relatively low; also the mean age of samples is rather low, compared to at risk ages for BN. However, to date, the evidence for increased risk for BN in wrestlers is not compelling.

Military life

It has been suggested that military life provides an environment in which eating disorders will thrive. The US Navy, for example, has weight regulations/restrictions that limit promotion and transfers. There is also considerable pressure for conformity. Military women must also meet weight standards, and are physically very active.

A questionnaire (with over an 80% response rate), followed by interviews, found that only three military women had DSM-IV bulimia nervosa (0.7%). A high number, however, had a sub-clinical disorder, 3.1% (Lauder *et al.* 1999).

A questionnaire study of female nurses in the Navy found that 12.5% had DSM-IV bulimia nervosa (McNulty 1997)—although the response rate was low. It was suggested that nurses in the Navy might experience a clash between a demand for conformity and professional individuality, and self-accountability. Few studies have been conducted but the methodologically more robust study does not (at present) suggest a greater prevalence of BN in the military.

It is important to note that in all these studies the direction of causality is not clear. There are three possibilities. It could be that those with BN are attracted to certain careers and interests because of their concerns; that their concerns develop after exposure to the field; or that both processes take place.

Cultural differences

Early studies on the prevalence of BN did not generally provide information on ethnicity. Cross-cultural studies also often look at levels of eating disorder related behaviour, e.g. dieting, weight, and shape concern, and compensatory behaviours,

Table 6.6 Minority cultures studied by those interested in BN

Ethnic minorities in majority cultures
Non-Caucasian—mixed groups
Black—USA and UK
Asian—USA and UK
Chinese

rather than diagnosis. While the latter usually roughly mirror the former, some studies find that high levels of related behaviours are not reflected in high levels of diagnosable eating disorder. Some studies also look at sub-clinical rates—usually these do seem to reflect diagnostic levels.

Studies that focus on ethnic or cultural differences have all the problems associated with the studies discussed above, i.e. related to diagnosis and methodology. In particular, comparability of measures and symptoms in different settings and different populations cannot be assumed.

Cultural studies are of two kinds. First are reports of BN in ethnic minority groups in a larger majority culture. Second are reports from non-Westernized majority cultures. The different cultures considered below in these two groups are summarized in Table 6.6.

Ethnic minority groups

An early study to report ethnicity, and to find some bulimic minority sufferers, reported that 14% of Caucasian women (in a USA sample) had bulimic symptoms, compared to 2.7% of Asian-Americans (Nevo 1985). In other words the rate was much lower in the Asian-Americans than in the Caucasians.

Studies have subsequently looked at different ethnic minority groups in several different countries.

Non-Caucasian: all groups

Some studies in the USA have not separated out different ethnic minority groups. One study, for example, surveyed 1152 students, 95.6% of those who attended class. They used DSM-III-R criteria. Some of the questionnaires had data on sensitivity and specificity, mostly from other studies. Over 50% of the sample were non-white. Overall, 0.9% met DSM-III-R criteria, 1.3% female, 0.2% male; of these 1.5% were white, and 0.4% were non-white, i.e. rates were lower in the non white (Pemberton et al. 1996).

Black

BN has been studied mostly amongst blacks, of all the minority groups, in the USA. One study, on 507 college students, used DSM-III criteria. There was an almost 100%

response rate and data were compared with 339 Caucasian college students in a previous study (Gray & Ford 1985). Prevalence of bulimia nervosa was 3% (1.5% when Russell's criteria were used). The prevalence was much lower than in Caucasians, and did not seem to be explicable by socio-economic differences (Gray *et al.* 1987).

A lower prevalence in black women seems to fit with differences in attitude to weight and shape. For example, black women seem to have more positive attitudes to obesity than Caucasian women. Black women are also more likely to be obese, in all social classes (Kuczmarski *et al.* 1994). While they do not necessarily report less pressure to be thin, they endorse more positive attitudes about overweight, and are less likely to perceive themselves as being overweight (Wilfley *et al.* 1996). They also seem to have less body dissatisfaction, fewer weight concerns, and a more positive self-image (Crago *et al.* 1996)—these are often considered to be protective factors against developing an eating disorder.

Evidence also suggests that eating disorders are more common if black women are younger, well-educated, and more acculturated, i.e. identified with white middle class values (Crago *et al.* 1996).

Some studies do suggest, however, that there is no difference in prevalence of BN in black and Caucasian women (for a review see: Crago *et al.* 1996). This was the case, for example, in a two-stage UK study of family planning clinic attenders. Although more African-Carribean women had a diagnosis (2.2%) than white British women (0.5%), this was not statistically significant (Reiss 1996). However, some of these studies are relatively small, and may lack power to detect differences.

Asian

There are few studies in the USA, but reviews suggest that Asian women seem to have low rates of BN (e.g. Crago *et al.* 1996; Nevo 1985), although some studies find rates to be similar to those of the majority culture (e.g. Gross & Rosen 1988). Again, some of these studies are small in scale, and may lack power. They generally use DSM-III criteria.

There are several studies of British Asians and, in contrast to the USA studies, these tend to find similar or higher rates. One study of 12–18-year-old girls, using DSM-III criteria, found no differences in diagnosis between Asian and British girls (Furnham & Patel 1994). A one two-stage study of 14–16-year-olds found a high prevalence of bulimia nervosa (3.4%) compared with white girls (0.6%) (Mumford & Whitehouse 1988). It was suggested that this was due to Asian girls increasingly adopting Western patterns of reacting to stress. However, both studies were small, and both used DSM-III criteria, which may over-estimate BN. Both greater Westernization (Crago *et al.* 1996) and greater conflict, including inter-generational conflict, have been suggested as causal factors in Asian women and girls (Mumford *et al.* 1991).

Chinese

A study of Chinese students in Hong Kong, using a two-stage design, found no cases of bulimia nervosa, although it did find three partial syndromes (Lee 1993).

Is BN the same in minority groups?

A few studies (see Smith 1995), have looked in detail at the demographic and clinical features of black bulimics, e.g. weight, fear of fatness, distorted body image. One study found that, although they were more likely to have been self-referred (Holden & Robinson 1988), have lower education levels, and lower social class, they were similar to other groups in clinical features. Little is known about this in other minority groups.

South and Eastern Europe

Most epidemiological research in bulimia nervosa focuses on the USA or northern Europe, often the UK. There are also northern European studies in France (Tordjman *et al.* 1994), and Switzerland (Steinhausen *et al.* 1997).

Recently, there have been studies looking at areas of Europe that have rather different types of society. These cultures are summarized in Table 6.7

Southern Europe

One study, in southern Italy, found a prevalence of 2.3% for BN using DSM-IV diagnostic criteria (Cotrufo *et al.* 1998). Generally, rates are similar in northern Italian studies (e.g. Cotrufo *et al.* 1997; Santonastaso *et al.* 1996). This may appear surprising, given the relatively recent modernity of southern Italy. However, it has been suggested that the finding may be due to the lower self-esteem and presence of other eating disorder-related features in the sample from southern Italy, i.e. the samples are not strictly comparable (Ruggiero *et al.* 2000).

A study in Portugal, in the Azores, found no documented cases of BN. A subsequent survey identified only two cases (0.30% of girls, no boys) (de Azevedo & Ferreira 1992). It was suggested that the low rate may be due to the community being isolated and relatively free from socio-cultural pressures focused on weight and shape.

Eastern Europe

A few studies have been conducted in the former socialist countries in Eastern Europe. Using data collected before the radical changes in 1989, one group of researchers

Table 6.7 Less Westernized European and former Eastern European countries studied by those interested in BN

Less Westernized European cultures
Southern Italy
Portugal
Former Eastern European cultures
Hungary
German Democratic Republic
Poland

simulated DSM-III-R diagnoses in a group of medical students. They estimated rates of bulimia to be 1% in Hungary, and 0% in the German Democratic Republic (Rathner *et al.* 1995).

A more recent study in Warsaw, Poland, on adolescent girls, using DSM-III-R criteria, and with a good response rate, found no cases of bulimia nervosa, although it did find sub-clinical disorders in 2.34% (Wlodarczyk-Bisaga & Dolan 1996). A second study also failed to find any diagnosable cases (Boyadjieva & Steinhausen 1996).

A two-stage study in a Hungarian college and adolescent sample, with a rather low response rate, found no cases in a school sample and a rate of 1.3% in females in college (0.8% in males) (Szabo & Tury 1991).

The results of these studies suggest that rates of BN in former Eastern European cultures are relatively low.

Non-European societies

There have only been a few studies of BN in non-European societies. Those where BN has been studied are listed in Table 6.8.

A recent study in Japan, in a non-metropolitan area, found a point prevalence for females of 1.02 per 100 000 (5.79 for 15–29-year-olds) (Nakamura *et al.* 2000).

A recent survey in China, with a 100% response rate, found 1.1% met DSM-III-R criteria (including both males and females) (Chun *et al.* 1992).

A study of schoolgirls in Lahore, Pakistan, found a prevalence of 0.3% for a DSM-III-R diagnosis (Mumford *et al.* 1992). The schools were all English speaking, and in a relatively wealthy area. There was some suggestion that the most Westernized girls had higher EAT scores (measured by eating Western food, and speaking English at home).

Another study of schoolgirls, using DSM-III-R criteria, found a prevalence of 0.4% (Choudry & Mumford 1992). However, it was noted that several respondents had some difficulty understanding the concepts associated with eating disorders.

A study of 3100 schoolgirls in Iran, using a DSM-IV diagnosis, found a lifetime prevalence for bulimia of 3.23% (Nobakht & Dezhkam 2000). It was suggested that conflict between conformity with Islamic values and Western values may contribute to its prevalence.

Table 6.8 Non-European countries studied by those interested in BN

Non European Countries
Japan
China
Pakistan
Iran
Egypt
Israel

A study of Arab female students in London and Cairo found that six in London had bulimia nervosa (Russell's criteria), but none in Cairo had an eating disorder (Nasser 1986). It was suggested that exposure to Western culture may affect the development of eating disorders.

More recently, a study of secondary school girls, in Cairo, suggested 1.2% had bulimia nervosa (Russell's criteria) (Nasser 1994).

A study of Jewish adolescents in Israel found a mean annual incidence of 8.6 for BN (Mitrany *et al.* 1995).

The results for non-European cultures produce mixed findings. Some cultures appear to have rates comparable to those observed in Westernized cultures. It seems likely that there are two reasons for this. Many of these countries have had considerable contact with Western culture, and many of those surveyed are relatively well-educated. No studies have yet been conducted, but it would be useful to study rates in less developed countries, e.g. South America and African societies with more traditional ways of life. It seems likely that rates will be much lower here.

Why does BN occur in some cultures and not others? A cognitive analysis

There are five main reasons, taking a cognitive perspective, why BN only occurs in some cultures and not others (see, for example: Cooper 2001). These reasons are summarized in Table 6.9.

1. The meaning of fat and thin may be different—as described above, in a broad sense fat may be associated with bad and thin with good in modern, Westernized societies. Fat is stigmatized and evaluated negatively—even young children in Western cultures attribute negative qualities to larger body shapes (e.g. Staffieri 1967). It has been suggested that this trend is linked to post-World War II concerns of life insurance companies that being overweight was associated with increased mortality. In contrast, non-Western societies associate plumpness with wealth, fertility, strength, and prosperity (e.g. Buhrich 1981).

2. Cognitive structures may be different. In particular, cultural selfways (Markus *et al.* 1997) may differ—characterized by a drive to fit in and be part of the group in

Table 6.9 Reasons why BN may occur in some cultures but not others

The meaning of fat and thin differs
Cognitive structures differ
Context-dependent thinking differs
Cognitive processes differ
Food and eating habits are different

non-Western societies. This may mean that low self-esteem (manifest as negative beliefs about the self) is less likely to develop in non-Western cultures.

3. Cultures may differ in the link between fat and thin and dispositional factors; non-traditional societies may prefer contextual explanations (e.g. Miller 1984)—this may mean a link between self-worth, and weight and shape is less likely to develop. This may be linked to a more holistic world view that promotes context-dependent thinking (Shweder & Bourne 1982).

4. Cognitive processes may also differ, e.g. the self-serving bias may differ. Non-Western societies tend to explain success in terms of situations, whereas failure is often explained as lack of effort or ability in the West. This, in turn, seems linked to child-rearing practices. It may mean, for example, that non-Western cultures are less likely to endorse 'if I'm thin I'm successful'.

5. Finally, as Gordon (2001) points out, there are also differences in food consumption and habits across cultures—in many cultures obesity is a health problem, and the target of much attention; fast food is also more freely available in some cultures (Gordon 2001).

It has been suggested that changes are occurring in many countries as they become more Westernized—socially, economically, and politically, and/or, in some cases, undergo rapid change. As cultures change, they may take on more Western values and acquire Western-style cognitive structures and processes. A detailed account has been written, for example, of some of the recent changes in Eastern European countries, especially the rise of commercialism (Catina & Joja 2001; Rathner 2001), and how this might affect the incidence of eating disorders. These are not purely 'cognitive' accounts, but it seems likely, for example, that increased focus on the body through the marketing of the thin ideal will alter the meaning societies attach to weight and shape (Rathner 2001). It may also change meanings and values in relation to women's contribution to society, and self-perception, in ways that could increase vulnerability to BN.

Social class differences

The socio-cultural argument suggests that higher rates of BN might be expected in higher social classes because the pressures associated with eating disorders are more prevalent there.

Initial papers on bulimia nervosa suggested that it was more common in higher social classes (e.g. Fairburn & Cooper 1984; Johnson et al. 1982). However, this impression may be due to a bias in referral rates, or methodological problems in research.

One study, the Minnesota Adolescent Health Survey, of 17 571 females, found no relationship between parental social class and eating disorder symptoms, e.g. vomiting once a week, abuse of laxatives, or diuretics. However, diagnosis of BN was not assessed (Rogers et al. 1997).

A study of a community population of women found DSM-III and DSM-III-R BN were both slightly more common in lower income groups (Pope *et al.* 1987a). One possible explanation for this finding is that change or conflict with new values is important, and that BN is more common amongst an aspirational group.

Urban vs. rural differences

Rural urban differences have been found for several psychiatric disorders, e.g. Lewis *et al.* 1992. Some of the studies described above have also found rates of BN to be higher in cities than in rural areas or small towns (e.g. Hoek 1991). One possibility is that 'modern' life pressures are less in rural settings.

A large Dutch GP study also found differences in the incidence of cases by setting. Overall incidence was 9.7 per 100 000 person years, using DSM-III-R criteria (9.1 if DSM-IV was used). It was 6.6 in rural areas, 19.9 in urbanized areas, and 37.9 in large cities (Hoek *et al.* 1995). The differences were not related to age—one possibility is that the young drift to cities. It may be, however, that the aspirational are more likely to move to cities.

Age: late and early onset

BN seems to be rare below the age of 14 years and even rarer pre-pubertally. Only a very few reports exist of BN before age 12 years, or pre-menarche (see Kent *et al.* 1992; Stein *et al.* 1998).

BN is also rare over age 40. A case series of 11 late onset (mean age 60) has been reported. It seems similar to bulimia in younger women, but the impression is that treatment may be more complicated (Beck *et al.* 1996).

Men

Case studies of men with BN began to appear in the 1980s (e.g. Henderson *et al.* 1987; Pope *et al.* 1986a).

A recent review suggested a mean prevalence of 1.1% in young men. Applying modified DSM-III (with a minimum specified binge-eating frequency) it was 0.5%; and using Russell's or DSM-III-R it was 0.2%. Most of these cases were detected by self-report questionnaire (e.g. Pyle *et al.* 1983). One study used a two-stage design, screening plus interview of potential cases (but no evaluation of the screening instrument) (Whitehouse & Button 1988). Only a small number of studies have interviewed the whole sample, or were two-stage studies that evaluated the screening instrument.

One large study, the Mental Health Supplement to the Ontario Health Survey, surveyed ages 15–65 years, using DSM-III-R and Russell's criteria, and trained interviewers. Lifetime prevalence for bulimia nervosa in men was 0.1% (Garfinkel *et al.* 1995).

Another large study, of in-patients at VA hospitals, age 40 and younger, found a lifetime prevalence of 0.03% (Streigel-Moore *et al.* 1999).

Two studies report on the incidence of BN in men. One study of men aged 16–24 years found no cases (Cullberg & Engstrom-Lindberg 1988), while another of male college students found a one-year incidence of 0.2% (Striegel-Moore *et al.* 1989).

Studies on males have similar problems to those conducted on females. There are also other difficulties. It has been suggested that men make up approximately 10–15% of bulimics in the community, but only 6% in the clinic (Soundy *et al.* 1995). Clinicians are not often used to identifying bulimia in males, and may only find the most severe cases. Men may be embarrassed at having a 'female' disorder, and be less likely to seek treatment.

Overall, it seems that the prevalence of BN in men may be 0.2% or less. In general, studies have not focused on factors that may affect male risk of developing bulimia.

Evidence for an increase

It may be hard to tell whether BN is increasing because so many different methodologies and diagnostic criteria have been used. Moreover, one possibility is that once it has been widely described, increased numbers are typically reported, both in the community and clinic. There may be better recognition and identification, as well as changes in referral practice and in the use of diagnostic criteria.

If the incidence of a disorder remains relatively stable in the years following its recognition, and identification, then true changes in incidence are unlikely. One study examined this using the Mayo Clinic register, in Rochester, Minnesota. Rates of BN were very low initially, peaked in 1983 (a clinical trial was being carried out), then declined and remained steady. The incidence rate (age and sex adjusted) rose from 7.4 per 100 000 in 1980 to 49.7 in 1983, then was relatively constant for the remainder of the study (Soundy *et al.* 1995). However, the study involved retrospective recall, and the results could be due to age-related forgetting (unlikely, because the decline starts early), or unreliable reporting of lifetime occurrence (more likely, see: Bushnell *et al.* 1990).

Fombonne (1995, p.295) concluded that 'a conservative conclusion … is … that bulimic disorders have not increased over the time period for which data are available to assess time trends'.

However, a more recent Japanese study found that the total number and percentage of all patients with BN increased, particularly from 1988 to 1992 (Nadaoka *et al.* 1996). This study, together with a suggestion of a small increase in prevalence rates (noted earlier) since Fairburn & Beglin's (1990) estimate was published, provides some tentative support for an increase.

Summary

This chapter has discussed the epidemiology of BN. In part one the different ways in which epidemiological research can be useful were outlined. These include service planning, prevention, and developing causal models. Identification of contextual factors—social, political, and economic—may also add to our understanding of the disorder.

Part two suggested that it can be difficult to compare prevalence and incidence studies of BN. Nevertheless, it was concluded that, although BN remains a rare disorder in absolute terms, it is particularly common amongst young women (and less common amongst men). Prevalence rates are not dissimilar to those of 1–2% proposed by Fairburn & Beglin (1990), although recent, well-designed studies suggest that a slight increase may have occurred. Reasons for a higher prevalence in young women (vs. older women and men), taking a cognitive perspective, were summarized.

Part three examined BN in 'at-risk' populations. The evidence is sparse to date, and at present it is mostly unclear whether it is more common in certain groups than others. For example, the evidence for IDDM is unclear. However, it seems to be more common in some sports than others. Possible risk factors in different groups were noted.

Part four suggested that only limited data is available on older women and men—where it seems much less common but possibly, in the case of men, often unrecognized. Prevalence rates in men seem to be 0.2% or less.

Cultural differences were explored in Part five. BN seems less common in minority groups, and in non-Western and less traditional societies. The link to social, economic, and political development was highlighted. A possible cognitive basis for differences between cultures was also discussed, focusing on the meaning of the key features of the disorder.

Finally, in part six, research relevant to an increase in BN was discussed. Again, there is some suggestion it may have increased recently, although not all the evidence supports this.

Chapter 7

Non-cognitive theories of bulimia nervosa

Overview

This chapter presents the main theories that have been influential in bulimia nervosa.[1] Part one will describe psychodynamic theories and the contributions made by Mara Selvini Palazzoli and Hilde Bruch. Part two will describe socio-cultural models, including a recently developed integrative model. Part three will outline the general influence of feminism and the potential contribution of female psychology. Part four covers family or systems theories. Part five will cover behavioural and other theories, including the anxiety reduction model. The plan for the chapter is summarized in Table 7.1.

Psychodynamic

Early psychodynamic models were developed primarily for anorexia nervosa, although there was some reference to bingeing and vomiting in so far as it occurred as a symptom of AN. A detailed psychodynamic model of BN is still lacking. The accounts presented below typically refer to binge-eating in the context of AN, although some object relations and self-psychology theorists have written more specifically on BN. A summary of the key psychodynamic approaches, and relevant influential writings is presented in Table 7.2.

Psycho-analytic

Early psycho-analytic models of AN drew on Freud's equation of eating with sexuality (Freud 1918/59). During the oral stage of psychosexual development, which occurs in the first year of life, the infant derives most gratification of id impulses from around the mouth, i.e. from eating. Anorexia nervosa was thought to reflect difficulties during this stage of development, i.e. internalized sexual conflict. These were activated when the individual was confronted with adolescent demands for mature sexuality. Some very detailed, and specific, accounts of the characteristic symptoms of AN were developed.

---

[1] Except for cognitive theory, which will be presented in a later chapter.

Table 7.1 Summary of plan for Chapter 7

Psychodynamic theory
Socio-cultural theory
Family/systems theory
Behavioural theory
Other theories

Table 7.2 Psychodynamic approaches and key writings in BN

Psychoanalytic—Kaufman & Heiman 1965
Ego psychology—Casper 1983
Object relations—Sours 1980; Sugarman & Kurash 1982
Object relations+adaptations for eating disorders—Bruch 1973; Selvini-Palazzoli 1978
Self psychology—Goodsitt 1980; Swift & Letven 1984
Relational—de Groot & Rodin 1998

For example, one popular view was that symptoms reflected oral ambivalence, and refusal to eat was a defence against phantasies of impregnation (Freud 1958; Szyrynski 1973). Within this context, there were also some detailed accounts of bulimia. For example, it was thought to be a breakthrough of unconscious desires for oral gratification, i.e. phantasies or wishes for oral impregnation (Kaufman & Heiman 1965). The vomiting that typically followed was then seen as a defence, i.e. it was designed to protect from the anxiety that this wish caused by desexualizing it. Other libidinal energies were also thought to be important by some writers. For example, eating or not eating, in general, could also be an expression of hostility or aggression (Kaufman & Heiman 1965). The idea that symptoms have meaning, and 'make sense' given certain beliefs, also characterizes developments in cognitive theory of BN. However, in cognitive theory the meaning is not thought to be unconscious. Neither is it often thought to be sexual, aggressive or hostile in content.

Ego psychology

Ego psychology emphasized the importance of the rational part of the mind. This negotiates between basic wishes (e.g. libidinal demands, such as sexuality) and the demands of the external world, represented in the superego. However, problems can arise as the ego attempts to balance internal id and external superego demands. In particular, anxiety can develop, often referred to as 'neurotic anxiety'. This is likely to happen, for example, when the individual wishes to express an id impulse that has, in the past, been punished. Defences may then develop to ward off or avoid the anxiety that results.

Unlike traditional psycho-analytic theory, ego psychology (e.g. Casper 1983) views bingeing as defensive; it functions to regulate and alleviate internal defects and anxieties (in BN, intolerable inner states). Vomiting then undoes the dependence on food by expelling (rejecting) it. This has some parallels with developments in cognitive theory—where bingeing in particular is seen as a way to deal with internal states, both emotional and cognitive.

Object relations

In object relations theory, symptoms (e.g. bingeing) are symbolic expressions of 'object' representations. These are representations of the self (including motives and emotions) in relation to other people (objects). They develop in early childhood and have an important influence on later experience. The way in which these develop, as the child separates from the mother, can help explain the development of later symptoms.

For Sours (1980), bingeing represents fantasized union with the idealized mother, and vomiting enabled the patient to get rid of hated food. For Sugarman & Kurash (1982), bingeing allows a fleeting experience (sensori-motor representation) of the mother. This is followed by dread of fusion, among other psychodynamics, and leads to vomiting (also a bodily action). Cognitive representations of these relationships are also thought to be important.

Developments in cognitive theory also have a role for cognitions about relationships, and a role for early experience, including relationships within the family, in the development of these in BN; although the latter is not yet well-formulated. Recent work linking attachment to cognitive development in normally developing children (see Chapter 5) may help to elucidate this.

Only two psychodynamic theorists have written in great detail about eating disorders. They are Mara Selvini Palazzoli and Hilde Bruch. Both wrote primarily about AN but they have also had a significant influence on those interested in BN. Both drew on ego psychology and object relations theory. Bruch was also very influenced by cognitive psychology, and drew, for example, on work conducted by Piaget.

Selvini-Palazzoli

Selvini-Palazzoli (1978) was particularly influenced by object relations theory. Early separation/individuation experiences mean that the anorexic is poorly equipped to meet the challenge of establishing autonomy, a sense of mastery, and an independent identity. Early on, the infant splits off an internal representation of the mother (containing unacceptable negative feelings that might facilitate separation) and the image remains unintegrated throughout childhood. At puberty, change in the body (occurring with increased demand for separation) is experienced as the return of the archaic mother— in its overpowering, negative aspects—and the anorexic tries to control the mother by mastering her body. The theory also emphasizes ego functions, such as ego weakness, perceptual distortions, and interpersonal disturbance.

Bruch

Bruch's theory departed more significantly from traditional analytic ideas. Again, it was largely developed for anorexia nervosa, though some of Bruch's patients had bulimic symptoms.

Bruch (1973) argued that early maternal deprivation creates permanent ego deficits, leaving the individual unable to cope with the demands of adult life. In development, the child's needs have been subverted to what the mother feels is appropriate. Consequently she has no sense of individuation and struggles for self-assertion and identity. Arrest in cognitive development occurs at the pre-conceptual stage of concrete operations (in Piagetian terms). The child grows up feeling helpless and confused, unable to distinguish hunger and satiety from other needs and discomforts, dependent on others to clarify and label her needs and feelings instead of relying on internal cues. Unlike early theorists, Bruch argues that biological needs, including hunger, are unidentified, and that children need to learn how to organize them (Bruch 1969). This sets the scene for potential misinterpretation and misuse of bodily functions in emotional and interpersonal situations. Often a façade of adequate coping is maintained until faced with a situation where, forced to rely on her own internal cues, the patient discovers the extent of her lack of self-awareness. She may adapt by being overly compliant to the needs of others.

Bruch had an important influence on early cognitive theory of AN (i.e. Garner & Bemis 1982), on which that of BN is based. She first suggested that symptoms had important meaning in the 'here and now', and reflected day to day struggles to achieve, assert the self, and establish a sense of identity. Many of the meanings she wrote about, particularly the link between dieting and self-definition, are also highlighted in cognitive theory. For example, she described distorted attitudes and beliefs about food, eating, weight, body image, perfectionism, achievement, and the value of exercise. She also described inability to reason in an abstract logical way. In Piagetian terms the anorexic remained at the level of concrete operations, rather than the abstract, formal operational level more typical of adolescents and adults. She departed particularly from traditional theory in taking a non-interpretive approach to symptoms, i.e. they were not necessarily seen as symbolic of unconscious conflicts.

Other themes have emerged in the psychodynamic literature on eating disorders and BN. Some object relations theorists, for example, emphasize feelings of emptiness and persistent struggles to establish autonomy (Masterson 1977). Fear of abandonment may also be important. Others focus on use of the body as a transitional object (Johnson & Connors 1987). Fixation on one's own body, for example, occurs at the expense of external objects, because of separation–individuation problems. Sugarman & Kurash (1982) also emphasize the body as the first transitional object.

Self psychology

This emphasizes the subjective experience of self. If the child experiences poor or inconsistent nurturing, she may develop a 'basic fault' (Balint 1968), a defect in cohesiveness of the self. Symptoms are attempts to restore a sense of wholeness and effectiveness, and to drown out painful self-states (rather than primarily to convey symbolic meaning—although they may do this as well). The principles of self psychology—the focus on identification and validation of subjective experience—has much in common with Bruch's emphasis on helping patients to rely on their own inner experience.

Goodsitt (1985) argues that food soothes, calms, comforts, and regulates painful emotions in those with an eating disorder. The person relies on food because she cannot get her self-object needs met from people. Geist (1989) argues that she feels empty because the self is under-developed. As a defence, she eats and controls feeling of emptiness by vomiting. Eating is the most closely related activity to filling up or emptying, thus it becomes the self-object symbolically. It is also something she has control over. Sands (1991) adds that food is a common substitute because it is the first medium through which soothing and comforting experiences were transferred from parental figures. It functions to prevent total fragmentation and disintegration. At the same time, the person gives up the option of relating to people as a source of comfort, calming, and soothing. Swift & Letven's (1984) view is similar—food functions to alleviate tension, bridge the 'basic fault' (Balint 1968), and consolidate the self.

Sours (1980) notes that the bulimic also turns primitive rage against the self. Bodily sensations and impulses must be curbed and punished. Kernberg (1994) also sees eating disorder psychopathology as an attack on the body.

The self has become important in developments in cognitive theory, not simply as a link to eating behaviour, but in its own right (see Chapter 8). Self psychology also identifies a link between the self and disturbing affect, e.g. in the notion of inability to self-soothe. This fits with developments in cognitive theory that emphasize negative self-beliefs as an important precursor of binge-eating. The notion of self-soothing is also echoed in some of the bulimic's characteristic cognitions (see Chapter 8).

Relational theories

These emphasize the relational nature of subjective experience, e.g. de Groot & Rodin (1998). In particular they highlight the system of mutual influence seen in the mother–infant dyad. Much of woman's self-worth comes from feeling she is part of, and is taking care of, relationships, and bulimia is seen to result from the absence of mutual relationships. It functions to preserve a sense of self and connection to others, while also keeping the person disconnected (Tantillo 1998).

The relational nature is echoed in developments in cognitive therapy in the importance given to beliefs about others, e.g. to weight and shape as a means to acceptance by others.

Current practice is often to use elements of all four of the main dynamic schools (drive, ego, object relations, self), to inform therapy (see for example: Fallon & Bunce 2000). There may be emphasis on the idiosyncratic (including symbolic) meaning of the symptoms, as well as focus on early environment, the parenting received, meeting of emotional needs, use of food to meet these needs, early separation, and individuation issues, including symptoms as control or organizers. Socio-cultural or familial emphasis on weight and shape may also have a role.

Many of these themes are echoed in developments in cognitive theory. However, unlike most cognitive theory of BN, the body has an explicit role in the development of the psyche. The world is perceived through the body, and body sensations are important to early development. As a result, mental processes, for example, are initially structured round eating/feeding. The link between body and mental processes is relatively neglected in cognitive theory of BN, although in other disorders (e.g. panic, social phobia) body sensations play an important role in the construction of beliefs relevant to cognitive theory. A possible link between these in BN will be discussed in Chapter 13.

Empirical evidence for psycho-analytic theories

Ego functioning

A small number of studies look at defence style in eating disorders, i.e. the mechanisms that protect from anxiety. It seems that eating disorder patients have a more immature defence style than controls (Steiger *et al.* 1989, 1990). However, there were no differences between subgroups of patients, or between eating disorder patients and a general psychiatric control group (Steiger *et al.* 1990). One study shows that excessive parental control during childhood is a negative predictor of mature defences, while physical abuse is a positive predictor of immature defence style in patients with eating disorders (Schmidt *et al.* 1993b). In this study, immature style included somatization, denial, acting out, isolation, and rationalization.

Ego functioning has also been found to predict outcome at one year, although different eating disorder syndromes were not linked to different levels of ego functioning (Sohlberg & Norring 1989). Over 6 years improvement in eating disorder symptoms, and general psychological functioning, were also associated with ego function changes (Sohlberg & Norring 1995), suggesting that it was important to build ego strength.

A specific defence—binge-eating as a defence against unconscious fears of abandonment (Sugarman & Kurash 1982)—has also been investigated (Patton 1992) in high EAT scorers, not patients. In support of the suggested relationship, those who saw a subliminal message related to abandonment ate more crackers in a taste test. However, it is not clear whether similar findings would emerge with patients.

Object relations

Becker *et al.* (1987) found greater ambivalent interpersonal relations and fear of object loss, including conflicting wishes for merger and autonomy, in bulimic groups than non-eating disordered groups.

Heesacker & Neimeyer (1990) integrated object relations and social cognition theory (influenced by Guidano & Liotti 1983). Using Repertory Grid techniques they looked at differentiation and integration, i.e. tightly organized but poorly differentiated social-cognitive schemas. They found that object relations (and cognitive structural features) both contribute to the prediction of disordered eating.

Self

Some studies indicate difficulties with self-soothing (often referred to as narcisstic dynamics). These studies overlap with those on personality functioning (see Chapter 6)—especially the assessment of narcisscism—though many studies focus on grandiosity, the presenting symptomatology, not the underlying feelings of vulnerability and low self-esteem (which are thought to be most typical of eating disorder patients).

A relationship between bulimic symptoms and self-soothing has been found in a non-clinical group (Steinberg & Shaw 1997). In a clinical group, there also seems to be a link between self-soothing, greater aloneness, and lack of evocative memory (Esplen *et al.* 2000).

One study also provides some evidence to suggest that a weak or disturbed sense of self-identity underlies eating problems in bulimia nervosa (Schupak-Neuberg & Nemeroff 1993). The study assessed disturbed identity, escape from self-awareness during bingeing, desire to separate from contact with people, and the mother, including on a physical level. Support was found that all three were disturbed in BN.

Parental bonding studies also provide some relevant evidence (object relations patterns usually refer to relationships with parents). These studies are discussed in Chapter 5.

Socio-cultural

Socio-cultural factors often provide a perspective rather than a coherent theory, like feminism, to which they are often related. They usually include some analysis of social and cultural influences on gender, to help explain why eating disorders are more common in women. However, they have a much wider focus than feminist perspectives or theories. Like these, they are not necessarily incompatible with other theories, e.g. cognitive theories, with which they may share common themes.

Traditionally, epidemiological research, e.g. showing that the disorder is more common in certain groups, cultures, countries, etc., is used to support the importance of socio-cultural pressures in BN. Some of this research is discussed in Chapter 6. How these factors relate to the individual, especially those with a clinical disorder, or to specific eating disorder symptoms, rather than common concerns with dieting, has not often been studied.

The two components of this perspective, i.e. social factors—social roles, and cultural factors—effect of modernization/Westernization on values, are usually examined together.

A summary of key approaches and themes identified in different socio-cultural perspectives, with key writings highlighted can be seen in Table 7.3.

Stice's contribution

Existing social and cultural factors have recently been put together into a detailed model (Stice 1994). This model has also been tested at the individual level. It focuses

Table 7.3 Key approaches and writings in socio-cultural models of BN

Stice's model—Stice 1994
Feminist approaches—Gilbert & Thompson 1996
Feminist psychodynamic—Boskind-Lodahl 1976; Bloom 1987

on weight, shape, and eating factors as being socially and culturally influenced.[2] It draws on a variety of theories for moderating and mediating influences, e.g. restraint theory, the affect hypothesis.

Stice highlights three themes in the literature: the thin-ideal body image espoused for women; the importance of appearance in the female gender role; and the importance of this for societal success. He then attempts to explain how these factors lead to bulimia in a subset of women. Socio-cultural messages are carried by family, peer, and media through social reinforcement and imitation; then pressures are internalized. Low self-esteem and identity confusion increase the likelihood of internalization. This leads to body dissatisfaction, moderated by weight, which leads to restrained eating, thus increasing bingeing. Modelling of bulimic behaviours also increases this outcome. Body dissatisfaction can lead to depression being internalized—which regulates affect. Deficits in coping skills increase this possibility.

The model is an eclectic model, drawing on several theories. It links epidemiological findings and study of social trends, with studies showing a link between carriers of these trends (family, peers, media) and the individual's attitudes. It does not offer an account of how social and cultural factors could enhance existing cognitive models—elements in the model are not typically at the same level, i.e. reduced to cognition and behaviour. Indeed, little attempt has been made in the literature to express socio-cultural influences in cognitive terms, and to link these with the individual personal beliefs and attitudes identified in cognitive theories.[3]

Stice's model is also potentially compatible with other theories, e.g. in psycho-analytic theory, to socio-cultural differences in child-rearing and attachment patterns. Other factors that may be important include conflict between cultural values.

One important feature is that, unlike many socio-cultural perspectives, Stice's model is multifactorial rather than purely continuum-based.

Evidence for Stice's model

Social trends provide relevant evidence for Stice's model. The disorder is socially and culturally dispersed—with low rates in ethnic minorities, non-Western countries, and a relationship to degree of Westernization. There is also an age, sex, and (possibly)

---

[2] However, it does not address social and cultural factors affecting for example, low self-esteem.

[3] An example of an attempt to achieve this can be seen in Cooper (2001).

social class bias. This evidence is discussed in more detail in Chapter 6; it provides only indirect evidence for the model. More direct evidence will be considered below.

Stice suggests family, peer, and media transmit relevant concerns. These are then moderated and mediated by various factors. There is some (anecdotal) evidence for the role of these influences in bulimia, and for links between them, and various moderating and mediating factors,[4] in BN.

Family influences

Bulimics often report starting to diet after pressure from family to lose weight (e.g. 55% of patients: Mitchell *et al.* 1986b). However, this could be because they are heavier, and the relationship is between weight and disorder, rather than family and disorder. There are no empirical studies of the link in bulimia.

Peer influences

Anecdotally, friends often suggest patients should diet. In one study, 45% said binge-eating and vomiting started after pressure from a friend to lose weight (Mitchell *et al.* 1986b).

Media influences

There is some suggestion that reading weight-loss articles/women's magazines makes women feel worse about their looks and lower in self-esteem (Then 1992, in Stice 1994). However, nothing seems to have been written on this in BN.

Mediator: internalization of socio-cultural ideals

Evidence suggests that bulimics endorse socio-cultural pressures regarding thinness and attractiveness more than controls, i.e. they score higher than controls on the drive for thinness scale of the EDI (Garner *et al.* 1983b).

Moderator: self-esteem and identity confusion

Bulimics have lower self-esteem than controls (e.g. Dykens & Gerard 1986), also greater identity confusion and instability in self-concept (e.g. Schupak-Neuberg & Nemeroff 1993), but it is not clear whether this leads to greater internalization of socio-cultural pressures.

Mediator: body dissatisfaction

This is widely known to be associated with bulimia nervosa, but there are no studies of, for example, its causal link to BN.

Moderator: weight

This is thought to interact with internalized ideals to produce body dissatisfaction. BN patients sometimes have a history of overweight (e.g. Fairburn & Cooper 1982, 1984)

---

[4] Moderators are factors that reduce the effect of a preceding factor. Mediators are factors that form a connecting link between other factors.

but there has not been a direct test of its relationship to eating disorder, or of the idea it interacts with internalized ideals to produce body dissatisfaction.

Mediator: restrained eating

Body dissatisfaction may produce bulimia via restrained eating. There are lots of evidence for an association between dieting and bulimia (but also some evidence that the relationship is not necessarily causal—see Chapters 2 and 3). Body dissatisfaction may also produce bulimia via negative affect, or via restraint leading to negative affect then bulimia. There is some evidence that bingeing is used to regulate affect (e.g. Heatherton & Baumeister 1991).

Moderator: social learning

This may link restraint and bulimia. Modelling may be particularly important here, from families, peers, and the media. There is some anecdotal evidence that vomiting can be used to control weight following family, peer, or media suggestions (e.g. Chiodo & Latimer 1983). Coping skills and impulsivity may also be modelled, and may interact with restrained eating and depression to produce bulimia. There is some evidence that bulimics have heightened impulsivity (see Chapter 4).

Only a few studies have looked at whether socio-cultural factors are linked to, or predict, bulimic behaviours (and none have looked at whether they predict the onset of bulimia nervosa). Stice (1998) looked at whether socio-cultural factors predicted the onset of binge-eating and purging. In this study he found that both family and peer social reinforcement predicted the onset of binge-eating and purging, while family and peer, but not media, modelling of abnormal eating behaviour also did. Paxton *et al.* (1999), found that similarity was greater within than between girls' friendship cliques for extreme weight-loss behaviours, but not for binge-eating. However, use of extreme weight-loss behaviours by friends predicted an individual's own level of use, including vomiting.

Experimental studies

Some studies have looked at the effect of exposure to media messages on body size estimation in bulimic patients, and found an effect (Waller, Hamilton & Shaw 1992), but other studies have not found a relationship (Waller *et al.* 1994). No studies have looked at the effect of manipulations or exposure on core bulimic symptoms in bulimics.

There are also no studies of involvement in socio-cultural factors in bulimics.

Stice's theory does not really explain why BN is more common in women. Others, however, have made relevant suggestions. Selvini-Palazzoli (1978), for anorexia, highlighted the new and often contradictory roles and expectations for women (also failure of the family to adapt to changing demands), though others, (e.g. Garner *et al.* 1983a) disagree that these are crucial. Further, social roles are no longer clear or prescribed, and need to be produced from within. This may mean that girls feel overwhelmed, and feel the need for internal restraints. As suggested above, Stice's theory neglects the potential role of socio-cultural influences on the development of general psychological factors, such as self-esteem, that are important in BN. It is also important to explain why women tend to suffer more from low self-esteem more than men. Difference in the upbringing of boys and girls is one possible explanation. Stress at puberty—which tends to be more difficult for girls, may also play a role.

Socio-cultural theories are often rather limited in their analysis of relevant social and cultural factors, e.g. the influence of specific aspects (work, schools, etc.) is not considered in detail.

It is important to recognize that cognitive theories typically acknowledge that social and cultural factors can play a role in BN, e.g. a career that demands emphasis on weight and shape may exacerbate the disorder. The solution proposed, however, is usually individual rather than social or cultural.

Feminist

It is important to remember that feminism is a political movement. There is also no one feminist theoretical model that can be tested. Most models are also best described as perspectives—none are articulated in detail. A lot of the evidence cited in their support is also used to support socio-cultural theories. In most cases, the political interpretation placed on it, which makes it a distinctively feminist as opposed to a general socio-cultural model, has not been 'proved'.

Themes in feminist perspectives

Gilbert & Thompson (1996) identify four themes in feminist perspectives. These themes, and relevant evidence, are outlined below.

Culture of thinness

To control women, patriarchal society glorifies thinness and stigmatizes fat. This functions to silence women's freedom, and control women's general behaviour—the anorexic figure symbolizes patriarchal society's belief that woman is inferior and needs to be controlled. An important motive is money. As the women's movement grew, there was decreased spending on clothing and fashion, so advertising focused more on diet and cosmetics. This made many women anxious, tense, and preoccupied with their body, food, and appearance.

Evidence In support of the culture of thinness, there is evidence that media images are getting thinner, e.g. beauty pageant winners, *Playboy* centrefolds, fashion models (Garner *et al.* 1980; Wiseman *et al.* 1992; Morris *et al.* 1989). There is also a relationship between the number of advertisements and articles on dieting and weight in women's magazines and men's magazines, and the incidence of eating disorders in the two groups (Anderson & DiDomenico 1992). Those under pressure to conform also have more disordered eating, e.g. dancers and fashion models (Garner & Garfinkel 1980). Experimental studies (discussed earlier) show that exposure to media images of thin and attractive women produces an immediate increase in body dissatisfaction and dysphoric mood. However, there is, as yet, no evidence of a causal link between BN and the belief that women are inferior, etc., or any explanation of how such a link might work. Evidence relevant to this would need a more detailed study of beliefs and values (if we assume these are conscious) in society, both generally in men and women, and specifically in BN patients. Such evidence could be collected within a cognitive framework.

Weight as power and control

This view argues that weight (loss) offers either a sense of power and control, or protection from being viewed as a sex object.

Evidence This tends to be anecdotal (Bruch 1973; Selvini-Palazzoli 1978), resting on the suggestion that thinness is pursued by women to undo feelings of ineffectiveness, and block attempts to control them. A link is then hypothesized between this and eating disordered symptoms/attitudes. This hypothesis is not easy to test. It would be necessary to show that weight loss has this meaning, and that it is linked causally to external pressures, e.g. to control women. Attitudes (and behaviour) related to the latter could be investigated as suggested above.

Anxieties about female achievement

Four possibilities have been suggested. Eating disorders may be an attempt by successful women to escape the negative stigma associated with women's achievement—and to achieve femininity. Women may become thinner to take up less space, thus reducing the symbolic threat to male dominated society. It may be an attempt for a woman to succeed in the only way she knows how—weight loss is a concrete achievable goal. It may be an attempt to minimize femaleness, which appears to be an impediment to success.

Evidence There is some support for the idea that eating disorders occur in women who value intellectual and professional achievement, but who feel impaired in these because of being female. Again, the links between BN and external forces, and a possible mechanism, have not been investigated.

Self-definition

In this theme the body offers a sense of identity. Food is used as a form of emotional regulation, i.e. as an escape from uncomfortable self-awareness states. The goal is to escape from the female role of wife and mother, a role that is devalued by society. Alternatively, it may be a denial of neediness/failed attempt to deny needs for nurturance.

Evidence There is some evidence that bulimics have a poorly developed sense of self, and use bulimia to cope with cognitive and emotional states. Issues of nurturing and caretaking are also often problematic in eating disorder families. However, this evidence does not provide support for the specific interpretation, e.g. to escape from the role of wife and mother.

Female psychology

Female psychology has also been drawn upon by some theorists to help understand BN. Like feminism, it can be used in conjunction with any theory. For example, it has been used explicitly by de Groot & Rodin (1994), with self psychology. Here, gender-related differences in relatedness, affectivity, and sense of agency, may help to explain why more women than men have eating disorders. Female identity is tied more to relationships than it is for men—thus identity may be less separate, and women may have less sense of individuality. This may contribute to greater capacity for empathy in females. For example, girls are more likely to respond to the crying of another infant by crying themselves, than boys (Sagi & Hoffman 1976). Women also have greater emotional awareness (capacity to experience, identify, and regulate affect), but may have better awareness and knowledge of others' emotions than of their own. Their sense of agency also tends to differ; a contributing factor might be that boys are given opportunities for more activity away from the mother, thus more opportunities for external reinforcement (Olesker 1984).

The feminist themes identified above can be seen most clearly in psycho-analytic theories, where they have been most often integrated. However, they could also be integrated into other models, including cognitive models. Alternatively (or as well), female psychology could be integrated with other theories—to help explain why women are particularly vulnerable to BN. An initial linking of this with cognitive theory has been described (Cooper 2001), but a detailed analysis of possible links has not yet been undertaken (either focused on weight and shape or on more general aspects of BN).

Feminist psycho-analytic theories

Several authors have taken up the role of women in society as important in the development of eating disorders, usually also in the context of AN (e.g. Chernin 1985; Orbach 1983). This has often been in a psycho-analytic context.

Boskind-Lodahl

Boskind-Lodahl (1976) has developed one of the few formulations specifically for BN. In her work, BN develops from an exaggerated striving to achieve the feminine ideal: to achieve and to attract a suitable man. The eating disorder is triggered by perceived rejection. The potential bulimic then tries to protect herself against future rejection—and becomes defensively preoccupied with weight. Bingeing is a release, one of the few things in a tightly regulated life that she can indulge in excessively. It brings about a union between mind and body—a complete loss of control (ego) and a kind of ecstasy. But it leads to guilt because of socialization and cultural pressures. Purging is a punishment for being assertive and rebellious, and an anticipation of rejection for having a fat body—which threatens to bring about ego dissolution and social humiliation. Purging also separates mind from body by focusing on the shame of being out of control. Fasting is a struggle for power and control over bulimic behaviour, i.e. against part of the self, rather than a struggle towards a self (Bruch 1973). She may also be asserting ownership rights over her body—this is a part her parents cannot control.[5]

Bloom

Bloom (1987) is more explicit about inequalities and the subordination of women. Her ideas also have much in common with those of self psychology—especially ideas of self-soothing and nurturing as a reason for bingeing. The bulimic feels not entitled to her needs and desires, to separation and autonomy. Not happy, she fastens on weight. Culturally good is losing weight, bad is associated with bad feelings, with weight gain, and being fat. The binge–purge cycle functions to repeat early needs that were not met—yearnings, loss, and disappointment. It links to food because early needs for soothing were met by food. But, unable to accept needs for nurturing and comfort, the bulimic vomits. The eating disorder is a way of taking power—something she can do about her predicament.

Like self psychology, there is some convergence between feminist analytical and cognitive theory, particularly with recent developments in meaning, e.g. of dieting and of not eating. A political dimension (Bloom's interpretation) can be attached to individual meanings, but there is no empirical evidence that this is a correct interpretation.

Family systems

The family systems approach is a general approach that focuses on the complex inter-relationships within families. It is based on systems theory—which is part of a wider movement in biology and communications research (e.g. Bateson 1973). It is a general way of thinking about family difficulties. Within the general framework, different approaches can have particular theoretical slants—often shared with those of specific individual theories. In general, they aim to identify the function of the symptom in maintaining the family system and (in treatment) identify alternative and more adaptive ways in which needs can be satisfied. Two well-known approaches are the structural (Minuchin 1974) and strategic (Haley 1976).

Two family therapists have been particularly influential in family therapy for eating disorders: Salvador Minuchin and Mara Selvini-Palazzoli. The former is associated with the structural approach. The latter is associated with the systemic or Milan approach. A summary of the key approaches and writings in this are can be seen in Table 7.4.

Structural theory

In Minuchin's approach (Minuchin *et al.* 1978), the patient is seen as the scapegoat for family psychopathology. Symptoms emerge in a particular ecological context and act

---

[5] Orbach, by contrast, emphasizes eating disorders as protest against conformity and stereotyping (Orbach 1983).

Table 7.4 Key systems and family approaches and key writings in BN

Structural—Minuchin, Rosman & Baker 1978
Systemic—Selvini-Palazzoli 1978
Interpersonal—Fairburn 1993

to stabilize disordered family patterns—ensuring family homeostasis and continuity. The family is organized 'structurally' and works to accomplish goals of maintaining integrity as a unit, promoting individual development, and allowing for the negotiation of affection, intimacy, and mutual respect. Hierarchy in the system provides leadership, direction, and reflects the different skills, abilities, and responsibilities of family members based on age and developmental stage. The family is then organized into smaller sub-systems based on function and role. Boundaries around the family and within it between sub-systems are the patterns of family interaction, which allow for the independent and effective functioning of each of the units. Negotiation, resolution of disagreement, and commitment to the achievement of goals, are necessary for effective functioning of the family and its sub-systems. The anorexic family (the model has mostly been used with anorexics, not bulimics) shares typical patterns of family interaction with other psychosomatic families including enmeshment, over-involvement, over-protectiveness, rigidity, and poor conflict-resolution. One problem with the model is that there is no account of how family patterns of interaction begin or how they lead to an eating disorder in one particular member.

Other family characteristics have been added to this model, e.g. isolation, consciousness of appearance, and a special meaning attached to food and eating (Schwartz *et al.* 1983). Identification with the dominant culture has also been emphasized. For example, it has been suggested that the family structure has failed to adapt to the structure of present day society. In particular it contains features that are adaptive for life in a stable kin network that no longer exists for them.

Systemic theory

Selvini-Palazzoli's model (1978) grew out of earlier models—both strategic (e.g. Haley 1976) and structural. It was also very influenced by Bateson's ideas, particularly the idea that communication and behaviour act to maintain certain rules. The way to eliminate the symptom is to change the rules. Micro-elements of interaction receive less emphasis, rather the therapist searches for the nodal point, where the maximum number of functions essential to its existence converge. Change here is believed to lead to change throughout the system.

This model emphasizes ambivalence about change, the consequences of change, and the importance of sequences of interactions and thinking that surround the system (Schwartz *et al.* 1983). Fear of change—in the daughter of giving up symptoms and in the parents of allowing their daughter to grow up—tends to be important in anorexic families.

Currently, there is much combination of theories (and therapies) in systems approaches. Therapists tend to be less split into distinctive schools now than previously. Schwartz *et al.* (1983), for example, combine both systemic and structural schools. Structural family therapy/theory (the treatment has a large behavioural component) has also been combined with analytic theory, e.g. with emphasis on the unconscious meanings ascribed to eating (Dare 1997; Forisha *et al.* 1990). Russell (e.g. Russell *et al.* 1987) draws on ideas from psychodynamic, cognitive, and behavioural theory in the family therapy approach he outlines. Emotionally focused family therapy (Johnson *et al.* 1998) has also been used in BN. Based on an attachment framework, it focuses on separation distress and attachment insecurity.

Empirical evidence

There is some support for the theories outlined above in a small number of empirical studies. This research has mostly been conducted in the context of Minuchin's ideas. For example, anorexic families seem to be more enmeshed, lack conflict resolution, focus on the daughter, and have parents that rarely talk directly to one another, than non-eating disordered families (Kog & Vandereycken 1985). One study operationalized four features of Minuchin's theory in detail. The features were: enmeshment, rigidity, over-protectiveness, and lack of conflict resolution. Enmeshment refers to lack of boundaries; rigidity refers to adaptability of them; over-protectiveness refers to a high degree of concern for each other's welfare, especially physical welfare; while lack of conflict resolution refers to absence of negotiation of conflicts or absence of divergence of opinion. In a mixed group of families, the features seemed to occur along dimensions (Kog *et al.* 1985), although Minuchin had described them as categorical. The four concepts tended to overlap. Over-protectiveness lacked convergent and discriminant validity, but there was support for the concepts of boundaries, adaptability and conflict.

There is, however, currently no evidence for a distinctive and consistent pattern of family structure and functioning in bulimia compared to other disorders (Johnson *et al.* 1998). This may be because so few relevant studies have been conducted. However, some have suggested that differences found between patients with eating disorders and controls may be the result of severe and chronic illness, i.e. not consistent aetiological factors, and just as likely to be typical of other disabling disorders (Dare & Eisler 1995). Other family factors, however, do seem to contribute to bulimia nervosa—both its development and/or maintenance (see Chapter 5).

Family work can also be conducted in the context of individual therapy. This may be important for patients who have significant family issues but do not want to involve their families or who live away from their families. Interpersonal psychotherapy (IPT), developed by Klerman *et al.* (1984) for depression, and adapted for BN by Fairburn (e.g. 1993), is one such therapy. It is based on ideas from the interpersonal school (Sullivan 1953)—the basic difficulty is misperception of reality (parataxic distortions) stemming from disorganization in the interpersonal relations of childhood, primarily those between child and parents. This is a traditionally Freudian view, but Sullivan placed more emphasis on current problems in interpersonal behaviour. Theoretically, relationships are seen as important antecedents to illness, an assumption shared by many family therapies, as well as by IPT.

Behavioural

There are several behavioural models. Some of the main ones, and key associated writings, are summarized in Table 7.5.

The anxiety model

This forms the basis for exposure plus response prevention. It is based on an anxiety model, derived from learning theory principles. Eating elicits anxiety (bingeing dramatically so). Vomiting has an anxiety reducing function similar to that of compulsive handwashing and checking rituals in OCD. Once it has been learned that vomiting leads to anxiety reduction, rational fears no longer inhibit it. The driving force of behaviour is vomiting not bingeing—bingeing might not occur if the person could not vomit afterwards (Rosen & Leitenberg 1982).

The model makes two main predictions. If there is no opportunity to vomit, food intake and associated thoughts and feelings about weight gain will provoke anxiety. Repeated exposure to feared stimuli (eating without vomiting) will eventually lead to decreased anxiety while eating, and increased ability to eat more normal amounts of food. Five single case studies provide some support for the model (Leitenberg *et al.* 1984). In treatment sessions, while subjects were eating, self-reported anxiety and the urge to vomit increased. After they had stopped eating, anxiety and urge to vomit increased. However, anxiety and urge to vomit eventually declined when they were not allowed to vomit. Across treatment sessions, the mean anxiety provoked by eating tended to decrease as did the mean urge to vomit. At the same time the mean amount of calories consumed tended to increase. Self-statements about eating problems also tended to become more positive and/or less negative as treatment progressed. Binge-eating also declined, even though the focus was on decreasing vomiting.

Hsu

A behavioural model has also been described by Hsu (Hsu & Holder 1986, based on work by Garfinkel & Garner 1982). In this model dieting leads to starving, and to feeling hungry and deprived. This leads to binge-eating, feeling guilty, and full, and then to

Table 7.5 Key behavioural models and writings in BN

Anxiety model—Rosen & Leitenberg 1982
Behavioural—Hsu & Holder 1986; Laessle *et al.* 1987a
Classical conditioning—Jansen *et al.* 1989a

vomiting, abuse of laxatives, and fasting. Binge-eating as a response to starvation is also important. The cycle seems to be based (implicitly) on learning theory; no role is given to cognitions.

Laessle

Another behavioural model proposes that over-eating is a learned reaction to several internal and external stimuli, reinforced by positive short-term consequences. It is an inadequate coping strategy to manage stressful situations or interpersonal problems. As well as learning principles, it also draws on restraint theory—restrained eating is a trigger for binge-eating—and highlights the importance of attitudes to weight and shape (Laessle et al. 1987a). One small study suggests treatment based on the model is helpful (Laessle et al. 1987a).

A classical conditioning model

One study makes the theoretical links very explicit (Jansen et al. 1992a). This draws on a Pavlovian conditioning model, and provides a model for binge-eating (Jansen et al. 1989a). Excessive food intake is the unconditioned stimulus (US). Stimuli repeatedly associated with this (view, taste, emotional states, time of day) become conditioned stimuli (CSs). There is evidence from animal studies that eating can be triggered by cues repeatedly associated with food consumption (Wardle 1990). Drawing on conditioning models for addictions, the model further suggest that CSs predict excessive food intake (US) and elicit physiological responses subjectively experienced as craving, i.e. an irresistable urge to eat. Cue exposure is thus the logical treatment. Moreover, this theory predicts that avoiding the cue using self-control (a common strategy) will not reduce cue reactivity or craving—thus the response will not be extinguished.

Behavioural theory has had an important influence in many treatment programmes, usually combined with cognitive principles. It shares the cognitive theory assumption that much behaviour (also beliefs and cognitions) is learned. But, unlike behaviour theory, cognitive theory gives a key role to cognition as a mediator and cause of behaviour.

Other models

A selection of miscellaneous models (that do not fit very easily into the categories used above), and their key associated writings are listed in Table 7.6.

Escape model

Escape from aversive self-awareness (Heatherton & Baumeister 1991) is a theory of binge-eating rather than of bulimia nervosa. People sometimes find it aversive to be aware of themselves, so they seek to escape from it. A common way to do this is to narrow the focus of attention to the present and immediate stimulus environment. This keeps self-awareness at a low level and avoids meaningful thought about ongoing identity and the implications of various events. Self is reduced to body and experience is reduced to

Table 7.6 Key other models and theoretical writings in BN

The escape hypothesis—Heatherton & Baumeister 1991
Addiction—Holderness *et al.* 1994
Physiology—Davis & Claridge, 1998
Stress—Cooper & Baglioni, 1998
Depression—Hudson *et al.* 1983a

sensation, and action to muscle movement. The idea of escaping the self by shifting levels of awareness has been applied to other phenomena besides binge-eating, e.g. alcohol, suicide. Particularly relevant to binge-eating is the effect on inhibitions— the shift to a low level of awareness removes inhibitions, which exist primarily at high levels of meaning. Shift to low level of awareness also deconstructs the troublesome meaning of such acts, removing intrapsychic obstacles and making the person more willing to commit them. A series of predictions can be made (see a summary of these in Heatherton & Baumeister 1991), and there is some evidence for them all. For example, there is evidence (mostly indirect) for high standards and expectations, high and aversive self-awareness, negative affect, cognitive narrowing, removal of inhibitions, and irrational beliefs in BN. However, research is needed to test the application of the model to binge-eating directly.

Treatment implications suggest a need to focus on cognitive processes and causes that set the escape pattern in motion, not just or primarily on stopping the behaviour—which could leave the causes in place and lead to some other self-destructive form of escape. This could be achieved by trying to alter high standards, self-acceptance, self-esteem, irrational cognitions about the self, and related affect. It may involve searching for 'some effective means of stopping unwanted thoughts and controlling their mental processes' (Heatherton & Baumeister 1991, p.102).

Addiction

Bulimia nervosa has been conceptualized as an addiction, not least because there is co-morbidity between it and substance-related disorders (for a review see: Chapter 1, and Holderness *et al.* 1994). For example, the two disorders have been seen as two different manifestations of an underlying predisposition to addictive behaviour, either through genetic vulnerability or common personality style (which may also have a biological component). The notion of the addictive personality has also been popular (Brisman & Siegel 1984), but there is little evidence it exists.

Physiological

One suggestion is that BN is an addiction to the body's endogenous opioids—specifically the beta-endorphins. This is known as the auto-addiction theory. It is largely based on animal research findings (e.g. Davis & Claridge 1998), not human research.

Some cognitive theorists have explicitly dissociated themselves from addiction models. The idea of BN as an addiction does not usually form part of the assumptions of cognitive theory.

Stress

A model to describe the relationship between stress, coping, social support, personality, and disturbed eating patterns was first proposed by Cooper & Baglioni (1998). It consists of three models: a person stress model; dispositional theory model; and indigenous model. There is no empirical evidence for it yet.

Depression model

The depression model, which links bulimia and depression through a biological mechanism (e.g. Hudson *et al.* 1983a), is now largely discredited.

Summary

This chapter has described the main theories of bulimia nervosa (with the exception of cognitive theory). In the first part, psychodynamic theory was outlined. The contributions of Mara Selvini Palazzoli and Hilde Bruch, which have had an important influence on cognitive theories of eating disorders, were noted. Bruch's contribution, in particular, has been important through its impact on early cognitive theories of anorexia nervosa. It was noted that some of the psychodynamic themes have echoes in developments in cognitive theory of BN.

Socio-cultural theories were considered in part two. A recent model, developed by Stice, which brings together many important socio-cultural factors, was outlined in detail. This model highlights the importance of the thin ideal, body image, and appearance in the female gender role for later BN. Unlike other socio-cultural models, it has been tested at an individual level, and there is evidence to support some of its hypotheses. It is also of note that it is potentially compatible with many other theories.

Feminist influence was covered in part three. Four main areas of influence were outlined: the culture of thinness; weight as power and control; anxieties about female achievement; and self-definition. The political nature of this influence (and its implications) was noted. Specific evidence is yet to be gathered. The potential (and largely unexplored) contribution of female psychology was noted. The influence of feminism on psychodynamic theory was explored. Although not necessarily incompatible with other approaches, this is where it has had its main influence.

Family and systems theories were described in part four. These have been largely developed for AN. Recently, integrative/eclectic models have been developed (e.g. incorporating psychodynamic theory). These also focus particularly on AN. Those that have been applied to BN were outlined, together with the available evidence that supports them.

Behavioural theories were outlined in part five. Behavioural theory in general has had an important influence in many cognitive therapy programmes. The anxiety model (the basis of exposure and response prevention) is the most well known in BN, but a conditioning model also exists. Finally, three other models, which do not fit easily into existing categories, were outlined, including two that have generated a fair amount of research, but which have had less influence on treatment.

Chapter 8

Cognitive theory

Overview

The first part of this chapter will introduce cognitive psychology and important trends in it that are relevant to BN. Part two will describe initial accounts of cognitive features in BN. This will include descriptions of weight- and shape-related attitudes and beliefs. Part three will summarize the current state of cognitive theories of BN. The main cognitive (or cognitive-behavioural) theory of BN that currently exists will be presented in some detail. New developments in theory that are relevant to BN will be outlined next. This will be followed by an account of a revised model. Part four will highlight some of the issues raised by cognitive psychology, and the newer cognitive psychotherapies, that require further investigation in BN, and that may need to be integrated into existing theory. The plan for the chapter is summarized in Table 8.1.

It is important to note that the application of cognitive theory (and therapy techniques) to BN has lagged behind that in many other disorders, especially the anxiety disorders. Throughout the chapter, novel issues raised by recent general developments in cognitive theory, and the cognitive psychotherapies, that are relevant to the understanding and treatment of BN will be identified and discussed.

Cognitive psychology

Cognitive psychology is an offshoot of 'experimental psychology'. It made its first appearance in the mid to late 1950s. The publication of Neisser's book *Cognitive Psychology* in 1967, helped establish the field, and in the 1970s the so-called 'cognitive revolution' took place (Dember 1974). Interest in mediational models grew; described by some as a major paradigm shift in Kuhnian terms. Others, perhaps more accurately, have seen it as a return to the concerns of the 'introspectionists'. Nevertheless, interest in cognition grew rapidly, and the dominant paradigm in psychology is now the cognitive one.

Table 8.1 Summary of plan for Chapter 8

Cognitive psychology
Cognitive features in BN
Cognitive theories of BN
Recent developments in theory
A revised cognitive model
New ideas in cognitive theory

Within the cognitive paradigm there are many theoretical approaches, and a wide range of phenomena are investigated—including perception, attention, memory, language, and thinking. These all focus on the study of the internal psychological processes that are involved in making sense of the environment. Traditionally, cognitive psychologists have been relatively less interested in motivation and emotion (often described as the other two main branches of psychology).

Although it can be difficult to describe the field coherently (Eysenck 1993), most cognitive psychologists are currently united in their use of the information processing paradigm. Within this framework, two important trends can be identified that have had an impact on psychotherapy, and on the development of clinical theories and research. One trend is the idea that information in the environment is processed by a series of processing systems (e.g. attention, short-term memory). These alter the information we see in some way, so that, for example, three connected lines are seen as a triangle (Eysenck 1993). Both structures and processes are thought to be important in this transformation. A second trend is the idea of stimulus-driven processing (as opposed to the idea that all information comes in directly through the senses). This is the idea that prior knowledge and experience determines what is experienced, i.e. knowledge is actively constructed. The mind is thus not (only) a passive repository of representations, but a self-organizing system (Mahoney 1993). Both themes are echoed in the cognitive psychotherapies, and both are relevant to theoretical developments in BN. For example, a range of different structures and processes are implicated in cognitive theories of BN. Construction of self-related experience is also important, particularly in recent developments in the field. The main themes in cognitive psychology relevant to clinical cognitive psychology are summarized in Table 8.2.

The major cognitive psychotherapies began to develop around the time that cognitive psychology was gaining in popularity. Early examples were the personal construct therapy of Kelly (1955), and Rogers' client-centered therapy (1951). Both were based on basic models of personality that took cognitive factors into account.

Subsequently, Ellis developed rational emotive therapy (1962), and Beck began to develop his cognitive therapy (1963). An important feature of Beck's therapy (unlike that of Ellis) was that it was based on a detailed theoretical model. Currently, there are a wide variety of different cognitive therapies.

Cognitive disturbance in AN

Although BN was not formally identified until much later, early reports of 'cognitive' disturbance in AN began to appear from the 1960s onwards. Initially, these descriptions

Table 8.2 Relevant themes for clinical cognitive psychology in cognitive psychology

The information-processing framework—that information is processed by a series of systems, e.g. attention, memory
Stimulus-driven processing—that prior knowledge determines what is experienced

were not only or explicitly cognitive. For example, the term 'weight phobia' was used (Crisp 1967), with implied reference to emotional and motivational, as well as to cognitive, aspects. Description of what was feared, i.e. adolescent maturity, or 'growing up' and all that entails, was also not clearly expressed by Crisp in cognitive terms (Crisp 1967). An exception to this general trend can be found in a book, which refers to weight as 'an outstanding concern, ... a "core" value' (Bliss & Branch 1960, p.59). It also describes 'the basic postulate ... that obesity is anathema and slimness is desirable' (p.38) and, importantly, some of the specific meanings associated with fatness (and which are still valid), e.g. 'to be obese takes on the meaning of ugliness, social isolation ... unpopularity' (p.60). This account has been relatively neglected. One reason for this may be that the authors included descriptions of all types of weight loss, not just that due to anorexia nervosa, as it would be defined today.

The most influential early writer in this area, however, was undoubtedly Hilde Bruch. She provided the first detailed cognitive account of AN. Bruch noted that three cognitive features seem to be disturbed in the disorder (Bruch 1973). These were:

(1) belief about weight and shape—she describes distorted attitudes and beliefs about food, eating, weight, body image, e.g. she describes 'a disturbance of delusional proportions in the body image and body concept' (Bruch 1973, pp.251–2);

(2) the self—she refers to 'cognitive distortions'(Bruch 1977, p.236), in relation to this; and

(3) interpretation of internal body stimuli, where she notes 'a disturbance in the accuracy of the perception or cognitive interpretation of stimuli arising in the body' (particularly signs of hunger and satiety) is common (Bruch 1973, p.252).

Bruch also reported that her patients often had a distorted sense of reality, and were unable to reason in an abstract, logical way (Bruch 1979).

Cognitive disturbance in BN

In BN, the terms 'attitudes' and 'concerns' were frequently used to describe the cognitive disturbance. Both terms also imply an emotional and motivational component. Most descriptions focused on weight, shape, and eating attitudes. Russell (1979, p.432), for example, describes a 'morbid fear of becoming fat'. He also notes that 'patients were abnormally concerned with their body size, fearing fatness which they describe in excessively harsh terms out of keeping with sensible standards'. Later in the same paper (Russell 1979, p.348), he remarks 'the preoccupation with body size and fatness consisted of overvalued ideas rather than obsessional ruminations, for the patients usually remained convinced of the danger and odiousness of fatness'. Others made similar observations. Mitchell & Pyle (1982, p.61) in a review note that 'these patients are very concerned about their weight'. Fairburn et al. (1986a, p.394) note that 'perhaps the most striking feature of bulimia nervosa is the intensity and prominence of these patients' concerns with their shape and weight'.

Fairburn and colleagues (Fairburn *et al.* 1986a) provide the first detailed cognitive account of BN. They describe beliefs and values, or 'unarticulated rules', that patients use to assign meaning and value to their lives. Typical beliefs include 'to be fat is to be a failure, unattractive, and unhappy' (Fairburn *et al.* 1986a, p.399). Patients also have strong views about food and eating, for example, they see a variety of foods as 'bad' or 'fattening', and may be convinced that if they eat meals or snacks without vomiting they will gain weight.

Although most early reports noted the presence of depression, unlike in anorexia there was little report of distorted beliefs and attitudes in areas other than food and eating (although Fairburn *et al.* 1986a, did note the importance placed by patients on self-control). This contrasts with AN, where beliefs about the self were thought to be important. The reason may be that early emphasis was on identifying the specific psychopathology of the disorder in relation to depression (as well as anorexia nervosa). Moreover, depression, with which such distorted beliefs might be linked, soon came to be seen as secondary to the disorder, thus relatively less important than the eating, weight and shape concerns.

Early research

A small number of early studies drew on Personal Construct methodology to investigate the way that attitudes to weight and shape are 'construed' in AN.[1]

These studies map onto later studies investigating the extent to which the self is evaluated in terms of weight and shape, and studies that look at the content of beliefs focused on the meaning of being fat or thin. A study of grids in 12 patients with anorexia nervosa, for example, found that the self was construed in terms of shape and weight, and that patients differed from controls in the meaning attached to being fat (Fransella & Crisp 1979). In particular, being fatter was seen as sexually attractive by AN patients, but not by controls. The way experiences and problems are construed in terms also seemed to change with treatment (Fransella & Button 1983). Initially, although 'thin self' was seen as undesirable, 'self at thinnest' was overall more meaningful than self at normal weight. Decrease in the meaningfulness of the fat–thin construct (i.e. a move to less extreme self-ratings) was associated with better outcome. Looser construing (less variance explained by a single component) was also linked with good outcome. The authors described ways in which the findings could be applied in therapy, to help 'elaborate person construing'. For example, for a patient for whom gaining weight meant being conspicuous, the aim might be to find what that means, and then to find that there are some aspects of being conspicuous that are not all bad. Personal construct writers also note that weight control offers meaning and predictability (Button 1983). More generally, personal construct theory draws attention to dichotomous thinking—the idea that for every assertion there is an implied negative assertion. Both these ideas are echoed in later cognitive theories of BN.

---

[1] Constructs are used for categorising experience, and for channelling behaviour.

Cognitive theory

Early descriptions of bulimia nervosa appeared at the time when Beck's cognitive theory was beginning to gain popularity, particularly that of depression (Beck 1976; Beck, Rush, Shaw & Emery 1979). Originally trained in psycho-analytic methods, Beck investigated some of the assumptions made by psycho-analysis in depression, e.g. that depression is anger turned against the self. Looking at themes in patients' thoughts, he found no evidence that this might be important. Instead, he found themes of loss. This research, and conversations with psychologists interested in cognition, became the basis for his cognitive theory of depression.

Beck offers a detailed conceptualization of depression that identifies two cognitive structures or levels: negative automatic thoughts and beliefs, as well as characteristic cognitive processes. He also employs the idea of content specificity—with cognition in depression being centered on themes of loss (and in anxiety on threat). Negative automatic thoughts are self-statements, the moment to moment, often fleeting, things people say to themselves. We all have them—but in depression they tend to be negative in tone. These thoughts trigger moods, in depression this is a negative mood. Thoughts and feelings then operate in vicious circles to maintain depression. Negative thoughts also lie behind the behaviours that are characteristic of the disorder, e.g. inactivity. Underlying negative automatic thoughts are beliefs. These include rules, assumptions, and should statements, e.g. 'if I make a mistake I've failed'. They also include negative beliefs about the self, e.g. 'I'm useless', and negative beliefs about the world, future, and other people, e.g. 'other people can't be trusted'. These are often formed in early childhood, from difficult or traumatic experiences, and they are responsible for triggering negative automatic thoughts. A typical Beckian model for depression can seen in Fig. 8.1.

Assumptions of cognitive theory

Beck's cognitive theory draws on several assumptions. These are summarized in Table 8.3.

First, it draws on those inherent in cognitive science. These tend to be rationalist in emphasis. For example, (from logical empiricism) it views the individual as a scientist, i.e. logical, rational, and hypothesis testing. It also assumes that there is external validity for one's observations, i.e. an objective reality. It further assumes that the individual can be understood in an information-processing framework, using a computer analogy.

However, Beck also drew on developmental ideas from Piaget, for example, the idea of 'primitive' and 'mature' thinking (Piaget 1932), and on the concept of schemas—the idea that meanings are constructed by the person. Thus, while treatment included strategies based on 'reality testing', it also drew on constructivist principles. Meanings are constructed by the individual and, in treatment, are correct or incorrect in relation to a given context or goal, i.e. in the context of the larger social and physical environment of the person (Alford & Beck 1997). Both subjective reality, as well as objective reality, are thus important.

The theory has developed in many ways since the early days (see below), but it was this basic form that was the initial impetus for the application of cognitive theory to eating disorders.

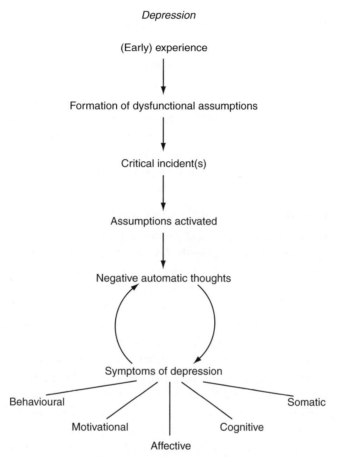

Fig. 8.1 A typical Beckian model for depression. Reproduced with permission from Melanie Fennell, from Keith Hawton *et al.* (1989). *Cognitive Behaviour Therapy for Psychiatric Disorders: A Practical Guide*. Oxford: Oxford University Press.

Table 8.3 Key assumptions of Beckian cognitive theory

Man is a scientist—logical, rational, hypothesis testing
External validity exists for man's observations—there is an objective reality
The computer analogy—information is processed
Developmental issues are important—e.g. thinking can be primitive or mature
Schema are crucial—meaning is constructed by the person, i.e. subjective reality is important

Anorexia nervosa: Garner & Bemis (1982)

Cognitive theory was first applied to anorexia nervosa by Garner & Bemis (1982), and the initial application to BN is based on this work. Garner & Bemis (1982) highlighted three key elements: negative automatic thoughts, beliefs, and information processing. Its application was based very closely on Beck's conceptualization of depression. Clearly, the main content of thoughts is different from depression (as Beck would predict), and Garner & Bemis (1982) describe the fundamental premise that 'thinness is a value of inestimable worth' (p.128), as the pivot of the disorder. This belief then accounts for the subsidiary beliefs and behaviours. However, the structures and processes are essentially similar in form to those described by Beck for depression.

Bulimia nervosa: Fairburn and colleagues

A cognitive theory of bulimia nervosa (Fairburn *et al.* 1986), based closely on Garner & Bemis's theory of AN, was subsequently developed. As in Garner & Bemis's model, patients' attitudes to weight and shape are central to the maintenance of the disorder. Like patients with anorexia nervosa, patients tend to evaluate their self-worth in terms of their shape and weight, which has the advantage of providing a simple and immediate measure of personal strengths and weaknesses. They view fatness negatively, and thinness and self-control positively. These attitudes are implicit and are based on unarticulated rules by which patients assign meaning and value to their experiences. They are dysfunctional because they are rigid and extreme, and hold excessive personal significance. Beliefs and values reflect the operation of certain dysfunctional styles of reasoning or disturbances in information processing. They include dichotomous thinking, over-generalization and errors of attribution, e.g. the belief that foods can be simply categorized as 'fattening' or 'non-fattening'. Beliefs and values are reflected in thoughts that explain patients' behaviour, such as frequent weighing or, alternatively, active avoidance of weighing. Reduction of food intake may also be directly attributed to thoughts concerning weight and shape. There is also a cognitive link between strict dieting and episodes of over-eating, in which intense concern with shape and weight leads patients to adopt extreme dieting rules that are impossible to obey. Inevitable minor deviations from these self-imposed rules are seen as catastrophic and evidence of weakness, so as a result patients temporarily abandon all controls over their eating and episodes of binge-eating occur. The typical model, as outlined by Fairburn and colleagues, and which is used to guide treatment is shown in Fig. 8.2.

More recently, Fairburn (1997b) has emphasized the role of dichotomous thinking more and added perfectionism to the model. In this account, the intensity and rigidity of dieting is seen to result from a combination of these. Perfectionism is also evident in other areas of a patient's life. Additionally, it is noted that binge-eating is more likely to occur at times of negative affect, and that bingeing also moderates negative affect. This model can be seen in Fig. 8.3.

In everyday treatment, however, it is usually the original model that is employed.

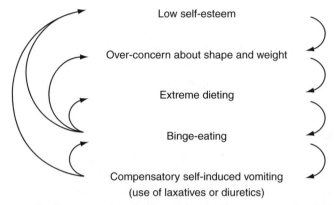

Low self-esteem

Over-concern about shape and weight

Extreme dieting

Binge-eating

Compensatory self-induced vomiting
(use of laxatives or diuretics)

Fig. 8.2 Fairburn and colleague's original BN model. © Keith Hawton *et al.*, 1989. Reprinted from *Cognitive Behaviour Therapy for Psychiatric Disorders: A Practical Guide* by Keith Hawton *et al.* (1989) by permission of Oxford University Press.

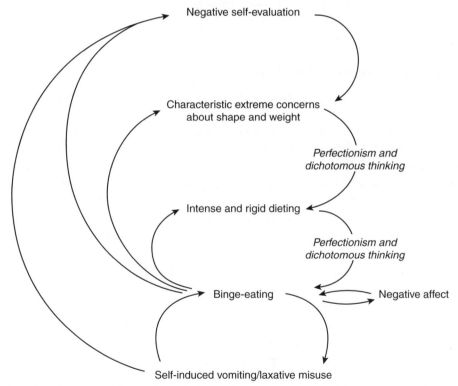

Negative self-evaluation

Characteristic extreme concerns
about shape and weight

*Perfectionism and
dichotomous thinking*

Intense and rigid dieting

*Perfectionism and
dichotomous thinking*

Binge-eating — Negative affect

Self-induced vomiting/laxative misuse

Fig. 8.3 Fairburn's model revised. © Clark & Fairburn, 1997. Reprinted from *Science and Practice of Cognitive Behaviour Therapy* by Clark & Fairburn (1996).

Fairburn and colleagues highlight the same features as Garner & Bemis—automatic thoughts (concerned with weight, shape, and eating), beliefs (the importance of weight and shape), and biases in information processing (the tendency to interpret things in terms of weight and shape). For some time it was the only cognitive theory of the disorder and, until recently, theory in BN had not taken full advantage of recent developments in the field.

Assumptions of cognitive theory of BN

Fairburn and colleagues have not elaborated on the assumptions of their theory. Since it is derived from Beck's theory of depression, it seems likely that similar assumptions hold (although it is important to note that some of Beck's writing on these has appeared since the BN theory was described and, unlike Beck's work, the latter has not been updated). The idea of an objective reality is evident in descriptions of beliefs as 'distortions', i.e. from a 'norm' or 'real' situation. However, the theory also has a role for beliefs as active determinants of experience—they influence what is attended to, perceived, and remembered, i.e. they play a role in constructing experience.

Fairburn and colleagues' theory also draws on restraint theory (this is discussed in more detail in Chapter 3).

First- and second-order change

Fairburn's theory tends to emphasize change in current beliefs, rather than creating a different world-view. In its extreme form this has been called 'first-order change' in beliefs (Lyddon 1990). The aim is to make beliefs more realistic and driven by data or facts. These facts may be testable in the 'objective' sense, e.g. 'if I eat a bar of chocolate, I'll gain two pounds'; or they may be 'subjective' facts, e.g. the reasons why someone did not speak to you in a particular situation. However, both can be tested against a criterion that is external to the person. Treatment thus remains essentially 'rationalist' in emphasis (even while acknowledging that experience may be constructed). This differs from some recent developments in cognitive theory and therapy (e.g. the focus on the self, and the use of strategies such as imagery modification), which may start to tap into what has been called 'second-order change' in beliefs (Lyddon 1990). Rather than 'correcting' distortions, the aim here is to 'create' or foster change in the core ordering processes (Neimeyer 1993). Cognitive theory for BN, as described by Fairburn and colleagues, does not focus a great deal on these self-beliefs and how they act to construct experience (construction of experience is confined to assumptions related to weight and shape). Although there is a role for self-esteem, this is not conceptualized in cognitive terms, and it is not given a great deal of emphasis. The possibility of working directly on second-order change is, therefore, likely to be limited within this framework.

Fairburn and colleagues' theory is an important one; it provided the first cognitive theory of bulimia nervosa. It has been the basis of most of the cognitive-behavioural treatment conducted with patients.

It easily generates testable hypotheses (see Chapter 9), and has been the impetus for a great deal of high quality research. This includes many studies conducted within an information-processing framework. These have investigated both structures and processes in BN. They have looked, for example, at attention, memory, and interpretive biases. Research has also tested the content-specificity hypothesis. This has identified different types of thought, including NATS, and underlying assumptions or beliefs focused on weight, shape, and eating. Fairburn's theory also has very clear implications for treatment (see Chapter 10).

Young's contribution

Young's work on early maladaptive schemas has had an influence on recent developments in cognitive theory of BN. This focuses on the self—and is an elaborated schema theory. Early maladaptive schemas are 'templates for the processing of later experience' (Young 1990, p.9). The idea that we each construct our own reality, particularly at the level of self-processing, is given particular emphasis.

Schemas are thought to develop during childhood and are elaborated on throughout life. They tend to reflect very stable and enduring themes, referred to as a 'metaphysical hard-core' (Lakatos 1974, in Guidano & Liotti 1983, p.66). They comprise unconditional beliefs about oneself, are highly resistant to change, dysfunctional, and usually they are tied to high affect. Young proposed that schema theory, and the therapy based on it, is particularly suitable for understanding and treating personality disorders, and those with long standing and chronic difficulties. Eating disorders often fall into at least one of these categories (e.g. the mean duration of illness before seeking treatment is often lengthy).

Young uses the term core beliefs, which seems to refer to the content of schema (Beck & Freeman 1990). Schema processing refers to three processes (avoidance, compensation, and maintenance) that act to keep schema intact. Young also gives a prominent role to early experience. Schema typically develop in early life as a result of negative experiences with caregivers, peers, or siblings.

Vitousek & Hollon's contribution

Vitousek and Hollon do not attempt to develop a theory, but describe a framework for guiding research (Vitousek & Hollon 1990). Like Young they draw on schema theory and they conceptualize eating disorders in these terms, drawing particularly on work in experimental cognitive psychology. They identify three features of eating disorders: low self-worth (self-schemata); attitudes to eating, weight, and shape (weight-related schemata); and evaluation of the self in terms of weight and shape (weight-related self schemata). They suggest that patients develop organized structures around issues of weight and its implications for the self that influence perception, thought, affect, and behaviour. This represents the core psychopathology of eating disorders and accounts for their persistence, e.g. by determining selective attention and memory. Importantly (and here there are echoes of the earlier work carried out by personal construct therapists) these also function to simplify, organize, and stabilize the individual's experience of herself and the environment. This, they argue, may be formless and chaotic in eating disorders.

The emphasis here, as in Young, is also on the construction of experience, on 'top down', schema-driven processes. Particularly novel, as far as eating disorders is concerned, is the idea of the self as an active processor or schema; including the idea of the self as an 'organizer', or control system. Like Beck, however, Vitousek & Hollon also appear to consider that objective reality is important—and that the primary aim in cognitive therapy is to look for facts and data to confirm or disconfirm beliefs. Thus, like Beck, they draw on both rationalist and constructivist perspectives.

Guidano & Liotti's contribution

This work focuses largely on anorexia (and is based on Bruch's work) but is included here because it has influenced current thinking on the development of bulimia nervosa (see below).

Guidano & Liotti describe a 'structural-developmental' theory. They propose a core that acts as a main control structure, which generates the rules we live by, and affects assimilation of further knowledge and behaviour. The core provides a sense of stable identity, and affects our sense of control or power. There is also a link between problem-attachment patterns and self-development. In this account, the self appears to be equated with identity, indeed it is conceptualized as a set of 'personal identity' structures.

Although the theory is primarily focused on anorexia nervosa, the authors assume that all eating disorders share the same underlying cognitive structure. The 'personal identity structures' consist of beliefs and rules around which individuals operate and around which they organize their lives. They tend (in anorexia) to be characterized by beliefs of general ineffectiveness and failure, that it is dangerous or useless to tell others about feelings or opinions, and the expectation of criticism or rejection. Anorexics also have an imprecise attributional style.

Importantly, Guidano & Liotti provide a detailed developmental account of eating disorders. This includes failure to develop autonomy, individuality, and self-expression in childhood. Their theory also draws on Bowlby's attachment theory to explain how identity structures are formed. The theory is constructivist in emphasis—especially when outlining the role of the self. However, the authors talk of 'creating' a different world view, i.e. treatment is less based on empiricism or reality testing, and is particularly interested in second-order change.[2]

---

[2] The equation of the self with personal identity raises the question (not so clearly an issue in previous accounts) of what is left when self-beliefs have been challenged, if self-beliefs are the individual's identity. This may have implications for change, and may tap into illness identity. For example, patients may fear they will be left with nothing if their beliefs (or at a general level, their eating disorder) are 'taken away'.

Constructivism, such as that outlined by Guidano and Liotti, has led to emphasis on an individual approach to research. For example, process research, and other qualitative research (e.g. looking at change events: Greenberg & Safran 1987) has developed from this area. To date, these approaches to research have had little impact on research conducted into BN. The link to attachment theory, e.g. as outlined in Guidano & Liotti's work, is also little investigated in BN (though see Chapter 5).

Guidano & Liotti's contribution also taps into a recent trend evident in cognitive psychotherapies and that is relevant to BN. This is interest in embodiment—the bodily origins of higher mental processes, or body basis for, and means of, experiencing (Guidano 1987). This theme will be picked up in Chapter 13.

The approach also highlights emotional processes rather more than previous theoretical contributions. This provides a link to those who have tried to integrate emotional theory and cognitive theory (e.g. Greenberg & Safran 1987), and to more experiential therapies. This issue, and the use of experiential strategies in cognitive therapy, will be discussed below, and in Chapter 13.

The cognitive theories outlined above have had some difficulty in explaining why some patients with dysfunctional weight- and shape-related beliefs binge, and others successfully restrict. They have also found it difficult to explain why an eating disorder, as opposed to some other kind of disorder, develops. Family, individual, social, and cultural factors have been mentioned but their relationship to the development of the disorder has not generally been specified in detail. Current developments (see below), however, have a contribution to make here, and may help answer these questions.

Bulimia Nervosa: Cooper and colleagues' model

Recently, an updated cognitive theory has been proposed (Cooper *et al.*, in press). These revisions make use of new data in BN, and recent general developments in cognitive theory. Importantly, the new model provides an account of both the maintenance and development of BN. The model is shown in Fig. 8.4.

Developmental processes

In the model, negative or traumatic early experiences lead to the formation of core beliefs (particularly negative self beliefs). Early experience that gives rise to these may be extreme, e.g. sexual, physical, or emotional abuse, or less extreme, e.g. neglect of indifference. To cope with these negative beliefs about the self, schema-compensation strategies develop (reflected in underlying assumptions). These typically involve two types of belief: that dieting will ensure the person is accepted by others, 'if I lose weight others will accept me more'; and that dieting will ensure that she is acceptable to herself, e.g. 'if I lose weight, it means I'm a better person'. There are usually negative counterparts to these (e.g. 'if I gain weight, then others won't respect me'; 'if I gain weight, I can't feel good about myself'). There may also be underlying assumptions linking eating behaviour with negative self-beliefs (e.g. 'if I don't eat, then I'm more worthwhile'). The latter can also be related to self and other acceptance. These types of belief are usually

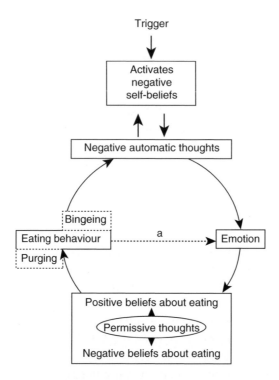

Note a = Distracting effects of eating on emotional intensity
= Direct physiological effects on feeling states/interoception

Fig. 8.4 Cooper and colleagues' model for BN.

conclusions reached as a result of particular experience whilst growing up. They could be learned within the context of the family, peers, or absorbed from the media.

Maintenance processes

A specific event or experience will trigger the maintenance portion of the model. This could be a remark about the person's weight, shape, or eating, or it could be something unrelated to this. The event activates a negative self-belief (e.g. 'I'm no good', 'I'm a failure'). This gives rise to one or more negative automatic thoughts, and to one or more associated emotions (e.g. anxiety, guilt). At the same time, two dissonant sets of beliefs are activated. First, there are positive beliefs about eating—centered on how eating will help with the negative thoughts activated in the trigger situation. These are typically of two types: how eating will help with the negative thoughts and feelings; and fears about what will happen if eating doesn't take place. A common fear is that the person will lose control of her thoughts and feelings and that she will not be able to cope with the distress that will result. Second, negative beliefs about weight and shape are activated. Beliefs about the negative consequences of eating, are typically, 'I'll get fat' or 'I'll gain weight'. Dissonance between these two sets of beliefs causes great distress. This is resolved by permissive thoughts, e.g. 'I'll just have one biscuit...'.

Permissive thoughts can include thoughts of no control—'I just can't stop myself'. Once permissive and thoughts of no control are activated, eating takes place. Eating then serves to reduce cognitive and emotional distress, and decreases arousal; it also prevents the initial automatic thought from being challenged; both thus reinforce eating, and eating therefore continues. When the positive thought, 'I'll get fat', starts to predominate, vomiting occurs, and the vicious circle is terminated.

Background: recent developments

Cooper and colleagues draw on several recent developments in general cognitive theory, and in BN. These are summarized below. More specific details on relevant BN research will be provided in Chapter 8. A summary of some of the more novel features of the theory, compared to existing theory, can also be seen in Table 8.4.

A clear distinction has recently been made between underlying assumptions and core beliefs (Padesky & Greenberger 1995). Initially, the two types of belief were not clearly distinguished. Now there are two types of belief in many theories. These are underlying assumptions, or conditional if-then statements, e.g. 'if I get fat then it means I'm a failure', and core beliefs (Young's term), e.g. absolute beliefs such as, 'I'm no good'. Conditional beliefs leave the way open for the person to do something to improve the situation. Core beliefs do not—nothing can be done. Assumptions link into core beliefs—they provide a bridge between automatic thoughts and core beliefs. Recent developments in cognitive theory also identify three or four types of core belief—about the self, world, others, and the future. Clinically, beliefs about the self are usually more evident and rather more important in bulimia nervosa. Cooper and colleagues distinguish between these two types of belief.

Young's schema theory identifies three processes that keep core beliefs alive. Compensation and avoidance are particularly important in bulimia. Compensation involves a way to overcome, or make up, for the core belief, e.g. 'if I lose weight I'll be more successful'. These are positively phrased expressions of underlying assumptions. Avoidance involves a way to avoid the belief and associated emotion.

Table 8.4 Novel features of Cooper and Colleagues' model for BN

Makes a clear distinction between underlying assumptions and core beliefs
Distinguishes different types of core belief
Identifies schema-driven processes, especially avoidance and compensation
Places greater emphasis on emotion
Argues early experience is important in the development of core beliefs and underlying assumptions
Includes cognition, behaviour, emotion, and physiology, and the links between them, in the maintenance cycle
Identifies different types of maintaining (automatic) thought
Suggests underlying assumptions can be examples of schema driven processes
Identifies three types of underlying assumption

It is important not to forget emotion—this is often relatively ignored in bulimia (it is not allocated a specific role in early cognitive formulations), although BN is an extremely distressing disorder, and there are often high levels of anxiety, depression, and despair. Core beliefs in particular are typically associated with much emotion—this link is included in the vicious-circle maintenance portion of the model, where binge-eating can function to reduce emotional distress. Emotion also has a specific role in the maintenance cycle.

Early experience is thought to be important in the development of underlying assumptions. However, not much attention has been paid to their origins in cognitive models. Clinical experience in BN suggests they are usually formed rather later than core beliefs, often in early teens or just before. Like core beliefs they also arise as a result of early experience—often with family or peers. In BN this experience often focuses around weight and shape issues.

Cooper and colleagues' model provides a detailed model including cognition, behaviour, emotion, and physiology. It has been argued that a good formulation includes an account of all these (Butler 1998), although early accounts in BN did not encompass all four elements. A good model should also specify the nature of the relationship between these elements (Butler 1998), and their typical content. Several models encompassing all these features now exist in other disorders, especially anxiety disorders (Wells 1997). Cooper and colleagues provide such a model for BN.

Cooper and colleagues identify different types of cognition involved in the maintenance cycle. Early theories did not identify different types of cognition, despite evidence that various types were implicated in the bingeing vomiting cycle. These include positive and negative thoughts about eating, thoughts of no control and permissive thoughts.

The theory also identifies underlying assumptions as examples of schema driven processes—see above. Note that there is an overlap between schema compensation and underlying assumptions—the former are an example of the latter.

Three different types of underlying assumption are also identified: one is focused on self-acceptance—'if I lose weight it means I'm more successful'; one on acceptance by others—'if I lose weight others will like me more'; and one on eating—'if I eat, it means I lack self control'.

New ideas in cognitive theory

Recent developments in cognitive theory have many implications for BN. Some have been incorporated into recent theory for the disorder, as described above; others require further research and integration. Themes that remain to be integrated, or that are in the process of being integrated will be discussed below. They are summarized in Table 8.5.

Attention and memory

These have been studied in the information processing framework in BN, particularly that of attention. The focus, however, has been on selective attention or memory for food

Table 8.5 Themes that need to be or are being integrated into cognitive theory for BN

Attention and memory—especially subjective, internal evidence
Emotion schemes
Bodily sensations—including those involved in feeling fat
Meta-cognitions

and eating, weight and shape stimuli in carefully controlled experimental paradigms, and on 'objectively real' evidence. A rather different emphasis is proposed here. This is that studies should track the 'subjective' or internal evidence (e.g. body sensations) that patients use to support their beliefs. This approach might be particularly fruitful in relation to beliefs that are 'emotionally' strongly held. It could include beliefs such as 'feeling fat', and negative self-beliefs.

Memories might also be involved in maintaining beliefs—both those related to weight and shape, and those related to more general issues. This internal and subjective focus is proving fruitful in other disorders, e.g. social anxiety, panic disorder, and PTSD, and makes clinical sense in BN, where attention to internal body sensations (see below) may be relevant, and where memories may also play a role, for example, in maintaining self-beliefs.

Cognitive/affective emphasis

As noted above, there has been an attempt to integrate theories of emotion and cognition (Greenberg & Safran 1987). Work on emotion schemes has been linked into work on cognitive schemas. Together they are thought to equate to the core sense of what is experienced as the self. In turn, this is thought to be founded in the affectively toned expressive and sensori-motor patterns of early life that begin the process of ordering experience (Stern 1985). Therapy based on such a model thus aims to change the complex cognitive, affective, motivation, and relational action components of action schemes. The whole response complex is activated, and tackled in treatment. This approach has not yet been applied to BN, either theoretically or therapeutically. However, it has features in common with the idea of 'emotional' belief, and is compatible with interest in imagery work in the disorder (see Chapter 13), where changing the meaning inherent in a relevant early memory appears to change many aspects of an experience, including cognitive and affective features.

Bodily sensations

This is a relatively neglected area in cognitive theory of BN, although Cooper and colleagues have a role for physiological factors, including sensations of hunger, satiety, and arousal. Some constructivists, however, highlight it as a key area. In particular, they emphasize the body basis of experience (e.g. Guidano 1987). In BN, understanding of body based sensations or experience may help explain a rather neglected puzzle, the experience of 'feeling fat' (see Chapter 13). It also draws attention to the experience of hunger and satiety, which has been relatively neglected in recent years, although given an important role by Bruch (1973). In particular, although Cooper and colleagues include the meaning of eating and not eating as possible assumptions relevant to BN, it has been rather neglected at the level of sensation in cognitive theory. This focus links into more experiential therapies, which place emphasis on facilitating the synthesis of new meaning from bodily felt experience. It links particularly into the notion of the 'embodied self' (Mahoney 1993)—the idea that there is a fundamental connection between mediated and immediate experience, and that mental activities have a bodily origin (thus challenging mind-body dualism). It also opens up use of experiential techniques, e.g. use of the felt sense, and focusing-oriented psychotherapy (Gendlin 1996). These issues will be discussed further in Chapter 13.

Other trends in cognitive psychology may also be relevant. For example, the area of meta-cognition (see, for example, Wells 2000) is probably relevant to BN. This is the idea that we act on our own perceptions and thoughts, and create new meaning from them. This has not been studied and integrated into cognitive theory of BN. Clinically, however, it seems that patients with BN do reflect on their experience; for example, they may believe that worrying about food stops them from over-eating.

Recent developments may help us to begin to answer the two questions posed above. The first question was as follows: Why do some patients with dysfunctional assumptions about weight and shape binge, and others successfully restrict? The difference would seem to lie in the specific cognitions identified in BN, and that maintain the bingeing vicious circle. In particular, the relative balance of cognitions is important. Different cognitions are associated with restriction (negative thoughts about eating) and over-eating (positive thoughts about eating). Clearly this needs further testing.

The second question was: Why do patients develop an eating disorder as opposed to some other kind of disorder? Here, it seems that the answer is that patients will develop BN rather than another disorder, when they have both negative self-beliefs, and weight- and shape-related beliefs. It is the conjunction of the two that is important. This begins to help explain why not everyone with weight and shape beliefs develops an eating disorder.

Specific, testable hypotheses can be derived from Cooper and colleagues' theory. Research focused on these may help elucidate further the difference between bulimia and anorexia, and help distinguish bulimia from other disorders, and from the weight-preoccupied or those who are dieting. The idea of a straightforward cognitive continuum no longer seems feasible—at least two different types of belief are involved, and these are unlikely to be at opposite ends of a continuum. In addition, eating disorders themselves are unlikely to be on a simple or straightforward continuum either, at a cognitive level several qualitatively different types of cognition seem to be involved.

Cooper and colleagues' work has implications for treatment that differ from that of Fairburn and colleagues. It is also in line with recent developments in cognitive therapy. For example, it draws attention to the role of emotion, the self, and attachment—which opens the way for more experiential approaches, e.g. use of imagery, metaphor, and work with early memories, as well as use of techniques designed to challenge core beliefs, such as cognitive continua.

Summary

This chapter has described cognitive theory in BN. Part one identified two important trends in cognitive psychology that are relevant to BN: information processing and constructivism. Part two reported on early accounts of cognition in BN, including descriptions of weight- and shape-related attitudes and beliefs, as well as disturbed information processing and self-beliefs.

The framework for the main cognitive model of BN was outlined in part three—it draws on Beck's cognitive theory of depression, and on Garner & Bemis's cognitive theory of AN. The model developed by Fairburn and colleagues, particularly that which has been most influential in guiding treatment, was then described. Recent developments in cognitive theory, and in eating disorders were outlined. A revised model, drawing on these (and on recent research), developed by Cooper and colleagues, was then described, and some of it's novel features outlined.

Finally, new ideas that may need to be, or which are being, integrated into cognitive models of BN were outlined in part four, including issues related to attention and memory, emotion, body sensations, and meta-cognition.

Chapter 9

Evidence for cognitive theories

Overview

This chapter will summarize and discuss the evidence that supports cognitive models of BN. Part one will discuss the different types and sources of evidence that exist in BN. A set of predictions or hypotheses derived from existing models will be presented. Part two will present evidence to support hypotheses about the content of cognition in BN. Part three will discuss the evidence that supports characteristic styles of information processing.

Part four will present relevant evidence from longitudinal (and treatment) studies. Part five will present evidence on the causal role of cognition in BN. The plan for the chapter is summarized in Table 9.1. Throughout, the evidence will be critically evaluated and, where appropriate, ideas for research that will provide further tests of the models will be suggested.

Sources of evidence and predictions

Most of the evidence gathered in support of cognitive models in BN has been cross-sectional, thus making it difficult to draw inferences about the extent to which cognitions are causally related to eating disorder behaviours, such as binge-eating. Two clearly articulated cognitive models of BN currently exist: that developed by Fairburn and colleagues; and that developed by Cooper and colleagues. Other models also include some reference to cognition, or present ideas that have had an influence on the

Table 9.1 Summary of plan for Chapter 9

Sources of evidence and predictions

Evidence—content of cognition
    automatic thoughts
    underlying assumptions
    negative self beliefs

Evidence—information processing   schema driven processes

Evidence—causal role of cognition
    treatment studies
    experimental paradigms

development of these models, but are much less clearly articulated. This includes, for example, work by Heatherton & Baumeister (1991), Grilo (Grilo & Shiffman 1994), and Root and colleagues (Root *et al.* 1986). It has been suggested that a set of hypotheses or predictions can be derived from Fairburn's model (see Cooper 1997). At least six predictions can be formulated; these are summarized in Table 9.2.

Recently, Fairburn (1997) has proposed a slightly revised model in which dichotomous thinking is given a more prominent role, and perfectionism (general and specific) also has a role. Perfectionism slots into predictions 5 and 6 (Table 9.2), where it is thought to have a causal role in both dietary restraint and binge-eating. Negative affect as a trigger and consequence of binge-eating is also highlighted. This is not dissimilar to predictions 5 and 6 below (Table 9.3), which are generated by Cooper's theory, although the role of cognition is not highlighted, as it is in Cooper's theory. Although perfectionism has been studied in BN (see Chapter 4), its potential role in Fairburn's theory has not yet been studied in cognitive terms, and will not be considered further here.

The revised model developed by Cooper and colleagues makes many similar predictions, or is consistent with many of the predictions made by Fairburn's model. However, it also makes much more specific and precise, as well as additional, predictions.

Table 9.2 Predictions derived from Fairburn's model

1. Treatment based on the model, i.e. cognitive therapy, will be effective.

2. Self-statements or automatic thoughts will reflect concern with food and eating, weight, and shape.

3. Underlying assumptions reflecting concern with food and eating, weight, and shape will be strongly endorsed.

4. Dysfunctional styles of reasoning or information-processing errors and biases will be found in food and eating, and in weight and shape concerns.

5. There will be a causal relationship between underlying assumptions and self-statements, and eating behaviour, particularly dietary restraint.

6. Dietary restraint, mediated by dichotomous thinking, will result in episodes of binge-eating.

Table 9.3 The more specific predictions derived from Cooper's model

1. Self-statements or automatic thoughts will include positive and negative thoughts about eating, thoughts of no control, and permissive thoughts.

2. Core beliefs will reflect global negative evaluation of the self.

3. Schema-driven processes will be evident in areas of core belief concerns.

4. Early experience will be important in the formation of core beliefs.

5. Bingeing will be preceded by negative cognition and emotional distress.

6. Bingeing will be followed by negative cognition and emotional distress.

Table 9.4 The causal predictions derived from Cooper's model

1. There will be a causal relationship between the different types of automatic thought specified in the model and binge-eating.
More specifically, two more precise predictions can be made, which are as follows:
2. Negative thoughts about eating will be causally related to vomiting (or other compensatory behaviour).
3. Positive thoughts about eating will be causally related to binge-eating.

Some of these predictions draw on features highlighted by other writers (as suggested above), and are also consistent with recent ideas, such as those outlined by Waller (e.g. Waller *et al.* 2000) on core beliefs. The great advantage of Cooper's theory, compared to that of Fairburn however, is that it makes more specific (not necessarily competing) predictions, thus it potentially has greater explanatory power. These more specific (and additional) predictions are summarized in Table 9.3.

Although many of Fairburn's broader predictions also hold for the model developed by Cooper and colleagues, the prediction 6 (Table 9.3) that dietary restraint has a causal role in binge-eating is not considered necessary, or essential. Instead, it is considered that cognition (with or without dietary restraint), including the different types of automatic thought specified in the theory, will predict bingeing. This is the main point where the two theories lead to rather different predictions, one general and two more specific ones. These are outlined in Table 9.4.

Cooper's revised model also takes a dimensional perspective; eating in BN is on a continuum with behaviours found in the normal population (see also Chapter 2). Thus it also follows (or is predicted) that positive thoughts will be linked to eating, and negative thoughts to not eating. Note that this does not mean that 'normal' eating is determined primarily by these specific cognitions, or that bingeing is on a continuum with dieting (see Chapter 2). While the form of cognitions is likely to be similar (e.g. instrumental in nature for initiating eating), the precise detail of the content may be different.

More specific predictions across the eating/bingeing cycle may also be possible, though not yet developed in detail. For example, it may be that positive thoughts are associated with the onset of eating, permissive and control thoughts with its maintenance once begun, and negative with cessation of eating or compensation behaviour.

Many different methods have been used to assess or test the different features of cognitive models of bulimia. These include self-report questionnaire studies, and studies that have used various techniques from experimental cognitive psychology. These techniques include thought listing and concurrent verbalization strategies, and also attention and memory paradigms. Attention paradigms, particularly the Stroop test, have been extremely popular. Most studies also focus primarily on assessment. Few longitudinal studies or experimental paradigms have been used to test causal links in the model, despite their apparent suitability for this (e.g. experimental paradigms could be used to manipulate cognitions and then to assess resulting behaviour and feelings). Most studies have also focused primarily on the characteristic weight and shape, food and eating content evident at the automatic thought or underlying assumption level. Until recently, few studies looked at the nature of the self, and its organization in BN. This, however, is beginning to change, and the recent developments in this area will also be reported below.

The development of reliable and valid methods of assessing cognition is crucial for the development of cognitive theory and therapy. This was noted early on in the history of cognitive therapy (Kendall & Korgeski 1979) and seen to be one of the major tasks facing cognitive therapists. Although some progress has been made in BN this is, arguably, still true. While a lot of effort has been directed into attentional paradigms (primarily the modified Stroop task: Stroop 1935), relatively little work has been focused on developing adequate measures of cognition that are specific to eating disorders. While several measures of behaviour or 'concerns' have been published (e.g. the Body Shape Questionnaire: Cooper et al. 1987; the Weight and Shape Concern subscales of the EDE: Cooper & Fairburn 1987; the Weight and Shape Based Self-esteem Inventory: Geller et al. 1997), there have been few purely cognitive measures that tap the constructs of Beckian cognitive theory and therapy directly. This may reflect the fact that, until relatively recently, the key cognitions in BN have not been specified precisely, either in detail, or in clear cognitive language.

Why assess cognitions? The reasons for assessing cognitions in any disorder (which may include BN) have been summarized elsewhere (see for example: Kendall 1981; Kendall & Korgeski 1979; Shaw & Dobson 1981). They include: to describe the nature and type of cognitions, particularly important in a new area; to find cognitions unique to particular disorders; and to elucidate their role in the development (and maintenance) of the disorder, and their relationship to prognosis. Their assessment is also necessary to confirm treatment mechanisms, to determine the process of change and to discover risk factors. Ultimately, the results of assessment will feedback into and help to improve treatment.

The evidence presented below that is relevant to the hypotheses outlined above will be divided into three sections: content, information processing, and causal links. It will address each of the hypotheses or predictions listed above. As noted above, it is important to remember that the two models are not necessarily competing; that developed by Cooper is often simply more specific and precise (and therefore may have greater explanatory power) than that developed by Fairburn. It is also expressed in more explicitly cognitive language.

Content of cognition

Fairburn's model includes evidence that automatic thoughts and underlying assumptions reflect concern with eating, weight and shape (predictions 2 and 3, Table 9.2). Cooper's model also includes the more specific prediction that there are four different types of automatic thought in the bingeing vicious circle: positive thoughts, negative thoughts, lack of control thoughts; and permissive thoughts (prediction 1, Table 9.3). Cooper's model includes evidence that core beliefs, particularly self-beliefs, are global and negative in content (prediction 2, Table 9.3). Evidence relevant to prediction 1 (Table 9.2), that treatment based on the model will be effective, will be considered in Chapter 10. This is primarily confined to treatment based on Fairburn's model. To help the reader navigate through the different sources of evidence for different elements of the two models, a summary of the type of evidence supporting each component can be seen in Table 9.5.

Automatic thoughts

There is considerable clinical and anecdotal evidence that, as predicted by Fairburn, self-statements or automatic thoughts, in BN reflect concern with food and eating, weight and shape. Evidence in support of this has been collected using a variety of paradigms, and by self-report questionnaire, or semi-structured interview. It includes (primarily anecdotal and clinical) evidence that dichotomous thoughts (as predicted by Fairburn) are one important self-statement.

Questionnaire studies

Self-statements focused on patients' characteristic concerns have been assessed in one questionnaire study (Phelan 1987). The Bulimic Thoughts Questionnaire has three factors: self schema (e.g. 'I'm so fat', 'I feel good about my body'), self efficacy (e.g. 'I can lose a few pounds if I want to'), and salient beliefs, e.g. ('I always fail on diets; why even try'). In this study patients with bulimia scored more highly than female controls on all three sub-scales. Salient beliefs also distinguished obese women from bulimics (bulimics had a higher score). However, the measure has not been much used in research, and does not appear to have been developed beyond this initial study. The sub-scales do not map onto the cognitive constructs identified as important in more specific cognitive theories of bulimia nervosa, although inspection of the items suggests that the three sub-scales do seem to measure typical self-statements. Its use in testing more specific cognitive models of BN, as opposed to providing general support for these theories, is, therefore, likely to be limited.

Recently, a study has been conducted that attempts to test the specific types of automatic thought identified by Cooper and colleagues (Cooper et al., submitted a). Thoughts from the four key domains hypothesized to exist were sampled, and a questionnaire developed. Factor analysis revealed three types of thought. These corresponded to positive thoughts (e.g. 'if I eat it will all hurt less inside'), negative thoughts (e.g. 'I'm going to go on getting heavier and heavier'), and a category including no control thoughts (e.g. 'I've no self control), and permissive thoughts (e.g. 'One more bite won't hurt' and 'I deserve something nice'). The measure has promising psychometric properties, including good internal reliability, and construct validity. Although not yet given to a clinical sample, the sub-scales of the measure were highly correlated with,

Table 9.5 Sources of evidence supporting different components of the two models

	Fairburn's general model	Cooper's specific model
Content		
Automatic thoughts	Self-report questionnaires.	Self-report questionnaire.
	Experimental psychology paradigms: thought listing, concurrent verbalization.	Anecdotal evidence (by product of other studies). Identifies four specific types of thought.
	Identifies broad category of thoughts.	
Content		
Underlying assumptions	Self-report questionnaires.	Self-report questionnaire.
		Semi-structured interview.
	Identifies broad category.	Identifies specific types.
Role of early experience	Not considered.	Semi-structured interview.
Content		
Negative self-beliefs	Not considered.	Self-report questionnaire.
		Semi-structured interview.
Role of early experience	Not considered.	Semi-structured interview.
Information processing — assumption level	Interview.	
	Self-report questionnaires.	
	Thought sampling.	
	Attention and memory paradigms.	
	Provides broad support.	General evidence also consistent with specific model.
Information processing — core-belief level	Not considered.	Self-report questionnaires.
		Cognitive psychology tasks.
Causal role of cognitions		
Self-statements link to restraint/bingeing	Treatment outcome studies.	Semi-structured interviews.
	Treatment follow-up studies.	
Negative self-beliefs link to eating behaviour	Experimental study.	Semi-structured interviews.
		Experimental study— consistent with negative thoughts link to restricting.

NB Evidence for Cooper's model highlights studies providing more specific evidence—this model is also broadly consistent with much of the evidence that supports Fairburn's model.

and also predict (in a multiple regression analysis), score on a measure of eating disorder symptoms (Cooper *et al.*, submitted a).

Other studies have been conducted that assess generic negative self-statements in BN, i.e. with content not unique to eating disorders. For example, two studies have used the Automatic Thought Questionnaire (ATQ: Hollon & Kendall 1980), to assess negative self-statements that are characteristic of depression (Franko *et al.* 1986; Schlesier-Carter *et al.* 1989). High levels of negative cognitions have been found but, where this has been assessed, these generally link to depression, and not specifically to eating disorder symptoms.

Further research is needed to develop measures of the specific cognitions associated with BN, including the four dimensions hypothesized by Cooper and colleagues. A measure based on recent theoretical developments, the Thoughts Questionnaire (Cooper *et al.*, submitted a) is promising, but needs much further development and study. This would enable it to be used to test specific (as opposed to general) theoretical predictions, and the outcome of treatment based on Cooper and colleague's more specific theory.

Techniques from experimental psychology

These include a wide range of techniques, from carefully controlled experimental paradigms to relatively unstructured techniques.

Unstructured techniques have several advantages, particularly in a relatively new field of research (Cooper 1997). The detailed information obtained can help develop hypotheses, for example, about differences between BN and AN. This is not yet much investigated, or very successfully investigated, in eating disorders—perhaps because theories have not, until relatively recently, been very clear about the cognitive difference between the two disorders. Information obtained can then provide a useful basis for the development of more structured measures.

Thought sampling is a technique in which thoughts are self-monitored at intervals in everyday life. In one study (Zotter & Crowther 1991), bulimia nervosa patients self-monitored their thoughts every 30 min for two randomly selected days. The patients had a greater proportion of weight- and shape-related cognitions than repetitive dieters and female controls, both of which groups had relatively more eating related thoughts.

Concurrent verbalization, or 'thinking aloud' is a technique in which all thoughts experienced are collected at the same time as a task or series of tasks are performed. In one study (Cooper & Fairburn 1992b) information was collected on self-statements in three behavioural tests. These were eating a chocolate, looking in a mirror, and weighing. Participants carried out 'thinking aloud' and rated thoughts on a checklist for frequency, duration, and belief. Patients with bulimia (and anorexia) had more negative self-statements about eating, weight, and shape than normal controls, while dieters occupied an intermediate position. In bulimia nervosa, concern with weight and appearance distinguished them most clearly from dieters. The pattern of concerns in controls and dieters was also similar to that found in the patients with bulimia nervosa.

Although potentially very useful, unstructured assessment is time-consuming. The latter study investigated thoughts in different tasks, as well as separating out different areas of concern to patients, but different types of thought were not assessed separately. This is important, since different types (as well as, or instead of, content) of thought could link separately to different behaviours (as suggested by Cooper and colleagues above in identifying four types of automatic thought). It was suggested, for example, that bingeing may be linked to positive thoughts and vomiting or not eating may be linked to negative thoughts. This way of classifying thoughts might also help identify differences between type of eating disorder. In so far as BN is related to bingeing, positive thoughts may be more common in BN, and in so far as AN is related to restricting, negative thoughts may be more common in AN. The causal relationship of thoughts to specific behaviours can also be examined or tested if these ideas are followed through.

One *in vivo* study of cognition, using a self-report measure to assess cognitions, has attempted to separate a mixture of different content and different types of thought in bulimic cognitions. This study used the Bulimic Cognition Inventory (BCI: Bonifazi & Crowther 1996). However, unlike previous studies, it used a college rather than a clinic sample of bulimics. The measure has three parts: food and eating concern; weight and body shape concern; self-efficacy and need for approval concern. Each included a negative, positive, and two distorted cognitions (e.g. reflecting all or nothing thinking, or overgeneralization). These thoughts were sampled in a natural setting and in the laboratory while eating a test meal. Bulimics, compared to non-eating disordered, non-dieting controls, had more thoughts in each content area, and more negative and distorted thoughts. They also rated their thoughts as more intense when they occurred. However, on many variables the bulimics were not always different from restrained eaters; thus the cognitions were also typical of those who were not necessarily bulimic. The measures taken (e.g. distorted cognitions) also overlap with information processing measures (see below).

Other *in vivo* studies have been conducted by Rosen *et al.* (1985a), and Willmuth *et al.* (1988). These have also recorded food-, eating-, weight- and shape-related thoughts during test meals, using thinking aloud, but have not separated types (or content) of thought. These studies did not set out to answer any specific research questions about cognitions, and did not have control groups, so it was not possible to tell whether the high levels of negative thoughts identified were also typical of, for example, dieters.

Unstructured assessment is a useful basis for developing new measures but to date, the analysis of these studies has generally been limited to general content of thoughts (i.e. weight, shape, and eating) rather than type of thought (e.g. loss of control, permissive thoughts). This may be because characteristic types of thought have only been highlighted in relation to theory relatively recently. Future studies, however, might usefully investigate whether such thoughts are frequent in thinking aloud or other unstructured paradigms, both to confirm the validity of (for example) the thoughts questionnaire, and test the theoretical importance of the different thoughts identified by Cooper and colleagues. The paradigms described here could be adapted to do this.

Types of automatic thought

Although few studies have investigated types of automatic thought in relation to theory (e.g. as hypothesized by Cooper and colleagues), there is some evidence in existing studies that supports the theoretical distinction into positive, negative, no control, and permissive thoughts. This evidence is summarized below, for each of the types of thought that have been identified.

Positive thoughts

These are thoughts that eating will help with, or distract from, unpleasant cognitions and emotions. There is considerable evidence that binge-eating provides a way of decreasing or distancing from distress, particularly emotional distress. It has been noted to give relief from anxiety (Kaye *et al.* 1986), while depression also decreases as a binge proceeds and before vomiting occurs (Hsu 1990). The associated cognitions have not yet been assessed in BN patients, but work outside eating disorders supports the notion of eating as instrumental, i.e. associated with certain cognitions about the anticipated consequences of eating (see Chapter 2). This supports the theoretical idea of positive thoughts as 'helping with' or distracting from distress (as identified by Root *et al.* 1986 and Heatherton & Baumeister 1991, respectively). This notion is also incorporated into the idea that bingeing is associated with aversive self-awareness, although the precise nature of the relevant cognitions is not specified (Heatherton & Baumeister 1991).

One relevant study has been conducted with eating disorder patients. This applied expectancy learning theory, and assessed the reinforcement obtained from eating and from dieting (Hohlstein *et al.* 1998). A measure was developed and tested. It had five sub-scales for eating. These were:

(1) eating manages negative affect;

(2) eating is pleasurable and useful as a reward;

(3) eating leads to feeling out of control;

(4) eating enhances cognitive competence;

(5) eating alleviates boredom.

It also had a scale for dieting, i.e. dieting leads to over-generalized self-improvement. Bulimics differed from controls, normal and psychiatric, on three eating sub-scales (eating helps manage negative affect, leads to feeling out of control, alleviates boredom), and on dieting expectancies. This study maps onto positive thoughts about eating—especially the sub-scales eating as a way to manage negative affect, and alleviate boredom. (Dieting expectancies also map onto underlying assumptions about the meaning of dieting and weight loss.) This provides some support for the specific types of thought identified by Cooper and colleagues.

Negative thoughts

These are extremely common anecdotally, e.g. 'I'll get fat, or gain weight', are very commonly linked to binge-eating as well as 'normal' eating in BN patients. They have been assessed on many self-report questionnaires, usually as one of many thoughts, e.g. in the study on thinking aloud conducted by Cooper & Fairburn (1992b), as 'I'll get fat'. They were also evident in the transcripts of patients' concurrent verbalizations in the three tasks, e.g. 'makes me feel fat now', 'I'm so huge', 'it really is revolting (when I am fat)', (Cooper 1991; Cooper & Fairburn 1992b). However, the different types of thought were not separated out in the analysis of this study and examined separately.

Permissive thoughts

These are also typically assessed together with other cognitions, e.g. on self-report questionnaires (Phelan 1987). Phelan's questionnaire includes thoughts such as 'I don't care enough about myself to resist the temptation to eat'. Again, examples of these thoughts were evident in Cooper & Fairburn's (1992b) thinking-aloud tasks, e.g. 'I wonder if they'd notice if I removed half of them [the chocolates]'. Again, they were not separated out and analysed separately.

Thoughts of no control

Again, these are also typically assessed together with other cognitions on inventories, including the EAT (Garner & Garfinkel 1979), e.g. 'feel that food controls my life'. Phelan's questionnaire includes the thoughts 'I can stop eating', and 'I am in control of my eating'. Examples are also evident on the EDI (Garner *et al.* 1983b), e.g. 'I stuff myself with food'.

As suggested above, more research is needed, e.g. using the thoughts questionnaire to confirm the role of these thoughts in BN, including research with alternative assessment paradigms, to confirm their validity in the disorder. However, there is some preliminary support for the specific automatic thoughts outlined by Cooper and colleagues.

Underlying assumptions

The content of underlying assumptions is also hypothesized to reflect general food and eating, weight and shape concerns (prediction 3, Table 9.2). Fairburn's more recent revisions also suggest that thoughts reflecting perfectionism should exist at this level. Cooper and colleagues, however, make much more specific predictions about different types of beliefs. Self-report questionnaires have most commonly been used to assess these in BN. There are four relevant measures. While general perfectionism has been found to be relevant to BN (see Chapter 4), eating disorder-specific perfectionism has not yet been assessed.

Bulimics score lower than controls on the self-assessment scale (ReynaMcGlone *et al.* 1986), as predicted, while restricting anorexics, unlike bulimics, scored in the normal range (ReynaMcGlone *et al.* 1986). Examples of items include 'if you should gain a few pounds, how sure are you that you can continue to feel good about yourself?'. Bulimics also scored higher on the Attitude and Belief Survey (Scanlon *et al.* 1986), and the Bulimic Cognitive Distortions Scale (Schulman *et al.* 1986). Typical items are: 'if I gain weight I must be out of control'—from the Attitude and Belief Survey, and 'if I overeat

I've blown it'—from the Bulimic Cognitive Distortions Scale. One measure (unlike the other two mentioned), the Anorectic Cognitions Scale (Mizes 1988), has been more extensively investigated, in a series of studies conducted by Mizes and colleagues. Using a psychiatric control group Mizes (1992) found bulimics scored more highly than a non-eating disordered group. There were, however, no differences between a bulimic and anorexic group (Mizes 1992). Typical items include, 'when I see someone who is overweight I worry that I will be like him/her' and 'no matter how much I weigh, fats, sweets, breads, and cereals are bad food because they always turn into fat'. The difference between the findings of ReynaMcGlone and colleagues, and Mizes, may be because the self-assessment scale focuses particularly on eating, especially the ability to control eating, while Mizes's measure is relevant to weight and shape, as well as to eating and food.

The weight and shape assumptions of Fairburn's theory, are assessed on two sub-scales of the EDE and EDE-Q (a semi-structured interview and self-report questionnaire, respectively). However, the scales seem to reflect 'concern' rather than beliefs, and the items are not phrased in terms of cognition.

While the measures described above all provide some support for the general importance of weight, shape, and eating in assumptions or attitudes, they do not assess its specific content.

The Eating Disorder Belief Questionnaire (EDBQ: Cooper et al. 1997) also assesses underlying assumptions. One advantage of this measure is that it separates weight and shape from food and eating (of theoretical importance in Fairburn's account as it is weight and shape assumptions that are thought to be key in driving behaviour in BN). In addition, two types of assumption emerged in factor analysis. These were weight and shape as a means to self-acceptance, and weight and shape as a means to acceptance by others. Items are also expressed in a form that is compatible with cognitive therapy and, in particular, the developments in theory outlined by Cooper and colleagues. Thus it can provide a specific test of the suggestion that there are different types of assumptions, as well as (ultimately) of the specific effects of therapy on assumptions.

The identification of two types of assumption, self and other related, is consistent with research suggesting that the dimensions of sociotrophy and autonomy may be relevant to bulimia nervosa (Friedman & Whisman 1998). These reflect themes of, respectively, acceptance and approval, and themes of independence and achievement. However, this research was conducted on bulimic students, not patients.

Underlying assumptions about eating are also identified by the EDBQ. Two types can be evident—these have been termed first- and second-order assumptions. The first order are at the level of automatic thoughts—these are often centered around the meaning of eating or not eating, and that eating will or will not make the person fat. Unlike second-order eating assumptions, these do not link to core beliefs. Both have been very clearly identified in AN (Turner & Cooper, 2002), and also seem to be evident in bulimics (Cooper et al. 1998). The meaning of eating has been relatively neglected in bulimia.

Overall, the research supports the theoretical suggestion of Cooper and colleagues that underlying assumptions can be broken up in meaningful ways.

The role of early experience in the development of underlying assumptions has not been much investigated, and is relatively ignored in Fairburn's theory. Evidence suggests that childhood experience of enhanced attention to, or interest in, weight and shape, food and eating, may be linked to the development of beliefs, or underlying assumptions, about weight or eating, but this is largely anecdotal (Cooper *et al.* 1998). Data on the relationship between parental and peer concerns also suggests that early experience, or exposure to certain values and associated behaviours, may be important in the development of these beliefs (see Chapter 5).

In summary, underlying assumptions related to weight and shape seem typical of BN. Different types also seem to exist—including those concerned with self and other acceptance. Assumptions related to eating merit further investigation—they are not adequately assessed at present, and little studied. The link between assumptions and early experience also merits systematic study.

Negative self-beliefs

Although long thought to be important, the self has not received much empirical attention in BN. Some studies, using well-validated measures, show that patients with bulimia nervosa have low self-esteem (Jones *et al.* 1993), often as low as those with major depression.

There has, however, been little interest in the cognitive correlates of low self-esteem in Fairburn's theory of bulimia. Cooper, however, (prediction 2, Table 9.3), suggests that core beliefs will reflect global negative evaluation of the self. The EDBQ includes a scale that assesses these beliefs—the negative self-beliefs scale. Items include 'I'm unloveable', and 'I'm a failure'. Research shows that scores on this sub-scale are higher in bulimia nervosa than controls (Cooper *et al.* 1997) but, as predicted, are similar to those of women with a diagnosis of major depression (Cooper & Hunt 1998).

The Young Schema Questionnaire has also been used to investigate cognitive content in binge-eaters—including in a bulimia nervosa group. The measure assesses a broad range of beliefs, and was not developed specifically for eating disorders. In one study, a BN group had particularly high defectiveness/shame (perceived defects that make one unlovable), insufficient self-control (cannot or need not control impulses and feelings), and low failure to achieve scores (inadequacy leading to failure to meet goals) (Waller *et al.* 2000). In the whole sample, frequency of bingeing was also predicted by emotional inhibition (emotional expression has adverse consequences), while frequency of vomiting was best predicted by defectiveness/shame. The link between emotional inhibition and bingeing is not inconsistent with the idea that bingeing serves to block negative thoughts and feelings and, importantly, the suggestion that thoughts about the negative consequences of not bingeing are important. Both these ideas are consistent with Cooper and colleague's theory.

The content of core beliefs in different clinical groups has also been compared. In one study, clinical groups (restricting anorexics, bulimic anorexics, bulimia nervosa) differed only on entitlement (Waller *et al.* 2000, above). Another study (Leung *et al.* 1999) found only three beliefs distinguished the groups studied. These were defectiveness/shame, failure to achieve; and insufficient self-control. In another study, there were no differences between bulimic and anorexic patients, but there were differences between anorexic and bulimic groups in the pattern of association with eating symptoms. Eight of the 16 core beliefs were associated with symptoms in the bulimia nervosa group—in particular the frequency of bingeing was linked negatively with social undesirability beliefs, whereas no beliefs were linked to symptoms in the AN group (Leung *et al.* 1999). These studies are not necessarily tightly theoretically driven, i.e. no very specific predictions are made about which beliefs link to bingeing, but the fact that links have been found is consistent with Waller's suggestion that such beliefs are important, and also consistent with their role in Cooper's theory.

There is some preliminary evidence that negative self-beliefs are relatively more important than other types of core belief (i.e. about others, and the world) in BN patients (Cooper *et al.* 1996a).

There is also some evidence relevant to prediction 4 (Table 9.3), that early (negative) experience is important in the development of core beliefs in BN.

There are anecdotal reports of early childhood trauma and early negative experiences in BN (Guidano & Liotti 1983). Childhood sexual abuse is common though not specific to eating disorders (Welch & Fairburn 1994); as is physical and emotional abuse (Rorty *et al.* 1994). These experiences also seem to be linked to the development of negative self-beliefs (Cooper *et al.* 1998).

One study recently looked at the relationship between core beliefs and experience in the first few years of life, using the Parental Bonding Instrument (Parker 1983; Parker *et al.* 1979). This study found some associations in a bulimic group (e.g. low maternal care predicted the emotional deprivation belief) (Leung *et al.* 2000a).

One study of family factors, using structural analysis of social behaviour (Benjamin 1993), found that bulimics perceived both parents as hostile and disengaged. Self-concept was also associated with perceptions of parental attack/friendliness (Wonderlich *et al.* 1996a).

Interest in the study of core beliefs in BN is growing. Initial and promising attempts have been made to identify the beliefs characteristic of the disorder, and also the early experiences that may be related to the development of these beliefs. More work is needed in this important area of research.

Information processing

Schema-driven processes

Schema-driven processes have been predictioned to exist in BN (prediction 4, Table 9.2), in weight and shape concerns, and (in prediction 3, Table 9.3) associated with core beliefs. The latter includes a mechanism linking core beliefs to dieting.

Clinically, there seems to be a link between dieting and the importance of judging self-worth in terms of shape and weight (Fairburn & Cooper 1989), and a link between weight and shape concerns and feelings of ineffectiveness and worthlessness in BN (Fairburn & Cooper 1989). Prediction 4 (Table 9.2) is consistent with the observation that there is a link between thinness and happiness or success in BN (Lacey 1984). Other findings are also relevant: for example, the factor structure of the shape- and weight-based self-esteem inventory (Geller *et al.* 1997) is consistent with such a link. Scores in a mixed group of eating disorders, for example, were higher than in normal and psychiatric controls—after controlling for demographic variables, depression, and self-esteem—suggesting it is specific to the eating disordered (but see below) (Geller *et al.* 1998). Self-esteem and body dissatisfaction in bulimia are also correlated in BN (Joiner *et al.* 1997c). While these studies provide general support for the link suggested by Fairburn, none of them express self-esteem or the implied assumptions in cognitive terms. Expressing these concepts cognitively, Cooper *et al.* (1998) have found some support for such links, specifically for underlying assumptions as a reflection of schema compensation. Other work also suggests another schema-driven process, cognitive and emotional avoidance, may be reflected in binge-eating (Spranger *et al.* 2001). In this study, bulimic women reported greater use of all types of schema-avoidance strategies than comparison women.

Self-report questionnaires

These provide some evidence for cognitive processes, e.g. general information processing biases, in areas of concern with food and eating, weight and shape. There are two such measures (Franko & Zuroff 1992; Thompson *et al.* 1987) that assess styles of reasoning at the underlying assumption level. These measures include items containing characteristic distortions, e.g. over-generalization, perfectionism, and dichotomous thinking. In both of the studies cited, high levels of distortions have been found in BN. One study also discriminated those with 'bulimic-like' symptoms from those with a diagnosis (Thompson *et al.* 1987). The other found that bulimics reported higher levels of distortions than depressed college students and obese subjects (Franko & Zuroff 1992). Typical items on these measures include, 'if I eat a piece of cake, it seems to turn into fat immediately'—from the measure used by Thompson *et al.*, the Food and Weight Cognitive Distortions Survey; and 'I ought to be thinner than I am'—from the Bulimic Automatic Thoughts Test (Franko & Zuroff 1992; Franko *et al.* 1986).

One study used self-verification theory (e.g. Swann *et al.* 1992) to explore schema-driven processes in relation to weight and shape. This theory suggests that people strive to attain and preserve predictable, certain, and familiar self concepts. They thus actively seek out self-confirming interpersonal responses from others. Bulimics (not a patient sample) expressed more interest in receiving negative feedback in several domains, including, but not only, body appearance. This study concludes that this process may be involved in the development and persistence of bulimic symptoms and body dissatisfaction, and that bulimic symptoms may also be increased via increases in body dissatisfaction (Joiner 1999). This provides some general support for Fairburn's theory, but does not test the more specific processes (e.g. schema compensation, avoidance, and maintenance) predicted by Cooper.

Experimental psychology techniques

These have also been used to investigate information processing. A study using thought-sampling (Zotter & Crowther 1991), for example, found more dichotomous thinking relevant to concerns with eating and weight in bulimics than repetitive dieters and normal controls.

Most studies have, however, used selective attention paradigms, usually the modified Stroop (1935) task.

There are several versions of this in existence. Two have generally been used in bulimia nervosa (one developed by Fairburn and colleagues, the other by Ben Tovim and colleagues). Initial studies were rather poor methodologically, and in terms of data analysis. The materials consist of words written in different colours, relevant to food and eating, weight and shape. The task is to name the colour of the ink in which the word is written. The measure is the time taken to do this. Those with BN are typically much slower at colour-naming words relevant to their concerns with food and eating, weight and shape than words that are not relevant. It is thought that the reason for this is that they attend selectively to these words. Studies with bulimics typically show they are slower to colour name these words than control subjects (Ben-Tovim & Walker 1991; Ben-Tovim et al. 1989; Cooper et al. 1992; Fairburn et al. 1991a).

Control groups used in these studies include dieters. One study found disturbed information-processing in patients and dieters with some symptoms of an eating disorder. Normal dieters, however, were no different from the non-dieting controls (Cooper & Fairburn 1992a). Patients also differ from adolescent females concerned about their shape and weight (Ben-Tovim & Walker 1991). Other studies find no differences between bulimics and restrained eaters (e.g. Black et al. 1997).

Several studies have included words relevant to eating, weight, and shape, without separating them into different areas of concern, e.g. food and eating from weight and shape (Channon et al. 1988). These studies find that bulimics, but not anorexics, are slowed on shape-related words (Ben-Tovim et al. 1989; Channon et al. 1988); and anorexics, but not bulimics, are slowed on food and eating (Perpina et al. 1993). Black et al. separated out food and weight and shape but found no differences between a bulimic and a restrained group. One study separated out the three concerns, food and eating, weight, shape in a single study (Cooper & Todd 1997), and found that bulimics were slowed on all three types of word compared to controls.

There are lots of methodological differences between these studies. The method employed varies (computer vs. card presentation of stimulus words): the cards used differing in number and exact words used to sample the domains; whether word frequency matching is carried out or not for control words; whether balanced order of presentation is used; data analysis; and criteria used for selecting groups, especially for dieters, restrained eaters, and normal controls.

A few studies have looked at the relationship between symptoms and colour naming. In one study, frequency of purging, not general psychiatric disturbance, was the best predictor of interference (Cooper & Fairburn 1993). However, while EAT score and interference were correlated in another study, the relationship disappeared when level of depressive symptoms was controlled (Cooper et al. 1992).

There are other measures of selective attention. One of these, the dichotic listening task, has also been used in BN. This study found that bulimics attended to the word fat more often than to a control word (Schotte et al. 1990).

A visual probe detection task has also been used (Rieger et al. 1998). This found that bulimics direct attention away from words related to a thin body shape and towards words related to a fat body shape (the latter was a non-significant trend).

A small number of studies have examined selective memory (Hunt & Cooper 2001; King et al. 1991; Sebastian et al. 1996). King et al. looked at person memory in restrained eaters but also included a small number of eating disordered patients. Patients had better recall for weight- and food-related information than other information. Sebastian et al. found that a mixed group of eating disordered patients recalled more fatness-related words than normal and weight-preoccupied controls. Only one study has included an eating disorder group that contains only those with bulimia nervosa (Hunt & Cooper 2001). It also included a depressed control group. The bulimia nervosa group demonstrated a bias to recall positive and negative weight- and shape-related words compared to emotional words, but not compared to neutral nouns and body words. A memory bias for food-related words was found, but this was also found in depression, and was related to level of hunger in both groups. The authors conclude that this study provides partial support for memory biases for weight- and shape-related information in bulimia nervosa.

There is a relatively large body of work supporting information processing biases in BN. Further work might usefully add to the studies using paradigms from experimental psychology, to help identify the precise nature of the different biases characteristic of the disorder. More detailed study of characteristic thoughts might also help identify which type of distortions in thinking are typical of BN. Some may be more common in BN than others (see for example: Cooper, Todd & Wells 2000). The evidence to date provides only general support for the two theories. At the automatic-thought level (and core-belief level, see below), more information is needed about what types of thought are linked to information processing.

There is some evidence for Cooper's prediction 3 (Table 9.3), that schema-driven processes will be evident in areas of core belief concern.

Young (1990) identifies three processes associated with schemata that keep them unchallenged and unchanged. Evidence that all three operate in BN was obtained in a semi-structured interview study (Cooper et al. 1998). Underlying assumptions about weight, shape, and eating seemed to link self-statements with core beliefs.

Schema compensation (dieting) was a way to overcome, or make up for core beliefs. Binge-eating also seemed to function as schema avoidance; it was a way to escape from unpleasant thoughts and feelings about the self.

A recent study has used the Young–Rygh Avoidance Inventory, a measure of Young's concept of schema avoidance (YRAI: Young & Rygh 1994; Spranger *et al.* 2001). This study found that a small number of bulimics scored more highly than comparison women on all subscales of schema avoidance.

There is also a small number of studies looking at schema-driven processing that have used the Stroop task, using typical core-belief content (also called ego or self-esteem threats) as stimulus words (Heatherton & Baumeister 1991).

One study found that a mixed group of bulimics (all patients but not all with a BN diagnosis) had greater interference with processing of threat information than controls (there was no psychiatric control group). They were slower on all types of threat, particularly autonomy threat, discomfort anxiety threat, ego others threat, and also socio-trophy threat and ego self-threat (compared to controls). The content of the ego self-threat is similar to that of core or negative self-beliefs (e.g. failure, inadequate). There was also a strong association between self-directed ego threats and bulimic characteristics (McManus *et al.* 1996).

There are a small number of other studies but these have not been conducted on patients or on those with bulimia nervosa. One study, for example, has investigated the priming of self-esteem in a highly restrained (but non-clinical) group. This study found that priming increased the accessibility of subliminally presented body weight and shape stimuli, thus supporting a potential causal link (Meijboom *et al.* 1999).

It has been suggested that bulimia nervosa patients have an attentional bias towards such threats, but may also show cognitive avoidance of these threats. The two biases seem to be related, and may have a temporal pattern—an initial orientation towards the threat, then avoidance of it. Which is found may depend on the task used to assess them (Waller & Meyer 1997). The process proposed is similar to that outlined for anxiety (Beck & Clark 1997). When information is aversive there is an initial automatic response (attentional bias), which will then be followed by more purposive processing (avoidance of the aversive material, or cognitive escape). This proposal has not yet been investigated in BN.

Schema-driven processing (at core belief level) is a new area in BN. Preliminary work by Cooper and Waller suggests that there is some support for these processes. It seems likely that further systematic and detailed study will help identify which processes are typical of BN.

Causal role of cognition

Treatment studies

A small number of treatment studies provide some general evidence relevant to prediction 5 (Table 9.2), that attitudes (underlying assumptions) have a causal role in BN. In one study, residual level of attitudinal disturbance at the end of treatment predicts outcome, defined in behavioural terms, at 12 months (Fairburn *et al.* 1993c). However, this finding has not been replicated (Cooper & Steere 1995), possibly because of restricted assessment of the cognitive disturbance. It may be that the measure used in this study (the EDE) does not capture the cognitive variables changed by treatment, or the cognitions that are most important.

One study measuring core beliefs using the YSQ found that pretreatment levels predicted outcome, in group cognitive behaviour therapy for bulimia nervosa (Leung *et al.* 2000b). Less healthy beliefs generally predicted lower gains on bulimic behaviours, vomiting, and bulimic attitudes. Thus it seems that generic beliefs, as well as specific ones, may be causally related to outcome.

There is also some (indirect) support for the causal role of cognitions from treatment follow-up studies. For example, one study found that gains made with CBT are more likely to be maintained than gains made with other treatments (Thackwray *et al.* 1993).

Fairburn's revised model includes perfectionism (at the assumption or attitude level) as a causal agent in binge-eating. Although there is no work on this in BN, a study in a non-clinical group suggested that perfectionism, together with perceived weight, predicted binge-eating (Vohs *et al.* 1999).

Treatment studies could help the investigation of cognition in BN by including appropriate measures of cognition, which would then facilitate these sorts of analysis. To date, many treatment studies have not assessed cognitions directly.

A general prediction is made (prediction 5, Table 9.1), that underlying assumptions and self-statements (plus more recently by Fairburn), perfectionism will be causally linked to eating behaviour. There is some general evidence for this link in a study conducted by Cooper, Clark & Fairburn (1993). More specific predictions are made about the links between cognition and behaviour and emotion in predictions 5 and 6 (Table 9.2), and 2 and 3 (Table 9.4).

There is as yet little evidence for the links in the vicious circle of maintenance proposed by Cooper and colleagues (predictions 5 and 6, Table 9.3). However, there are some relevant studies.

There is some evidence that a wide variety of situations seem to trigger binge-eating, including both eating-related situations (eating anything at all, thinking of food) and others (going home, being alone, going out with a member of the opposite sex). Events may also be either external or internal. It seems that triggers are usually associated with negative feelings (Abraham & Beumont 1982). This is also consistent with Fairburn's recent note about the role of negative affect in binge-eating, although unlike Cooper there is no reference to the role of cognitions.

One study, using an experience-sampling procedure, found that binges were preceded by a more negative self-concept and by negative moods (Steiger *et al.* 1999a). Participants were bulimic, although not all were bulimia nervosa patients. Participants were hypersensitive—there were larger increases in self-critical thoughts as a function of increasingly negative social interactions in the bulimics than controls. This effect was also present in the formerly bulimic.

There are lots of evidence that immediately after bingeing, and before purging, negative emotions increase, especially depression (De Elmore & Castro 1990; Hsu 1990). Negative emotions focused on self-loathing, especially guilt and disgust, also intensify, as do negative cognitions (Cooper *et al.* 1988).

Experimental paradigms

There are very few studies that have attempted to manipulate or activate beliefs in BN, and measure the effect of this on behaviour and emotion (predictions 5, Table 9.2, 2 and 3, Table 9.4). An early study showed that activating beliefs in patients with bulimia nervosa led to greater negative self-statements, and greater restriction in a taste test, i.e. beliefs affect behaviour, as predicted (Cooper *et al.* 1993). No similar studies seem to have been conducted.

The causal role of dieting in maintaining binge-eating (prediction 6, Table 9.2) has not often been studied longitudinally, and not specifically linked to BN. One study, in a community sample, found that whereas dieting predicts the onset it does not predict the maintenance of bulimic behaviours (Stice & Agras 1998). Other relevant studies are discussed in Chapters 2 and 3.

As yet there is no evidence specifically relevant to predictions 2 and 3 (Table 9.4). However, the study conducted by Cooper *et al.* (1993) is consistent with the prediction that activating negative thoughts about eating is causally linked to decreased eating. The beliefs activated in this study were primarily about the negative consequences of eating, weight, and shape—this led to decreased eating in the experimental, compared with the control, condition. There was also no evidence that the patients in the experimental condition went on to binge in the following 24 h—a finding that might be thought contrary to the restraint prediction.

Much more research is needed to investigate the causal links in cognitive models. The link initially proposed by cognitive theory between dieting and binge-eating remains unclear—recent studies have not found that dieting is involved in the maintenance of binge-eating (see Chapter 2 for further details). The role of cognition in the binge cycle requires further investigation. Some very specific links have now been proposed by Cooper and colleagues, including between different types of automatic thought and different eating behaviour. However, these have not yet been much studied. Experimental paradigms, as well as longitudinal studies, could usefully test these links. Unlike Fairburn's theory, the predictions are much more specific and expressed in more precise cognitive terminology. Additional predictions are also made. To date, there is some evidence for the validity of these more specific predictions, and for some of the additional predictions.

Summary

In part one, sources of evidence for cognition in BN were identified. This includes self-report questionnaires and experimental psychology techniques. A set of predictions was then derived from existing cognitive theories, focusing on the two most articulated theories that currently exist.

In part two, evidence to support the content of automatic thoughts, underlying assumptions, and core beliefs in BN was presented. As Fairburn's more general theory would predict, this is typically concerned with weight, shape, and food and eating (for automatic thoughts and underlying assumptions) and, more relevant to Cooper's theory, negative self-evaluation (for core beliefs). As Cooper's more specific theory would predict, automatic thoughts also seem to include positive thoughts, negative thoughts, no control, and permissive thoughts. Preliminary studies have also looked at different types of core belief, although no specific predictions have been made about their typical characteristics in BN.

Part three considered information-processing biases and schema-driven processes. As Fairburn would predict, general information-processing biases related to food, weight, and shape exist in attention and memory. This evidence is also consistent with Cooper's theory. To date, there is relatively little evidence for different types of characteristic process in these, although there is some recent relevant work in schema processing. Here, both Waller and Cooper have found support for some specific predictions about types of processing, an issue that is not addressed in Fairburn's theory.

Part four presented the evidence from longitudinal and treatment studies, indicating that cognitions predict eating disorders and eating disorder-related behaviour. This is limited to date, and sometimes contradictory.

Part five summarized evidence for the causal links in cognitive theory. This includes a very small amount of experimental evidence. Most of the evidence is derived from anecdotal report, and from studies in which the main hypotheses were not directly relevant to understanding the causal role of the specific cognitions associated with BN. However, the findings are consistent with underlying assumptions, and automatic thoughts, as causal. This evidence is consistent both with Fairburn's model and Cooper's more specific theory.

Chapter 10

Non-cognitive treatment of bulimia nervosa

Overview

This chapter describes some of the different psychotherapeutic approaches to the treatment of BN (with the exception of cognitive therapy, which will be discussed in Chapter 11). Evidence for their effectiveness will also be considered.

Part one will consider psycho-analytical and psychodynamic approaches. This will include object relations and self-psychology treatment. It will also discuss Bruch's work. Part two will discuss treatment based on socio-cultural theories. This will include prevention programmes, and the role of public health. Part three will discuss educational approaches. Part four will consider the influence of feminism on the treatment of BN. Part five will consider family therapies. This will include systemic and structural family therapy, as well as the combined treatments often employed in practice. Part six will discuss behaviour therapy, particularly exposure and response prevention. Part seven will consider some of the combination treatments that have been described in the literature, some of which have also been evaluated. The plan for the chapter is summarized in Table 10.1.

Throughout the chapter, ways in which treatments have been adapted for BN will be considered, together with any issues that are specific to the disorder.

Table 10.1 Summary of plan for Chapter 10

Psycho-analysis
Psychodynamic treatment—object relations, ego psychology
Bruch's approach
Psychodynamic treatment—self psychology, relational approaches
Socio-cultural approaches—prevention programmes
Psycho-educational approaches
Feminist influences on treatment
Family therapy—systemic, structural
Behaviour therapy—exposure and response prevention, cue exposure
Combination treatments

Psychodynamic therapy

Pine makes a useful distinction between psycho-analytic theories—they can be broadly divided up into drive, ego, object relations, and self theories (Pine 1988). Therapy associated with each is rather different; how each has been applied to BN will be discussed below. To provide a summary, the main goals of the different dynamic therapies and key features and strategies employed are set out in Table 10.2.

Psycho-analysis

BN is not widely discussed in the literature in relation to psycho-analysis, the therapy associated with drive theory. There do not seem to be any very detailed accounts of its application to BN.

The goal in psycho-analysis[1] is to make the patient conscious of the repressed conflicts that lie behind her behaviour, and cause her symptoms. This is typically referred to as 'insight' and takes place in a gradual process of 'working through'. In sessions the patient examines the problem, understands her symptoms as an attempt to deal with conflict, and is then able to resolve it without denial or distortion, i.e. without using unhelpful defence mechanisms.

Traditionally, treatment involves frequent meetings (often several times a week). Free expression (or free association) in sessions is emphasized to help recover unconscious material, that might otherwise be censored. The analyst remains anonymous, and neutral. This means not gratifying, confronting, or suppressing the patient's unconscious desires. It also means that the therapist does not help the patient in practical ways with everyday problems, e.g. she will not offer advice. Rather, the therapist reflects back what is going on, from the patient's point of view, and makes interpretations. These may include commenting on the patient's behaviour in a way that is new, linking the present with the past, and using the past to illuminate the meaning of the present. Throughout, the analyst and patient work with the transference. (Transference is the idea that the patient reacts to the analyst in a similar way to important figures from the past—and thus recreates the earlier emotional state). Because this parallels previous relationships that the patient has had, it can be used to help work out the reasons for the patient's defences, i.e. what the conflicts are. Once insight is achieved, the therapist helps the patient deal with the underlying conflict that has been revealed in a more rational, mature way.

Johnson (1995) suggests that the use of psychodynamic techniques, including psycho-analysis, is most relevant to those with BN who do not respond fully to briefer

---

[1] The term psycho-analysis will be confined to therapy based on drive theory. Psycho-analytical psychotherapy will be used for therapies derived from this, e.g. that practised by Klein, Fairbairn, & Winnicott (see Avery 1996). Analytical psychotherapy refers to that based on Jungian principles. Psychodynamic is used as an umbrella or generic term.

Table 10.2 Goals, strategies, and features of dynamic therapies

Goals	Strategies and features
Psychoanalytic:	
Insight—to make repressed conflicts conscious.	Working through; frequent meetings; symptoms are symbolic of sexuality; free association; interpretation, use of transference; focus on past relationships; use of unconscious.
Ego psychology and object relations:	
Insight—to reveal repressed conflicts; reduce need for defences; take in good aspects of therapy relationship.	Working through; focus on early mother and child relationship and on social relationships; transference; interpretation; symptoms symbolic of eating object relations; here and now important.
Bruch:	
Develop more competent, less painful, and more effective way of handling problems.	Fact finding; here and now; focus on actual experience; explore, examine and reinterpret cognitive distortions; early mother and child relationship important (but not symbolic); focus on unrealistic self-appraisals.
Self psychology:	
Restore confidence in capacity to form and have mature relationships; to acknowledge and deal with distressing moods.	Self-object transference—self-object needs identified, experienced, fulfilled; moods and unmet needs interpreted; has a new experience when these are understood and attended to; interpretative (of unmet needs for human connection).
Relational:	
To create mutually empathic and empowering relationships with others.	Here and now; often group work; focus on links with others (and food), and self; self-monitoring, record thoughts and feelings, links eating to wider problems; discover self and others.

approaches, or to medication. He notes that such patients often have personality difficulties or personality disorders. He also suggests that some of the features of traditional psycho-analysis may require modification for patients with BN. For example, the therapist may be advised to maintain less of a neutral stance. She may, on occasion, offer specific symptom-management strategies—either cognitive-behavioural, psycho-educational, or psychopharmacological. Johnson argues that this may help further analysis of the transference, for example, giving up bingeing and purging may allow feelings and awareness of conflicts to surface more readily—these can then be worked through. At the same time as offering advice, however, analysis of the patients' behaviour (including any resistance to practical suggestions) remains central. Johnson notes that analysis of the transference tends to be more important in BN than is sometimes assumed, particularly the analysis of how the patient understands and experiences the therapists' actions. Counter-transference (the therapist's response to the patient's transference) is also important and provides a particularly useful source of information to help the therapist understand the patient with BN.

Ego psychology and object relations

Ego psychologists place greater emphasis on the external world, including social relationships, than drive theorists. This emphasis is shared by object relations therapists. In addition, object relations therapists focus particularly on the early mother–child relationship.

Treatment based on ego psychology and object relations has similar aims to that of psycho-analysis. The goal is insight—to reveal repressed conflicts, which will reduce the need for defences, and enable the patient to feel and behave differently. As in psycho-analysis, change is achieved primarily through the transference relationship. Free association is also encouraged, and the therapist makes interpretations, e.g. of the transference and of defences. Another goal (unlike that of psycho-analysis) may also be for the patient to become able to take in good aspects of the interaction with the therapist. This facilitates change; by taking in new meanings and messages, the patient becomes less trapped by archaic ways of relating and being. The symbolic nature of symptoms remains important, but these now represent early object relations (such as fantasized union with the idealized mother: Sours 1980), rather than sexuality. Ego analysts also place rather more emphasis on the here and now relationships in a patient's life.

Although several therapists have written theoretical papers on they dynamics of BN from ego psychology and object relations perspectives (see Chapter 7), there has been very little written on treatment using these principles. This makes it difficult to work out exactly how treatment has been applied to BN. Even the papers that include case reports are not very enlightening on this point, but are essentially descriptive, and discuss dynamics rather than precisely how treatment was carried out, or what techniques were used.

Bruch

Bruch (1973) was influenced by object relations and ego psychology. However, she developed an approach to therapy that is unlike psycho-analysis and psycho-analytic psychotherapy—and that has much in common with modern cognitive therapy approaches. Although other analysts do not seem to have drawn much on her work, and she worked primarily with anorexic patients, her thinking has had an impact on cognitive therapists who work with BN thus her work will be discussed briefly here.

Bruch (1973) aims 'to assist (the patient) in developing a more competent, less painful, and less ineffective way of handling their problems' (p.337). Her approach was not interpretive—but fact finding. It attends to the way the patient misperceives or misinterprets events and body sensations. It has a 'here and now' focus, with an initial aim of finding out what the patient is currently experiencing. The therapist then explores and examines alternatives, and helps the patient repair cognitive distortions (rather as in cognitive therapy). She also helps the patient learn to rely on her own thinking, and become more realistic in her self-appraisal. Bruch noted that interpretation (the traditional tool of psycho-analysis) was problematic in eating disorders, and part of the problem. Too often others have told the patient what she must be thinking and feeling, and she has never had an opportunity to find this out for herself—it is not, therefore, helpful for the therapist to do this. Although Bruch attended to the early mother–child relationship, and emphasized its importance, she did not suggest a symbolic representation of this in patients' symptoms, as did the object relations therapists. The mechanism in Bruch's treatment, like that of cognitive therapy, lies in correcting distorted cognitions, and unrealistic self-appraisals.

Other dynamic therapies have occasionally been applied to BN and written about in the literature. An account of Adlerian therapy, for example, is contained in Miller & Mizes (2000), while Woodman (1980) has written about Jungian therapy with eating disorder, including probable BN, patients.

Self psychology

Goodsitt (1985, 1997) provides an account of self psychology in the treatment of eating disorders, including BN. The aim of treatment is to restore confidence in the capacity of close human relationships to calm and deal with distressing moods. Therapy works with the self-object transference, within which self-object needs (e.g. for attunement, validation, etc.) are identified, experienced, and fulfilled. Needs and unmet needs are also interpreted. Self psychology departs from analysis and analytical therapy in several ways. For example, it does not aim to rework past traumatic experiences, rather the patient must have a new experience in which self-object needs are understood and responded to. The concept of psychological holding (described by Winnicott) becomes important here, as the patient requires support in her attempts to gain a new experience, and regulate tension in a new way. Like traditional analysis, self psychology uses interpretation but, consistent with its theoretical basis, the content of the interpretations focuses on unmet needs for human connection, and not on sexuality or object relations. Meeting unmet (self-object) needs (e.g. for empathic understanding) may also be more important than insight via interpretation, although both may effect, and be responsible for, change.

Others have written on self psychology in BN. Geist (1989), for example, writes within a self psychology framework, but he also uses symbolic representation from object relations theory. Sands (2000) presents a readable account of self psychology in an eating disorder patient. She describes how girls are vulnerable to eating disorders (i.e. using their body in a maladaptive way), as a result of early difficulties in mirroring and idealizing (Sands 1989). She also discusses ways in which therapy may need to be modified for patients with an eating disorder. This includes acknowledging that eating disordered patients may find the development of the self-object transference particularly difficult, and that this may be preceded by a transference to food and eating, which also needs to be understood. An important process may also be desomaticizing (Brickman 1992), in which the body becomes separated from affect (affect is sometimes thought to have been somatized, e.g. Sands 2000), through affect attunement, and is then reintegrated in a way that allows for the body self and psychological self to be differentiated.

Kohut (1971) divides self psychology work into two phases: the empathic mirroring phase (understanding); and the interpretation phase (explaining). The first is thought to be particularly important for eating disordered patients (Goodsitt 1997). In the second, explaining phase, the therapist interprets from within, i.e. from the patient's perspective, thus evoking the self-object experience and encouraging self-growth. The therapist conveys awareness of her own repeated potential failures of empathy, by interpreting them to the patient. Later on in therapy, the patient talks about hurt feelings, rather than trying to restore a sense of cohesion through bingeing and vomiting (Bachar 1998).

Combination dynamic treatments

These generally draw on relational and self theories (de Groot & Rodin 1998; Tantillo 1998). Some (e.g. Tantillo 1998) use group treatment.

Relational treatment

The goal of treatment based on relational principles is to create mutually empathic and empowering relationships with others. Tantillo (1998) adapts this approach for BN. Therapy pays explicit attention to connections between a persons' relationships with food and with self and others. Treatment promotes four healing factors: validation, self-empathy, mutuality, and empowerment. It includes work on food and eating, e.g. self-monitoring, and recording thoughts and feelings before and after eating. Once the patient can see how her eating patterns link to wider problems, the group moves on to other issues, e.g. the disconnection, relational dilemmas, and images and meanings that precipitate and maintain disconnection from self and others. Treatment focuses on the here and now, as well as earlier relationships.

Self and relational therapy

De Groot & Rodin, (1998) present an argument for treatment that combines elements of the self and relational approaches. The patient's focus on weight and shape wards off emotional experience that is uncomfortable or threatening. Initially, therapy should help the subjective world to emerge, e.g. validate it, and facilitate creative self-reflection through providing a 'transitional space' (Winnicott 1953). The therapist may need to provide some structure, verbal interaction, direction, and possibly behavioural interventions—not least so that the patient sees the therapist involved in a meaningful way. The therapist may also need to engage directly with the patients' somatic concerns—and then shift gradually to the emotional problems. The patient may need help to learn to identify feelings, before meaning can be understood. An initial idealized experience of the therapist is common in eating disorders, it may be helpful, and may reflect an unmet developmental need to experience a parental figure in positive terms (and not a defence against hostile or competitive feelings). The patient will need help to identify her own feelings and goals, and disentangle them from those of others. Empathic responsiveness is very important, more so than interpretation/insight. The aim is not to uncover what is repressed but to help the patient understand and organize her experience. There should be collaboration, and a joint construction of meaning. It is also important for the patient to feel understood. Later in treatment, psychological and interpersonal issues take up most of the time.

There is little empirical evidence for psychodynamic treatment in BN. Only three reports could be found.

A study of psychodynamic group psychotherapy (nine young women) conducted treatment using a 'traditional psychodynamically oriented group psychotherapy approach ... with the emphasis on self exploration and identification and resolution of conflicts, both at the level of the group and the individual' (p.154). Improvement was obtained on several self-report measures over an average of 16 sessions (O'Neil & White 1987).

Another study evaluated psychodynamic in patient treatment. Not many details were provided of the treatment, apart from the note that it assumed that intrapsychic conflicts are responsible for the symptoms. It focused more on low self-esteem, interpersonal problems, and core conflicts, than on eating attitudes and behaviour. Bingeing and vomiting decreased significantly in the experimental and control treatments, and the number abstinent from bingeing and vomiting continued to increase during the following two years. Both core symptoms and associated symptoms improved. There was some suggestion that there was a delayed effect, as for other non-symptom focused treatments, e.g. interpersonal therapy, suggesting it may operate by creating positive changes in relationships, which then initiate other positive changes, including eating improvement. Overall, the in-patient analytic fared slightly better, but neither treatment produced effects consistently related to the theoretical origin of the therapy (Jager *et al.* 1996).

One study compared in-patient analytic with systemic, out-patient therapy. The analytic consisted of four group sessions a week in a 2-month programme. Both groups improved (Liedtke *et al.* 1991).

Socio-cultural

Socio-cultural theories are usually aetiological theories and thus have particular relevance to prevention. Some programmes have been developed to try to reduce the incidence of eating disorders, including bulimia nervosa.

Based on a detailed theoretical formulation, Stice (1994) recommends that such programmes should aim to decrease internalization of socio-cultural pressures. This might be achieved by enhancing self-esteem, highlighting the mismatch between biology and the thin ideal, and stressing the health risks of extreme thinness. Programmes might also try to improve body satisfaction, educate about the consequences of dieting, and teach alternative coping skills to dieting.

Prevention may be seen as a triad (Caplan 1964), of primary, secondary and tertiary levels. Primary prevention is aimed at those who do not yet show signs of illness. It can be divided up into reactive and proactive strategies (Catalano & Dooley 1980). Reactive prevention is use of strategies to improve coping responses and increase resistance to potentially harmful stressors—this can occur before or after the stressor. Proactive prevention is use of strategies to eliminate causal agents—this avoids the stressor altogether. Eating disorder prevention programmes usually use reactive strategies, targeted at the individual. In other health problems, e.g. smoking, public health effort goes into changing the environment, by restricting advertising, and changing social norms. However, this has not generally happened in eating disorders.

Most programmes have not been very successful. The main goals, features, and strategies of treatments based on socio-cultural models are summarized in Table 10.3.

The relevant studies have recently been reviewed (Austin 2000). Austin identified 20 studies in eight countries over two decades. They were varied in content, theoretical framework, and methodological rigour. Results were discouraging, only four studies showed positive behaviour change, while four found some worsening of symptoms, together with some improved knowledge and attitudes about weight and shape. He commented on the format of the programmes—these were usually didactic, even though public health research suggests that participatory intervention strategies are most effective. Only a small number tried to change the social environment, including parents and school staff. Few studies had a theoretical rationale for the intervention. Those that did usually used cognitive behaviour theory—which was consistent with their focus on the individual, rather than on broader factors.

Leaving the burden of change to the individual has been considered unethical. It has been suggested that we need to make a switch from clinical treatment to a public health perspective, and set up primary prevention programmes. This presents a challenge for researchers. We will, for example, need tools to measure the environment relevant to eating disorders.

Table 10.3 Goals, strategies and features of socio-cultural approaches to treatment

Goals	Strategies and features
To decrease the internalization of socio-cultural pressures (Stice 1994).	Public health strategies—prevention; education; coping skills; generally targeted at the individual.

The programmes that have been run generally provide psycho-educational material about the symptoms of eating disorders, consequences of behaviour, risk factors, and healthy weight-control techniques. Some also teach socio-culture pressure resistance techniques.

But, education alone may not be sufficient—as has been found, for example, in substance abuse prevention programmes (Moskowitz 1989). Programmes may also need to be targeted at those most at risk to have a significant effect, i.e. at those already struggling with some weight/shape related issues. Finally, given that they often discuss eating disorder behaviours, such as use of vomiting, and laxatives for weight control, they may encourage their use in those who are unhappy with their weight and shape.

A theoretical model of socio-cultural factors has long been needed—Stice provides a comprehensive model that could be used to guide interventions, and a study has been conducted using this model (Stice *et al.* 1996b). It focused on reducing the thin-ideal internalization that occurs early on in the development of an eating disorder. A dissonance-based approach (Festinger 1957) was used, including counter-attitudinal role play and essay writing. The study had some success, and the intervention led to a decrease in thin-ideal internalization, body dissatisfaction, dieting, negative affect, and bulimic behaviours. Most effects remained at one month follow-up.

A range of strategies follow from Stice's model, in addition to focus on change in the thin-ideal internalization. They include to reduce obesity, for example, with regular exercise and low fat diets, and education about the dangers of unhealthy weight-loss strategies (which may be particularly helpful at the secondary prevention stage, in those who show early signs of an eating problem). Interventions also need to make people more resilient to socio-cultural pressures to be thin, e.g. they could generate thoughts that counter pressures from family, peers, and the media. They could teach critical thinking skills, e.g. in media literacy programmes, reduce the pressure by working through families, teach assertiveness skills, and advocate political pressure to boycott ultra thin images in the media. The thin ideal might additionally be tackled using reverse role play, and motivational interviewing, e.g. reviewing the costs of trying to be ultra thin. Cognitive interventions could also be used, to change body dissatisfaction, and target negative thoughts. Education about norms might be useful, together with reducing dieting, use of food diaries, regular eating, and exercise (Stice 1999).

Psycho-educational

Educational components have often been included in individual treatment programmes, and there have been some evaluations of these programmes delivered as the primary treatment. Typically they focus on weight and shape, and eating (and not on other components, e.g. self-esteem). The main goals, features, and strategies of these programmes are outlined in Table 10.4.

Psycho-education for eating disorders was first outlined in detail by Garner *et al.* (1984b). It was suggested as a supplement to psychotherapy, not a replacement for it.

Table 10.4 Goals, strategies and features of psycho-educational approaches to treatment

Goals	Strategies and features
To educate about causes of binge eating and wider social and cultural context.	Education—about cultural pressures, binge-eating, dieting, obesity. Includes education about a weight range, stopping dieting, meal planning, relapse prevention.

It is now very commonly employed, and it has been estimated that it is mentioned in about 75% of the published treatment studies for bulimia nervosa (Olmsted & Kaplan 1995). It was originally seen as an important part of cognitive behavioural therapy (based on the premise that some maladaptive beliefs are the result of faulty information or lack of information), but is now often included in other treatment approaches. It is based on several assumptions—many shared with cognitive behavior therapy (CBT). These include: dieting can cause binge-eating; body weight resists change and is regulated physiologically round a set point, or weight that the body seeks to defend. One aim is to educate about this, and about the wider cultural context. Cultural factors include: pressure on women to achieve unrealistic thinness; the harmful effects of dieting; glorification of youth; glamourizing of anorexia nervosa; and prejudice against obesity. Other assumptions include that dieting can lead to bingeing, as well as preoccupation with food and eating, emotional changes, social and sexual changes, cognitive and physical changes, e.g. metabolic adaptations to dieting. The relative ineffectiveness of weight-loss strategies, such as vomiting, laxatives, and diuretics, are also highlighted. This approach leads to several therapeutic suggestions, or interventions. For example, choosing a goal weight range not a specific weight. For controlling bingeing and vomiting, it suggests that patients must stop dieting, as well as understand the biological and cultural factors that contribute to disturbed eating. Meal planning—quantity, quality, spacing, record-keeping—may also be helpful to interrupt the binge cycle. Education about the dangers of bulimia, and teaching techniques for relapse prevention, may be useful.

Several different programmes have been reported in the literature. One programme has been outlined in some detail (Weiss *et al.* 1985). It consists of: goals for change, information on bulimia, development of alternative coping strategies, changing thought patterns, self-esteem, perfectionism, anger, and assertiveness, societal expectations, enhancing body image, summary, going forward, and relapse prevention.

Although the primary role of psycho-education is to act as a foundation or structure for other interventions (Olmsted & Kaplan 1995), it has been suggested that it may be a cost-effective first step in a stepped-care approach. Ideally it is delivered in a group format, and this can be in a large group.

The Toronto group have conducted most of the research into psycho-education as a treatment in its own right. Their programme focuses on psychological and physiological sequelae, the multi-determined and self-perepetuating nature of the disorder, regulation of body weight, and the consequences of dieting, a non-dieting approach to eating, and coping with change. They provide information and advice on self-care strategies, including self-monitoring, meal planning, stimulus control, problem solving, and cognitive restructuring. Treatment is conducted in five 90-min sessions over 4 weeks. In an evaluation of the programme, they found a clinically significant change in symptoms of eating disorders, including behaviour, although scores on measures of personality disturbance were little changed. At follow-up over 3–5 months (of 76% of the sample), they found reductions in frequency of bingeing and vomiting were generally maintained (Davis *et al.* 1990b).

This approach has been compared with individual CBT. CBT was better only for patients who had more severe symptoms, though CBT was better overall. The authors suggest a sequencing model for treatment (Garner, Garfinkel & Irvine 1986)— educational treatment then psychotherapy for those who need it (Olmsted *et al.* 1991).

Another study found no additional benefit from seven extra sessions of psychotherapy, using a group CBT approach (Davis *et al.* 1997b).

Psycho-education has also been computerized, and evaluated in a mixed group of eating disorder patients. The aim was health education, rather than symptom reduction, i.e. to change attitudes and knowledge. Information was provided, then tests and feedback, with information not learned being repeated. It covered similar areas to those covered by the Toronto group, except for coping strategies. Evidence suggested that it improved knowledge and attitudes (Andrewes *et al.* 1996).

An Australian group has used a version of psycho-education called nutritional counselling. This aimed to modify restrained eating. It was primarily educational, with some behavioural and cognitive elements. It included: information on the consequences of bingeing and vomiting; information and discussion of metabolic processes, energy requirements, effects of starvation, body weight, meal planning; advice on meals, quantity, content, frequency, stimulus control; meal preparation advice, introducing feared foods; information about foods. It had a theoretical rationale—restrained eating causes bingeing. Treatment took place in groups, with 15 2-h sessions, over 3 months. It was compared with stress management. Both treatments were effective, but the nutritional management group responded more rapidly, and bingeing decreased faster (Laessle *et al.* 1991).

This treatment has been compared with fluoxetine. While there was some additional benefit of fluoxetine during active treatment, the results suggested that stopping the drug may lead to increase in symptoms (Beumont *et al.* 1997b).

The Australian group have described their treatment in detail (e.g. Beumont *et al.* 1997a; Beumont & Touyz 1995). It involves taking a detailed dietary history, including eating patterns, weight fluctuations from childhood to now, methods of weight control, foods avoided, reason for avoidance, purging, and binge-eating. This should also identify beliefs about nutrition and attitudes towards eating, of the patient, and of other family members. Education is used to correct faulty nutritional knowledge, e.g. about energy and nutrient requirements. It can be conducted individually or in a group. Topics to cover include energy input, activity, and weight control; nutrient content of foods; dangers of dieting and purging; nutritional requirements for good health and weight maintenance; role of dieting in triggering bingeing; role of normal eating in reducing urge to binge. Patients keep a food diary, plan meals, use stimulus-control strategies, introduce feared foods, learn how to deal with lapses, and how to plan for dealing with relapse. Key family members are involved. Unlike the Toronto group's programme, it includes behavioural interventions in addition to simple education.

At present, it is not known whether psycho-education is a necessary part of treatment when used with other interventions. The relevant 'dismantling' studies have not been conducted. Its mechanisms of action are also unclear.

Feminist treatments

These are not tied to a single theory or approach, although they are often associated with dynamic therapies. Some general principles may be extracted, however, and these are considered below. The main goals, features, and strategies are summarized in Table 10.5.

Treatment usually encourages women to reject cultural norms on a personal and political level, and to derive self-worth from things other than social norms for female attractiveness. It encourages women to change culturally prescribed roles that are oppressive to women, and to develop strengths that are often devalued by culture, e.g. they may support women's decisions to deviate from prescribed social norms. Some argue that women should also become politically active—to change the oppressive cultural standards responsible for distress in women. In treatment, feminists try to minimize the traditional power differential between therapist and client. They place emphasis on empowerment—including self-differentiation and self-determination. There tends to be greater attention to relationships, use of groups, and more interest in the therapeutic relationship. Some have focused particularly on the treatment of sexual and other forms of abuse, e.g. inadequate fathering, conflicting messages about sexuality, differential treatment of sons and daughters, and the assumption daughters serve as emotional caregivers. Feminist therapists may be more self-disclosing in treatment, more informal, more willing to be nurturing, and to advocate on behalf of patients. They often try to re-value affect—and this has led to interest in experiential therapies,

Table 10.5 Goals, strategies and features of feminist approaches to treatment

Goals	Strategies and features
To encourage right to reject cultural norms (personal and political), derive self-worth from things other than social norms for attractiveness	Minimize power difference between patient and therapist; encourage self-determination and self-differentiation; emphasize relationships; often use groups; focus on abuse; interested in experiential therapies.

such as art therapy (Rust 1995), music therapy (Slobada 1995), and psychodrama (Levens 1995) (for examples of the use of these see: Dokter 1995; and Lawrence 1987). They note how therapist gender can influence the content and process of therapy, e.g. in disclosure of sexual abuse.

Feminist researchers have also questioned the objectivity of research, and the automatic generalization of research findings based on samples of men to the female population (Gilbert & Thompson 1996).

Feminist influences are evident in all treatments, but are particularly apparent in dynamic therapy, where they have been explicitly developed and formulated. For example, there is a detailed account of feminist psycho-analytic treatment for BN in Orbach's edited book (Bloom 1987). Treatment had three themes or tracks. They were:

(1) understanding that the symptom had a function, i.e. that it was an attempt to take care of herself, and a way to avoid the pain of aloneness, conflicts, pressures, etc.;

(2) learning to take in food according to bodily needs; and

(3) to take in and hold onto the pleasure and satisfaction that can come from self-nurturance.

Work took place through the transference, and an important component was to give a different experience of a relationship—one that was consistent, reliable, and caring.

Family therapy

This has traditionally been considered important in the treatment of anorexia, especially young anorexics still living at home with their families. Models developed by two main groups, structural (Minuchin *et al.* 1978) in Philadelphia, and strategic (Selvini-Palazzoli 1978) in Milan, have typically been employed. The goals, features, and strategies of these approaches are outlined in Table 10.6.

Structural therapists are symptom orientated—they seek to change symptoms with an active, directive approach, not through insight. Strategic therapists are also symptom

Table 10.6 Goals, strategies and features associated with family therapy approaches to treatment

Goals	Strategies and features
Structural:	
To modify system and subsystem boundaries of the family.	Symptom focused; active; directive; paradoxical interventions; therapist joins the family; focus on structure.
Strategic:	
To find the interventions or perturbations that bring about desired change.	Symptom focused; look for hidden family gain; paradoxical interventions; indirect working; team working; focus on process.

oriented but they look for hidden family gain. Both may use paradoxical interventions. There are many other types of family therapy, e.g. behavioural family therapy (Falloon 1988), developed for schizophrenia, but these have not generally been widely used in clinical practice in BN.

Structural family therapy

This is concerned with subsystems within families, with the boundaries between the different subsystems, and those between the family system and wider environment. The therapist 'joins' the family and takes part in its transactions. She observes boundaries between people, alignments (coalition and alliances), and notes who has the power, and who makes the decisions. She also needs to know the functions available to the family—do they always operate in the same way or do they use a variety of functions to suit different circumstances. It is also helpful to know about flexibility or rigidity, coherence or incoherence—how drastic changes are when they do occur in family functioning. Once the therapist has an idea of its structure, then she needs to decide how far the problem they are seeking help for is related to their way of functioning. If it is, then she needs to intervene to alter the structure. Work then takes place to modify the system and subsystem boundaries.

Strategic family therapy

This is also referred to as systemic—though looking at systems is part of most family therapy.[2]

This aims for second-order change. It uses indirect methods and focuses on process, and the interaction in which the symptom exists. The symptoms of the identified patient are expressions of the way the whole family system is functioning. Focus on the symptom may make it worse, and may reinforce the idea that the patient is the problem, not the family system. The therapist devises a plan, and may use reframing—give new meaning to the behaviours and attitudes of family members. Therapists tend to work in teams, and may use one-way screens to observe sessions, so that one therapist can offer advice to the therapist with the family. The family is seen as a unit with certain properties that will respond in certain ways to particular interventions. The therapist must find the interventions or 'perturbations' that will bring about the desired change.

Often the distinctions between the different types of family therapy are not at all clear. For example, direct methods of change can be systemic, and strategic if they focus on the family as a whole, and are designed to produce change in the way the family functions as a group.

The Maudsley hospital in London has been a centre of family therapy for eating disorders, mostly focused on anorexia nervosa, but also BN. A variety of approaches are

---

[2] Most family therapies could also be called strategic, because the therapist is likely to use some strategy to produce change.

used, including a family meal, to help assess the family structure and organization. The approach is influenced by both Minuchin and Selvini-Palazzoli—especially the idea that the family is organized round the symptoms of the patient. It also draws on non-systemic techniques. Direct techniques are used (with an emphasis on parental consistency), to help parents manage the patients' symptoms, together with indirect methods, paradoxes, behavioural strategies, and psychodynamic interpretations. It has two components—helping parents manage the child's problem, and the more traditional family therapy interventions.

Emotionally focused family therapy has also been described for BN (Johnson *et al.* 1998). This is based on attachment theory. It aims to modify the distressing cycles of interaction that create and maintain attachment insecurity in family members, particularly in the patient, and foster positive cycles of accessibility and responsiveness. First it is important to identify the attachment patterns and negative cycles associated with the problem. This may involve a combination of dyadic, triadic, and individual and family sessions. The therapist identifies the negative emotion that primes this cycle, and reframes the problem in the context of attachment needs. This de-escalates negative interactions and helps elicit cohesion and collaboration. The therapist must then explore and engage with the disowned or unformulated attachment emotions and needs, and integrate them into the family system, so that new problem-solving occurs. Both experiential—for exploring and reformulating intrapsychic responses—and structural family therapy techniques—for changing interactions—are used. The main techniques for exploring intrapsychic experience are: focusing on and reflecting experience; validating the individual's perspectives and responses; expanding experience by evocative exploration using open questions; heightening such responses by use of imagery, repetition, and empathic interpretations. For restructuring interactions, the main techniques are: reflecting and describing cycles of interaction and their impact on the family; framing individual responses in the context of cycles and attachment needs; and directly shaping interactions.

A small pilot study suggested treatment was effective, but many declined to participate in family therapy, either because they did not want their family involved, or because they had not told their family about the problem.

The Maudsley group included a small number of bulimic patients in a study of family therapy for anorexia nervosa. Family therapy was no more effective than individual psychotherapy, and most had a poor outcome (Russell *et al.* 1987). Other studies with (mostly) low-weight bulimics produce inconsistent findings (Dare & Eisler 1995). A small open study of bulimics (adolescents) (Dodge *et al.* 1995) suggests that it can be effective (but there were only eight patients and no comparison treatment).

Vandereycken (1987) suggests that restructuring family interactions is not usually enough on its own for eating disorder patients—and a more intensive, multimodal approach is needed. Indeed, family therapy is now often part of a multimodal treatment programme. This may include techniques from different schools, and also some individual work.

Interpersonal

This is a short-term focal psychotherapy. The aim is to identify and modify any inter-personal problems accompanying the eating disorder, rather than the eating disorder itself. It is non-directive and non-interpretive, and was originally devised for the treat-ment of depression (Klerman *et al.* 1984). Its main goals, features and strategies are summarized in Table 10.7.

Interpersonal problems are identified by studying situations in which binge-eating occurs. Treatment then focuses on ways to change these problems. Finally, there is a review of what has been learned and discussion of ways to apply it in the future (Fairburn *et al.* 1986b). It seems to be an effective treatment (Fairburn *et al.* 1991b). Changes are slower to develop than in CBT but they continued during follow-up, of 12 months (Fairburn *et al.* 1991b). Problems are usually in one of four areas: grief, interpersonal role disputes, role transitions, or interpersonal deficits. There is not always a clear relationship between the interpersonal problems and eating disorder. The focus is on the present, and the therapist is active but not directive. The focus is on attempts to change, and the aim is to clarify, summarize, and stress the need to change—to provide general encouragement, not encouragement to do specific things. It has been suggested that it may work through realization that change elsewhere can be achieved in the eating problem too. Mood and self-esteem improvement may decrease the tendency to diet, while increased social activity reduces unstructured time and the opportunity to binge. Finally, reduced interpersonal stress may reduce direct triggers (Fairburn 1997).

Others have suggested that the coping model is central to IPT (and CBT), and provides an explanation for change (Christiano & Mizes 1997). IPT (and CBT), for example, may both work by facilitating accurate appraisal and adaptive coping.

Behavioural

Early on there were a few single case studies of behavioural techniques. Kenny & Solyom (1971) used a form of aversion therapy to treat binge-eating. Linden (1980) used a combination of meal planning, stimulus control techniques, and alternative responses. Two studies used relaxation (Mizes & Fleece 1986; Mizes & Lohr 1983), although not with great or lasting benefits. The main goals, features and strategies of behavioural treatments are summarized in Table 10.8.

Table 10.7 Goals, strategies and features associated with interpersonal therapy

Goals	Strategies and features
To identify and modify any interpersonal problems accompanying the eating problem.	Non-directive; non-interpretive; identify problems binges occur in and change the problems—grief, interpersonal role deficits, role transitions, interpersonal deficits; provide general encouragement.

Table 10.8 Goals, strategies and features associated with behavioural therapies

Goals	Strategies and features
Exposure and response prevention:	
Exposure to feared stimuli and prevention of habitual escape response.	Focus on control over vomiting; use exposure to food, settings; graded hierarchy to feared foods, may challenge cognitions; exposure outside sessions.
Cue exposure:	
To identify conditioned stimulus (CS) for binge-eating; break CS–UCS (unconditioned stimulus) link.	Bulimia is an addiction; exposure to cues while preventing eating.

The most popular behavioural treatment has been exposure and response prevention (ERP), based on the anxiety reduction model. The format of this treatment is based on the treatment of obsessive-compulsive disorders. It has two main components. The first is exposure to the feared stimulus in the presence of the therapist, i.e. eating particular foods or amount of food. The second is prevention of the habitual escape response, vomiting. Unlike CBT, it focuses on gaining control over vomiting, not binge-eating. Repeated exposure to anxiety provoking eating situations will elicit distressing feelings. These extinguish as the patient discovers that the feared consequences do not occur, or that it is possible to control these feelings without vomiting. ERP usually begins as an intensive treatment, with three sessions a week, to speed learning. Treatment can be individual or group. Patients are encouraged to eat an amount that causes a strong urge to vomit, then not allowed to vomit. Sessions are relatively lengthy, up to two hours. Patients are advised to practice the technique with several feared foods, eating normal amounts or just above normal amounts, i.e. enough food to get anxious. A graded hierarchy may be used to tackle different feared foods, and the therapist may also encourage the patient to challenge cognitions during the session, e.g. about food and nutrition, weight, physical appearance, vomiting, binge-eating, dieting, and pressure to be thin. Exposure is required at home, once gains have made in the session, to encourage transfer of learning (Leitenberg & Rosen 1986).

Treatment studies

Some single case studies, with promising outcomes, have been conducted (Rosen & Leitenberg 1982). A series of five patients, for example, found four out of five improved in eating behaviour and attitudes, depression, and self-esteem.

But some aspects of the model were not supported. Heart rate did not rise and fall in parallel with eating, except in one subject. Not all subjects reported an increase in anxiety prior to vomiting. There was no evidence that an increase in 'normal' eating was linked to reduced anxiety, or vice versa (Leitenberg, *et al.* 1984).

Giles *et al.* (1985), in an open trial, found treatment based on Rosen & Leitenberg's model to be effective.

In a controlled (group) study, exposure and response-prevention groups did slightly better than a CBT group on vomiting and amount of food consumed in one of the test meals, but all treated groups improved on behaviour, attitudes, self-esteem, and depression (Leitenberg *et al.* 1988).

One study compared exposure and response prevention of bingeing and ERP of vomiting. They produced similar results (Schmidt & Marks 1988), but some patients reported that exposure to vomiting was aversive (Rossiter & Wilson 1985), and there was a high drop out in the treatment (Schmidt & Marks 1989).

Other behavioural treatments

Hsu based treatment on the binge cycle modified from Garfinkel & Garner (1982). The focus was on binge-eating. Patients received instructions on balanced meals and meal planning. Antecedents of bingeing were identified and alternative strategies, and inter-personal problem-solving, were taught. About half the sample improved markedly, but this was not a controlled trial (Hsu & Holder 1986).

Cue exposure

Cue exposure has been used as a treatment (Jansen *et al.* 1989b). This is based on the conceptualization of bulimia as an addiction. The therapist identifies the conditioned stimuli for binge-eating, then aims to break the CS–UCS link. Patients are exposed to the contextual cues that precede a binge, while prevented from eating. Exposure sessions take place daily. Patients may also eat a preload of binge food (the UCS) in a place not predicting a binge, then confront herself with the binge food and contextual cues without eating. Treatment was successful in a single case (Jansen *et al.* 1989b). The frequency of binge-eating decreased, mood improved, and self-talk became less dichotomous and irrational. Craving also declined within and between sessions.

A small controlled study has also been conducted in obese binge-eaters. Both experimental and control treatment were effective in reducing binge frequency, but cue exposure produced abstinence in all six (vs. 33% in the other group) after treatment and at 1-year follow-up (Jansen *et al.* 1992a).

Differential reinforcement

This has also been used successfully as a stimulus control procedure to treat bingeing and vomiting (Posobiec & Renfrew 1988).

Eclectic treatments

A wide variety of eclectic treatments have been proposed for BN. These draw on a wide variety of models. Some have been described in detail, and some have also been evaluated.

Lacey (1983) describes a programme that makes use of behavioural and counselling techniques, then moves on to insight-oriented psychotherapy in half-hour individual sessions. Patients also attend an insight-oriented group for one and a half hours. Treatment lasts 10 weeks. The aim is to remove all symptoms of the eating disorder, and enable the patient to deal with emotional and relationship problems. No formal evaluation was conducted but all had fewer symptoms after treatment, and 24 out of 30 had stopped bingeing and vomiting (Lacey 1983).

Lacey (1995) also describes an intensive in-patient treatment (for multi-impulsive bulimia), with follow-up day-patient programme. Behavioural strategies are used, there is an occupational therapy programme round food and eating, and the unit is run on milieu lines—the staff try to explore underlying psychological processes in patients' interactions with peers and staff. There are psychodynamic groups, CBT groups, and individual psychodynamic therapy using the transference, art therapy, psychodrama, and education. The programme has been evaluated (Lacey 1995) and seems effective.

An intensive out-patient group treatment, based on an Alcoholics Anonymous model, and on behavioural and cognitive models, has been described. It includes educational techniques, self-monitoring, behavioural analysis, stimulus control, alternative behaviours to deal with antecedents, stress management, assertiveness, reward and reinforcement, and cognitive change (Mitchell *et al.* 1983a).

An out-patient programme, a combination of individual, group, and body image work has been described. Body image therapy aims to create a greater awareness of body image distortion, to lessen it and clarify the relationship between negative body image and disordered eating. It also heightens awareness of relationships between the mother's body image and her daughter's, and decreases boundary diffusion with significant others. Exercises are designed to help patients describe and interpret their own internal sensations, the ways they use bodies as expression—such exercises often focus on differentiation from the mother. Treatment also uses imagery, art and movement to assess feelings about the body and rework past material related to the development of body image. This work also serves to increase control of perceptions and feelings about her body image, using imagery, movement and art exercises (Wooley & Wooley 1984). A residential programme has similar content but is more intensive.

An in-patient programme based on an anxiety reduction model and exposure has been described (Tuschen & Bents 1995). It also included cognitive interventions.

A behaviourally oriented group treatment has also been described. This included problem-solving, coping skills training, and detailed behavioural analysis. It sought to modify the stimulus conditions and consequences of stressful situations. It included role play, relaxation, planning, and problem-solving, communication skills and expression of feelings, as well as altering dysfunctional attitudes. It also had a nutritional aspect—planned eating, with reinforcements, information on nutrition, and consequences of inadequate diet/bulimic behaviour. In a small study it was more effective than being on the waiting list, at the end of treatment and at 3 and 6 month follow-up (Laessle *et al.* 1987a).

There are also other amalgams, e.g. developmental-systemic-feminist (Bryant-Waugh 2000). Some specific treatments have also been evaluated (although not described in detail), mostly showing some effect. This includes supportive-expressive therapy (Garner *et al.* 1993; Wilfley *et al.* 1993). Motivational enhancement therapy has also been used (not as a treatment by itself but to enhance commitment, and reduce drop out) (Treasure *et al.* 1999).

Summary

Part one of this chapter considered psychodynamic approaches. Ego psychology, object relations, and self psychology contributions were summarized. Bruch's influence and ideas were also considered. These depart from traditional dynamic treatment, and have much in common with cognitive therapy.

Part two considered treatment based on socio-cultural theories. This included prevention programmes, and the role of public health. To date, such programmes have not been very effective. The recent development of a more comprehensive and detailed theory may be helpful with this.

Part three considered psycho-educational programmes as a primary treatment for BN. These may be particularly important in a stepped care approach.

Part four discussed the influence of feminist principles on treatment. Although these have had an impact on all treatments for BN, they have had a particular impact on dynamic therapy.

Part five considered family therapy approaches—structural and strategic, and recent studies that have combined elements of both. These approaches are not particularly common in BN. A related treatment, which focuses on interpersonal problems (interpersonal psychotherapy) was also considered.

Part six discussed behaviour therapy, particularly exposure and response prevention, but also other behaviourally based treatments (e.g. cue exposure). These treatments are not currently very widely used in clinical practice.

Part seven considered some of the amalgams of different approaches that have been described, and in some cases, evaluated in the literature.

Chapter 11

Cognitive therapy

Overview

This chapter describes and presents examples of cognitive behaviour therapy (CBT) and cognitive therapy (CT) for BN. It is in two parts, with detailed clinical material used to illustrate the two approaches. Part one presents treatment based on Fairburn's model. Part two presents treatment based on the model described by Cooper and colleagues.

Treatment based on Fairburn's model

The model for this treatment is outlined in Fairburn *et al.* (1986a). The typical treatment based on it is outlined in several places, including the following articles or book chapters (Fairburn 1985; Fairburn & Cooper 1989; Fairburn *et al.* 1993b). It is also described in two self-help books (Cooper 1995, revised version; Fairburn 1995). The approach outlined here is similar to, and based on, these outlines. The approach has been employed in several treatment trials, initially by Fairburn *et al.* (1991b) and subsequently, for example, by Agras *et al.* (2000b), and others.

Practical points

Patients are usually seen for a fixed number of sessions, typically 20, and for a limited number of follow-up appointments for review. Treatment lasts about 20 weeks. If the eating problem is severe, they may be seen twice a week at first, particularly if they are bingeing several times a day. If they have days free from bingeing, then it is more usual (or possible) to see them once a week.

General principles

The treatment is based on Beck's cognitive therapy of depression, and shares many of its' principles. For example, it is problem-focused, and concerned with the present and future rather than the past. It focuses on maintaining factors, and not aetiology. Treatment is an active process. It is collaborative, and mutual trust and respect are important. The therapist also needs to be knowledgeable about bulimia, including its physical complications, and about body weight regulation, dieting, and body image disturbance.

Assessment

Before treatment a thorough assessment is recommended. This involves a full history, and mental state examination, as well as an assessment of physical health—to check that the patient can be seen as an out-patient and does not need in patient care. Fairburn identifies four indications for hospitalization. These are as follows: very depressed, risk of suicide, pregnant and in first trimester (because of the risk of spontaneous abortion), failure to get better as an out-patient. Such indications tend to be rare.

Outcome measures

Assessment should typically include self-report measures, to help assess outcome. In practice, several different measures can be used. Usual measures in routine clinical practice may include: the EAT (Garner & Garfinkel 1979), a measure of the symptoms associated with eating disorders; the Beck Depression Inventory (BDI) (Beck *et al.* 1961), a measure of the symptoms of depression; and the Rosenberg Self-esteem Scale (RSE) (Rosenberg 1965), a brief measure of self-esteem. This is probably a minimum. Measures should be given after assessment and then again at the end of treatment. One additional useful but longer measure is the EDI (Garner *et al.* 1983b). Outcome can also be assessed by examining behaviours recorded in the eating diary—a key aspect of treatment. The patient is asked to record all episodes of bingeing and vomiting (and other things) in a daily diary. The frequency of bingeing and vomiting at the beginning and end of treatment is an important measure of progress.

Referral

Susie was referred by a specialist in psychiatry, alerted by her GP, because she had problems with her eating. She had been seen together with her husband by the counsellor at the GP surgery for the past three months for help with relationship difficulties. The counselling had been helpful—Susie and her husband were arguing less, but she now wanted to focus on her eating problem, which had not improved during this time.

Current problems

When seen, Susie said that her main problem was definitely her eating (and not her relationship). She described it as 'uncontrollable' and said that it ruled her life. She was experiencing frequent episodes of binge-eating, during which she felt that she had lost control over her eating. At such times she would eat large quantities of food, usually in a relatively short space of time. She binged on sweet foods and confectionery—including biscuits, cake, and chocolate. She tried to counteract the effects of bingeing by vomiting—to make sure she got rid of all the food she had eaten. She binged between one and two times a day, usually in the evenings, sometimes in the early morning, and always when she was alone.

Susie was preoccupied with food and eating. She was constantly dieting and set herself a variable limit of 400–1200 calories each day—depending on how 'good' she had been the previous day. She was also preoccupied with critical thoughts about her weight and shape, describing herself as 'grotesquely fat'. She weighed herself up to 10 times a day, and exercised to lose weight. She went swimming, cycling, or jogging for 2–3 hours, three to four times a week.

Susie also reported being depressed—primarily about her inability to control her eating, but also about the constant thoughts of food and eating. She said that she occasionally wished that she could fall asleep and not wake up (always after a 'bad food day'). However, these thoughts were always short-lived, and she said that she would never do anything to harm herself.

Background information

Susie was aged 30. She was married, and worked as a physiotherapist in a general hospital. Her husband was away a lot, but they usually managed to spend weekends together. They did not have any children. Susie felt a bit isolated, they had only recently moved to the area, and had not yet made many friends. However, she was enjoying her job. She was in good physical health, and the report from her GP indicated that her electrolyte levels were in the normal range. She was keen to start a family, but said she wanted to overcome her eating disorder first. Plans for a baby had been an important factor in her decision to seek help.

Recent therapy

Counselling had been 'helpful' in talking over the difficulties between Susie and her husband, but it had not helped the eating problem.

Past treatment

In the past (before her marriage), Susie had had treatment for severe and disabling panic attacks. She had spent seven weeks as an in-patient in a psychiatric hospital. Her eating problem came to light after she took an overdose, triggered by the fear that she would never be able to stop bingeing and vomiting. She was offered follow-up, focused on her eating problem, but when the therapist left after only a few weeks, no further treatment was arranged, and Susie did not seek out further help.

View on CBT

Susie did not initially seem very optimistic about changing—she had had the problem for over ten years, and had tried several times to sort it out herself. However, she wanted a practical approach focused on her eating. She was able to establish good rapport, and was motivated by plans for a family. She was realistic about the likely speed of change, and the need to put a great deal of effort into treatment.

History

Susie had first tried to diet when she was 9 years old. When she was 14 she was sent away to school where she dieted and lost weight. Between the ages of 14 and 18 she probably met DSM-IV criteria for anorexia nervosa (American Psychiatric Association 1994). She started to binge soon after leaving school, and rapidly gained weight. After a few months, worried about the weight increase, she started to vomit after bingeing. She had continued to binge and vomit, and diet, ever since. Her symptoms had fluctuated over the years, but never entirely disappeared. They tended to increase with external stress, including problems at work and difficulties with her husband.

Current coping

To control her bingeing Susie tried to avoid food and eating. She also tried to keep busy so that there would be little or no opportunity to binge.

Weight

Her weight was currently in the normal weight range; her BMI[1] was 23.

Family background

Susie described her father as distant. He had emphasized sporting and academic achievement to Susie. She spent more time with her mother, but described her as rather detached, and unable to provide much emotional support. An older brother had died aged two before Susie was born. Susie's husband knew about the eating problem, but no one else did.

Assessment

A general assessment was conducted. A detailed assessment of Susie's eating behaviour was then completed. This covered the areas recommended by Fairburn *et al.* (1993), including current state of the eating problem, its history, current adjustment, previous treatment experience, personal and family history (see details above). Susie also completed the EAT, BDI, and RSE. There were no indications that she was unsuitable for out-patient help.

Diagnosis

Susie had a DSM-IV bulimia nervosa diagnosis (American Psychiatric Association 1994). Her questionnaire scores indicated rather more distress (EAT score = 56; BDI score = 34) and lower self-esteem (RSE score = 20) than is typical of the average patient with bulimia nervosa.

Goals for treatment

Susie wanted to stop bingeing and vomiting, and she wanted to be less preoccupied with food and eating.

Explanation of treatment

The structure and content of treatment was explained to Susie. The three stages to treatment were then explained. The first would be to explain the rationale for the treatment, and help Susie regain control over her eating. The second would be to deal with factors maintaining the problem. The third would be to make sure the changes were maintained, and would continue to be after treatment ended. Susie was told that

---

[1] kg/m^2.

most people improve greatly with this treatment, and stay improved once it ends. She was also told that while it was usual to still have some problems at the end of treatment, it was also usual to continue to improve after treatment had ended. She was told that a total 'cure' was unlikely, her eating was likely to remain 'an Achilles heel' but that, although it might be problematic at times of great stress, this should only be temporary. She was told that she was also likely to remain more sensitive than most people about food, eating, weight, and shape. The need to put maximum effort and commitment into treatment, including into homework, was emphasized.

Susie thought that the treatment might well be helpful. The therapist also thought that she might be helped by the approach. It coincided with what she was looking for, after having received non-directive counselling, during which very little attention had been paid to her eating problem. She seemed well-motivated. She also seemed realistic about the likely speed of change, and recognized that she would have to work hard. The idea of her eating as an Achilles heel made sense to her. Her marriage was no longer a source of major stress, and she could concentrate fully on her eating problem. Her husband was supportive of her attempts to change, and they both had plans for the future. She was very motivated by the thought of starting a family.

Stage 1: sessions 1–8

This stage of treatment had two aims. The first was to explain the CBT rationale. The second was to replace binge-eating with a stable pattern of regular eating.

Session 1

The rationale was explained, using Susie's terms and words, as a series of vicious circles. These were as follows:

• Vicious circle: binge-eating leads to vomiting (see Fig. 11.1).

Susie nearly always vomited following binge-eating, to compensate for having eaten so much, and to make sure that she did not gain weight. If she managed not to vomit (e.g. if there were people around) then she compensated in another way, usually by going for a long run.

• Vicious circle: vomiting encourages overeating (see Fig. 11.1).

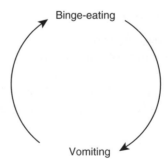

Fig. 11.1 Binge-eating and vomiting vicious circle.

Susie was aware that knowing that she could vomit often meant that she ate more than she might otherwise have done. She would often find herself thinking 'I can always get rid of it afterwards'.

• Vicious circle: bingeing leads to dieting (see Fig. 11.2).

Each time that Susie binged she resolved to cut down on her eating. Immediately after bingeing she would avoid eating, to make sure that she did not gain weight.

• Vicious circle: dieting encourages binge-eating (see Fig. 11.2).

Susie had noticed that on 'successful' diet days (i.e. when she ate very little), she nearly always had a binge in the late evening.

Fairburn (1995) identifies three types of dieting: avoiding certain 'banned' foods; going for a long time without eating; and eating only small amounts. Susie recognized that she engaged in all of them at different times.

Two other key links in the model were also explained. These were as follows:

• Link: dieting increases concern about shape and weight (see Fig. 11.3).

Susie readily saw that avoiding eating, or limiting her food intake, increased her preoccupation with food and with eating, weight, and shape.

• Link: low self-esteem leads to dieting (see Fig. 11.4).

Susie recognized that she often did not feel very good about herself, and when this happened she would usually think of going on a diet.

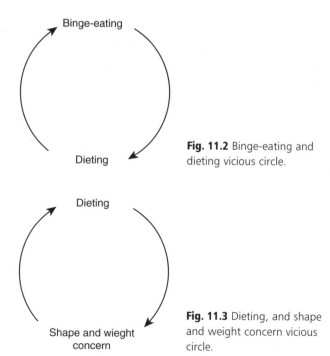

Binge-eating

Dieting

Fig. 11.2 Binge-eating and dieting vicious circle.

Dieting

Shape and wieght concern

Fig. 11.3 Dieting, and shape and weight concern vicious circle.

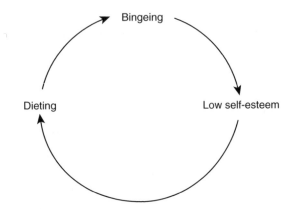

Fig. 11.4 Dieting, self-esteem and binge-eating vicious circle.

• Link: bingeing leads to low self-esteem (see Fig. 11.4).

Susie saw a connection between bingeing and feeling bad about herself. Feeling bad was her usual reaction after bingeing and vomiting

Socratic questioning (see Beck *et al.* 1979) (and a recent example of when Susie had binged and vomited) were used to help Susie to identify the vicious circles, and links described above, in her own behaviour and experience.

Susie and her therapist then identified three aspects to focus on in treatment. The first was her eating; the second was dieting; and the third included thoughts and feelings or concerns about weight and shape.

The initial focus was on Susie's eating. Monitoring was introduced, and the rationale for it was explained. This included finding out what, how much and when Susie was eating, and the circumstances in which eating was a problem.

Susie was reassured to learn that many people with an eating disorder feel very ashamed of what, and how much, they eat in a binge. She was give written instructions on how to monitor and prepare sheets to record her eating on. She was also asked to record any other important events, feelings or thoughts that occurred. It was emphasized it was important to fill the records in immediately after eating, or when key events occurred (for accuracy). Some of the potential difficulties with this were identified and coping strategies worked out.

Session 2

Much of the second session (and each session thereafter) was spent reviewing the monitoring sheets. A typical day for Susie can be seen in Table 11.1.

The therapist also helped Susie identify any additional thoughts during, or at the time of, the episodes of bingeing Susie had recorded. Links between thoughts, feelings, and behaviour were also sought. Standard cognitive therapy prompts, e.g. 'what was going through your mind as you ate this?', 'how did that make you feel?' and 'what did you do then?' were used.

Table 11.1 A typical eating day for Susie

Date	Time	Food and liquid consumed	V	P	Context
26/8	7.00	Coffee, skim milk×2		K	
	9.15	Coffee, skim milk		W	
	10.00	Half a biscuit			Should not be having this biscuit.
		4 biscuits			
		2 chocolate muffins			
		packet of sweets			
		2 bars of chocolate	V	W	
	11.30	Diet coke			
	12.20	Tuna salad			Trying to be good.
		Apple		W	
	1.45	Diet coke			Argued with Karen over rota.
		2 eclairs			
		2 iced buns			
		2 apple turnovers			
		bar of chocolate	V		
	3.00	coffee, black		W	
	4.00	orange juice			
	7.00	risotto			Couldn't stop eating, I hate myself
		salad			
		banana		K	
		half a loaf of bread—toast with butter and jam	V		

V=Vomiting; P=Place; K=Kitchen; W=Work.

Susie had completed her monitoring sheets, including a great deal of helpful detail. They confirmed what she had said at assessment—she was bingeing once or twice a day, often in the evenings, and always when she was alone. She had not binged at all over the weekend. Binges varied in size, but were often large, consisting of several thousand calories, and often consisted of confectionery, biscuits, cake, and chocolate. She had also eaten a lot of cereal, toast, and jam. She had also noted down a few thoughts, and triggering situations. There were two types of trigger: difficult situations at work; and concern that she had gained weight. Typical thoughts associated with bingeing were 'I'm so fat', 'I must eat less', 'I'm just going to go on getting heavier and heavier', 'I can't control my eating', 'I look disgusting', and 'I hate myself'. She had also recorded some feelings—'I feel so miserable', 'I'm down, depressed', and in relation to work stress—'I can't stop feeling so panicky, I'm really worried'.

Helped by the therapist, and Socratic questioning, Susie could see how her thoughts, feelings, and eating in these binge situations might be connected to each other.

Weekly weighing

Susie usually avoided weighing herself. As part of treatment she was asked to weigh herself once a week on a morning. Two main reasons were given for this. First, people who are trying to change their eating are usually very concerned they will gain weight once they stop vomiting, so it is useful to see what happens to their weight. This reflected Susie's fear that her weight would balloon if she stopped vomiting. Second, at a later point, reactions to weighing will be examined (and thoughts challenged). Thus it is useful to start to note down thoughts when weighing.

Sessions 3–8

Sessions followed a set format from session 3. First, Susie's monitoring sheets were reviewed, followed by any homework tasks set (i.e. strategies suggested for getting back control over eating). There followed discussion of any problems and progress. Finally, new homework tasks were assigned.

The model was continually reinforced when reviewing records, and setting homework tasks. The therapist highlighted any vicious circle links, and also asked Susie to identify these.

Education

Susie was given information on BMI ranges for under-weight, normal, and over-weight, and told what her own BMI was. She was advised to accept a range, not an absolute weight, above 18. She was given advice on the problems of low weight—physiological and psychological. She was also advised not to choose a weight range that could only be maintained by strict dieting. It was suggested that it might be better to decide on this after treatment, once she was eating properly. She was told that her weight was unlikely to affected by treatment. Advice that vomiting and laxative abuse are ineffective ways to control weight was given. Susie was also advised that vomiting is habit-forming—it encourages over-eating because the tendency is to think that you can eat more if you are going to vomit, and then to find that you need to eat more because vomiting is easier with a full stomach. Susie was also advised that dieting might have some adverse effects. The idea of a set-point weight that the body tries to defend was discussed.

To back up all this advice, Susie was given Garner's chapter (Garner *et al.* 1984b) to read for homework. This covers most of these topics, plus some socio-cultural issues.

Susie found the information helpful—she had lots of misinformation about dieting and weight control.

Advice on eating, vomiting, and laxative use

Susie was given advice on regular eating, i.e. three planned meals and two or three planned snacks per day. She was advised to go no longer than three hours between eating episodes. This plan was to be given high priority, whatever she was doing. She was advised to plan ahead, e.g. the night before, what she was going to eat the next day, and when she was going to eat it.

Susie's bingeing was quite severe, and she had few or no normal meals or snacks in her day (at weekends she 'picked' at food, and generally ate very little). She decided to introduce regular eating gradually, starting with breakfast. Once this was achieved she worked through the rest of the day. With her therapist she agreed on the food and amount she felt able to eat without vomiting first thing in the morning. This was a small bowl of cereal (with low fat milk) and one slice of toast (diet bread and low fat spread, at first). Initially Susie planned her morning breakfast the night before—she set out bowl and plate, cutlery, and a mug for coffee. She wrote down on her monitoring sheets exactly what she planned to eat. In the morning she practised stimulus control to lessen the chance of bingeing. She took out just enough for breakfast, then put the packets and loaf of bread where she could not see them, before starting to eat. At times when she felt she might binge, i.e. immediately after finishing her breakfast, she practised alternative activities. For example, she decided to spend some time in her garden, either weeding, or mowing the grass, to fill the time before leaving for work.

Susie continued to build up a pattern of normal eating and snacks, in small steps, using planning ahead, alternative behaviours (e.g. trips to the cinema, telephone calls, reading, television) and stimulus control (e.g. not buying binge foods, asking her husband to prepare his own packed lunches, cook his own supper).

As she gradually built up normal eating, Susie's bingeing decreased. She had some set-backs along the way, and found it difficult to make progress some days. These problems were reviewed in detail, to assess what had gone wrong, and to plan how the problem could be dealt with if it arose again. If a difficult situation was anticipated, advance planning was emphasized. Susie was advised that an up and down pattern of progress was more usual than a steady uphill course.

Susie's husband (Stephen) already knew about the problem, but the therapist wanted to make sure he understood the treatment, so that he could best support Susie. He had already read the educational chapter, as well as a book on eating disorders. He attended one session with Susie. Susie had a good grasp of the treatment and the rationale, and was able to explain it clearly to him. Stephen was anxious to know how he could best help. He confirmed that they were getting on better since Susie had been for counselling—there were fewer arguments. He had noticed a change in her since she had started to tackle her eating—she was less down, and a lot more confident. Susie was encouraged by this feedback.

Stage 2: sessions 9–16

This stage tackled dieting, concerns about weight and shape, and more general cognitive distortions. It also taught problem-solving—to deal with triggers for bingeing.

Treatment sessions followed the same pattern as before. Monitoring sheets were reviewed, then new topics introduced, followed by setting homework.

Dieting

Not eating for long periods had been tackled by planned eating. Next, avoidance of specific foods, and overall low-calorie intake were tackled. For specific avoided foods Susie created a hierarchy, from easiest to most difficult to eat. She then planned to introduce the easiest food, step by step, until she was able to eat a normal amount of it without feeling anxious. Other controls also needed to be relaxed, e.g. avoidance of eating food she had not prepared, and eating food at parties, and in restaurants.

Susie avoided most of the foods she binged on. She also ate lots of low-calorie foods, and tried to eat less than 1200 calories a day. She did not like eating food when she did not know how many calories were in it—this meant that she could not usually eat out. Together with her therapist, she prepared hierarchies—for specific avoided foods, for eating outside the home, and for foods that others had prepared. Susie gradually introduced these foods, starting with the least difficult. She also phased out diet food and substituted normal foods.

The seven steps of problem-solving, to deal with external triggers of bingeing, were taught. Susie first completed an example in a session, then went away to practice the technique for homework.

Susie's records suggested that stress at work was a major trigger for bingeing. The example worked on in the session took a recent situation of this from her records. She was then asked to implement the strategy if difficulties arose, and record it on the back of her monitoring sheets, together with the outcome.

In the next session, Susie had several examples of using problem-solving. One involved having to deal with an angry client, and another having to deal with a double-booking (not her fault). In both situations she had been tempted to binge. Instead she brainstormed possible solutions, weighed up the likely effectiveness and feasibility of each, and chose a solution. Then she defined the steps needed to carry out the solution, carried them out, and then evaluated the entire process. An example for the angry client can be seen in Table 11.2.

Shape and weight concern

Cognitive restructuring was used, initially in sessions, to deal with problematic thoughts, i.e. as identified from weekly weighing. A four-step approach was used. The thought was written down, evidence that supports it was identified, then evidence against it, then a reasoned conclusion was reached, even if this was not yet believed. Susie was also given assignments for homework that might provoke relevant thoughts. These included looking in a full-length mirror, trying on clothes in a shop, and putting on tight clothes.

Table 11.2 An example of Susie's problem solving

Problem:

Very angry client—the special equipment on order had not arrived. Did not like being shouted at when it was not my fault. Tempted to go off to lunch early, and binge.

Possible solutions:

Find someone to talk to, and let off steam.

Make a cup of coffee.

Tell client how to complain to the right person.

Go for a short walk outside.

Treat myself to a biscuit.

Phone Stephen.

Go off early, and do some shopping.

Evaluation:

Making coffee will give me a break but it will take me near food, and eating a biscuit will make it easier to binge. Shopping for something nice to wear will cheer me up, and be a treat after having a hard time, but it will also take me near food. A walk would be nice, but if I am by myself it will be easy to go to the shop and buy chocolate. Stephen will be too busy to talk to me. Telling the client how to complain will take the pressure off me. Finding someone to let off steam to will make it seem less awful.

Solution:

Give the client the name of the person to direct complaints to. Find Kerry, and tell her all about it.

Steps:

Look up name of person to complain to, write it out for the client. Call Kerry and see if she is free to have a chat.

Possible problems:

Kerry might be busy.

Possible solution:

Ask her to come over later when she is free.

Evaluation: Gave client name of the person to complain to—she actually seemed pleased I had bothered to find it. Kerry was busy, but said she would come over at 2 pm for a chat.

The thoughts Susie had centered on, 'I'm fat', and were all variations of this theme. A completed example of the four-step approach can be seen in Table 11.3, for a thought that Susie had when she tried on a tight skirt.

Attitudes

Susie's attitudes about weight and shape were identified. With the therapist she then looked at the advantages and disadvantages of holding them.

Table 11.3 Thought-challenging example for Susie

Thought:
I am so fat.

Evidence for:
I have gained two pounds this week.
I feel fat.

Evidence against:
Two pounds in one week is only a normal fluctuation—it will probably go down again.
Just because I feel fat, it does not mean I am fat.

Table 11.4 An example of challenging beliefs for Susie

Belief:
My weight and shape are the most important thing about me.

Disadvantages:
A person is more than their weight.
I overlook other (more important) qualities in myself.
When my weight goes up I feel terrible.

Advantages:
It is a quick and easy way to make a judgement about myself.
It makes life simple.

Susie had several beliefs, e.g. 'thinness is a good thing', 'if I get fat, everyone will despise me', 'fat is disgusting', 'my weight and shape are the most important thing about me'.

An example of how she looked at the advantages and disadvantages of the latter belief can be seen in Table 11.4.

Susie was also encouraged to examine how one really evaluates self-worth, initially in relation to her own view of others. She generated a long list of things on which self-esteem could be based, apart from weight and shape.

Stage 3: sessions 17–19

These last sessions were spaced out over several weeks. The aim was to make sure progress was maintained.

Susie was quite realistic about the future. She felt that she would always be vulnerable and would need to be careful. However, she said she would feel devastated if she had another binge. The difference between a lapse, a relapse, and a set-back was discussed and she was encouraged to think of a binge in the future as a set-back, and get back to normal as soon as possible. The idea of a review to learn the reason for it, so that it could be prevented next time, was introduced. The dangers, and indications for, dieting in the future were discussed.

Susie completed the questionnaires again—her scores were now all in the normal range. Her monitoring sheets indicated that she had not had any binges for four weeks. A follow-up appointment was arranged for a month's time. Susie was pleased with her progress. She subsequently decided to work further on building her self-esteem, using a self-help book based on cognitive therapy principles.

Treatment based on Cooper and colleagues' model

The model for this treatment is outlined in a self-help book (Cooper *et al.* 2000), and in a theoretical paper (Cooper *et al.* in press). Useful information on the developmental aspect of the formulation can be found in Cooper *et al.* (1998). See also Chapter 8, for more detail and differences between this and Fairburn's model.

Practical points

Treatment is usually for a fixed number of sessions, up to 14, with a number of follow-up appointments for review. Sessions are weekly to begin with, then spaced out once work on assumptions and beliefs begins (change is generally slower during this work, and more time is needed to practice exercises). Towards the end of treatment, there may be three or even four weeks between sessions. Treatment is based on the principles outlined by Beck for depression (Beck *et al.* 1979) and anxiety (Beck *et al.* 1985). It also draws on those outlined by J. S. Beck, particularly for assumption and core belief work (Beck 1995), but also in the general style and format of treatment sessions. It is problem-focused, and concerned with the present and future rather than the past (though it does also attend to this). It focuses primarily on maintaining factors (but also attempts to understand the development of the problem). Treatment is an active process, it is collaborative, and mutual trust and respect are important. It makes extensive use of Socratic questioning, guided discovery, behavioural experiments, thought-challenging using verbal (and written) strategies, summaries by therapist and patient, requests for feedback, regular homework, and audio-taping of sessions (for the patient to listen to each week and provide comments and feedback). Sessions have an agenda with the patient taking increasing responsibility for bringing items as the treatment progresses. The therapist needs to be knowledgeable about bulimia, including its physical complications, common eating and dieting myths, relevant recent research on weight and eating, and socio-cultural pressures related to weight and shape. Treatment attends to the principles identified as important on the cognitive therapy rating scale (Beck *et al.* 1979). This can be used by therapists (and their supervisors) to rate treatment sessions, and is an important part of self-supervision, continued learning and reflective practice. Supervision with experienced cognitive therapists is also recommended (and advisable).

Before treatment a thorough assessment must be undertaken, if this has not already been done. This should include a full history, mental state examination, and an assessment of physical health. A check should be made that the patient can be seen on an out-patient basis, i.e. no serious physical complications, or significant suicide risk. The therapist should also check that bulimia nervosa is the primary problem (eating difficulties may be secondary to other significant problems). The patient should desire help with this (even if doubtful about the possible benefit and usefulness of treatment), and be willing and able to commit to treatment at present (practical problems such as childcare may need to be overcome). The therapist should also try to assess whether the patient has major depression that requires treatment in its own right (this can be difficult to assess, but if it seems to be the case then this may also need to be a focus of treatment).

Assessment should always include self-report measures, both to help identify treatment targets and to assess outcome. This might include the EAT (Garner & Garfinkel 1979), BDI (Beck *et al.* 1961), and RSE (Rosenberg 1965) as a minimum. It is also helpful to give measures of cognition and behaviours derived from the model. Two cognitive measures are useful—the Eating Thoughts Questionnaire (Cooper *et al.* submitted a), a measure of three key types of automatic thought, and the Eating Disorder Belief Questionnaire (Cooper *et al.* 1997), which assesses negative self-beliefs and underlying assumptions characteristic of eating disorders. Also useful is a measure of behaviours that help maintain the disorder—the Eating Behaviours Questionnaire (Cooper *et al.* submitted a). Weekly assessment of bingeing and vomiting and laxative abuse should also be made. This can be done using a brief questionnaire—the Eating Disorder Rating Scale (Cooper *et al.* unpublished), which assesses weekly change in key behaviours and thoughts. It is usually given at the beginning of each treatment session.

If the therapist is not medically qualified, then a physician should do a physical check, and take responsibility for monitoring important physical parameters, including electrolyte levels.

Referral

Becky was referred to a specialist eating disorder service. She had recently been to see her GP, feeling depressed, and desperate about her inability to control her eating.

Current eating problem

When seen, Becky said that she felt as though she was 'bingeing all the time'. Her eating felt 'completely out of control'. She had two types of bingeing episode. In one she ate a normal meal then continued eating. In the other she bought lots of chocolate, sweets, and biscuits, and ate them over the course of an hour or so. Both involved 'objectively' large amounts of food (as defined by the EDE (Cooper & Fairburn 1987). She had two to three binges each day, and rarely went a day without at least one binge.

Becky also felt fat, despite knowing that she was not. She did not often weigh herself (a small weight increase made her very miserable) and she went to the gym whenever she had a spare moment, and was exercising two to three hours a day. She wanted to be thinner (thinner than was probably healthy). She occasionally took laxatives to lose calories and prevent weight gain.

Other problems

Becky's mood fluctuated from day to day. Sometimes she felt weepy and tearful, and sometimes she felt very angry 'for no particular reason'. She had no thoughts of self-harm. Most of the time, however, she said, 'I hate myself'.

Partner

Becky had a boyfriend, but said she 'wondered why he was interested in her'. He seemed worried about her, and had visited the GP with her.

Background

Becky was aged 24, and worked as a PA to a successful businessman in a small company. She was not happy in her job—she felt it was not challenging enough, but had little idea what she would enjoy doing.

Previous treatment

Becky had not had any psychological treatment for her eating problem, although her GP had treated her with Prozac for several weeks (for the mood disturbance and for the bulimia). Becky felt this had not helped much, and she had stopped it. The GP had then tried several anti-depressants for her depressed mood, but these had given her lots of side-effects. She was not currently on any medication.

Becky had a long history of eating problems (see below), including a period of severe anorexia nervosa during her teens, for which she had been hospitalized.

Family

Becky was reluctant to talk about her family when first seen. She lived with her mother and step-father, and no longer had contact with her father. Her mother had a long history of mental health problems.

View of treatment

Becky liked the description of treatment, and thought it was 'worth a go'. She felt that she had reached 'breaking point' and 'had to do something'. She liked the idea that treatment would focus on how she saw herself, as well as her eating. She said her self-esteem had always been very low. She often felt 'like attacking myself', although she had never self-harmed.

History of eating problem

Becky had first become weight-conscious at age 5, but had not dieted until age 11 or 12. Food then became a battleground at home—with Becky refusing to eat and her mother trying to force her to do so. This continued for several years. At one stage her weight became so low that she was admitted to hospital for re-feeding. On leaving home for university she started bingeing and, despite regular vomiting, she gained weight. Since then her weight had fluctuated, but had never dipped below what was normal for her height and age. The bingeing and vomiting had continued, and remained fairly constant, unless she had no opportunity to carry it out for a few day, e.g. on a recent trip to Thailand with friends.

Coping

Becky reported that she now made little attempt to control her eating. She coped by 'getting on with things' and ignoring it. She kept busy and belonged to several clubs, including a choir group.

Strengths

Becky had done well at school; she had a job and a supportive partner. She also had friends and many interests.

Weight

This was in the normal weight range, and her BMI was 22. Becky's mother and her partner knew that she still had an eating problem, but she had not told any of her friends. Becky was advised to ask for a full physical assessment, including blood count, from her GP. These indicated low but normal electrolyte levels.

Diagnosis

Becky had a DSM-IV bulimia nervosa diagnosis. She also met criteria for major depression. However, she felt the eating disorder was the primary problem.

Self-report questionnaire measures

Becky's scores on the self-report measures were: EAT = 54, BDI = 30, RSE = 16. These scores were all rather higher (in the case of the RSE, lower) than is usual for bulimia nervosa patients. The same was true of her EDBQ sub-scale scores. Her scores on the Thoughts and Behaviours Questionnaire sub-scales were also high.

Goals for treatment

Becky had clear goals. She wanted to stop bingeing and vomiting. She wanted to be able to eat normally—like her friends, and with her partner. She also wanted to feel better (less down), particularly about herself.

Table 11.5 Session plan for Becky

Complete weekly rating scale.
Set agenda.
Feedback on last session.
Reactions to the tape.
Review homework.
Main topics: brought by patient and therapist.
Setting of homework.
Feedback on session.

Treatment, and what it would involve—the structure and content—was explained to Becky. It included an explanation of regular audio-taping of sessions. Becky was given written information to back up the verbal explanation. This introduced her to the main principles of cognitive therapy for BN, and started the socialization process.

Fourteen sessions, weekly at first, were agreed. The format of sessions was explained; this included agenda setting, and feedback on the audio-tape of the previous session. The collaborative nature of the treatment was explained, together with the importance of active participation, and regular homework. Becky was asked to read the written information as part of her first homework assignment. The format agreed for sessions can be seen in Table 11.5. Treatment had five stages.

Stage 1

The aim was to increase motivation, introduce the cognitive model, and give understanding, and hope.

Becky had read the information on the content and style of treatment prior to attending the first treatment session. She said she thought it all sounded 'fine', and that she was willing to give it a go. Her partner had also read the information.

The therapist agreed a detailed problem list with Becky, and also the aims or goals of treatment. These were made specific and detailed, concrete and objective.

Problems were identified in several areas, including bingeing, vomiting, trying hard not to eat, and concerns with being, and feeling, fat. Becky was also exercising excessively, and occasionally abused laxatives.

Becky was able to generate goals for each of her problems. These were to stop bingeing and vomiting; to exercise 'only when I want instead of when I feel I should'; to eat normally 'like people at work'; to reduce the amount of time taken up ('wasted') by worrying about being fat. For each goal specific objectives were generated. Those for eating normally can be seen in Table 11.6. A detailed list of such objectives was compiled for each goal.

The therapist also watched out for any unrealistic objectives. For example, one of her goals was 'never to eat chocolate, sweets, biscuits, and cakes again'. Socratic questioning

Table 11.6 One of Becky's goals

Goal:
To eat normally.
Specific objectives:
To eat meals in restaurants and at friends' houses.
To eat sensibly at work—to stop 'snacking' on sweets and chocolate, and replace these with more healthy foods.
To take sandwiches to work.
To eat brunch at weekends without thinking 'I'll get fat'.

was used to ascertain whether this was a realistic or very helpful goal. Becky looked at the advantages and disadvantages, and considered what she would say to a good friend. She decided that, on balance, perhaps she should aim to allow herself small, but regular treats of these instead.

The idea of a therapy file—a box or file to keep all her therapy paperwork in—was introduced, and the therapist suggested Becky should aim to bring it to each session. The usefulness of referring back to points and exercises was discussed.

The advantages and disadvantages of change, both in the short term and the long term, were then considered. A wide range of factors was covered—Becky was asked to think about health, weight, social life, friendships, career, family, and relationships.

Becky identified several advantages of changing. She was particularly worried about her health—she had felt faint and dizzy recently. Her GP thought this was due to her eating habits, and frequent vomiting. One advantage therefore might be improved physical health. She also thought that she would generally feel better about herself, i.e. more in control, and more on top of things; also less embarrassed and ashamed of herself, i.e. 'for running to the bathroom to throw up in secret'. Friendships would also be easier if she could eat with other people—she would not need to make excuses to avoid social events involving food and eating.

Becky also identified several disadvantages. She was worried that she would not cope very well with 'problems' or 'life' if she could not binge. She would have to do something about the lack of satisfaction in her job—she would not have bingeing, her 'problem', as an excuse.

The gap that would be left by not bingeing and vomiting, was explored. Becky was worried that she would not be able to deal with distress if she could not binge. The need to seek a new job also worried her greatly.

Discussion with Becky suggested that some of these fears might be realistic. She had little experience of coping with distress without bingeing. She also lacked confidence to apply for more challenging jobs.

The advantages and disadvantages of change in the light of this were discussed with Becky, using Socratic questioning. Becky decided, on balance, that it might be helpful

Fig. 11.5 A vicious circle for Becky.

to learn how to deal with distress in other ways—and this could be another goal of treatment. She thought, on balance, that she would like to learn to believe more in herself (and perhaps get herself a more satisfying job).

Becky read about the physical and psychological problems associated with bingeing and vomiting, dieting, and other methods of weight control, for homework.

The basic vicious circle formulation for bingeing was introduced. Using detailed questioning, and a recent example, the vicious circle was drawn out for Becky. Care was taken to use her words, and to determine whether this was a typical example.

An example of one of Becky's vicious circles can be seen in Fig. 11.5.

The implications for treatment were elicited. Becky readily saw that one way to approach her problem was to work on changing her thoughts, i.e. the automatic thoughts she had in the vicious circle. The central role of thoughts in maintaining negative emotions and problem behaviour was discussed in some detail with her. The four different types of thought in the bingeing vicious circle—positive thoughts about eating, negative thoughts about eating, permissive thoughts, and thoughts of no control—were identified. Examples of these for Becky can be seen in Figure 11.5.

Stage 2

The aim was to challenge the myth of lack of control, and to identify and challenge other automatic thoughts in the vicious circle, i.e. positive thoughts, negative thoughts, and permissive thoughts.

A mixture of verbal challenging and behavioural experiments was used. Specially designed modified thoughts records were used to record evidence for and against thoughts (see Cooper *et al.* 2000). The lack of control thoughts were the first to be tackled.

Becky identified evidence for the thought that she had no control over her eating. Then she challenged the evidence, using questions, on a modified thought record. Becky's main piece of evidence was, 'I binge all the time'. She believed it 100%. She then used questions to challenge it, and finally concluded, 'I'm not bingeing every single moment of the day—there are times when I'm not bingeing, or eating anything at all'. Her belief in the thought then fell to 30%, and she concluded, 'I need to work on increasing the time that I'm not bingeing'.

As well as examining the evidence, Becky was helped to identify thinking errors. Types of thinking error in BN include catastrophizing, selective attention, emotional reasoning, and double standards. For example, Becky ate a pastry in the office at coffee time. She used this as evidence she could not control her eating, even though she did not think the same about the colleagues who were also eating them. Identifying when she was making a thinking error helped her gain a sense of perspective.

Becky then carried out a series of behavioural experiments to confirm and build up a sense of control. At first she did not really believe that she could go for long without bingeing—she thought three hours was her limit—and her belief that she could control her eating was 10%. With her therapist she drew up a hierarchy, a series of experiments, of increasing lengths of time during which she would not binge. (This makes use of the binge-postponement strategy—delaying bingeing for increasing lengths of time—see Cooper *et al.* 2000). She then treated each step as an experiment, starting with the easiest step first. Each time she conducted a step or experiment in the hierarchy she considered likely problems, devised strategies to deal with them (e.g. saying no firmly to the offer of a cream cake at work when she had just eaten her lunch). Then she carried out her experiment, reviewed the outcome, and re rated her belief in the initial prediction or belief. Using this strategy, Becky gradually built up her confidence that she could control her eating, without bingeing. After three experiments, in which she gradually increased time without bingeing to eight hours (all day at work), her belief in control rose to 85%.

An example of one of Becky's experiments to build up her sense of control can be seen in Table 11.7.

Table 11.7 An example of Becky's experiments to build up a sense of control

Thought to be tested: I can't control my eating

Belief that the thought is true (0–100%): 85%

Experiment to test thought	Likely Problems	Strategies to deal with problems	Date of experiment	Outcome of experiment	Belief in thought (0–100%)
Postpone bingeing for an hour after lunch.	I'll buy sweets from the shop next door. Someone will offer me a biscuit, or a piece of Katy's birthday cake.	Go to work that day without any money. Say, no thank you, I've just eaten lunch.	Tuesday, 6 May.	Was tempted to go to the shop—having no money helped. Peter asked if I wanted a biscuit—I said no, I have just eaten.	60%

Becky then moved on to challenge her positive thoughts. These focused on the thought that bingeing would make her 'feel better', i.e. take away bad feelings or distress. A modified thought record was used here too, and she was taught to ask a series of questions to help her challenge these thoughts. An example of a completed worksheet can be seen in Table 11.8, for an occasion when she babysat her two nephews.

Particular attention was paid to any 'yes, but' statements. These are often important in bulimia, and Becky had lots of these. For example, she came up with the challenge, 'I know I'm not fat' (to a negative thought, 'I'm far too fat'), but qualified it with, 'but I still feel as though I am'. This thought then also needed to be challenged.

Becky's permissive thoughts, e.g. 'now I've started eating, I might as well go on', were challenged in a similar way, using questions, and modified thought records. The role of thinking errors was also addressed. One error Becky made, was jumping to conclusions that were not entirely justified by the evidence. She learned to recognize when she was doing this.

Stage 3

The aim was to identify and change behaviours that maintain bingeing, and weight and shape preoccupation.

Becky identified the behaviours that might be maintaining her bingeing and her preoccupations (including from the Eating Behaviours Questionnaire). These included eating diet foods, avoiding tight clothing, not eating sweet foods, chocolate, or snack foods. Experiments were used to illustrate how the behaviours might be contributing to her difficulties. This included a focused-attention experiment (Cooper *et al.* 2000), and several experiments in which she compared old and new behaviours. For example,

Table 11.8 An example of challenging positive thoughts for Becky

Situation	Feelings and sensations	Positive thoughts about eating	Evidence that does not support the hot thought	Alternative, more helpful thought	Belief in alternative thought
Just back from shopping, felt tired. The children had all their toys over the floor —the house was a mess, and Jim was asleep.	Cross, annoyed, angry.	I should not be annoyed, Jim has had a hard week. Eating will help me feel less angry. If I do not eat something I'll explode, lose it completely	Being angry cannot make you lose it, i.e. go mad.	It is better to be angry than to binge— and Jim did offer to look after things while I went out.	55%
When was it?		What were you saying that made it easier to start eating?			
Where were you? Who were you with? What were you doing? What were you thinking about?	How did you feel? What body sensations did you notice?	Identify and circle the hot thought. This is the thought that makes it most likely that you will start eating and go on the binge	Use the questions in Boxes 13.1* and 13.2 to challenge your hot thought.	Write down an alternative, more helpful thought.	Rate how much you believe this thought to be true on a scale from 0 to 100%.

*From Cooper et al. 2000, Chapter 13.

she discovered that checking repeatedly how she looked in the mirror (old behaviour) made her feel much fatter than not doing this (new behaviour).

Becky's fears about giving up the behaviours were identified—these were often about weight gain. For example, she believed that if she ate normally, i.e. without vomiting, she would gain a large amount of weight. The advantages and disadvantages of continuing with this belief were identified. One advantage was that it helped her to avoid eating high-calorie foods. A big disadvantage, however, was that it stopped her joining in when food was around; she also felt deprived and resentful, and this had been known to trigger a binge, 'to spite myself'.

Specific behaviour changes, e.g. eating a small piece of chocolate twice a day (so that she would not feel deprived) were agreed and carried out. Where possible these were also set up as behavioural experiments. Becky's prediction was that she would gain at least six pounds if she did this for a week—belief 95%. After one week she found that she was two pounds heavier. But she was able to use a pie chart to work out the most likely reasons for this (see Wells 1997), a strategy she had learned earlier in treatment.

She concluded that the weight gain was most likely to be a normal fluctuation. Her belief in the original thought fell to 35%.

Fears about giving up food and eating related behaviours, weight- and shape-related behaviours, and dieting related behaviour (all of which might contribute to problem behaviours and concerns) were all dealt with in this way.

One of Becky's goals was normal eating. This was tackled, through graded introduction of normal food and eating patterns, in the form of a series of behavioural experiments. In Becky's case these tested the prediction, 'I'll get fat [gain a stone in two weeks] if I eat as much as the girls at work'. Becky initially believed this 95%, but after two weeks of relatively normal eating her belief was 20%.

Becky also had some meta-beliefs. For example, she believed that if she stopped worrying about her weight she would gain several pounds in a week. This belief was also tested, using behavioural experiments, and these enabled her to give up worrying.

Stage 4

This aimed to identify (and formulate) and challenge underlying assumptions, and core beliefs.

Becky's assumptions and beliefs were identified from themes in her thought records, by using the downward arrow technique, and from the EDBQ. Her assumptions

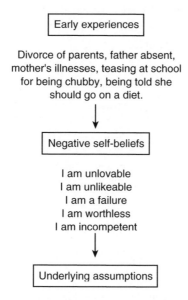

Early experiences

Divorce of parents, father absent, mother's illnesses, teasing at school for being chubby, being told she should go on a diet.

Negative self-beliefs

I am unlovable
I am unlikeable
I am a failure
I am worthless
I am incompetent

Underlying assumptions

If I gain weight no-one will like me, it means I am not loveable, it means I have failed.

If I lose weight, I will be more successful, people will like me more, accept me more.

Fig. 11.6 Development of Becky's eating problem.

included the beliefs, 'If I eat it means I've failed' and 'if I get fat, no one will like me'. Her beliefs about herself included, 'I'm unloveable, and I've failed'.

The role of these in the development of her disorder was conceptualized, and the early experiences that might have led to their development were identified. Fig. 11.6 shows an example of this for Becky. Several of her early experiences, including the divorce of her parents, disappearance of her father from her life, and her mothers' illnesses seemed to be linked to the development of the negative self-beliefs. Early teasing for being 'chubby' at school also seemed important. One particular memory from that time was a teacher telling her mother that she ought to put her on a diet.

Assumptions were then challenged by considering the evidence for and against them, and identifying the advantages and disadvantages of continuing to believe in them. An example for Becky's assumption, 'if I gain weight, no one will like me' can be seen in Table 11.9.

The main advantage she identified for continuing to believe in this was that it gave her a simple answer to the question, 'why can't I keep friends or relationships?'. The main disadvantage was that it stopped her from dealing with the real problem—widening her circle of friends.

Alternative beliefs were identified, e.g. 'just because I'm heavier, it doesn't mean I have to stop seeing people', and Becky also planned behavioural experiments to put the new belief into practice. For example, she started to get back in touch with friends that she had not seen lately.

The link between bingeing, dieting, and negative self-beliefs was discussed. Becky believed 'if I lose weight, I'll be more successful'—her assumption was a way to change the negative self-belief she had, 'I'm a failure'.

Table 11.9 Challenging one of Becky's assumptions

The assumption I hold is: If I gain weight it means I have failed.

Belief in the assumption (0–100%): 90%

Advantages	Disadvantages
I can be certain when I have done something wrong.	It means I often feel bad—and end up having mood swings that puzzle everyone around me.
I do not have to think about why I might really have done badly, e.g. in a job at work.	I do not tackle the real reasons for getting something wrong—that gets me into trouble at work.
It gives me an excuse—a reason—for not doing well.	It keeps me focused on my weight, and on how I look.

Outcome:
The belief has some advantages, but these are mostly very short-lived. At the end of the day I have not tackled the real reasons why something has gone wrong. I also get very moody, and people around me find it difficult to know me—that is putting a strain on my friendships.

Belief in the assumption now (0–100%): 30%

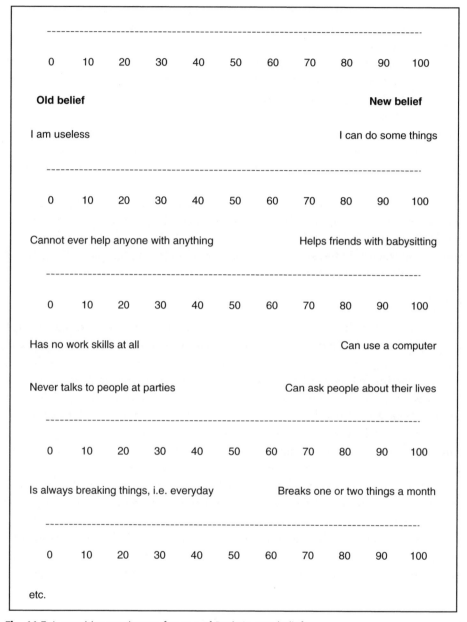

Fig. 11.7 A cognitive continuum for one of Becky's core beliefs.

The idea of schema and schema-driven processes (things that act to keep the negative self-beliefs going) was discussed with Becky. She had many negative self-beliefs and these were tackled over several weeks. Becky found cognitive continua particularly useful in weakening beliefs such as 'I'm worthless, incompetent'. A partially completed example of the use of this strategy for 'I am useless' can be seen in Fig. 11.7. She also found positive data logs, and flashcards with the key evidence for new beliefs recorded on them useful.

Becky also contemplated, and began to make, some lifestyle changes. For example, she found it particularly difficult to be assertive, or to say what she thought. With her therapist she explored ways to overcome this, and began to put them into practice in specific situations, with some success.

Discussion of schema-driven processes that prevent effective challenging of core beliefs—avoidance, compensation, and maintenance—helped Becky identify why she was finding it difficult to look for an alternative job. One fear was that, in a more challenging job she would be exposed as incompetent. Becky recognized that she could start to challenge this belief by taking steps to look for alternative employment.

Stage 5

This involved relapse prevention. A blueprint, or summary, of what Becky had learned in treatment and what had been particularly useful was developed. This included any early warning signs of problems, so that action could be taken quickly. In Becky's case, this was starting to buy diet foods, and taking increased interest in how she looked. The importance of continuing with belief change was emphasized. Becky planned to continue with her positive data log, and to review her notes on schema at regular intervals. Becky thought ahead to likely difficulties she might face, including the possible temptation to resume bingeing, and how she might handle this. An important strategy was to read over her notes and use things that had helped before.

Becky stopped bingeing and vomiting halfway through treatment. At the end of treatment her scores on all the self-report measures were in the normal range. Her problems were not completely over—she felt that she still needed to work on being more assertive, and on being more confident. She had not yet tackled her job, but had set up an appointment with a careers advisor to explore options. She was pleased with her progress, and felt that she could use the skills she had learned to make further progress.

Summary

This chapter has described treatment for BN using standard cognitive behaviour therapy, based on Fairburn's model, and treatment using a revised model developed by Cooper and colleagues. Case examples were used to illustrate typical treatment strategies and progress.

Chapter 12

Cognitive therapy outcome

Overview

This chapter will present cognitive therapy outcome studies for BN, and some of the issues that arise from these studies. Part one will discuss the problems with CT outcome studies, results of early reviews, the untreated prognosis, and results of naturalistic studies. Predictors of outcome in these studies will also be identified. Part two will cover more recent review studies, meta-analyses, and recent individual and group treatment studies. Part three will discuss studies that have attempted to identify the active ingredients of CT for BN. Part four will cover self-help studies, and in-patient treatment outcome. It will also cover some of the predictors of outcome that have been identified in cognitive therapy treatment studies. Part five will draw together the theoretical, and other, implications of CT outcome studies for BN. The effectiveness of CBT, as currently delivered, will be assessed. The plan for the chapter is summarized in Table 12.1.

Outcome of BN

There are several problems with assessing outcome in cognitive therapy for BN. Early studies did not have access to EDNOS or BED criteria, so figures could under-estimate those who continue to have problems after treatment and at follow-up. Changes in diagnostic criteria, e.g. from DSM-III to the more restrictive DSM-III-R or IV, might also affect numbers given a diagnosis at follow-up. Many different measures of symptoms and key constructs have been used—making it difficult to compare studies. While some report abstinence rates for key symptoms, others report percentage reduction in symptoms. Typically, abstinence rates at the end of treatment and follow-up are disappointingly high. Some derive an overall outcome score or put people in outcome categories, but most do not use the same variables when making this judgement. It has been suggested that researchers need to take account of both severity of symptoms and duration of improvement (Herzog *et al.* 1991b) in assessing outcome, but few have done this. Very few studies have included measures of cognition, even when cognitive treatments have been included in the study. Data may be interview or questionnaire, or may be obtained over the telephone—thus data may differ in quality. Studies also have different rates of participation, and different lengths of follow-up. Some only assess a very few aspects of outcome—this is often just behaviour or psychiatric indicators, and not attitudes, concerns, or dieting. This then restricts the number of variables that can

Table 12.1 Summary of plan for Chapter 12

Cognitive therapy outcome
Problems with outcome studies in the field
Early reviews
Untreated prognosis
Predictors of outcome in early studies
Recent reviews
Meta-analyses
Individual treatment studies
Group treatment studies
Identifying the active ingredients of CT for BN
Self-help treatment
In-patient outcome
Predictors of outcome in recent studies
Implications of treatment outcome studies

then be entered into analysis of predictors of outcome. There are no studies of an untreated sample reported in the literature, so the untreated course of BN cannot be determined accurately. This means that we cannot compare treatment efficacy directly with untreated outcome. Cross-sectional sampling (most commonly used) also does not give any information on the course of the disorder, i.e. it is unclear whether the person is fully recovered or in remission. Most patients also come from secondary or tertiary services—these sources might be associated with different outcomes from those recruited, for example, from primary care. All these points need to be considered when evaluating the research reported below.

Reviews of outcome

A summary of the findings from early outcome studies can be seen in Table 12.2. They are discussed in more detail below.

Initial reports suggested that BN was a chronic condition (Russell 1979), and that outcome was often poor. The first follow-up review of bulimia (mean duration of follow-up at least one year, seven studies included) concluded that it is 'episodic with remissions and relapses' (p.142) and that at least one-third were still ill at several years follow-up (Herzog *et al.* 1988). No agreed predictors of outcome could be identified. Outcome seemed better than that for anorexia nervosa (Herzog *et al.* 1993), even taking into account the fact that bulimics relapse at high rates (Keller *et al.* 1992). Worryingly, residual symptoms persisted in a third of those who had recovered, e.g. restrictive dieting, compulsive exercise (Keller *et al.* 1992). Recovery also tended to occur early on in the follow-up process, or not at all.

Table 12.2 Summary of BN from early outcome studies

Chronic
Poor outcome—including development of other eating disorders and depression
Often relapses
Residual symptoms are common
High treatment drop-out rate
Improvement tends to occur early on, if it happens at all
In-patients do particularly poorly

A second review, including 32 studies conducted between 1976 and 1986, found approximately 40% were abstinent from bingeing at follow-up. No one treatment seemed more effective but most studies were not of high quality (the authors were more liberal in their inclusion criteria than Herzog *et al.* 1988). The authors drew attention to the high drop-out rate and relatively short length of follow-ups (Cox & Merkel 1989).

More recently, a review has been conducted of 88 studies with participants followed up for at least 6 months (Keel & Mitchell 1997). Long-term follow-up (5–10 years) found that approximately 50% had fully recovered, while 20% still met diagnostic criteria for the disorder. Those who had received treatment (psychological or pharmacological) did better in the short term, but it seemed not to alter outcome after 5 years. The study also suggested that there is a high relapse rate—near to 30%, over 6 months to 6 years.

Naturalistic studies

There are several naturalistic studies of BN, although none consisting wholly of untreated participants. All the relevant studies suggest that bulimia nervosa tends to persist over time. One recent study, for example, found that at 5-year follow-up, 15% (14/92) of those with an initial BN diagnosis met DSM-IV criteria for bulimia nervosa. A further 36% (33/92) met criteria for another type of eating disorder (2% with anorexia nervosa and 34% with ED-NOS), while 8% met criteria for binge-eating disorder. Only 41% were fully abstinent, i.e. had no objective bulimic episodes, self-induced vomiting, or laxative abuse over the preceding three months. At follow-up, 40% also met criteria for major depressive disorder, self-esteem remained low, and social adjustment had not changed. Most of the improvement in symptoms occurred in the first 15 months, and each year about one-third remitted, and one-third relapsed (Fairburn *et al.* 2000). These findings are broadly consistent with the results of Keel & Mitchell's (1997) review.

Another study (of 110 women with BN seeking treatment) followed up participants on average for 7.5 years. While 73.8% achieved full recovery at some point (no or minimal symptoms for at least 8 weeks), and 99% achieved partial recovery at some point, 35.3% relapsed (return of full criteria for at least 8 weeks following full recovery). Recovery tended to happen early on; the recovery curve levelled off, with no new relapses after 400 weeks. No predictors of outcome were found, but the range of potential predictors was relatively limited (Herzog *et al.* 1999).

A more recent study, with a 98% follow-up rate over 5 years (better than either of the two studies above), found 22% had a DSM-IIIR diagnosis of an eating disorder at follow-up. Eight per cent met criteria for BN, 1% for AN, and 13% for EDNOS (Ben-Tovim *et al.* 2001). Outcome was better than for AN (where 35% met diagnostic criteria for a DSM-IIIR eating disorder diagnosis at follow-up). This study presents a rather better outcome than that of the reviews and two recent empirical studies mentioned above, but the outcome is still relatively poor. Predictors of outcome were also examined. Importantly, the study found that treatment (of various kinds and including psychotherapy) made no difference at all to outcome. Those who had received treatment, of varying levels of intensity, did not do better when followed up. However, psychosocial functioning and body related attitudes did predict outcome. The latter relationship provides some suggestion that cognitions may be important in predicting outcome.

The studies reported above suggest that relapse (from recovery) is common, and that reporting of diagnosis alone may mask the fact that many continue to have symptoms. Indeed, one study found that only 19% were continuously free from bulimic behaviour since finishing treatment (Mitchell *et al.* 1989); attitudes, which may also continue to be problematic, were not measured in this study.

Outcome for in-patients looks rather worse. In one study (mean 3.3 years after presentation), 50% had a DSM-IIIR diagnosis (Swift *et al.* 1987). In a second study, at 2–9 year follow-up, mean 4.5 years, 41.3% (19/46) of in-patients met DSM-III-R criteria. Of 18 fully recovered at follow-up, 14 (77.8%) had relapsed to full or partial bulimia at least once since discharge. Predictors of good outcome were shorter duration of bulimia before hospitalization, increased length of time since discharge, history of laxative or diuretic abuse, and greater weight fluctuation in the follow-up period (Fallon *et al.* 1991).

Outcome with cognitive therapy

A recent Cochrane review—the most comprehensive review of psychotherapy for bulimia nervosa to date—suggests CBT for BN does make a difference (although it also includes binge-eating disorder and EDNOS bulimia). Twenty-five studies were evaluated, and strict inclusion and exclusion criteria were used. Results suggested that CBT is superior to a waiting-list on abstinence of bingeing, and just fails to be superior to other psychotherapies, but not to pure self-help, or if exposure therapy is added to treatment. Non-CBT psychotherapies were also better than waiting-lists, but relatively few of these studies have been conducted. The authors conclude that CBT for BN is effective, but that it is not necessarily the only effective treatment, and not clearly the most effective, especially in the longer term (Hay & Bacaltchuk 2000).

There have been some previous meta-analyses of treatment studies focusing specifically on BN (Cox & Merkel 1989; Hartmann *et al.* 1992; Laessle *et al.* 1987b; Lewandowski *et al.* 1997). These all support the effectiveness of CBT, but have less stringent inclusion criteria than the review conducted by Hay & Bacaltchuk (2000). A summary of the findings from meta-analytic studies can be seen in Table 12.3.

One meta-analysis compared the relative efficacy of medication and CBT. CBT produced greater effect sizes (magnitude of change from pre- to post-treatment) for all measures: binge frequency, purge frequency, depression, and eating attitudes (Whittal *et al.* 1999).

Cognitive treatment

CBT for BN has been delivered primarily in the form of individual therapy. Early on in the history of the disorder, several single case studies were reported (e.g. Grinc 1982; Long & Cordle 1982; Welch 1979), together with a multiple case series (Fairburn 1981). Although most of these studies included cognitive restructuring of weight and shape (of various kinds), none of the studies assessed cognition. As is usual in the history of treatment, uncontrolled studies were followed by more tightly controlled studies, and then by studies examining the active ingredients of treatment. The different types of study that have been conducted are discussed below, and summarized in Table 12.4.

Table 12.3 Conclusions from meta-analyses of CBT

CBT is an effective treatment
CBT is not necessarily more effective than other psychotherapies, especially IPT
CBT may not be the most effective treatment in the long term

Table 12.4 Types of studies evaluating CBT for BN

Single cases
Uncontrolled studies—individual and group treatment
Controlled studies—with no treatment or waiting-list comparison groups
Multiple baseline evaluations
Controlled (individual treatment) studies—with other active treatments (short-term focal psychotherapy, exposure and response prevention, non-directive psychotherapy, supportive-expressive psychotherapy, interpersonal psychotherapy)
Controlled (group) studies—with non-directive psychotherapy

Uncontrolled studies: individual studies

Uncontrolled studies (e.g. Giles *et al.* 1985; Johnson *et al.* 1986; Leitenberg *et al.* 1984; Rossiter & Wilson 1985) have used a variety of cognitive strategies, usually including some form of cognitive restructuring. Most studies also used behavioural techniques. The one study using purely cognitive techniques (Rossiter & Wilson 1985) found that these were not effective. This may have been because the treatment was very simplified, and also very brief.

All the remaining studies reported success in reducing binge-eating and/or vomiting with treatment. However, several had no formal measures of binge-eating and purging. Other symptoms (usually assessed with standardized measures) were also reported to improve, including depression and self-esteem (Giles *et al.* 1985; Johnson *et al.* 1986), and there was improvement in social adjustment (Giles *et al.* 1985; Johnson *et al.* 1986).

Cognitive aspects of BN were not measured formally in any of these studies. However, some studies noted that cognitive aspects of the disorder also improved. For example, Welch (1979) reported that intrusive thoughts (self-monitored) reduced; and Fairburn (1981) noted that change in bingeing and vomiting was 'accompanied by a reduction in the intensity of abnormal attitudes toward food, eating, body weight and shape' p.709).

Follow-ups (available for some seven studies) ranged from 3 to 35 months. Findings indicated that the gains were largely maintained, although, as before, key eating-disorder symptoms were not formally assessed.

Uncontrolled studies: group studies

There are also some uncontrolled group CBT studies (e.g. Connors *et al.* 1984; Dedman *et al.* 1988; Pyle *et al.* 1984; Roy-Byrne *et al.* 1984; Schneider & Agras 1985; Stevens & Salisbury 1984;Williamson *et al.* 1989).

These studies have also used a range of different types of cognitive techniques, though many used the approach similar to that of Fairburn (1981) for individual treatment. All studies report improvements in bingeing and vomiting, although the gains seem to be rather less than for individual treatment and, as before, systematic measures are not always used. Depression, self-esteem, assertiveness, and anxiety (more likely to be measured systematically) also improve. Information on cognition is not formally reported. Follow-up is shorter than for individual treatment, from 10 weeks to 6 months, but the gains made tend to be maintained (although these are not always systematically assessed).

---

[1] The EAT, used in some of the studies discussed in this chapter, is considered here to be a measure of key symptoms, rather than cognition. Inspection of the items suggests that is a more accurate interpretation.

No treatment/waiting-list studies: individual studies

Two studies of individual therapy have used no treatment or waiting-list control groups. Freeman *et al.* (1988) focused on 'patients' dysfunctional beliefs about, and preoccupation with, food, eating, weight, and shape' (p.522). They used graded behavioural tasks to test the alternative thoughts generated. Agras *et al.* (1989), used CBT based on Beck *et al.* (1979) and elements from behavioural treatment of obesity (Brownell & Wadden 1986). Their treatment was similar to that of Fairburn (1981). They self-monitored eating, focused on reducing dieting, and normalized eating using behavioural techniques, then expanded the range of foods, including gradual introduction of avoided foods. Cognitive restructuring, related to food and eating, and to body image, was carried out. Relapse prevention included problem-solving. Cognitions were not formally assessed in these two studies. Follow-up at 6 months (Agras *et al.* 1989) and one year (Freeman *et al.* 1988) found that gains were maintained.

No treatment/waiting-list studies: group studies

Five studies have used a group approach. Dixon & Kiecolt-Glaser (1984), used cognitive restructuring and insight-oriented techniques, self-monitoring, and behavioural interventions. Huon & Brown (1985), used techniques aimed at recovering a sense of control (Boskind-Lodahl 1976; Fairburn 1981; Palmer 1979). Lee & Rush (1986) taught relaxation, and patients learned to control negative feelings that precipitated binges, and changed dysfunctional attitudes and cognitions about eating and weight. Psycho-education was also part of challenging beliefs. Other group approaches are reported by Wolchik *et al.* (1986) and by Leitenberg *et al.* (1988).

Both individual treatments decreased vomiting, and the study by Freeman *et al.* also decreased bingeing. All group treatments decreased bingeing and/or vomiting. Scores on measures of depression, anxiety, and self-esteem also improved. Most studies took detailed measures of key symptoms, including bingeing and vomiting, so that degree of change could be accurately assessed. None took formal measures of cognition, but some reported cognitive change. For example, Huon & Brown (1985) wrote that patients described 'changed attitudes to their body' (p.482). Although improvements in behaviour were reported in all studies, inspection of the data suggests that many remained with significant symptoms at the end of treatment and at follow-up.

There has also been a multiple baseline evaluation (Hersen & Barlow 1976) of group CBT. Treatment was based on previously described CBT (Fairburn 1985; Garner *et al.* 1984b). Participants did not improve over the multiple baselines, but did improve with treatment. Importantly, this study also included a measure of cognition—the Mizes Anorectic Cognitions Questionnaire (Mizes & Klesges 1989)—and found these declined with treatment, although patients still scored above the normal control means (Kettlewell *et al.* 1992).

CBT vs. other active treatments: individual studies

These studies have produced mixed but very interesting findings. Some have found a clear advantage for CBT over other active treatments, but others have not. One study found little or no advantage for CBT (Fairburn et al. 1986b). This used short-term focal psychotherapy (Rosen 1976), as the comparison treatment. It was adapted for BN using Bruch's ideas in anorexia nervosa (Bruch 1973) and Stunkard's approach to overweight binge eaters (Stunkard 1976, 1980). CBT was similar to previously described treatments (Fairburn 1981). A version of the CBT manual has subsequently been published (Fairburn 1985). Both treatments resulted in improvement in eating disorder symptoms and social adjustment, although CBT did have a greater effect on depressive symptoms. A second study also found no advantage for CBT; exposure and response prevention (ERP) was as effective at the end of treatment as CBT (Cooper & Steere 1995), although those who did not get CBT were more likely to relapse by the 12-month follow-up. This study included a formal measure of attitudes—these were similar in the two groups at the end of treatment. However, the authors noted that this finding might be due to restricted assessment of cognition, rather than a true lack of difference. Two studies have found a clear advantage for CBT. Agras et al. (1989) compared CBT with self-monitoring to non-directive psychotherapy, and focus on the antecedents and consequences of binge-eating. CBT was as described by Agras et al. (1989). In this study, CBT was superior to the comparison treatment, both on eating disorder and depressive symptoms. Garner et al. (1993) compared CBT with supportive-expressive therapy (a brief psychodynamic therapy, based on Luborsky 1984), and supplemented by other psychodynamic writers on eating disorders (Goodsitt 1985; Lerner 1983; Sugarman, Quinlan & Devenis 1982). CBT was based on Fairburn (1985) plus modifications (Garner 1986; Garner & Bemis 1982; Garner et al. 1984b). The results favoured CBT, on both eating disorder and general symptoms. Patients were also more satisfied with CBT.

Two studies have used IPT as one of their comparison treatments. Fairburn et al. (1991b) compared: CBT, interpersonal psychotherapy (Klerman et al. 1984), and behaviour therapy, the latter a simplified version of CBT, containing all the elements of CBT except the cognitive procedures. A recent multi-centre study used the same design and the same three treatments (Agras et al. 2000b). In both these studies, CBT was superior to IPT at the end of treatment (in reducing vomiting, dieting, and attitudes to shape and weight in Fairburn et al.'s study; in reducing bingeing, purging, and dietary restraint in Agras et al.'s study). However, there were no differences between CBT and IPT at follow-up. Scores on general clinical state, including anxiety and depression, improved equally in both treatments, in both studies, as did social adjustment. The authors suggest that CBT may have a specific effect on the primary behavioural symptoms of bulimia nervosa, but that after treatment, the course of symptoms is similar. Thus the advantage of CBT, compared to IPT, may be that it works faster on key

Table 12.5 Conclusions from treatment studies

CBT is more effective then several other psychotherapies, especially in the short term
It is good at reducing eating related symptoms
It may have a specific effect on cognitions
It is not necessarily more effective than IPT, especially in the long term
CBT may, however, act more quickly on key eating behaviours than other therapies

symptoms (Agras *et al.* 2000). In both studies, cognitions were assessed and CBT was found to have specific effects on patients' concerns or cognitions (attitudes to weight and shape in Fairburn *et al.*, and dietary restraint in Agras *et al.*).[2]

CBT vs. other active treatments: group

One group study (Kirkley *et al.*1985b) compared non-directive psychotherapy plus self-monitoring with CBT. CBT was more effective in reducing bingeing and vomiting. Cognitions were not formally assessed.

Conclusion

To date, the results suggest that CBT is more effective than several other active treatments, particularly in the short term, and particularly in reducing key eating-related symptoms. The key features distinguishing CBT from other treatment outcomes are summarized in Table 12.5.

It may also have a specific effect on cognition, although few studies have assessed this. However, CBT may not be more effective than IPT in the long term, either in reducing general or specific eating-related problems—including both behaviour and cognition. The particular advantage of CBT (as currently delivered) may, therefore, be that it acts more quickly than other treatments on the key behavioural (and possibly cognitive) symptoms. However, caution must be exercised in generalizing from those studies that have assessed cognition—to date the assessment is relatively limited, and relies almost exclusively on a single measure—the EDE. More detailed assessment might reveal further cognitive differences between CBT and other treatments, e.g. at follow-up. Importantly, inspection of the data suggests, that despite its success, many patients are left with significant behavioural symptoms at the end of treatment and at follow-up.

Identifying the active ingredients

Controlled studies suggest that change with cognitive behavioural treatment is unlikely to be due to natural fluctuations in symptoms over time. But, it is not clear that

---

[2]   There was a treatment by site interaction for change in weight and shape concerns in Agras *et al.*'s study.

changes are due to cognitive as opposed to non-specific, behavioural elements of treatment or to elements specific to the comparison treatments (all of which were designed to be active treatments). Importantly, most of the comparison treatments included some behavioural techniques, including self-monitoring of eating in both treatments being compared. Thus change could be due to use of these.

Five studies have tried to determine what the active ingredients of CBT are, including studies that have investigated whether formal exposure with response prevention adds anything to simple CBT.

Full CBT compared with BT

Four studies have isolated cognitive components, comparing behavioural elements of CBT with the full CBT intervention. Two of these are individual treatments, and both found that bingeing, vomiting, and general psychopathology improved equally in the two treatments being compared (Fairburn *et al.* 1991b; Freeman *et al.* 1988). One, however, found that CBT was better than behaviour therapy at altering disturbed attitudes to shape and weight and in decreasing dietary restraint (Fairburn *et al.* 1991b). This suggests that CBT may add to treatment, and have a specific effect beyond that attributable to behavioural techniques. It suggests that it may, therefore, operate through cognitive rather than behavioural mechanisms. It also provides some preliminary support for the suggestion that cognitions are of primary importance, rather than epiphenomenal or secondary to behavioural disturbance.

Two other studies have compared behavioural and CBT treatments. Thackwray *et al.* (1993) used a behavioural treatment designed as an eating habit control programme (e.g. Brownell 1985; Mahoney & Mahoney 1976; Stuart & Davis 1972). CBT was an abbreviated version of Fairburn (1985), with more emphasis on homework. Both the CBT and BT groups maintained their gains at 6-month follow-up, but only the CBT group maintained its abstinence from bingeing and vomiting at 6-month follow-up. A group study (Wolf & Crowther 1992) compared behavioural and cognitive interventions. The behavioural emphasized bingeing as a learned behaviour maintained by reduction in negative emotions. It focused on self-monitoring, regular eating, stimulus control, goal setting, exposure to feared foods, self-reinforcement, and relapse prevention. Cognitive treatment included all these aspects plus a cognitive component, including cognitive restructuring. Both treatments reduced bingeing and use of extreme weight control measures. Behavioural treatment was most effective at reducing behavioural symptoms, and at maintaining this reduction over time. CBT was better at decreasing concern with dieting, identifying sensations of hunger and satiety, and maintaining reductions in general psychopathology.

There are some other relevant studies. For example, looking at the usefulness of adding exposure with response prevention (ERP) to CBT (e.g. Leitenberg *et al.* 1988; Wilson *et al.* 1986), or adding behavioural self-instruction derived from Goldfried & Davison (1976) to CBT (e.g. Yates & Sambrailo 1984). There is also a study adding planned binges (Steel *et al.* 1995). These have practical rather than theoretical implications.

Exposure and response prevention studies

The studies involving ERP can be summarized as follows: cognitive restructuring (minus behavioural assignments) is less effective than cognitive restructuring plus exposure and response prevention (Wilson *et al.* 1986). Adding in session exposure and response prevention did not improve the effectiveness of CBT (including behavioural assignments) (Wilson *et al.* 1991). Patients also tended to find it less acceptable. CBT with response prevention resulted in a worse outcome at end of treatment and 6-month follow-up than CBT alone (Agras *et al.* 1989), suggesting that ERP impaired the results of CBT. However, the latter study has been criticized (Leitenberg & Rosen 1989), for not adding ERP to CBT in an incremental way (as had been done previously), but including it in the CBT package without adding additional time. It was also introduced relatively late in treatment, which might affect its credibility (Leitenberg & Rosen 1989).

In most of these studies there is considerable overlap between conditions. This makes it difficult to determine whether adding ERP improves outcome or not. Results are conflicting. Theoretically, similar findings in the two conditions could be due to the similarity of ERP to self-administered exposure—eating three meals a day, including avoided foods without vomiting (which forms part of many BT and CBT interventions). Both could decrease anxiety and enhance self-efficacy (Wilson *et al.* 1991). Alternatively, similar findings could be due to the inclusion of some form of cognitive restructuring in both conditions (e.g. as in Leitenberg *et al.* 1988).

A recently conducted, large RCT study has attempted to answer more clearly the clinical question of whether adding ERP to a core of CBT (i.e. exactly the same CBT treatment in both conditions), improves outcome. This study found no advantage in adding exposure and response prevention (either exposure to pre-purging or pre-bingeing cues) to standard CBT (Bulik *et al.* 1998).

The addition of other interventions to CBT can be summarized as follows: self-instruction (Yates & Sambrailo 1984) added to CBT suggests that the combination may have had more effect on bingeing and purging frequency, but it is impossible to be certain. Planned binges (Steel *et al.* 1995) added to Fairburn's CBT approach, 'a behavioural-based cognitive challenge' also seem a promising strategy, although not yet evaluated in a trial.

CBT vs. drug treatment

There are also some studies comparing CBT with drug treatment. Intensive group-CBT resulted in greater improvement than drug (imipramine) alone, and adding drug to psychotherapy was no more effective than psychotherapy plus placebo in changing bingeing and vomiting, but did lead to more change in anxiety and depression

(Mitchell *et al.* 1990b). Medication also led to greater drop-out—due to side-effects of the drug. For example, 36 in drug vs. 10 in the placebo conditions (total recruited 155) (Mitchell *et al.* 1990b). Another study also found that CBT, and CBT and medication (desipramine) reduced bingeing and vomiting, whereas medication alone did not. CBT alone also resulted in rather better maintenance of gains at 6-month follow-up (on depression and self-esteem scores), including than CBT plus medication (Leitenberg *et al.* 1994). One study found that the combination of fluoxetine and CBT was not superior to CBT alone, including on EDE sub-scales (Goldbloom *et al.* 1997). Another study, however, found that combining CBT with medication was superior to medication in reducing vomiting. This study had a more sophisticated two-stage medication intervention, consisting of desipramine and fluoxetine (the other was used if either one was ineffective or poorly tolerated) (Walsh *et al.* 1997).

Drug studies in BN typically find that responders need at least 5–6 months of therapy, and that many later relapse. Indeed it has been suggested that patients need at least 1–2 years of treatment to obtain the full benefit (Pope *et al.* 1985a). There is often a high drop-out rate, and many patients with BN do not want to take medication. If the medication does work, it may operate differently to CBT. Patients on medication typically lose weight thus it may operate through an effect on appetite.

Adding nutritional therapy to CBT and medication has also been found to be effective (Brambilla *et al.* 1995; Laessle *et al.* 1991). The rationale for nutritional therapy is that malnutrition may be responsible for binge-eating. Cognitive and interpersonal therapy have also been combined in a group format (Roth & Ross 1988), focusing on self-referential beliefs and interpersonal belief (about other people), but the approach has not been evaluated systematically.

Brief and full CBT

Brief CBT has been compared with a full version in one study. Ordman & Kirschenbaum (1985) compared a full CBT intervention, including exposure and response prevention, with a brief version of the same treatment. The full intervention was more effective than the brief, on bingeing and vomiting, eating disorder symptoms (EAT), depression, and general psychological adjustment.

Group vs. individual CBT

Freeman *et al.* 1988, compared group therapy with individual CBT but the group treatment was not comparable. It focused on support and education, and consisted of non-directive discussions and behavioural homework tasks.

Other studies

One study has compared different forms of group CBT, differing in intensity and emphasis, on abstinence. All treatments used the same manuals—a healthy eating one and one outlining cognitive behavioural strategies. Intensive treatment, emphasis on early abstinence or intensive treatment, combined with early interruption of bingeing, produced the best results (Mitchell *et al.* 1993). Emphasis on abstinence is important—some preliminary evidence suggests that it may produce better long-term outcome (Maddocks *et al.* 1992).

Another study found that those in the action stage did better than those in the contemplation stage, in a study comparing motivation enhancement therapy with CBT. However, there were no differences between treatments (Treasure *et al.* 1999).

Long-term outcome of CBT

Most CBT studies have followed patients after treatment, usually for up to 6 months, and most find that gains are maintained, and that CBT remains superior to other treatments (except in the case of IPT). Most studies are open follow-ups, i.e. patients have been free to seek further treatment, so it is often unclear how much the maintenance of changes have been due to additional treatment. There are very few longer-term follow-ups (i.e. beyond 6 months), or closed follow-ups.

One small early study found gains made with cognitive restructuring plus exposure and response prevention were maintained at one year (Wilson *et al.* 1986). A study with a closed follow-up of 12 months found that the superior effect of CBT (over short-term focal-psychotherapy) was maintained (Fairburn *et al.* 1986b). Another, also with a one-year closed follow-up, found patients receiving CBT and IPT made similar and lasting changes in all areas, whereas few BT patients had a good outcome—and those who did tended to relapse. Effects were sustained for bingeing and purging, dietary restraint, attitudes to weight and shape, general psychiatric functioning, and social functioning (Fairburn *et al.* 1993a). Another one-year follow-up, but open study, found those who received 16 weeks of medication only tended to relapse—while gains made by other groups (CBT and CBT plus medication) were maintained (Agras *et al.* 1994).

The longer one-year follow-ups have mostly been of individual treatment. There is one brief report of outcome of group CBT, at 30 months, which found reasonable maintenance of gains (Luka *et al.* 1986).

There is only one much longer follow-up. At a mean of 5.8 years, over a third in each group (CBT; two forms of short-term psychotherapy; behaviour therapy, BT)) had received further psychiatric help. There were no differences between groups in presence of bulimia nervosa or anorexia nervosa at follow-up, but there was when all forms of DSM-IV eating disorder were considered together (CBT, 37%; psychotherapy, 28%; BT, 86%). The difference was due to the large number of the BT group having an EDNOS diagnosis; there was no difference between the other two groups. The study had a high follow-up rate (90%). The authors conclude that bulimia nervosa is not 'intractable' as suggested by Russell (1979)—overall only one in five still had a BN diagnosis. But if cases of EDNOS are considered, then the outcome looks much less positive—almost half had a DSM-IV eating disorder (Fairburn *et al.* 1995), including many who had received CBT.

Self-help

There is some preliminary evidence that patients with bulimia nervosa might benefit from CBT treatment in self-help form (Carter & Fairburn 1998). Most studies use either pure self-help (written materials only: Treasure *et al.* 1994) or guided self-help (written materials plus meetings or telephone calls from a lay or non-specialist helper (Cooper *et al.* 1996). Evidence suggests both forms may be effective (Cooper *et al.* 1994, 1996; Schmidt *et al.* 1993c; Treasure *et al.* 1994).

Pure self-help can involve individual or group interventions. Three manuals and programmes, or versions of these, have been evaluated in the literature (Cooper 1995; Fairburn 1995; Schmidt & Treasure 1993). All have a CBT basis.

Pure self-help has many advantages. It can be used with existing treatments to reduce therapist time, dependency on the therapist, and to allow time for work on more complex issues in sessions. It can be a first step, or it can make treatment available to those who might otherwise be unable to receive help. It can be used with trained or lay therapists—with the degree of support needed dependent on the severity or complexity of the patient's problem. It also has clear cost implications—being much less expensive than a therapist seeing a patient for individual sessions.

A pilot study (Schmidt *et al.* 1993c) and RCT (Treasure *et al.* 1994) have used Treasure's manual. The treatment seems effective. Two studies have used the manual developed by Cooper. In a pilot study, bingeing and vomiting decreased, although attitudes to weight and shape remained quite disturbed (Cooper *et al.* 1994). In a follow-up study, guided self-help decreased bingeing and vomiting, and patients also improved on EDE weight and shape sub-scales, and on depression. At follow-up one year later, gains were maintained—or improved (Cooper *et al.* 1996b).

No direct comparisons have been made, but inspection of the data suggests that guided self-help may be more effective than pure self-help. Overall, however, abstinence rates are often low at the end of treatment.

Two studies suggest that a manual may be as effective at reducing bingeing and weight control behaviours (apart from vomiting) as full CBT. Full remission was as follows in one RCT: in manual group, 22%; waiting-list, 11%; and full CBT, 24% (Treasure *et al.* 1994). A second study found that full CBT vs. the manual was better at the end of treatment at decreasing bingeing and vomiting (54.8% and 12.9%, respectively, had not binged or vomited in the last week of treatment). But at mean 43 weeks follow-up, this had increased to 70.8% and 60.9%, respectively—with no differences between the groups. There were also no differences in attitudes to weight and shape, or dietary restraint using the EDE (Thiels *et al.* 1998a).

Use of treatment manuals

Patients have to use manuals for them to be effective. Some initial findings suggest that those high on a measure of compliance, amount read, shared manual with someone else, number of exercises completed did better (40% vs. 5% achieved full remission). Those with greater distress about their weight and shape tend to use it less, but those who have been ill for longer are more likely to use it—perhaps reflecting greater readiness to change (Troop *et al.* 1996).

Much more research is needed to understand more about who is likely to comply, as well as what factors promote compliance. We also need to study what is helpful, not helpful, and what is motivating and not motivating. It is also helpful to consider what the aims of a self-help manual might be (Garvin *et al.* 1998). Some of the things identified in the self-help literature are decreasing social isolation, increasing knowledge, broadening coping skills, and improving self-esteem. This means it may be useful to broaden what is assessed when evaluating these manuals, e.g. changes in motivation for, or seeking of treatment might also be useful to know about. Such outcomes have been described anecdotally (Troop *et al.* 1996).

There is also an early suggestion that improvement may continue beyond treatment, unlike standard individual or group CBT (see: Thiels *et al.* 1998; Cooper *et al.* 1996). Despite these promising results, we need follow-up studies to see if patients maintain (or continue to improve on) their changes.

Cognitive therapy day programmes, or in-patient programmes, have not been systematically evaluated. The Toronto group uses CBT, but it is only part of multi-modal treatment. This will not be discussed in detail here, although it appears to produce good results. In patient programmes based on CBT principles have yet to be evaluated, although they have been described in the literature.

Predictors of outcome

Many studies have too few participants to identify reliable predictors of outcome. In addition, few prognostic factors have yet been replicated across studies. The differences found may be due to differences in the type of therapy, mode of delivery, nature of the sample, definition of treatment success, measures and variables considered. Sample size, type of analysis, sampling of predictor variables, variance on any one variable, may also contribute (Davis *et al.* 1992). There may also be a subject by treatment interaction; for example, Davis *et al.* suggest depression and borderline organization might differentially predict outcome in treatments that differ in emphasis on interpersonal processes, self-disclosure and corrective emotional experiences. They suggest that such patients may be more able to make changes (e.g. in psycho-educational programmes) when there is no demand for a therapeutic relationship (Davis *et al.* 1992).

Knowledge of predictors can help select likely responders, thus saving time, cost, and the frustration of failure. It can also help to identify reasons for a treatment's failure.

These considerations are particularly important in the context of managed care.

It has been suggested that predictors fall into seven categories (Bulik *et al.* 1998). These are as follows: demographic; behavioural symptoms; psychological or cognitive; axis I co-morbidity; axis II co-morbidity; personality; and family history. Other factors

Table 12.6 Factors found to be predictive of treatment outcome

Other disorders or symptoms: personality disorder, alcohol abuse, anorexia nervosa, depression, general psychiatric symptoms
Eating-related factors: frequency of bingeing and vomiting, high EAT score, longer history, in-patient treatment, low body weight, history of obesity, receipt of drug treatment for BN
Family and social factors: controlling family environment, social adjustment
Personality related factors: self-esteem, self-efficacy, high self-directedness
Attitude to change: readiness to change, ambivalence about change

Table 12.7 Factors found to predict relapse

Post-treatment bingeing and vomiting, restricting, urge to binge
Distorted body image
Pretreatment self-esteem
Younger age

may also be important though they are less studied in BN. McKisack & Waller (1997), in their review of factors influencing outcome of group psychotherapy, highlight 'therapy dose', number, length and frequency of sessions, therapist characteristics—gender, experience, source of referrals—and treatment location. Another factor that is not often considered is the client's assessment of outcome, including what aspects of therapy they found helpful (Rorty *et al.* 1993). Bulik *et al.* (1998) also note that it is important to distinguish between the temporal nature of the predictors used. Pretreatment variables reveal characteristics predictive of outcome, post-treatment reveal those relevant to relapse. Factors identified as potential predictors of outcome are summarized in Table 12.6, and discussed further below. Factors identified as potential predictors of relapse are summarized in Table 12.7.

In studies with smaller numbers, between-group analysis has been used to examine potential predictors in CT for BN.[3] These have mostly looked at the impact of personality variables or demographic features. Results are conflicting. One study found that those with a borderline personality disorder diagnosis had a worse outcome on general psychiatric symptoms, but not on eating disorder symptoms (Steiger & Stotland 1996). Another, however, found that those with a personality disorder had a poorer outcome on bulimic symptoms, and needed more sessions after the trial had ended. However, when differences in depression and BMI were taken into account, this difference disappeared (Fahy *et al.* 1993). When the borderline syndrome index (Conte *et al.* 1980) was used, score was related to later bingeing and vomiting frequency (Herzog *et al.* 1991a).

In a group seeking treatment, responders were more likely to have received drug therapy in the first 13 weeks (Herzog & Sacks 1993). Patients had a poorer outcome if

---

[3] In this section only studies in which some or all the participants received CBT will be considered.

they had a history of alcohol abuse or anorexia nervosa (Lacey 1983). However, those with a history of substance abuse (alcohol or drug) were not more likely to relapse to these problems once their eating had improved (it has been suggested that these behaviours may be interchangeable with bingeing for some patients) (Mitchell *et al.* 1990a).

Readiness to change seems to be associated with outcome; the better outcome group had higher scores on action (have a commitment to change and have begun to try to change their problem behaviours) (Franko 1997).

Larger studies have been able to make use of multiple regression or discriminant function analysis. An early study suggested that pre-treatment level of self-esteem was a predictor of outcome, including at 12 months (Fairburn, Kirk, Anastasiades & Cooper 1987), although it only predicted general psychiatric symptoms and depression, not eating disorder symptoms. Other studies, however, have found that pre treatment self-esteem also predicts eating disorder symptom outcome, both at the end of treatment and at three month follow-up (Baell & Wertheim 1992). A related construct, self-efficacy, was also associated with better outcome for three domains—controlling binge-eating in high-risk situations, use of stimulus control techniques to control bingeing, and forming satisfactory social relationships (Schneider *et al.* 1987).

Pretreatment binge and vomiting frequency have frequently been associated with outcome, with higher pretreatment levels linked to worse outcome (e.g. Fahy & Russell 1993; Turnbull *et al.* 1997; Wilson *et al.* 1999). High EAT scores at pretreatment, also interpersonal distrust (EDI), have also been linked to poor outcome (Bossert *et al.* 1992; Olmsted *et al.* 1994). Post-treatment vomiting frequency also predicted relapse (Olmsted *et al.* 1994).

Depression predicts outcome (Bossert *et al.* 1992; Davis *et al.* 1992), as does severity of initial psychiatric symptoms (Steiger *et al.* 1993). Relapse over two years, was associated with younger age (Olmsted *et al.* 1994). Longer history predicted poorer outcome (Fahy & Russell 1993; Turnbull *et al.* 1997). In one study, if treated 15 or more years after onset, the probability of recovery was only 20%, but 80% if treated in the first few years (Reas *et al.* 2000). Duration of previous in-patient treatments also predicts outcome (Bossert *et al.* 1992). Ambivalence or pessimism about change predicts poorer outcome (Mussell *et al.* 2000), as does history of low body weight (Davis *et al.* 1992). Other predictors include a history of substance abuse (Wilson *et al.* 1999).

Personality disorder predicts poor outcome (Fahy & Russell 1993), including Cluster B (Rossiter *et al.* 1993), and borderline characteristics (Steiger *et al.* 1993).

The therapeutic alliance also predicted remission, but it seemed that the change in symptoms influenced the alliance rather than the other way round (Wilson *et al.* 1999).

Social adjustment also predicts (Steiger *et al.* 1993). In one study dissatisfaction with body image was the best predictor of relapse (Freeman *et al.* 1985).

Signal detection analysis has also been used to investigate predictors. Here poor response was best predicted by social adjustment, and by lower body mass index (Agras *et al.* 2000a). The authors argue that this technique is particularly helpful in establishing cut off points for developing treatment algorithms.

Path analysis has also been used. This has suggested that a controlling family environment limits ability to make behavioural and cognitive change (Blouin *et al.* 1994).

One study has conducted a comprehensive survey of predictors in each category dividing predictors into pretreatment, post treatment and lifetime (including personality). Lifetime history of obesity predicted poor outcome, alcohol dependence decreased chances of poor outcome, and high self-directedness predicted good outcome at one year. Pretreatment global functioning and high bulimia scores on the EDI, and major depression, also predicted poor outcome. Post-treatment bingeing, restriction, urge to binge (on a cue reactivity test) all predicted poor outcome (Bulik *et al.* 1998).

Role of cognitions

The predictive value of cognitions in treatment is little investigated, despite its value in testing cognitive theory. The results are also conflicting, and at times counter-intuitive. In one study, for example, 12-month outcome was best predicted by attitudes to weight and shape, and by low self-esteem. Unexpectedly, those with more severe attitudes, and lower self-esteem, did best. However, as predicted by the cognitive model, attitudes at the end of treatment predicted outcome in those who had responded to treatment, i.e. more disturbed attitudes predicted worse outcome (Fairburn *et al.* 1993c). In another study, however, these same cognitive variables did not predict relapse (Cooper & Steere 1995). One possible explanation, considered by the authors, is that current assessments do not capture the relevant cognitions adequately.

Rapid responders

It has been suggested that it might be useful to identify the key characteristics of rapid responders (Wilson *et al.* 2000). This could save money, and also the frustration and demoralization that may result from failed therapy.

One study found that rapid responders were generally bingeing and vomiting less frequently before treatment. They were also less symptomatic at the end of treatment, and less likely to relapse over a 2-year follow-up (Olmsted *et al.* 1996). A second study also found that rapid responders were bingeing and vomiting less frequently before treatment; they were also less likely to be self-directed on a personality measure (Bulik *et al.* 1999a).

Drop-outs

It is also useful to be able to predict who will drop out. One study found that those who dropped out were younger, had experienced more parental breakup, more previous psychiatric treatment, and were more likely to be employed. Also important may be low or average severity, and failure to complete questionnaires properly (Mahon *et al.* 2001). Another study found that interpersonal difficulties discriminated completers from drop-outs (Blouin *et al.* 1995). Hopelessness and depression pretreatment, also higher level of ineffectiveness and higher external locus of control, were predictive in another study (Steel *et al.* 2000).

One study of six patients, who could not be engaged, found that they had a low desired weight, used more laxatives, had longer duration of illness, were more depressed, had lower self-esteem, and more 'impulsive' behaviour—self harm and substance abuse. More also had borderline personality disorder (Coker *et al.* 1993).

It has been argued that it is important to distinguish between failure to engage and drop-outs (Kazdin & Mazurick 1994). Failure to engage (those who did not come back after assessment) had more bulimic (perceived by the patient) and borderline pathology, and patients saw their families as relatively good at showing emotional concern for each other. Drop-outs (who attended some sessions) were similar but saw their families as poor on emotional concern (Waller 1997).

One study selected a group at risk of treatment failure or failure to engage in treatment. More in this group reported a history of sexual abuse (Gleaves & Eberenz 1994).

Theoretical implications

Few researchers have as yet assessed cognitive aspects of the disorder in treatment studies. Nearly all studies have relied on the EDE and, as has been suggested (Cooper & Steere 1995), this may not assess the full range of the key cognitive disturbance in BN. The theoretical implications of CBT studies are, therefore, currently limited. There is some preliminary support for the suggestion that CBT works by altering restraint and attitudes, thus supporting Fairburn's model, but this needs more work, using a range of cognitive measures, and assessing cognition during and after treatment. Single-case multiple baseline studies might be useful here—this would enable the key prediction that change in cognition (attitudes to weight and shape) is responsible for change in behaviour to be tested. Self-efficacy has also been suggested as a possible mechanism in CBT (Wilson & Fairburn 1993). CBT may, for example, enhance coping with specific situations that trigger binge-eating, or work to help patients cope with general stress, e.g. by problem-solving or relapse prevention. As yet there is no evidence for this.

Issues

The treatment studies discussed above raise several issues. In particular, it seems that overall success rate, even with what is generally accepted to be the best treatment, CBT, is relatively low. Recently, there has been interest in treatment choice when CBT fails.

What to do when CBT fails

One study gave non-responders IPT or medication (a staged intervention using two drugs, imipramine and fluoxetine). Neither were beneficial (Mitchell *et al.* 1999, in Wilson *et al.* 2000). Results using fluoxetine were more promising in a small study (Walsh *et al.* 2000). Those who had not responded to CBT or IPT did better with fluoxetine than placebo for 8 weeks however, some declined to take part.

Wilson (1996) suggests expanding the scope of CBT, when it fails. He argues that it may be useful to include more focus on interpersonal issues, and also to intensify cognitive restructuring. Adding in dialectical behaviour therapy techniques (see, for example: Linehan 1993), to address personality problems could also be useful, as could exposure to cues for bingeing. This might involve planned binges, akin to 'worry exposure' (Craske *et al.*1992), i.e. to thoughts and images of weight and shape.

The role of medication

The role of medication remains to be established (Wilson *et al.* 2000). In general, it is much less effective than CBT, more intrusive, less acceptable to many people, and there are no controlled studies of its long-term efficacy (Wilson *et al.* 2000).

The role of manualized treatments

It has been argued that idiographic formulation (not usual in manualized treatment for BN) would increase the effectiveness of CBT. In specific phobia, however, it was the use of a specific technique rather than individual formulation that produced better results (Schulte *et al.* 1992). While this suggests individual formulation may not be essential, specific phobia is usually a much more straightforward problem than BN.

The role of stepped care

Stepped care has become a popular concept in BN. One study has evaluated a self-help manual followed by a course of attenuated CBT, compared to standard CBT. The reduction in symptoms and abstinence was similar in the two groups (30% abstinent), and improvements were maintained at follow-up of 18 months (around 40% abstinent in either group). Twenty per cent of the patients had only the manual and did not need further treatment (Treasure *et al.* 1996).

Another study evaluated brief psycho-education plus individual cognitive behavioural therapy. The group receiving both did better than those who had psychoeducation alone, on bingeing and purging but not on attitudes or behaviours (EDE Global score) (Davis *et al.* 1999).

It has been suggested, based on studies such as these, that clinicians should provide treatments sequentially according to need. This should start with the lowest step—the simplest, least intrusive, and least costly, and then go on to more complex or intensive treatment if the patient does not respond (Wilson *et al.* 2000). The clinical needs of the patient, and responses to treatments, should also be taken into account.

There have been some attempts to combine stepped care with a clinical decision tree (see Garner & Needleman 1997). This has not been evaluated, and it may not be practical to do so. However, treatment sequences that are relevant clinically, e.g. CBT with systematic addition of other components, could be evaluated.

Maintenance of gains

One study has looked at the role of a support group, following treatment, in those who had responded. Most of those who had access to this did not relapse over a 6-month follow-up period (Pyle *et al.* 1990). This needs a controlled evaluation.

The role of clinical governance

Evidence-based medicine has become popular, and it is considered good practice to use empirically validated treatments. But persuading people to use these can be difficult. Persuading training courses to teach them is a further obstacle (Chambless *et al.* 1996). Few health and social care professionals are currently trained in CBT, the treatment of choice for BN—this may explain why it is used less often than seems appropriate. Indeed, it is often felt that CBT for bulimia nervosa is not well disseminated, especially in the USA (Wilson 1999). One study found only 7% of those who had received treatment for their bulimia had received CBT—although almost 97% had received some form of psychotherapy (Crow *et al.* 1999a).

Patients' perception of treatment

This has been neglected, as has the process of treatment. With emphasis on the consumer or user perspective in healthcare, this is likely to become more an important area for research.

Implications for primary care

One study developed a simple and brief form of CBT for use in primary care, although no formal cognitive restructuring was carried out. Eleven patients were treated by non-specialists, and six had a good outcome. This suggests some cases may not need specialist help (Fairburn & Peveler 1990). Thus CBT may be a useful treatment in primary care—where most patients with BN are likely to be found.

The role of cognition in CBT

Cognitions are an integral part of BN. Theoretically they are responsible for a great deal of patients' distress (and behaviour). The emphasis on behaviour—especially bingeing and purging—in treatment studies risks losing this important fact. Anecdotally, patients are distressed, not only by their behaviour, but also by their thoughts. However, most treatment studies have no formal measure of cognitive change with treatment—this is an important omission. It has been suggested that behaviour may be a poor marker of severity; it correlates poorly with other characteristics (Fairburn & Cooper 1984). It may also not provide a complete explanation for outcome—for example, in one study, only those whose body image had changed, as well as being abstinent from bingeing and purging at the end of treatment, maintained their gains at follow-up (Freeman *et al.* 1985). In many fields recent research suggests that cognitions are powerful predictors of behaviour and psychological distress, often more important predictors than general 'illness' or demographic variables. These need to be assessed in treatment studies, and their relationship to behaviour and psychological distress (including at outcome) needs to be evaluated.

The effectiveness of CBT

Although CBT is effective for some patients with BN, much more work is needed to improve its success rate. CBT for some other disorders has better outcome than CBT for BN. One possibility may be to use ideas from these other disorders to develop both the theory and treatment. An attempt to do this is presented in Chapter 8.

Summary

This chapter has presented and discussed cognitive therapy outcome for BN. Part one identified some of the problems with the relevant outcome studies, and presented results of naturalistic and early review studies. There are several problems with the studies available; but the evidence suggests that BN often has a poor outcome if untreated.

Part two reviewed existing cognitive therapy studies for BN, including individual and group treatment, self-help and other studies. While CT works for some people with BN, and is more effective than many other active treatments (with the possible exception of interpersonal psychotherapy), many do not recover or continue to have distressing symptoms. This is particularly true when long term follow-up is conducted.

Part three discussed initial attempts to identify the active ingredients of cognitive therapy for BN. The role of cognition was emphasized. It was concluded that much more work is needed on its role in BN. This may involve routine assessment of cognition in treatment studies, and use of a wider range of assessment measures.

Part four summarized research on self-help and in patient studies, and predictors of outcome in CT for BN. Research is limited, but severity of behavioural symptoms (as well as some other features) emerges as a significant predictor. The role of cognitions as a predictor of outcome was briefly considered. Again, there is little relevant research as yet. Related issues (e.g. predictors of drop out, what to do when CT fails) were discussed.

Part five summarized the effectiveness of CBT as currently delivered, and considered the theoretical and general implications of cognitive therapy treatment research. It was concluded that there is a need the further development of cognitive theory and therapy. This might usefully draw on some of the ideas used in the treatment of other disorders, and more recent theoretical developments in CT, as discussed in Chapter 8.

Chapter 13

The future

Overview

This chapter will discuss some of the current issues in BN, relevant issues in the field of mental health, and topics with roots in general (especially cognitive) psychology. The aim is not to provide an over-arching theory or detailed synthesis of the field. There is not nearly enough evidence on cognition in BN to do that yet. Rather, the aim is to highlight issues of relevance to clinicians and researchers working in the field, and to share some of my thoughts on future directions. Part one will, therefore, consider current 'hot' issues in BN.

Part two will consider relevant issues currently important in the mental health field. Part three will consider relevant issues from general psychology. Part four will provide a brief summary and assessment of current clinical practice guidelines for BN. Finally, the book will be briefly reviewed in the light of its aims. The plan for the chapter is summarized in Table 13.1.

Current issues in BN

A summary of the current issues to be covered in this section is presented in Table 13.2.

Schema-focused theory and therapy

Schema theory has only recently been applied to BN and much about it remains to be studied. The presence of core beliefs and underlying assumptions in BN is now well established (see work by Cooper and colleagues, and by Waller and colleagues), but little is known about their nature. For example, what is their characteristic content, and how does it differ, if at all, from that found in other disorders? A mechanism (schema compensation) has been identified (see work by Cooper and colleagues) linking dieting to negative self-beliefs, but how do different beliefs link to different

Table 13.1 Summary of plan for Chapter 13

Current 'hot' issues in BN
Issues important in mental health
Issues from general psychology
Clinical practice guidelines for BN
Review of book

Table 13.2 Current issues in BN

Schema-focused theory and therapy
Imagery interventions
Insights from cognitive psychology
Abstinence
Use of manualized treatments
Stepped care
Prevention

behaviours—particularly to bingeing and (particularly relevant to understanding how AN differs from BN) to restricting? Some of these issues are beginning to be addressed. For example, one study has investigated the specific content of core beliefs (Waller *et al.* 2001). This study suggested that bulimics might have more failure beliefs than depressed patients, but are similar on beliefs related to defectiveness/shame and social isolation. There are methodological problems with the study—it is not clear whether length of illness in the depressed and bulimic groups was the same; the depressed group tended to be older, and it is possible that the bulimics had a more chronic history. In addition, only 38.9% of the depressed group were correctly classified by the discriminant function analysis used, and 33.3% were put into the one of the bulimic groups. Nevertheless, the study is an important first step.

Another study suggests that there may be 'self-other' differences in core beliefs. In this study, sociotrophy (acceptance and approval) and autonomy (independence and achievement) were related to bulimic symptoms, but only sociotrophy was uniquely related to bulimia when the symptoms of depression were controlled (Friedman & Whisman 1998). This suggests that bulimics' self-esteem may be more related to interpersonal relationships than to self-oriented features, i.e. independence and achievement. Depression, however, may be related more to autonomy than to sociotrophy. Interpersonal or 'other' related beliefs may thus be particularly characteristic of depression. This apparent and intriguing difference between BN and depression needs further study.

One study has investigated schema-driven processes in BN, specifically avoidance—using the Young-Rygh Avoidance Inventory (Young & Rygh 1994). Both of its scales, cognitive and emotional avoidance, and somatic and behavioural avoidance, distinguished normals from bulimics—suggesting that, in addition to schema compensation, both of these types of avoidance are likely to be important in bulimia. Neither correlated with frequency of bingeing and vomiting in the clinical group—indeed there was a tendency to a negative association. There was a relationship in the normals—especially for behavioural/somatic avoidance—but with symptom and severity (not binge and vomit frequency). One possibility is that those with more severe bulimic pathology/behaviour avoidance are using other means of avoidance, i.e. more binge-eating. There are methodological problems with this study too—a mixed eating-disorder group was used, and this group was also much older and heavier than the controls (Spranger *et al.* 2001). The psychometric properties of the measure also remain to be established. Nevertheless, the study is an important first step, and raises issues that merit further study.

More research is needed into the specific content of core beliefs in BN, their associated processes, and the link between beliefs and key behaviours. If the model proposed recently is correct (Cooper *et al.*, in press) then this relationship should be mediated by positive thoughts (for binge-eating) and negative thoughts (for restricting). The latter may begin to provide a cognitive explanation of food restriction that can be applied to AN. One way to obtain some of this information, and to discover how BN patients differ in this from AN patients, and dieters, is to devise and use detailed semi-structured interviews. This may enable more accurate and finer differences and distinctions to be identified than is possible with structured measures, particularly as most of those used to date (e.g. the Schema Questionnaire and Avoidance Inventory) have not been designed with BN in mind. The EDBQ is an exception but, although developed for EDs, it is not designed to be specific to BN (and there may be important differences at this level between AN and BN that it cannot identify). Such interviews may help provide data for the development of BN specific measures. They have already begun to find intriguing differences between patients with AN and dieters (Turner & Cooper, 2002).

Schema-focused therapy is a relatively recent development in cognitive therapy. Evidence for the role of its key theoretical constructs in BN suggests that treatment based on it may be useful. There are now some descriptions of its application to BN, and suggestions for specific schema-focused techniques that may be helpful (see Chapter 11). However, it is important to remember that its use has not yet been thoroughly evaluated. The question of whether or not, and when, clinicians should be using it to treat patients with BN is considered below.

Imagery interventions

Imagery has not often been studied in bulimia nervosa. One study found that at least half of all bulimics reported (visual) images in conjunction with negative automatic thoughts, usually similar in content, i.e. focused on the negative consequences of gaining weight, or getting fat (Cooper *et al.* 1998).

However, characteristics of imagery in bulimia nervosa have not been explored in detail, in the way that they have begun to be studied in other disorders. Imagery in social phobia, for example, has been found to be spontaneous, negative, and viewed from an 'observer perspective', i.e. the self is seen as if from an external point of view (Hackmann *et al.* 1998). Images are found particularly when anticipating or recalling in social and not non-social situations (Wells *et al.* 1998). The effect of the observer perspective is specific to social evaluative concerns, and not also found in other phobias (Wells & Papageorgiou 1999). The implications of this bias are that patients with social anxiety may have little access to how others actually behave, instead they tend to focus on internal cues when making judgements about social situations. In social anxiety, this includes interoceptive cues. Attention to such cues might be important in the maintenance of the disorder; thus treatment may need to alter this. Vividness is another feature that may be important, and has been studied in relation to spider phobia (Pratt *et al.*, submitted; Watts *et al.* 1986). Detailed analysis of the dimensions and characteristics of imagery (along these lines) would be useful in BN. Clinical experience suggests that the observer perspective and attention to interoceptive cues may well be features of BN, and that both may play a role in the maintenance of the disorder.

Studies have also investigated the early memories associated with images in social anxiety. One study found that most participants had such memories, and that they tended to be negative, similar in sensory and interpersonal content to the images, and represented in the same sensory modalities. This suggests that spontaneous images may have their origins in childhood memories. The images also involved various modalities, especially bodily sensations, almost as often as visual (Hackmann, Clark & McMarus, 2000). This means that work on transforming memory in order to change the distorted meanings that still colour the present and give the image a meaning that is less distorted, may be helpful. This parallels recent work on PTSD (Ehlers 1999) and draws on techniques used in schema-focused therapy (Layden *et al.* 1993). Clinically, it seems likely that those with BN also have memories associated with their images, also that these are likely to reflect visual and kinesthetic sensations, in particular. Some preliminary work supports this suggestion (Cooper *et al.*, submitted b), and also suggests that imagery modification strategies can be used successfully to change the meaning of these early memories, and the core beliefs associated with them.

Imagery therapy of two types has been developed in BN. The first has been developed in a psychodynamic context. This is based on object relations, and self psychology formulations, which highlight difficulty in self-soothing, and the importance of a holding environment (Esplen & Garfinkel 1998). Two types of guided imagery exercises are typically used—to provide comfort and relaxation, and to promote self-exploration and self-experience. In these exercises patients are encouraged to interpret and contemplate the imagery, and are provided with a transitional object that can be internalized (Esplen *et al.* 1998). There is some evidence that treatment based on this is effective.

The second uses imagery in the context of schema-focused or CBT interventions (see Cooper *et al.*, submitted b). It is based on procedures described in Layden *et al.* (1993), and Edwards (1990), to modify deeper level beliefs, meaning, and assumptions. It may be particularly useful in modifying affect related to developmentally more primitive systems, i.e. preverbal ones. It can also be used to develop more adaptive beliefs (Smucker & Niederee 1995). This is the approach used in the preliminary study reported above (Cooper *et al.*, submitted b).

Why images rather than verbal thoughts? It has been suggested that images condense a great deal of information, and reveal idiosyncratic layers of meaning. Imagery is a major coding system in the brain (Paivio 1986), and images are often linked to greater emotional arousal than verbal thoughts. Thus changing them might be more likely to create a greater emotional shift than changing verbal thoughts (Hackmann 1998).

Work can take place at the level of automatic thoughts (not yet typically conducted in BN) or core beliefs. At the automatic-thought level, the patient can let the image run on—to see what actually happens, and to change the meta-meaning, of having the image, i.e. just because you have it does not mean it is true or that it is actually going to happen. The patient may need help to change the dimensions of the image, e.g. put it on a screen or change it to a field perspective. At the core belief level—work can take place with an early memory associated with it that comes to mind, including on repairing the memory, e.g. by highlighting coping factors, or presenting an adult perspective. This may also be the mechanism through which Esplen & Garfinkel's (1998), guided imagery works.

Imagery in BN needs further research. Clinically, the images patients with BN have in relation to their weight and shape are often very distressing, and seem to link to distress experienced about body shape and weight (affective and cognitive). This distress can be difficult to change using standard cognitive therapy strategies, and imagery modification may be particularly useful here. Distress associated with weight and shape may also be manifest as 'feeling fat', a phenomenon that is little understood in BN. It is possible that this, with its heightened awareness of body sensations, may also be helped by modifying aspects of imagery (particularly kinesthetic aspects). As for visual images, work at a meta-level might modify the belief that feelings are facts, or (see below) attentional processing. The use of imagery as a treatment tool is showing some promise clinically and needs to be evaluated further. Particular attention may need to be paid to modalities of images other than the visual in BN.

Insights from cognitive psychology

There is a lot of individual variability in reports of experienced imagery in cognitive psychology tasks. High imagers score differently on tests of spatial manipulation, i.e. they do better, than low imagers, e.g. Barratt (1953), but not on tests of reasoning. In manipulation tests (Shepard & Feng 1972), some use visual imagery but some use kinesthetic imagery, i.e. they imagine folding a cube. Performance also does not seem to be related to vividness of imagery in general but to quality while carrying out a specific task. This suggests that there may be individual differences in imagery in BN too, and that what may be most important is not their imagery ability in general but ability on specific key tasks. There is some evidence for this in spider phobia (Pratt et al., submitted). Different stimuli also differ in their ability to elicit images (Paivio et al. 1968. This suggests that certain cues may recur in association with imagery in BN. Clinically, an image of the self as overweight and fat was common in patients' images in BN (Cooper et al. 1998). Such images may be particularly easy to elicit, which makes it important to use control groups. However, in spider phobia, use of a control group suggested that images relevant to concern with spiders were less likely in the control group (Pratt et al., in preparation).

Theoretically, there seems to be some separation between images and propositions (verbal information). In his memory model, Baddeley (1986) includes a phonological loop that is separate from a visuo-spatial working memory. Dual coding (Paivio 1971), has also been suggested, with a verbal system specialized for serial or sequential processing, and an image system for simultaneous or parallel processing. This is partially supported by more recent research (e.g. Marschark *et al.* 1987), which suggests that there is a distinction between imaginal and verbal processing, but not between the two storage systems. Some separation between the two systems suggests a need for treatment procedures designed for each aspect. That is, if we are to change imaginal aspects, imaginal procedures may be needed. This may seem particularly relevant to disorders such as PTSD, where intrusive images or flashbacks are common. It may also be relevant to phenonema that standard CBT does not deal with very well at present. In BN this may include feeling fat and core (especially strongly held emotional) beliefs. The latter tend to be developmentally more primitive, and 'non-verbal' in character. Both are difficult to shift using standard CBT techniques; and may respond well to imaginal strategies. There is some preliminary evidence that imaginal strategies can successfully alter emotional belief in BN (Cooper *et al.*, submitted b).

Imageability is also a good predictor of memory (Paivio 1971). Selective memory has been studied in BN (Hunt & Cooper 2001). It is possible that there could be a link between selective memory and imagery in BN. This remains to be investigated.

In summary, details of schema content, processes, imagery characteristics, and their associated processes will need to be incorporated into a cognitive model of BN. Cooper *et al.* (in press) have recently provided a basic framework for this.

Abstinence

Most treatments for BN, including standard CBT, do not produce abstinence from bingeing and vomiting, despite the fact that it is associated with better long-term outcome. A rather higher rate of binge episodes is usually expected (and tolerated) at the end of treatment than might be acceptable, e.g. for panic episodes in panic disorder. There are several possible reasons for this. One possibility is that motivation for change is low in BN—and patients do not see maximum change as desirable. It is certainly true that drop out from treatment is high (which might support this suggestion). Therapists are beginning to pay attention to the issue of drop out, and some are adopting motivational interviewing before treatment commences (Schmidt & Treasure 1993), or devoting considerable space in treatment to enhancing motivation to change (Cooper *et al.* 2000). Another possibility is simply that standard treatments are less effective than they might be (and perhaps therefore, and also, less acceptable). Yet another suggestion is that because concern about weight and shape and eating is 'normative', the abstinence goal is unrealistic. The latter proposal ignores the fact that the vast majority of young adult women do not binge-eat and vomit (as defined in DSM-IV), and that most patients want to stop bingeing and vomiting, rather than merely decrease its frequency. It may be that recent advances in theory and treatment, particularly in cognitive theory and therapy, make this goal more attainable—the evidence suggests that it is a worthwhile goal, as well as being the aim of most patients. The relevant treatment studies urgently need to be done, based on these recent developments. Leaving patients symptomatic at the end of treatment is not acceptable. Residual or remaining symptoms may be just as distressing as the experience of a full-blown disorder. For example, there is some evidence that those with partial syndromes are cognitively as distressed as those who meet DSM-IV diagnosis for BN (Turner & Bryant-Waugh, submitted). One problem may be that number of treatment sessions is often limited by services or insurance (often to fewer than the number used in the major treatment studies), and full recovery in a relatively short space of time may be unrealistic. With current treatments this may leave many people with distressing symptoms.

Manualized treatments

It has been argued that the most effective treatment for bulimia nervosa is manual based CBT (Wilson & Fairburn 1998). However, CBT manuals, such as those developed for BN, have been criticized. In particular, it has been argued that manual-based treatments are incompatible with individualized formulations (Persons 1991). Wilson (1996; 1997) argues that manualized treatments are often more flexible than they seem but, nevertheless, diagnosis-based models, including early CBT models for BN, do tend to assume that all patients have the same reasons for their problems, and do not emphasize individual formulation. In recent developments in CT models, there is more space for individual differences, e.g. in content of thoughts and beliefs. Indeed, unlike the old model, an important feature of the revised model for BN is that it must always be individualized for the patient, and treatment cannot proceed until this has been achieved. This combination (basic model plus individual tailoring) has the advantage of drawing on empirical research, yet allowing for individual differences, thus introducing greater flexibility than was previously possible. Further research is needed to see if this is more effective than treatment packages, or existing self-help treatments. One recent book uses a combination of basic model plus individual formulation (Cooper *et al.* 2000), and this is need of evaluation.

Stepped care

This is the idea that treatment should start with a less intensive form, e.g. self-help or psycho-education, and only go on to more intensive treatment if the patient fails to respond. The alternative is to match the client to the treatment, e.g. self-help, individual cognitive therapy. The advantage of this is that it avoids the potentially demoralizing nature of the stepped-care sequence, which may then make a potentially effective treatment more difficult to implement.

Unfortunately it seems difficult to predict who will respond rapidly (or at all) to treatment (Olmsted *et al.* 1996). Indeed there has been little interest in studying those who fail to respond to different treatments. This seems an important omission, given that it has health policy implications—in terms of wasted resources and patient outcome, and also because there are many patients who have not responded to different treatments who could be studied. More work is needed here; particularly as only a very small number of patients seem to be helped by the first steps of treatment (self-help and psycho-education) based on current treatments, and there is considerable potential for failure experiences. This raises serious ethical issues; for example, are we justified in offering very basic self-help to someone with a very severe eating disorder? Currently, research does not help us to judge.

Prevention

Primary prevention programmes try to reduce factors that contribute to the occurrence or incidence of the disorder, secondary programmes try to reduce chronicity through early identification and intervention (Shisslak *et al.* 1987). Eating-disorder programmes have usually focused on primary prevention. To date, they have not been very effective. There is even some evidence that they increase dietary restraint (Carter, Stewart, Dunn & Fairburn 1997), and eating disorder symptoms (Mann *et al.* 1997). Secondary prevention programmes seem a little more promising (Stice *et al.* 2000), with decreases in thin ideal internalization, body dissatisfaction, dieting, negative affect, and bulimic symptoms being found in one programme (Stice *et al.* 2001).

One difficulty is identifying those at risk (both in primary or secondary programmes). It is not really quite clear what the (reliable) predisposing factors are that need to be identified. Given that eating disorders can be secretive, it might also be difficult to identify early cases for secondary prevention.

Huon suggests a focus on dieting as a necessary though not sufficient condition, and that the aim should be to prevent that behaviour. This should be part of a general programme to help young people respond positively to environmental challenges, including smoking, alcohol, drug related behaviour (Huon, Braganza, Brown, Ritchie & Roncolato 1998).

It has been suggested that Internet-based programmes, using computer-assisted education, may be one relatively inexpensive way to disseminate prevention programmes. One preliminary study found differences in body dissatisfaction and drive for thinness at follow-up (but not at the end of treatment: Winzelberg *et al.* 2000).

The best way to prevent bulimia is unclear. There have been some high-profile media campaigns in recent years. In one study, most men and women had heard of bulimia through the media. Over one-third of women said that this knowledge had affected their own eating or attitudes in some way, e.g. often made them cautious about dieting—usually in relation to knowledge of anorexia. But in a few cases it had encouraged extreme weight-loss behaviours, including vomiting, and use of laxatives. This suggests that careful thought and research is needed about the best way to use the media to prevent eating problems (Murray *et al.* 1990).

It has been argued (Battle & Brownell 1996) that instead of focusing on the individual, we need to focus on society, and use public health approaches. This might include modifying the environment (though the suggestions seem more relevant to obesity). This might involve regulating advertising of diets, cosmetics, and clothing, for example, to children, in the same way that cigarette and alcohol advertising is regulated. It could involve teaching psychological inoculation to aesthetic ideals, diet, cosmetic and food industries, as is being done for tobacco.

Others are pessimistic, and suggest that eating disorders cannot be prevented (e.g. Vandereycken & Meermann 1984), both because we do not know enough about their aetiology, and because the socio-cultural factors that contribute cannot be easily modified. Interestingly, most programmes have focused on weight and shape pressures, none have yet focused on broader self-esteem, or the conflicting role expectations, that have also been found to be important (Steiner-Adair 1989) in the development of eating problems. Given the role assigned to self-worth in recent cognitive theory for BN, it may be that enhancing self-esteem in girls might be a protective factor. This is an avenue for future research.

General mental health issues

A summary of the topics to be covered in this section can be seen in Table 13.3.

Case formulation

Case formulation provides a link between theory and practice (Butler 1998). It applies the theory, and research to the patient; and helps the therapist to structure information about the individual patient's problem. It also needs to explain all relevant aspects of psychological life (Butler 1998). This typically includes cognition, emotion, behaviour and physiology.

One of the problems with the initial cognitive theory of BN is that it did not do this. As suggested above, it also did not place great emphasis on individual formulation. Recent developments incorporate all aspects, and give individual formulation an important role.

It remains to be seen whether formulation-based treatment is more effective in BN than treatment that is not based on individual formulation. Studies of diagnostic-led interventions vs. problem-focused or problem-formulated interventions in other disorders are inconclusive. They often seem to have been conducted with relatively simple

Table 13.3 General mental health issues

Case formulation
Evidence-based practice
Psychotherapy integration
User perspectives
Clinical effectiveness

problems, e.g. phobias, where it may be difficult to demonstrate that formulation driven treatment is better.

Evidence-based practice

It has been argued that therapists have an ethical and legal obligation to offer empirically supported treatment. This is important for patients and also for those paying. Nevertheless, despite the evidence, CBT for bulimia nervosa is underutilized (Wilson 1998). The same is true of empirically supported psychotherapy in other disorders (Persons 1997).

Wilson suggested that there are two reasons for this; that RCTs are largely irrelevant to everyday practice, and that manualized therapies are too constraining.

Arnow (1999), however, argues that these objections may be overstated. He also suggests that the developers of the treatments must take some of the blame—often findings are not presented in a useful way for clinicians. For example, they do not tell you how to do the therapy, and there is often little opportunity to learn, or access to training. Therapists in trials often have extensive training, and it may be difficult for others to approximate their success rate. The manuals often focus on specific interventions but there are many other issues that arise, e.g. relationship issues, or the client gains lots of weight, or does not keep appointments. Studies are needed to look at how much flexibility is useful, and under what conditions (Eifert *et al.* 1997). More research is also needed on therapist and client characteristics, group vs. individual treatment, and application to culturally diverse groups (Iwamasa & Orsillo 1997).

More significantly, it has been argued that RCT efficacy is not adequate for general dissemination to be recommended (Persons 1997). Research needs to find if it is also effective first, i.e. useful in everyday clinical practice (although it is clearly better to use RCT data than nothing) (Persons 1997).

A complementary paradigm, practice-based evidence, has been suggested (Margison *et al.* 2000). This involves gathering good quality data from routine clinical practice, and it has been suggested that this evidence is needed together with RCT evidence. It is related to the issue of efficacy and effectiveness (Cochrane 1972). Efficacy usually refers to evidence obtained from carefully designed trials where threats to internal validity are minimized—the RCT is often the gold standard here. Effectiveness refers to studies with high generalisability, but greater compromise over internal validity. The latter refers to how useful the treatment is in everyday clinical practice. This has been relatively neglected in psychotherapy, including in BN. Rather worryingly, (and many clinicians will not be surprised at this), there is some evidence that effectiveness for psychotherapy in BN may be poor (Ben-Tovim *et al.* 2001). To date, the effectiveness of CBT has not been evaluated. It needs infrastructure—the USA practice research networks provide an example of how it might work. This is a network of clinicians who collaborate to gather data on real world practice. It also typically involves more than just 'outcome', e.g. adherence to treatment, acceptability of treatment, competence and skillfulness of the therapist also tend to be evaluated. This is in urgent need of research.

Treatment also needs to be disseminated. Factors that may affect dissemination include: lack of training in the protocols, and not valuing an empirical approach to treatment. Other key factors include: personal contact with developer or champion; fit with methods already using; provision of information; availability of videos, etc.; informing consumers of what is available; letters; talk shows; books for the lay audience (Persons 1997). Manualized treatments also need to be taught and integrated into graduate training programmes.

Psychotherapy integration

Cognitive therapy has a potentially key role in integration (Rimm & Masters 1979), given that it brings together internal and behavioural processes. It can incorporate a broad range of concepts from other therapies, including those that focus on internal and external processes. In the 1980s and 1990s, a growing number of therapists identified themselves as integrative or eclectic, and there were an increasing number of publications on integration (Hollanders 1996).

The term integration has many meanings (Albeniz & Holmes 1996), and a whole field of psychotherapy integration has emerged (Norcros & Goldfried 1992). Typically it refers to a combination of two or more forms of theoretically based psychotherapies. It differs from eclecticism, or the use of techniques and procedures, regardless of theoretical origin (Garfield 1994). Eclecticism has been referred to as the process of selecting out; and integration as the process of bringing together (Hollanders 1999; Hollanders & McLeod 1999).

Integrated treatments have not been much used in bulimia nervosa research, and have rarely been evaluated. However, it has been suggested that they have an important role in clinical practice (Garner & Needleman 1997), where a big issue is how to match patients to treatments. Treatment studies typically have narrow entry criteria; in clinical practice patients have other problems, different characteristics, and may fail to respond to standard treatment or relapse after it. It can be difficult to determine an appropriate treatment when the patient is not typical of those who have participated in a research trial. Garner & Needleman (1997) suggest a basic stepped-care approach should be tried initially. If that fails, then individual CBT, plus medication, and then IPT (if there are significant interpersonal problems), or if still not much improved, psychodynamic and family treatment, either with or without CBT and IPT (but only if longer term therapy seems warranted). Some of these combinations have been tried and reported in the literature.

An early example of integration was the use of behavioural and psychodynamic therapy (Lacey 1983).

Day and in-patient programmes often use several therapies together—possibly because patients needing this level of input tend to have complex and severe problems. CBT and dynamic therapy, with an interpersonal focus, has also been described (Steiger 1989), particularly for patients with characterological disturbances. CBT combined with dynamic therapy and medication has been described, integrated through the therapeutic relationship, the 'primary treatment matrix through which all other modalities are introduced and monitored' (Herzog *et al.* 1989). Other combinations include psychodynamic and feminist principles (Zerbe 1995), psychodynamic and 12-step approaches (Overeaters Anonymous) (Johnson & Sansone 1993). Often, however, it is not clear how far different treatments have been 'integrated' as opposed to delivered sequentially, or in relative isolation.

Cognitive theory and therapy in BN is increasingly taking on concepts and strategies previously typical of other forms of therapy—and, in some cases, translating them into cognitive terms where necessary. Thus, other approaches are fully 'integrated', within a general cognitive framework. Focus on the self, and on imagery, and early experiences are all examples of this. In addition, unlike some other theories and therapies, their use and application is based on a body of evolving empirical research.

User perspectives

Client perception of progress (and other aspects of the disorder) has rarely been investigated in bulimia nervosa. Despite the emphasis on user perspectives in the NHS, and existence of important self-help organisations, e.g. in the UK, the Eating Disorders Association, there is very little published research on user views in BN. Most that there is seems to be qualitative, and remains unpublished. Platt (1992, in Jarman & Walsh 1999), for example, suggests that clients see three stages of recovery, each a necessary precursor to the next. This involves seeing bulimia as an unwanted coping mechanism and commitment to change, to learning to tolerate uncomfortable psychological and physiological sensations and substituting alternative behaviours to developing more adaptive coping, caring for self and improving self-esteem. An important question is how client's views of progress, and their explanations of how this occurs and what has been helpful, map onto our theoretical understanding of bulimia. This could help inform theory, and treatment. For example, how does the process of change map onto cognitive theory? Some suggestions (from unpublished sources mainly) in Jarman & Walsh (1999) suggest that feeling of control over the process, changes in relationships, self-esteem, body image, and female identity are important. These could all easily be translated into and studied in cognitive terms.

The user perspective could also be employed in the development of research. Although not much done in eating disorders, users have a role to play in setting national priorities, commenting on individual studies, e.g. through ethics, critical review committees, and grant awarding bodies. For example, the best judge of whether research is reasonable or acceptable to bulimics may be to ask them, not to judge on their behalf.

Clinical effectiveness

Bulimia nervosa, as defined by DSM criteria, represents only a small and narrow subset of people with eating disorders who binge and compensate for bingeing. Yet most research is on this group. Some preliminary evidence suggests that the biggest group who present for treatment actually fall into the EDNOS category; in particular, they binge-eat and compensate but at a lower frequency than is needed for a BN diagnosis. It is not clear how suitable our models and treatments are for them. It is easy to assume that they are less severe cases of bulimia nervosa, but there is no evidence for this. Clinically, the presence or absence of bingeing and severe compensation seems to be an important marker, but this needs further research. Efficacy and effectiveness studies for this group are badly needed.

The general need for effectiveness studies was noted above. An important issue is acceptability of treatment. This may be less of an issue when treatment is being offered free (when it would not usually be, for example, in a research study). Patient choice (most have chosen to take part in research and get these particular treatments—lots contact or are assessed but only a small number are taken on) is also important. These sorts of factors may lead to over-estimation of effectiveness in clinical practice. Data analysis may also over-estimate effectiveness—for example, taking out the drop-outs, (who have not had the treatment) may increase the significance of the findings. A treatment is not good if large numbers do not want it, or only a few can tolerate it. It has also been argued that the inclusion and exclusion criteria for many treatment studies exclude those who are most difficult to treat (Mitchell *et al.* 1997).

General psychology issues

The topics to be covered in this section are summarized in Table 13.4.

Role of affect

Affect has been relatively neglected in cognitive models of bulimia nervosa. It has an important role in recent developments. For example, affect may be generated directly by core beliefs as well as by negative automatic thoughts. Ability to deal with emotions is also important. Bingeing is seen as a way to cope with unpleasant thoughts, feelings, and sensations, i.e. it is used as a form of emotional (and cognitive) regulation.

Emphasis on the development of affect provides a link to attachment theory. Identification and discrimination of feelings has been studied by those interested in

Table 13.4 General psychology issues

Role of affect
The self
Well-being
The future of cognition in BN
Theoretical implications
Clinical implications

early attachment. Response of mothers is thought to be important, particularly sensitivity, and synchronization (Oatley & Jenkins 1996). Many other processes within the attachment relationship are also important (Oatley & Jenkins 1996), including warmth and affection. There are also other factors—such as learning to speak about emotions, modelling, re-inforcement, meta-emotion (Hooven *et al.* 1995), parents' views on the expression of certain feelings, and mutual goal structures. Relationships with other people, e.g. peers, also have a role. This broadens the concept of attachment to include elements not necessarily highlighted by Bowlby. Some of these factors could usefully be incorporated into cognitively based theory.

The self

An important area that has not been much studied is the self concept. Although a crucial construct in analytic theories and therapies, it has been relatively ignored in CBT until recently. Experimental work on it has also been limited. Social cognitive psychology (see below) provides many opportunities for investigating it further, as does the developmental literature.

Well-being

Cognitive theorists and therapists have not generally studied well-being. In particular, there has been little research on the cognitive structures and processes associated with it. Well-being is difficult to define, and one possibility is that the positive negative dichotomy may not be interdependent, i.e. well-being may not simply be the opposite of disorder. In BN little is known about cognition, e.g. related to weight and shape, and the self, in those who do not have an eating disorder. More needs to be known. This might make it easier to set targets in therapy, e.g. should we be trying to eliminate the negative only, should we be actively trying to substitute positive thoughts, is working towards a balance between the two more appropriate? In mental health, well-being is often seen as simple absence of disorder. But the idea that it is rather more than just the opposite of ill-health is perhaps very relevant to BN, where patients not uncommonly worry what they will be left with, or how they will cope, if their illness or binge-eating is 'taken away'. Some therapists argue that there is usually a need to build the positive to decrease vulnerability (cf. Padesky, notes that an important goal is to build positive beliefs), although this has little empirical backing as yet. A preliminary study, however, shows that well-being therapy, which aims to increase self actualization, and potential, e.g. for creativity, love, and growth, (build the positive) seems to help patients with residual affective disorder, and may be more effective in this than CBT (Fava *et al.* 1998). One possibility is that this treatment might be useful for those with residual symptoms of BN, or that it might help prevent relapse in those who have recovered. It seems quite possible that 'well-being' could be interpreted cognitively, and integrated into cognitive treatment for BN.

Future of cognition in BN

The cognitive approach is dominant in contemporary psychology. One of its main strands is experimental cognitive psychology—the study of normal individuals in laboratory situations. Its influence is evident in several areas of psychology, including developmental, social, and clinical psychology. It studies internal processes using experimental tasks, and typically uses the scientific method taken from the older, more established sciences.

Many articles and several books have been devoted to its application to clinical psychology (see for example: Brewin 1988; and Williams *et al.* 1997).

Early on, its influence was reflected in the assessment of cognition—using methods taken from experimental psychology (see for example: Merluzzi *et al.* 1981; Kendall & Hollon 1979, 1981). Then came interest in information processing, again using paradigms developed in experimental cognitive psychology.

In BN there has been some interest in using assessment procedures, and information-processing paradigms (see Chapter 9). The former includes unstructured techniques such as thought-listing and thinking aloud. The latter include both attention (particularly the Stroop) and memory paradigms.

Cognitive psychology has considerably more potential than this, however. There are more paradigms that could be used to explore information processing, but there are many other constructs and concepts that could be transferred and applied to enhance our understanding of BN. This would help align it more closely with work in non-clinical groups. The benefits in increased richness and depth of understanding of the disorder are likely to be considerable. It is also important to broaden borrowing to include the social and developmental literature, where a large body of knowledge exists on cognition, and its origins.

The development of cognitive models may also be a fruitful area of study. Connectionism is currently popular, but recent theorists suggest that not all knowledge may be represented in logical argument, but in, for example, knowing how (Ryle 1949). There may also be some yet to be discovered modes of representation, beyond imagery and language/propositions. This broadening of representational systems is beginning to impact on clinical theories, and may have relevance to BN.

Several areas of social cognitive psychology can contribute paradigms and concepts that could be applied in BN. These include: attributional judgements; schemas—about the self, and about other people; judgemental heuristics; social identity theory (e.g. Tajfel & Turner 1979) and social categorization (classifying people into groups); research on the effect of mood on social cognition; social explanation or attribution theories; attitudes—including values; attitude change; and prejudice and discrimination.

Some relevant work has also been conducted on developmental aspects of these, for example, on attitudes of parents and children and on how a child's attitudes develop.

Theoretical implications

Two new theories deserve a brief mention. Both have considerable potential as a general framework within which to consider many of the new ideas and developments in the psychology of BN, including developments in cognitive and clinical cognitive theories.

The first is the interacting cognitive sub-systems theory (Barnard & Teasdale 1991; Teasdale & Barnard 1993). In this theory, emotion is conceived of as sense or feelings, due to activity in the implicational system, just as experience of pitch or timbre mark activity in the acoustic system (Teasdale & Barnard 1993, p.84). The implicational pattern (rather like a schema) can elicit emotions, derived from biological, and environmental experience, and can impact on meaning without going via a propositional system (Williams 1994). This theory has potential to explain much of the imagery findings, the difference between rational and emotional belief, also the 'feeling fat' phenomena in BN.

The second is the self-regulatory executive function model (S-REF) (Wells & Matthews 1994), which links schema theory with information processing. Emotional disorder is marked by chronic and self-focused attention. Treatment needs to modify the blueprint or plan for the processing routine. Modifying declarative (the content of) beliefs is knowing with the head, and modifying procedures is knowing with the heart. Treatment focuses particularly on attention training. New routines are developed, using combinations of strategies, e.g. a shift to the observer perspective, abandoning of safety behaviours, designed to decrease self focus. This theory also has potential to explain what we know about imagery, emotional and rational belief, and feeling fat, as well as body focus, and recent interest in meta-cognition (in relation to both imagery—see above—and propositional thought) in the disorder.

Other theoretical frameworks are also useful. Attachment theories, specifically working models of the mind, are particularly relevant, and help provide a framework for the development of cognition. They have generated a great deal of experimental cognitive research, e.g. so-called theory of mind studies. They might help to provide a detailed link between early experience and cognition that is lacking in current models. Some of the experimental studies, for example, conducted with children, may provide useful paradigms in BN.

Clinical implications

Clinical practice guidelines in the UK (Royal College of Psychiatrists 1992) recommend CBT as the treatment of choice; they also recommend a stepped-care approach. More recently, in the USA, APA guidelines (2000) note that CBT is the 'psychosocial treatment for which the most evidence for efficacy exists' (p.2). It also notes that interpersonal psychotherapy is effective. CBT is also recommended in practice guidelines for adolescents, although most of the relevant research has been on adults (Steinhausen 1997). Most practice guidelines also suggest a role for medication. However, as we have seen, the success of CBT based on early models is limited. Stepped care may not be ideal, we know little about clinical effectiveness, and the BN older models are limited in their explanatory power and as a basis for treatment. Some of the ways in which models could be developed further, and BN given a clearer cognitive framework with treatment implications, have been presented here.

Conclusion

This book set out to provide a wide-ranging, comprehensive, concise, and up to date review of psychological features in BN. The content ranges from psycho-analysis to behaviour therapy, from discussion of the historical context to recent experimental work on imagery. I hope the reader will agree that it is wide-ranging. It is based on a thorough review of the literature, and is as up to date as is possible, based on extensive literature searching, at the time of writing. Inevitably, not everything that was read and studied could be included, and I hope a (comprehensive), representative selection of studies and material has been retained. I hope too that it is sufficiently concise for the reader. As planned, it has focused particularly on cognitive factors, including cognitive theories, therapy and constructs—thus relatively more space and a greater number of chapters have been devoted to these. It has also drawn on research and theory in non-clinical groups.

Summary

Part one considered current issues in BN. The role of schema theory and therapy, including imagery, was discussed. Ideas for further research in this area were presented. Abstinence, use of manualised treatments and stepped care were considered. It was concluded that abstinence is a worthwhile goal, that research matching patients to treatment is needed, and that new developments in CT may help address important issues in these areas. Prevention was considered—it was suggested that work on enhancing self-esteem, as well as addressing weight and shape issues, might be useful.

Part two considered issues in the mental health field. Case formulation was discussed in the light of recent developments in CT, together with evidence based practice, clinical effectiveness and psychotherapy integration. It was noted that recent developments may provide a more comprehensive formulation of BN, and that CT for BN is not necessarily widely practised. There is currently no evidence for its clinical effectiveness. In clinical practice there is much interest in integrated treatments, and cognitive therapy is suggested as a useful integrative framework.

Part three considered issues from general psychology. The role of affect, the self, and well-being were considered. All have potential to contribute to the understanding of BN, particularly if approached from a cognitive perspective. The role of cognition was then highlighted. It was suggested that there are many paradigms and concepts in cognitive psychology, including in social and developmental psychology, that might advance our understanding of BN. Two new theories (together with insights from attachment theory) that can incorporate some of the newest developments were also highlighted.

Part four provided an assessment of current clinical practice guidelines for BN. It also provided an overall summary and conclusion for the book in the light of its aims.

References

Abbey, A., Abramis, D. J., & Caplan, R. D. (1985). Effects of different sources of social support and social conflict on emotional well-being. *Basic and Applied Social Psychology*, **6**, 111–129.

Abdu, R. A., Garritano, D., & Culver, O. (1987). Acute gastric necrosis in anorexia nervosa and bulimia. *Archives of Surgery*, **122**, 830–832.

Abraham, S. F. & Beumont, P. J. V. (1982). How patients describe bulimia or binge eating. *Psychological Medicine*, **12**, 625–635.

Abraham, S. F., Mira, M., Beumont, P. J. V., Sowerbutts, T. D., & Llewelyn-Jones, D. (1983). Eating behaviours among young women. *Medical Journal of Australia*, **2**, 225–228.

Abraham, S. F. (1998). Sexuality and reproduction in bulimia nervosa patients over 10 years. *Journal of Psychosomatic Research*, **44**, 491–502.

Adler, A. G., Walinsky, P., Krall, R. A., & Cho, S. Y. (1980). Death resulting from ipecac syrup poisoning. *Journal of the American Medical Association*, **243**, 1827–1928.

Agras, W. S., Schneider, J. A., Arnow, B., Raeburn, S. D., & Telch, C. F. (1989). Cognitive-behavioural and response prevention treatments for bulimia nervosa. *Journal of Consulting and Clinical Psychology*, **57**, 215–221.

Agras, W. S., Rossiter, E. M., Arnow, B., Telch, C. F., Raeburn, S. D., Bruce, B., & Koran, L. M. (1994). One year follow up of psychosocial and pharmacological treatments for bulimia nervosa. *Journal of Clinical Psychiatry*, **55**, 179–183.

Agras, S., Hammer, L., & McNicholas, F. (1999). A prospective study of the influence of eating disordered mothers on their children. *International Journal of Eating Disorders*, **25**, 253–262.

Agras, W. S., Crow, S. J., Halmi, K. A., Mitchell, J. E., Wilson, G. T., & Kraemer, H. C. (2000a). Outcome predictors for the cognitive behaviour treatment of bulimia nervosa: data from a multi-site study. *American Journal of Psychiatry*, **157**, 1302–1308.

Agras, W. S., Walsh, T., Fairburn, C. G., Wilson, G. T., & Kraemer, H. C. (2000b). A multicentre comparison of cognitive behavioural therapy and interpersonal psychotherapy for bulimia nervosa. *Archives of General Psychiatry*, **57**, 459–466.

Ainsworth, M. D. S., Blehar, M. C., Walters, E., & Wall, S. (1978). *Patterns of Attachment: A Psychological Study of the Strange Situation*. Hillsdale, NJ: Erlbaum.

Albeniz, A. & Holmes, J. (1996). Psychotherapy integration: its implications for psychiatry. *British Journal of Psychiatry*, **169**, 563–370.

Alford, B. A. & Beck, A. T. (1997). *The Integrative Power of Cognitive Therapy*. New York: Guilford.

Allerdissen, R., Florin, I., & Rost, W. (1981). Psychological characteristics of women with bulimia nervosa (bulimerexia). *Behaviour Analysis and Modification*, **4**, 314–317.

Altshuler, B. D., Dechow, P. C., Waller, D. A., & Hardy, B. W. (1990). An investigation of the oral pathologies occurring in bulimia nervosa. *International Journal of Eating Disorders*, **9**, 191–199.

American Psychiatric Association. (1952). *DSM-I*. Washington, DC: American Psychiatric Association.

American Psychiatric Association. (1968). *DSM-II*. Washington, DC: American Psychiatric Association.

American Psychiatric Association. (1980). *DSM-III*. Washington, DC: American Psychiatric Association.

American Psychiatric Association. (1987). *DSM-III-R*. Washington, DC: American Psychiatric Association.

American Psychiatric Association. (1994). *DSM-IV*. Washington, DC: American Psychiatric Association.

American Psychiatric Association. (2000). Practice Guideline for the Treatment of Patients with Eating Disorders (Revision). Washington, DC: American Psychiatric Association.

Ames-Frankel, J., Devlin, M. J., Walsh, B. T., Strasser, T. J., Sadik, C., Oldham, J. M., & Roose, S. P. (1992). Personality disorder diagnoses in patients with bulimia nervosa: clinical correlates and changes with treatment. *Journal of Clinical Psychiatry*, 53, 90–96.

Anastasi, A. (1988). *Psychological Testing*. New York: Macmillan.

Andersen, A. E. & DiDomenico, L. (1992). Diet vs shape content of popular male and female magazines: a dose response relationship to the incidence of eating disorders? *International Journal of Eating Disorders*, 11, 283–287.

Anderson, I. M., Parry-Billings, M., Newsholme, E. A., Fairburn, C. G., & Cowen, P. J. (1990). Dieting reduces plasma tryptophan and alters brain 5-HT function in women. *Psychological Medicine*, 20, 785–791.

Anderson, K. P., LaPorte, D. J. Brandt, H., & Crawford, S. (1997). Sexual abuse and bulimia: response to inpatient treatment and preliminary outcome. *Journal of Psychiatric Research*, 31, 621–633.

Andrewes, D. G., O'Connor, P., Mulder, C., McLennan, J., Derham, H., Weigall, S., & Say, S. (1996). Computerised psychoeducation for patients with eating disorders. *Australian and New Zealand Journal of Psychiatry*, 30, 492–497.

Andrews, B. (1997). Bodily shame in relation to abuse in childhood and bulimia: a preliminary investigation. *British Journal of Clinical Psychology*, 36, 41–49.

Arkes, H. R. (1991). Costs and benefits of judgement errors: implications for debiasing. *Psychological Bulletin*, 110, 486–498.

Armstrong, J. G. & Roth, D. M. (1989). Attachment and separation difficulties in eating disorders: a preliminary investigation. *International Journal of Eating Disorders*, 8, 141–155.

Arnow, B. A. (1999). Why are empirically supported treatments for bulimia nervosa underutilised and what can we do about it? *Journal of Clinical Psychology*, 55, 769–779.

Austin, S. B. (2000). Prevention research in eating disorders: theory and new directions. *Psychological Medicine*, 30, 1249–1262.

Avery, B. (1996). *Principles of Psychotherapy*. London: Thorsons.

Bachar, E. (1998). The contributions of self psychology to the treatment of anorexia and bulimia. *American Journal of Psychotherapy*, 52, 147–167.

Baddeley, A. D. (1986). *Working Memory*. Oxford: Oxford University Press.

Baell, W. K. & Wertheim, E. H. (1992). Predictors of outcome in the treatment of bulimia nervosa. *British Journal of Psychology*, 31, 330–332.

Bagby, R. M., Parker, J. D. A., & Taylor, G. J. (1994). The twenty item Toronto Alexithymia Scale: Item selection and cross-validation of the factor structure. *Journal of Psychosomatic Research*, 38, 23–32.

Bagley, C. & Ramsay, R. (1986). Sexual abuse in childhood: psychosocial outcomes and implications for social work practice. *Journal of Social Work and Human Sexuality*, 4, 33–47.

Balint, M. (1968). *The Basic Fault*. London: Tavistock.

Bardwick, J. (1971). *Psychology of Women: A Study of Bio-Cultural Conflicts*. New York: Harper & Row.

Barnard, P. J. & Teasdale, J. D. (1991). Interacting cognitive subsystems: a systemic approach to cognitive affective interaction and change. *Cognition and Emotion*, 5, 1–39.

Barratt, P. E. (1953). Imagery and thinking. *Australian Journal of Psychology*, 5, 154–164.

Bartlett, S. J., Wadden, T. A., & Vogt, R. A. (1996). Psychosocial consequences of weight cycling. *Journal of Consulting and Clinical Psychology*, **64**, 587–582.

Bateson, G. (1973). *Steps to an Ecology of Mind*. London: Paladin.

Battle, E. K. & Brownell, K. D. (1996). Confronting a rising tide of eating disorders and obesity: treatment vs prevention and policy. *Addictive Behaviours*, **21**, 755–765.

Baumeister, R. F. (1999). The nature and structure of the self: an overview. In *The Self in Social Psychology* (R. F. Baumeister, ed.). Hove, East Sussex: Psychology Press.

Beck, A. T., Ward, C. H., Mendelson, M. Mock, J., & Erbaugh, J. (1961). An inventory for measuring depression. *Archives of General Psychiatry*, **4**, 53–63.

Beck, A. T. (1963). Thinking and depression. *Archives of General Psychiatry*, **9**, 324–333.

Beck, A. T. (1976). *Cognitive Therapy and the Emotional Disorders*. New York: Meridian.

Beck, A. T., Rush, A. J., Shaw, B. F., & Emery, G. (1979). *Cognitive Therapy of Depression*. New York: Guilford.

Beck, A. T. (1983). Comparison of sociotrophy and autonomy in agoraphobics and other psychiatric patients. Unpublished study cited in *Anxiety Disorders and Phobias: A Cognitive Perspective*. A. T. Beck, G. Emery, & R. L. Greenberg (1985). New York: Guilford.

Beck, A. T., Emery, G., & Greenberg, R. L. (1985). *Anxiety Disorders and Phobias: A Cognitive Perspective*. New York: Guilford.

Beck, A. T. & Freeman, A. (1990). *Cognitive Therapy of Personality Disorders*. New York: The Guilford Press.

Beck, J. S. (1995). *Cognitive Therapy: Basics and Beyond*. New York: Guilford.

Beck, D., Casper, R., & Andersen, A. (1996). Truly late onset of eating disorders: a study of 11 cases averaging 60 years of age at presentation. *International Journal of Eating Disorders*, **20**, 389–395.

Beck, A. T. & Clark, D. A. (1997). An information processing model of anxiety: automatic and strategic processes. *Behaviour Research and Therapy*, **35**, 49–58.

Becker, B., Bell, M., & Billington, R. (1987). Object relations ego deficits in bulimic college women. *Journal of Clinical Psychology*, **43**, 92–95.

Beebe, D. W. (1994). Bulimia nervosa and depression: a theoretical and clinical appraisal in light of the binge-purge cycle. *British Journal of Clinical Psychology*, **33**, 259–276.

Beebe, D.W, Holmbeck, G. N., & Grzeskiewicz, C. (1999). Normative and psychometric data on the body image assessment—revised. *Journal of Personality Assessment*, **73**, 374–394.

Beglin, S. J. & Fairburn, C. G. (1992). What is meant by the term 'binge'? *American Journal of Psychiatry*, **149**, 123–124.

Bell, C. & Cooper, M. J. (submitted). Sociocultural predictors of eating disorder symptoms and cognition in young girls.

Bell, R. M. (1985). *Holy Anorexia*. Chicago: University of Chicago Press.

Bellak, L., Hurvich, M., & Gediman, H. (1973). *Ego Functions in Schizophrenics, Neurotics and Normals*. New York: John Wiley.

Bemporad, J. R. (1997). Self starvation through the ages: reflections on the pre-history of anorexia nervosa. *International Journal of Eating Disorders*, **19**, 217–237.

Benjamin (1993). *Interpersonal Diagnosis and Treatment of Personality Disorders*. New York: Guilford.

Bennett, W. B., & Gurin, J. (1982). *The Dieter's Dilemma: Eating Less and Weighing More*. New York: Basic Books.

Benton, A. L. (1974). *The Revised Visual Retention Test*. New York: Psychological Corporation.

Ben-Tovim, D. I. (1988). DSM-III, draft DSM-III-R, and the diagnosis and prevalence of bulimia in Australia. *American Journal of Psychiatry*, **145**, 1000–1002.

Ben-Tovim, D. I., Walker, M. K., Fok, D., & Yap, E. (1989). An adaptation of the Stroop test for measuring shape and food concerns in eating disorders: a quantitative measure of psychopathology? *International Journal of Eating Disorders*, **8**, 681–687.

Ben-Tovim, D. I. & Walker, M. K. (1991). Further evidence for the Stroop test as a quantitative measure of psychopathology in eating disorders. *International Journal of Eating Disorders*, **5**, 609–613.

Ben-Tovim, D. I., Walker, K., Gilchrist, P., Freeman, R., Kalucy, R., & Esterman, A. (2001). Outcome in patients with eating disorders: a 5-year study. *The Lancet*, **357**, 1254–1257.

Berger, D., Saito, S., Ono, Y., Tezuka, I., Shirahase, J., Kuboki, T., & Suematsu, H. (1994). Dissociation and child abuse histories in an eating disorder cohort in Japan. *Acta Psychiatrica Scandinavica*, **90**, 274–280.

Berkson, J. (1946). Limitations of application of fourfold table analysis to hospital data. *Biometric Bulletin*, **2**, 47–53.

Berndt, T. J. & Perry, T. B. (1990). Distinctive features and effects of early adolescent friendships. In *From Childhood to Adolescence: A Transitional Period?* (R. Montemayor & G. R. Adams, ed.). Thousand Oaks, CA: Sage Publications.

Berndt, T. J. & Savin-Williams, R. C. (1993). Peer relations and friendships. In *Handbook of clinical research and practice with adolescents* (P. H. Tolan & B. J. Cohler, ed.). New York: Wiley & Sons.

Bernstein, E. M. & Putnam, F. W. (1986). Development, reliability, and validity of a dissociative scale. *Journal of Nervous and Mental Disease*, **174**, 727–737.

Berrios, G. & Porter, R. (1995). *A history of clinical psychiatry*. London: The Athlone Press.

Beumont, P. J. V., Kopec-Shrader, E. M., Talbot, P., & Touyz, S. W. (1993). Measuring the specific psychopathology of eating disorder patients. *Australian and New Zealand Journal of Psychiatry*, **27**, 506–511.

Beumont, P. J. V. & Touyz, S. W. (1995). The nutritional management of anorexia and bulimia nervosa. In *Eating Disorders and Obesity: A Comprehensive Handbook* (K. D. Brownell & C. G. Fairburn, ed.). New York: Guilford.

Beumont, P. J. V., Beumont, C. C., Touyz, S. W., & Williams, H. (1997a). Nutritional counselling and supervised exercise. In *Handbook of Treatment for Eating Disorders* (2nd edn) (D. M. Garner & P. E. Garfinkel, ed.). New York: Guilford Press.

Beumont, P. J. V., Russell, J. D., Touyz, S. W., Buckley, C., Lowinger, K., Talbot, P., & Johnson, G. F. S. (1997b). *Australian and New Zealand Journal of Psychiatry*, **31**, 514–524.

Binswanger, L. (1944). Der Fall Ellen West. *Archives of Neurology and Psychiatry*, **54**, 69–117.

Birch, L. L. (1987). The role of experience in children's food acceptance patterns. *Journal of the American Dietetic Association*, **87**, S36–S40.

Birtchnell, S. A., Lacey, J. H., & Harte, A. (1985). Body image distortion in bulimia nervosa. *British Journal of Psychiatry*, **147**, 408–412.

Black, C. M., Wilson, G.T, Labouvie, E., & Heffernan, K. (1997). Selective processing of eating disorder relevant stimuli: does the Stroop test provide an objective measure of bulimia nervosa? *International Journal of Eating Disorders*, **22**, 329–333.

Blais, M. A., Becker, A. E., Burwell, R. A., Flores, A. T., Nussbaum, K. M., Greenwood, D. N., Ekeblad, E. R., & Herzog, D. B. (2000). Pregnancy: outcome and impact on symptomatology in a cohort of eating disordered women. *International Journal of Eating Disorders*, **27**, 140–149.

Blatt, S. J. (1995). The destructiveness of perfectionism: implications for the treatment of depression. *American Psychologist*, **50**, 1003–1020.

Bliss, E. L. & Branch, C. H. (1960). *Anorexia Nervosa: Its History, Psychology, and Biology*. New York: Paul B. Hoeber.

Bloom, C. (1987). Bulimia: a feminist psychoanalytic understanding. In *Fed up and Hungry: Women, Oppression and Food* (M. Lawrence, ed.). London: The Women's Press.

Blouin, J. H., Carter, J., Blouin, A. G., Tener, L., Schnare-Hayes, K., Zuro, C., Barlow, J., & Perez, E. (1994). Prognostic indicators in bulimia nervosa treated with cognitive behavioural group therapy. *International Journal of Eating Disorders*, 15, 113–123.

Blouin, J., Schnarre, K., Carter, J., Blouin, A., Tener, Zuro, C., & Barlow, A. G. (1995). Factors affecting drop out rate from cognitive behavioural group treatment for bulimia nervosa. *International Journal of Eating Disorders*, 17, 323–329.

Blumberg, H. & Morgan, J. P. (1985). Combining anorexiant studies for analysis: a statistical method. In *Clinical Pharmacology and Therapeutics*, Vol. 5 (J. P. Morgan, D. V. Kagan, & J. S. Brody, ed.). New York: Praeger.

Bo-Linn, G. W., Santa-Ana, C. A., Morawski, B. A., & Fordtran, J. (1983). Purging and calorie absorption in bulimic patients and normal women. *Annals of Internal Medicine*, 99, 14–17.

Bonifazi, D. Z. & Crowther, J. H. (1996). *In vivo* cognitive assessment in bulimia nervosa and restrained eating. *Behaviour Therapy*, 27, 139–158.

Booth, D. A. (1994). *Psychology of Nutrition*. London: Taylor & Francis.

Boskind-Lodahl, M. (1976). Cinderella's stepsisters: a feminist perspective on anorexia nervosa and bulimia. *Signs: Journal of Women in Culture and Society*, 2, 342–356.

Bossert, S., Schmoelz, U., Wiegand, M., Junker, M., & Kreig, J. C. (1992). Predictors of short term treatment outcome in bulimia nervosa inpatients. *Behaviour Research and Therapy*, 30, 193–199.

Bouquot, J. E. & Seime, R. J. (1997). Bulimia nervosa: dental perspectives. *Practical Periodontics and Aesthetic Dentistry*, 9, 655–663.

Bourne, S. K., Bryant, R. A., Griffiths, R. A., Touyz, S. W., & Beumont, P. J. V. (1998). Bulimia nervosa, restrained, and unrestrained eaters: a comparison of non-binge eating behaviour. *International Journal of Eating Disorders*, 24, 185–192.

Bowden, P. K., Touyz, S. W., Rodriguez, P. J., Hensley, R., & Beumont, P. J. V. (1989). Distorting patient or distorting instrument? Body shape disturbance in patients with anorexia nervosa and bulimia. *British Journal of Psychiatry*, 155, 196–201.

Bowlby, J. (1969). *Attachment and Loss, Vol. 1: Attachment*. New York: Basic Books.

Bowlby, J. (1973). *Attachment and Loss, Vol. 2: Separation, Anxiety and Anger*. New York: Basic Books.

Bowlby, J. (1980). *Attachment and Loss, Vol. 3: Loss, Separation and Depression*. New York: Basic Books.

Boyadjieva, S. & Steinhausen, H-C. (1996). The Eating Attitudes Test and the eating disorders in four Bulgarian clinical and non-clinical samples. *International Journal of Eating Disorders*, 19, 93–98.

Brambilla, F., Draisci, A., Peirone, A., & Brunetta, M. (1995). Combined cognitive behavioural, psychopharmacological and nutritional therapy in bulimia nervosa. *Neuropsychobiology*, 32, 68–71.

Brewerton, T. D., Hand, L. D., & Bishop, E. R. (1993). The Tridemensional Personality Questionnaire in eating disorder patients. *International Journal of Eating Disorders*, 14, 213–218.

Brewerton, T. D., Lydiard, R. B., Herzog, D. B., Brotman, A. W., O'Neil, P. M., & Ballenger, J. C. (1995). Comorbidity of Axis 1 psychiatric disorders in bulimia nervosa. *Journal of Clinical Psychiatry*, 56, 77–80.

Brewin, C. R. (1988). Attribution therapy. In *New Developments in Clinical Psychology*, Vol. 2 (F. Watts, ed.). New York: John Wiley & Sons.

Brickman, B. (1992). The desomatising self object transference: a case report. In *New Therapeutic Visions: Progress in Self Psychology*, Vol. 8 (A. Goldberg, ed.). Hillsdale: Analytic Press.

Briere, J. M. (1992). *Child Abuse Trauma: Theory and Treatment of the Lasting Effects*. Newberry Park, CA: Gage Publications.

Brisman, J. & Siegel, M. (1984). Bulimia and alcoholism: two sides of the same coin? *Journal of Substance Abuse and Treatment*, 1, 113–118.

Brody, M. L., Walsh, B. T., & Devlin, M. J. (1994). Binge eating disorder: reliability and validity of a new diagnostic category. *Journal of Consulting and Clinical Psychology*, 62, 381–386.

Brown, G. W., & Harris, T. O. (1978). *Social origins of depression: a study of psychiatric disorder in women*. London: Tavistock.

Brown, L. M. & Gilligan, C. (1992). *Meeting at the Crossroads: Women's Psychology and Girl's Development*. Cambridge, MA: Harvard University Press.

Browne, A. & Finkelhor, D. (1986). Impact of child sexual abuse: a review of the research. *Psychological Bulletin*, 99, 66–77.

Brownell, K. D. (1985). *The LEARN program for weight control*. Philadelphia: University of Pennsylvania Press.

Brownell, K. D. (1986). Public health approaches to obesity and its management. *Annual Review of Public Health*, 7521–7533.

Brownell, K. D. & Wadden, T. A. (1986). Aetiology and treatment of obesity. *Journal of Consulting and Clinical Psychology*, 60, 505–517.

Bruce, B. & Agras, W. S. (1992). Binge eating in females: a population-based investigation. *International Journal of Eating Disorders*, 12, 365–373.

Bruch, H. (1962). Perceptual and conceptual disturbances in anorexia nervosa. *Psychosomatic Medicine*, 24, 187–194.

Bruch, H. (1969). Hunger and instinct. *Journal of Nervous and Mental Disease*, 149, 91–114.

Bruch, H. (1973). *Eating Disorders*. Basic Books: New York.

Bruch, H. (1977). Psychotherapy in eating disorders. *Canadian Psychiatric Association Journal*, 22, 102–108.

Brumberg, J. J. (1988). *Fasting girls: the history of anorexia nervosa*. New York: Penguin Books.

Bryant-Waugh, R. (2000). Developmental-Systemic-Feminist Therapy. In *Comparative Treatments of Eating Disorders* (K. Miller & J. S. Mizes, eds.). London: Free Association Books.

Buhrich, N. (1981). Frequency of presentation of anorexia nervosa in Malaysia. *Australian and New Zealand Journal of Psychiatry*, 15, 153–155.

Bulik, C. M. (1992). Abuse of drugs associated with eating disorders. *Journal of Substance Abuse*, 4, 69–90.

Bulik, C. M., Sullivan, P. F., Epstein, L. H., McKee, M., Kaye, W. H., Dahl, R. E., & Weltzin, T. E. (1992). Drug use in women with anorexia and bulimia nervosa. *International Journal of Eating Disorders*, 11, 213–225.

Bulik, C. M., Sullivan, P. F., Carter, F. A., & Joyce, P. R. (1996). Lifetime anxiety disorders in women with bulimia nervosa. *Comprehensive Psychiatry*, 37, 368–374.

Bulik, C. M., Sullivan, P. F., Carter, F. A., & Joyce, P. R. (1997). Initial manifestations of disordered eating behaviour: dieting versus binging. *International Journal of Eating Disorders*, 22, 195–201.

Bulik, C. M., Sullivan, P. F., Carter, F. A., McIntosh, V. V., & Joyce, P. R. (1998a). The role of exposure with response prevention in the cognitive behavioural therapy for bulimia nervosa. *Psychological Medicine*, 28, 611–623.

Bulik, C. M., Sullivan, P. F., Joyce, P. R., Carter, F. A., & McIntosh, V. V. (1998b). Predictors of 1 year treatment outcome in bulimia nervosa. *Comprehensive Psychiatry*, 39, 206–214.

Bulik, C. M., Sullivan, P. F., Carter, F. A., McIntosh, V. V., & Joyce, P. R. (1999a). Predictors of rapid and sustained response to cognitive behavioural therapy for bulimia nervosa. *International Journal of Eating Disorders*, 26, 137–144.

Bulik, C. M., Sullivan, P. F., & Joyce, P. R. (1999b). Temperament, character and suicide attempts in anorexia nervosa, bulimia nervosa and major depression. *Acta Psychiatrica Scananivica*, **100**, 27–32.

Burks, N. & Martin, B. (1985). Everyday problems and life change events: ongoing versus acute sources of stress. *Journal of Human Stress*, **11**, 27–35.

Bushnell, J. A., Wells, J. E., Hornblow, A. R., Oakley-Browne, M. A., & Joyce, P. (1990). Prevalence of three bulimia syndromes in the general population. *Psychological Medicine*, **20**, 671–680.

Bushnell, J. A., Wells, J. E., & Oakley-Browne, M. A. (1992). Long-term effects of intrafamilial sexual abuse in childhood. *Acta Psychiatrica Sandanivica*, **85**, 136–142.

Bushnell, J. A., Wells, J. E., McKenzie, J. M., Hornblow, A. R., Oakley-Browne, M. A., & Joyce, P. R. (1994). Bulimia comorbidity in the general population and in the clinic. *Psychological Medicine*, **24**, 605–611.

Butler, G. (1998). Clinical formulation. In *Comprehensive Clinical Psychology*, Vol. 6 (A. S. Bellack & M. Hersen, ed.). Oxford: Pergamon.

Button, E. (1983). Personal construct theory and psychological well being. *British Journal of Medical Psychology*, **56**, 313–321.

Button, E. J., Sonuga-Barke, E. J. S., Davies, J., & Thompson, M. (1996). A prospective study of self-esteem in the prediction of eating problems in adolescent schoolgirls: questionnaire findings. *British Journal of Clinical Psychology*, **35**, 193–203.

Caplan, G. (1964). *Principles of Preventive Psychiatry*. New York: Basic Books.

Carter, P. I. & Moss, R. A. (1985). Screening for anorexia nervosa and bulimia nervosa in a college population: problems and limitations. *Addictive Behaviours*, **9**, 417–419.

Carter, F. A., Bulik, C. M., Lawson, R. H., Sullivan, P. F., & Wilson, J. S. (1996). Effect of mood and food cues on body image in women with bulimia and controls. *International Journal of Eating Disorders*, **20**, 65–76.

Carter, J. C., Stewart, D. A., Dunn, V. J., & Fairburn, C. G. (1997). Primary prevention of eating disorders? Might it do more harm than good? *International Jounral of Eating Disorders*, **22**, 167–172.

Carter, J. C. & Fairburn, C. G. (1998). Cognitive behavioural self help for binge eating disorder: a controlled effectiveness study. *Journal of Consulting and Clinical Psychology*, **66**, 616–623.

Carver, C. S. & Scheier, M. F. (1990). Origins and functions of positive and negative affect: a control-process view. *Psychological Review*, **97**, 19–35.

Cash, T. F. & Brown, T. A. (1987). Body image in anorexia nervosa and bulimia nervosa: a review of the literature. *Behaviour Modification*, **11**, 487–521.

Cash, T. F. & Deagle, E. A. (1997). The nature and extent of body-image disturbances in anorexia nerovsa and bulimia nervosa: a meta-analysis. *International Journal of Eating Disorders*, **22**, 107–125.

Casper, R. (1983). On the emergence of bulimia nervosa as a syndrome. *International Journal of Eating Disorders*, **2**, 3–16.

Casper, R. C., Hedeker, D., & McClough, J. F. (1992). Personality dimensions in eating disorders and their relevance for subtyping. *Journal of the American Academy of Child and Adolescent Psychiatry*, **31**, 830–840.

Casper, R. C. & Lyubomirsky, S. (1997). Individual psychopathology relative to reports of unwanted sexual experiences as predictor of a bulimic eating pattern. *International Journal of Eating Disorders*, **21**, 229–236.

Cassidy, C. M. (1994). Emotion regulation: influences of attachment relationships. *Monographs for the Society for Research in Child Development*, **59**, 228–283.

Catalano, D. & Dooley, R. (1980). Economic change as a cause of behavioural disorder. *Psychological Bulletin*, **87**, 450–468.

Catina, A. & Joja, O. (2001). Emerging markets: submerging women. In *Eating Disorders and Cultures in Transition* (M. Nasser, M. A. Katzman & R. A. Gordon, ed.). London: Routledge.

Cattanch, L. & Rodin, J. (1988). Psychosocial components of the stress process in bulimia. *International Journal of Eating Disorders*, 7, 75–88.

Chambless, D. L., Sanderson, W. C., Shoham, V., Johnson, S. B., Pope, K. S., Crits-Cristoph, P., Baker, M., Johnson, S. B., Woody, S. R., Sue, S., Beutler, L., Williams, D. A., & McCurry, S. (1996). An update on empirically validated therapies. *The Clinical Psychologist*, 49, 5–18.

Channon, S., Hemsley, D., & de Silva, P. (1988). Selective processing of food words in anorexia nervosa. *British Journal of Clinical Psychology*, 27, 259–260.

Chernin, K. (1985). *The Hungry Self.* London: Virago.

Chiodo, J. & Latimer, P. R. (1983). Vomiting as a learned weight control technique in bulimia. *Journal of Behaviour Therapy and Experimental Psychiatry*, 14, 131–135.

Chodorow, N. (1971). Being and doing: a cross-cultural examination of males and females. In *Women in Sexist Society* (V. Gornick & B. K. Moran, ed.). New York: Basic Books.

Choudry, I. Y. & Mumford, D. B. (1992). A pilot study of eating disorders in Mirpur (Pakistan) using an Urdu version of the Eating Attitudes Test. *International Journal of Eating Disorders*, 11, 243–251.

Christiano, B. & Mizes, J. S. (1997). Appraisal and coping deficits associated with eating disorders: implications for treatment. *Cognitive and Behavioural Practice*, 4, 263–290.

Chun, Z. F., Mitchell, J. E., Li, K., Yu, W. M., Lan, Y. D., Jun, Z., Rong, Z. Y., Huan, Z. Z., Filice, G. A., Pomeroy, C., & Pyle, R. L. (1992). The prevalence of anorexia nervosa and bulimia nervosa among freshman medical college students in China. *International Journal of Eating Disorders*, 12, 209–214.

Cicchetti, D. & Beeghly, M. (1987). Symbolic development in maltreated youngsters: an organisational perspective. *New Directions for Child Development*, 36, 47–68.

Cicchetti, D., Cummings, E. M., Greenberg, M. T., & Marvin, R. S. (1990). An organisational perspective on attachment beyond infancy: implications for theory, measurement and research. In *Attachment in the PreSchool Years: Theory, Research and Intervention* (M. T. Greenberg & D. Cicchetti, ed.). Chicago, IL: The University of Chicago Press.

Cicchetti, D., Ganiban, J., & Barnett, D. (1991). Contributions from the study of high-risk populations to understanding the development of emotion regulation. In *The Development of Emotion Regulation and Dysregulation* (J. Garber & K. A. Dodge, ed.). New York: Cambridge University Press.

Cicchetti, D. (1993). Developmental psychopathology: reactions, reflections, projections. *Developmental Review*, 13, 471–502.

Cloninger, C. R. (1986). A unified biosocial theory of personality and its role in the development of anxiety states. *Psychiatric Developments*, 3, 167–226.

Cloninger, C. R. (1987). A systematic method for clinical description and classification of personality variables. *Archives of General Psychiatry*, 44, 573–588.

Cloninger, C. R., Svrakic, D. M., & Przybeck, T. R. (1993). A psychobiological model of temperament and character. *Archives of General Psychiatry*, 50, 975–999.

Cochrane, C. T. (1972). Effects of diagnostic information on empathic understanding by the therapist in a psychotherapy analogue. *Journal of Consulting and Clinical Psychology*, 38, 359–365.

Cochrane, C. E., Brewerton, T. D., Wilson, D. B., & Hodges, E. L. (1993). Alexithymia in the eating disorders. *International Journal of Eating Disorders*, 14, 219–222.

Cohen, S. & Wills, T. (1985). Stress, social support and the buffering hypothesis. *Psychological Bulletin*, 98, 310–357.

Coker, S., Vize, C., Wade, T., & Cooper, P. J. (1993). Patients with bulimia nervosa who fail to engage in cognitive behaviour therapy. *International Journal of Eating Disorders*, 13, 35–40.

Collings, S. & King, M. (1994). Ten year follow up of 50 patients with bulimia nervosa. *British Journal of Psychiatry*, **164**, 80–87.

Connors, M. E., Johnson, C. L., & Stuckey, M. K. (1984). Treatment of bulimia with brief psychoeducational group therapy. *American Journal of Psychiatry*, **141**, 1512–1516.

Connors, M. E. & Morse, W. (1993). Sexual abuse and eating disorders: a review. *International Journal of Eating Disorders*, **13**, 1–11.

Conte, H., Plutchik, R., Karasu, T., & Jerrett, I. (1980). A self-report borderline scale. *Journal of Nervous and Mental Disease*, **168**, 428–435.

Conti, J., Abraham, S., & Taylor, A. (1998). Eating behaviour and pregnancy outcome. *Journal of psycosomatic research*, **44**, 465–477.

Cooke, E. A., Guss, J. L., Kissileff, H. R., Devlin, M. J., & Walsh, B. T. (1997). Patterns of food selection during binges in women with binge eating disorder. *International Journal of Eating Disorders*, **22**, 187–193.

Cooper, M. J., Todd, G., & Wells, A. (submitted a). Assessing eating disorder thoughts and behaviours: the development and preliminary evaluation of two questionnaires.

Cooper, M. J., Todd, G., & Turner, H. (submitted b). Using imagery to change core beliefs in bulimia nervosa.

Cooper, M. J., Wells, A., & Todd, G. (in press). A cognitive theory of bulimia nervosa. *British Journal of Clinical Psychology*.

Cooper, M. J., Wells, A., & Todd, G. (unpublished). The eating disorder rating scale.

Cooper, P. J. & Fairburn, C. G. (1983). Binge eating and self induced vomiting in the community: a preliminary study. *British Journal of Psychiatry*, **142**, 139–144.

Cooper, P. J. & Fairburn, C. G. (1986). The depressive symptoms of bulimia nervosa. *British Journal of Psychiatry*, **148**, 268–274.

Cooper, Z. & Fairburn, C. G. (1987). The Eating Disorder Examination: a semi-structured interview for the assessment of the specific psychopathology of eating disorders. *International Journal of Eating Disorders*, **6**, 1–8.

Cooper, P. J., Charnock, D. J., & Taylor, M. J. (1987a). The prevalence of bulimia nervosa: a replication study. *British Journal of Psychiatry*, **151**, 684–686.

Cooper, P. J., Taylor, M. J., Cooper, Z., & Fairburn, C. G. (1987b). The development and validation of the Body Shape Questionnaire. *International Journal of Eating Disorders*, **6**, 485–494.

Cooper, J. L., Morrison, T. L., Bigman, O. L., Abramowitz, S. I., Levin, S., & Krener, P. (1988). Mood changes and affective disorder in the bulimic binge-purge cycle. *International Journal of Eating Disorders*, **7**, 469–474.

Cooper, Z., Cooper, P. J., & Fairburn, C. G. (1989). The validity of the Eating Disorder Examination and its subscales. *British Journal of Psychiatry*, **154**, 807–812.

Cooper, M. J. (1991). Cognitive processes in anorexia nervosa and bulimia nervosa. DPhil Dissertation, University of Oxford.

Cooper, M. J., Anastasiades, P., & Fairburn, C. G. (1992). Selective processing of eating, weight and shape related words in persons with bulimia nervosa. *Journal of Abnormal Psychology*, **101**, 352–355.

Cooper, M. J. & Fairburn, C. G. (1992a). Selective processing of eating, weight and shape related words in patients with eating disorders and dieters. *British Journal of Clinical Psychology*, **31**, 363–365.

Cooper, M. J. & Fairburn, C. G. (1992b). Thoughts about eating, weight and shape in anorexia nervosa and bulimia nervosa. *Behaviour Research and Therapy*, **30**, 501–511.

Cooper, M. J., Clark, D. M., & Fairburn, C. G. (1993). An experimental study of the relationship between thoughts and eating behaviour in bulimia nervosa. *Behaviour Research and Therapy*, **31**, 749–757.

Cooper, M. J. & Fairburn, C. G. (1993). Demographic and clinical correlates of selective information processing in patients with bulimia nervosa. *International Journal of Eating Disorders*, 13, 109–116.

Cooper, P. J., Coker, S., & Fleming, C. (1994). An evaluation of the efficacy of supervised cognitive behavioural self help for bulimia nervosa. *Journal of Psychosomatic Research*, 40, 281–287.

Cooper, P. J. (1995). *Bulimia Nervosa and Binge Eating*. London: Robinson.

Cooper, P. J. & Steere, J. (1995). A comparison of two psychological treatments for bulimia nervosa: implications for models of maintenance. *Behaviour Research and Therapy*, 33, 875–885.

Cooper, M. J., Todd, G., & Cohen-Tovee, E. (1996a). Core beliefs in eating disorders. *International Cognitive Therapy Newsletter*, 10, part 2, 2–3.

Cooper, P. J., Coker, S., & Fleming, C. (1996b). An evaluation of the efficacy of supervised cognitive behavioural self help bulimia nervosa. *Journal of Psychosomatic Research*, 40, 281–287.

Cooper, M. J. (1997). Cognitive theory in anorexia nervosa and bulimia nervosa: a review. *Behavioural and Cognitive Psychotherapy*, 25, 113–145.

Cooper, M. J., Cohen-Tovee, E., Todd, G., Wells, A., & Tovee, M. (1997). The Eating Disorder Belief Questionnaire: Preliminary Development. *Behaviour Research and Therapy*, 35, 381–388.

Cooper, M. J. & Todd, G. (1997). Selective processing of three types of stimuli in eating disorders. *British Journal of Clinical Psychology*, 36, 279–281.

Cooper, C. L. & Baglioni, A. J. (1998). A structural model approach toward the development of a theory of the link between stress and mental health. *British Journal of Medical Psychology*, 61, 87–102.

Cooper, M. J. & Hunt, J. (1998). Core beliefs and underlying assumptions in bulimia nervosa and depression. *Behaviour Research and Therapy*, 36, 895–898.

Cooper, M. J., Todd, G., & Wells, A. (1998). Content, origins, and consequences of dysfunctional beliefs in anorexia nervosa and bulimia nervosa. *Journal of Cognitive Psychotherapy*, 12, 213–230.

Cooper, M. J., Todd, G., & Wells, A. (2000). *Bulimia Nervosa: A Cognitive Therapy Programme for Clients*. London: Jessica Kingsley.

Cooper, M. J. (2001). Eating disorders, culture and cognition. In *Cultural Cognition and Psychopathology* (J. F. Schumaker & T. Ward, ed.). Westport, CT: Praeger.

Cooper, M. J., Galbraith, M., & Drinkwater, J. (2001). Assumptions and beliefs in adolescents with anorexia nervosa and their mothers. *Eating Disorders: The Journal of Treatment and Prevention*, 9, 217–224.

Coopersmith, S. (1959). A method for determining types of self-esteem. *Journal of Abnormal and Social Psychology*, 59, 87–94.

Coovert, D. L. & Powers, P. S. (1988). Bulimia nervosa and enema abuse: a preliminary analysis based on four case reports. *International Journal of Eating Disorders*, 7, 697–700.

Corcos, M., Guilbaud, O., Speranza, M., Paterniti, S., Loas, G., Stephan, P., & Jeammet, P. (2000). Alexithymia and depression in eating disorders. *Psychiatry Research*, 93, 263–266.

Costa, P. T. & McCrae, R. R. (1988). *The NEO Personality Inventory Manual*. Odessa: Psychological Assessment Resources.

Cotrufo, P., Barretta, V., & Monteleone, P. (1997). An epidemiological study on eating disorders in two high schools in Naples. *European Psychiatry*, 12, 342–344.

Cotrufo, P., Barretta, V., Monteleone, P., & Maj, M. (1998). Full-syndrome, partial-syndrome and subclinical eating disorders: an epidemiological study of female students in Southern Italy. *Acta Psychiatrica Scandanivica*, 98, 112–115.

Cox, G. L. & Merkel, W. T. (1989). A qualitative review of psychosocial treatments for bulimia. *The Journal of Nervous and Mental Disease*, 177, 77–84.

Crago, M., Shisslak, C. M., & Estes, L. S. (1996). Eating disturbance among American minority groups: a review. *International Journal of Eating Disorders*, 19, 239–248.

Craske, M. G., Barlow, D. H., & O'Leary, T. (1992). *Mastery of your Anxiety and Worry*. New York: Graywind.

Crichton, P. (1996). Were the Roman emperors Claudius and Vitellus bulimic? *International Journal of Eating Disorders*, **19**, 203–207.

Crisp, A. H. (1967). The possible significance of some behavioural correlates of weight and carbohydrate intake. *Journal of Psychosomatic Research*, **11**, 117–131.

Crisp, A. H., Hsu, L. K. G., Harding, B., & Hartshorn, J. (1980). Clinical features of anorexia nervosa: A study of a consecutive series of 102 female patients. *Journal of Psychosomatic Research*, **24**, 179–191.

Crow, S., Mitchell, J., & Kendall, D. (1997). Levothyroxine abuse and bulimia nervosa. *Psychosomatics*, **38**, 151–153.

Crow, S. J., Mussell, M. P., Peterson, C. B., Knopke, A., & Mitchell, J. E. (1999a). Prior treatment received by patients with bulimia nervosa. *International Journal of Eating Disorders*, **25**, 39–44.

Crow, S., Praus, B., & Thuras, P. (1999b). Mortality from eating disorders—a 5 to 10 year record linkage study. *International Journal of Eating Disorders*, **26**, 97–101.

Cullberg, J. & Engstrom-Lindberg, M. (1988). Prevalence and incidence of eating disorders in a suburban area. *Acta Psychiatrica Scandanivica*, **78**, 314–319.

Cullen, W. (1780). *Synopsis Exibens … Systema Nosolgica*. Edinburgh: G. Creech.

Dale, K. S. & Landers, D. M. (1999). Weight control in wrestling: eating disorders or disordered eating? *Medicine and Science in Sports and Exercise*, **31**, 1382–1389.

Dancyger, I. F. & Garfinkel, P. E. (1995). The relationship of partial syndrome eating disorders to anorexia nervosa and bulimia nervosa. *Psychological Medicine*, **25**, 1019–1025.

Dansky, B. S., Brewerton, T. D., Kilpatrick, D. G., & O'Neil, P. M. (1997). The National Women's Study: relationship of victimisation and post-traumatic stress disorder to bulimia nervosa. *International Journal of Eating Disorders*, **21**, 213–228.

Dare, C. & Eisler, I. (1995). Family therapy and eating disorders. In *Eating Disorders and Obesity* (K. D. Brownell & C. G. Fairburn, ed.). New York: Guilford Press.

Dare, C. (1997). Chronic eating disorders in therapy: clinical stories using family systems and psychoanalytic approaches. *Journal of Family Therapy*, **19**, 319–351.

Davis, R., Freeman, R. J., & Garner, D. M. (1988). A naturalistic investigation of eating behaviour in bulimia nervosa. *Journal of Consulting and Clinical Psychology*, **56**, 273–279.

Davis, C., Fox, J., Cowles, M., Hastings, P., & Schwass, K. (1990a). The functional role of exercise in the development of weight and diet concerns in women. *Journal of Psychosomatic Reseaarch*, **34**, 563–574.

Davis, R., Olmsted, M. P., & Rockert, W. (1990b). Brief group psychoeducation for bulimia nervosa: assessing the clinical significance of change. *Journal of Consulting and Clinical Psychology*, **58**, 882–885.

Davis, R., Olmsted, M. P., & Rockert, W. (1992). Brief group psychoeducation for bulimia nervosa. II: Prediction of clinical outcome. *International Journal of Eating Disorders*, **11**, 205–211.

Davis, C., Katzman, D. K., Kaptein, S., Kirsh, C., Brewer, H., Kalmbach, K., Olmsted, M. P., Woodside, D. B., & Kaplan, A. S. (1997a). The prevalence of high-level exercise in the eating disorders: etiological implications. *Comprehensive Psychiatry*, **38**, 321–326.

Davis, R., Olmsted, M., Rockert, W., Marques, T., & Dolhanty, J. (1997b). Group psychoeducation for bulimia nervosa with and without additional psychotherapy process sessions. *International Journal of Eating Disorders*, **22**, 25–34.

Davis, C. & Claridge, G. (1998). The eating disorders as addiction: a psychobiological perspective. *Addictive Behaviours*, **23**, 463–475.

Davis, R., McVey, G., Heinmaa, M., Rockert, W., & Kennedy, S. (1999). Sequencing of cognitive behavioural treatments for bulimia nervosa. *International Journal of Eating Disorders*, **25**, 361–374.

Davison, G. C. & Neale, J. M. (1994). *Abnormal Psychology*. Wiley: New York.

de Azevedo, M. H. P. & Ferreira, C. P. (1992). Anorexia nervosa and bulimia: a prevalence study. *Acta Psychiatrica Scandanivica*, **86**, 432–436.

Dedman, P. A., Numa, S. F., & Wakeling, A. (1988). A cognitive behavioral group approach for the treatment of bulimia nervosa—a preliminary study. *Journal of Psychosomatic Research*, **32**, 285–290.

De Elmore, D. K. & Castro, J. M. (1990). Self rated moods and hunger in relation to spontaneous eating behaviour in bulimics, recovered bulimics, and normals. *International Journal of Eating Disorders*, **9**, 179–190.

Deep, A. L., Lilenfeld, L. R., Plotnicov, K. H., Pollice, C., & Kaye, W. H. (1999). Sexual abuse in eating disorder subtypes and control women: the role of comorbid substance dependence in bulimia nervosa. *International Journal of Eating Disorders*, **25**, 1–10.

de Groot, J. M. & Rodin, G. (1994). Eating disorders, female psychology, and the self. *Journal of the American Academy of Psychoanalysis*, **22**, 299–317.

de Groot, J. M., Rodin, G., & Olmsted, M. P. (1995). Alexithymia, depression, and treatment outcome in bulimia nervosa. *Comprehensive Psychiatry*, **36**, 53–60.

de Groot, J. M. & Rodin, G. (1998). Coming alive: the psychotherapeutic treatment of patients with eating disorders. *Canadian Journal of Psychiatry*, **43**, 359–365.

Dember, W. N. (1974). Motivation and the cognitive revolution. *American Psychologist*, **29**, 161–168.

Demo, D. (1985). The measurement of self-esteem: refining our methods. *Journal of Personality and Social Psychology*, **48**, 1490–1502.

Derogatis, L. R. (1977). *SCL-90 Manual*. Baltimore, Maryland: Johns Hopkins University.

de Sauvages, F. B. (1772). *Nosologie methodique ou distribution des maladies en classes, en genres et en especies*. Lyon: J-M. Bruyset.

Devlin, M. J., Walsh, B. T., Kral, J. G., Heymsfield, S. B., Pi-Sunyer, F. X., & Dantzic, S. (1990). Metabolic abnormalities in bulimia nervosa. *Archives of General Psychiatry*, **47**, 144–148.

Dixon, K. N. & Kiecolt-Glaser, J. (1984). Group therapy for bulimia. *Hillside Journal of Clinical Psychology*, **6**, 156–170.

Dodge, E., Hodes, M., Eisler, I., & Dare, C. (1995). Family therapy for bulimia nervosa in adolescents: an exploratory study. *Journal of Family Therapy*, **17**, 59–77.

Dokter, D. (1995). *Arts Therapies and Clients with Eating Disorders: Fragile Board*. London: Jessica Kingsley.

Dulit, R. A., Fryer, M. R., Leon, A. C., Brodsky, B. S., & Frances, A. J. (1994). Clinical correlates of self-mutilation in borderline personality disorder. *American Journal of Psychiatry*, **151**, 1305–1311.

Dunn, J. & Plomin, R. (1990). *Separate Lives: Why Siblings are so Different*. New York: Basic Books.

Dykens, E. M. & Gerrard, M. (1986). Psychological profiles of purging bulimics, repeat dieters, and controls. *Journal of Consulting and Clinical Psychology*, **54**, 283–288.

Edwards, F. E. & Nagelberg, D. B. (1986). Personality characteristics of restrained/binge eaters versus unrestrained/nonbinge eaters. *Addictive Behaviours*, **11**, 207–211.

Edwards, E. (1990). Cognitive therapy and the restructuring of early memories through guided imagery. *Journal of Cognitive Psychotherapy*, **4**, 33–50.

Ehlers, A. (1999). A cognitive approach to the understanding and treatment of posttraumatic stress disorder. In *The international handbook of road traffic accidents and psychological trauma: current understanding and law*. E. J. Hickling & E. B. Blanchard (eds). New York: Elsevier.

Eifert, G. H., Schulte, D., Zvolensky, M. J., Lejuez, C. W., & Lau, A. W. (1997). Manualised behaviour therapy: merits and challenges. *Behaviour Therapy*, 28, 499–509.

Ellis, A. (1962). *Reason and Emotion in* Psychotherapy. New York: Stuart.

Elmore, D. K. & De Castro, J. M. (1991). Meal patterns of normal, untreated bulimia nervosa and recovered bulimic women. *Physiology and Behaviour*, 49, 99–105.

Engstrom, I., Kroon, M., Arvidsson, C-G., Segnestam, K., Snellman, K., & Aman, J. (1999). Eating disorders in adolescent girls with insulin-dependent diabetes mellitus: a population-based case-control study. *Acta Psychiatrica Scandanivica*, 88, 175–180.

Eppright, E. S., Fox, H. M., Fryer, B. A., Lamkin, G. H., & Vivian, V. M. (1969). Eating behaviour of pre-school children. *Journal of Nutrition Education*, 1, 16–19.

Esplen, M. J. & Garfinkel, P. E. (1998). Guided imagery treatment to promote self soothing in bulimia nervosa. *The Journal of Psychotherapy Practice and Research*, 7, 102–118.

Esplen, M. J., Garfinkel, P. E., Olmsted, M., Gallop, R. M., & Kennedy, S. (1998). A randomised controlled trial of guided imagery in bulimia nervosa. *Psychological Medicine*, 28, 1347–1357.

Esplen, M. J., Garfinkel, P., & Gallop, R. (2000). Relationship between self-soothing, aloneness, and evocative memory in bulimia nervosa. *International Journal of Eating Disorders*, 27, 96–100.

Evans, J. & le Grange, D. (1995). Body size and parenting in eating disorders: a comparative study of the attitudes of mothers towards their children. *International Journal of Eating Disorders*, 18, 39–48.

Everill, J. T. & Waller, G. (1995). Reported sexual abuse and eating psychopathology: a review of the evidence for a causal link. *International Journal of Eating Disorders*, 18, 1–11.

Eysenck, H. J. & Eysenck, S. B. (1976). *Manual of the Eysenck Personality Questionnaire*. San Diego, California: Educational and Industrial Testing Service.

Eysenck, S., Pearson, P., Easting, G., & Allsopp, J. (1985). Age norms for impulsiveness, venturesomeness, and empathy in adults. *Journal of Personality and Individual Differences*, 6, 613–619.

Eysenck, M. W. (1993). *Principles of Cognitive Psychology*. Hove, East Sussex: Erlbaum.

Fahy, T. A. & Treasure, J. (1991). Caffeine abuse in bulimia nervosa. *International Journal of Eating Disorders*, 10, 373–377.

Fahy, T. & Eisler, I. (1993). Impulsivity and eating disorders. *British Journal of Psychiatry*, 162, 193–197.

Fahy, T. A., Eisler, I., & Russell, G. F. (1993). A placebo controlled trial of d-fenfluramine in bulimia nervosa. *British Journal of Psychiatry*, 162, 587–603.

Fahy, T. A. & Russell, G. F. (1993). Outcome and prognostic variables in bulimia nervosa. *International Journal of Eating Disorders*, 14, 135–145.

Fairbairn, W. R. D. (1993). *Psychoanalytic Studies of the Personality*. London: Routledge, Kegan & Paul.

Fairburn, C. G. (1981). A cognitive behavioural approach to the treatment of bulimia. *Psychological Medicine*, 11, 707–711.

Fairburn, C. G. & Cooper, P. J. (1982). Self-induced vomiting and bulimia nervosa: an undetected problem. *British Medical Journal*, 284, 1153–1155.

Fairburn, C. G. & Cooper, P. J. (1984). The clinical features of bulimia nervosa. *British Journal of Psychiatry*, 144, 238–246.

Fairburn, C. G. (1985). Cognitive behavioural treatment for bulimia. In *Handbook of Psychotherapy for Anorexia Nervosa and Bulimia* (D. M. Garner & P. E. Garfinkel, ed.). New York: Guilford Press.

Fairburn, C. G., Cooper, P. J., & Cooper, Z. (1986a). The clinical features and maintenance of bulimia nervosa. In *Physiology, Psychology and Treatment of the Eating Disorders* (K. D. Brownell & J. P. Foreyt, ed.). New York: Basic Books.

Fairburn, C. G., Kirk, J., O'Connor, M., & Cooper, P. J. (1986b). A comparison of two psychological treatments for bulimia nervosa. *Behaviour Research and Therapy*, 24, 629–643.

Fairburn, C. G. (1987). The definition of bulimia nervosa. *Annals of Behavioural Medicine*, **9**, 3–7.

Fairburn, C. G., Kirk, J., O'Connor, M., Anastasiades, P., & Cooper, P. J. (1987). Prognostic factors in bulimia nervosa. *British Journal of Clinical Psychology*, **26**, 223–224.

Fairburn, C. G. & Cooper, P. J. (1989). Eating disorders. In *Cognitive Behaviour Therapy for Psychiatric Problems* (K. Hawton, P. M. Salkovskis, J. Kirk & D. M. Clark, ed.). Oxford: Oxford University Press.

Fairburn, C. G. & Beglin, S. J. (1990). Studies of the epidemiology of bulimia nervosa. *American Journal of Psychiatry*, **147**, 401–408.

Fairburn, C. G. & Peveler, R. C. (1990). Bulimia nervosa and a stepped care approach to management. *Gut*, **31**, 1220–1222.

Fairburn, C. G., Cooper, P. J., Cooper, M. J., McKenna, F. P., & Anastasiades, P. (1991a). Selective information processing in bulimia nervosa. *International Journal of Eating Disorders*, **10**, 415–422.

Fairburn, C. G., Jones, R., Peveler, R. C., Carr, S. J., Solomon, R. A., O'Connor, M. E., Burton, J., & Hope, R. A. (1991b). Three psychological treatments for bulimia nervosa: A comparative trial. *Archives of General Psychiatry*, **48**, 463–469.

Fairburn, C. G., Peveler, R. C., Davies, B., Mann, J. I., & Mayou, R. A. (1991c). Eating disorders in young adults with insulin-dependent diabetes mellitus: a controlled study. *British Medical Journal*, **303**, 17–20.

Fairburn, C. G. & Cooper, Z. (1993). The Eating Disorder Examination. In *Binge eating: nature, assessment and treatment* (C. G. Fairburn & G. T. Wilson, ed.). New York: Guilford Press.

Fairburn, C. G., Jones, R., Peveler, R. C., Hope, R. A., & O'Connor, M. (1993a). Psychotherapy and bulimia nervosa: the longer term effects of interpersonal therapy, behaviour therapy and cognitive behaviour therapy. *Archives of General Psychiatry*, **50**, 419–428.

Fairburn, C. G., Marcus, M. D., & Wilson, G. T. (1993b). Cognitive Behaviour therapy for binge eating and bulimia nervosa: a comprehensive treatment manual. In *Binge Eating: Nature, Assessment and Treatment* (C. G. Fairburn & G. T. Wilson, ed.). New York: Guilford.

Fairburn, C. G., Peveler, R. C., Jones, R., Hope, R. A., & Doll, H. A. (1993c). Predictors of 12-month outcome in bulimia nervosa and the influence of attitudes to shape and weight. *Journal of Consulting and Clinical Psychology*, **61**, 696–698.

Fairburn, C. G. & Beglin, S. J. (1994). Assessment of eating disorders: interview or self-report questionnaire? *International Journal of Eating Disorders*, **16**, 363–370.

Fairburn, C. G. (1995). *Overcoming Binge Eating*. New York: Guilford Press.

Fairburn, C. G., Norman, P. A., Welch, S. L., O'Connor, M. E., Doll, H. A., & Peveler, R. C. (1995). A prospective study of outcome in bulimia nervosa and the long-term effects of three psychological treatments. *Archives of General Psychiatry*, **52**, 304–312.

Fairburn, C. G., Welch, S. L., Norman, P. A., O'Connor, M. E., & Doll, H. A. (1996). Bias and bulimia nervosa: how typical are clinic cases? *American Journal of Psychiatry*, **153**, 386–391.

Fairburn, C. G., Welch, S. L., Doll, H. A., Davies, B. A., & O'Connor, M. E. (1997). Risk factors for bulimia nervosa. *Archives of General Psychiatry*, **54**, 509–517.

Fairburn, C. G. (1997a). Interpersonal psychotherapy for bulimia nervosa. In *Handbook of Treatment for Eating Disorders* (2nd edn) (D. M. Garner & P. E. Garfinkel, ed.). New York: Guilford.

Fairburn, C. G. (1997b). Eating disorders. In *Science and Practice of Cognitive Behaviour Therapy*. D. M. Clark & C. G. Fairburn (eds). Oxford: Oxford University Press.

Fairburn, C. G., Cooper, Z., Doll, H. A., & Welch, S. L. (1999). Risk factors for anorexia nervosa: three integrated case-control comparisons. *Archives of General Psychiatry*, **56**, 468–476.

Fairburn, C. G., Cooper, Z., Doll, H. A., Norman, P., & O'Connor, M. (2000). The natural course of bulimia nervosa and binge eating disorder in young women. *Archives of General Psychiatry*, **57**, 659–665.

Fallon, B. A., Walsh, B. T., Sadik, C., Saoud, J. B., & Lukasik, V. (1991). Outcome and clinical course in inpatient bulimic women: a 2 to 9 year follow up study. *Journal of Clinical Psychiatry*, **52**, 272–278.

Fallon, B. A., Sadik, C., Saoud, J. B., & Garfinkel, R. S. (1994). Childhood abuse, family environment, and outcome in bulimia nervosa. *Journal of Clinical Psychiatry*, **55**, 424–428.

Fallon, A. & Bunce, S. (2000). The psychoanalytic perspective. In *Comparative treatments for eating disorders* (K. J. Miller & J. S. Mizes, ed.). New York: Springer Publishing Company.

Falloon, I. R. H. (1988). *Handbook of Behavioural Family Therapy.* London: Guildford Press.

Fava, G. A., Rafanelli, C., Cazzaro, M., Conti, S., & Grandi, S. (1998). Well-being therapy: a novel psychotherapeutic approach for residual symptoms of affective disorders. *Psychological Medicine*, **28**, 475–480.

Favaro, A. & Santonastaso, P. (1997). Suicidality in eating disorders: clinical and psychological correlates. *Acta Psychiatrica Scanadivica*, **95**, 508–514.

Favaro, A. & Santonastaso, P. (1998). Impulsive and compulsive self-injurious behaviour in bulimia nervosa: prevalence and psychological correlates. *Journal of Nervous and Mental Disease*, **186**, 157–165.

Favaro, A. & Santonastaso, P. (1999). Different types of self-injurious behaviour in bulimia nervosa. *Comprehensive Psychiatry*, **40**, 57–60.

Favaro, A., Rodella, F. C., & Santonastaso, P. (2000). Binge eating and eating attitudes among Nazi concentration camp survivors. *Psychological Medicine*, **30**, 463–466.

Favazza, A. R. (1989). Why patients mutilate themselves. *Hospital and Community Psychiatry*, **40**, 137–145.

Ferguson, J. M. (1985). Bulimia: a potentially fatal syndrome. *Psychosomatics*, **26**, 252–253.

Fernandez-Aranda, F., Dahme, B., & Meerman, R. (1999). Body image in eating disorders and analysis of relevance: a preliminary study. *Journal of Psychosomatic Research*, **47**, 419–428.

Festinger, L. (1957). *A Theory of Cognitive Dissonance.* Stanford: Stanford University Press.

Fichter, M. M., Quadflieg, N., & Brandl, B. (1993). Recurrent overeating: an empirical comparison of binge eating disorder, bulimia nervosa and obesity. *International Journal of Eating Disorders*, **14**, 1–16.

Fichter, M. M., Quadflieg, N., & Rief, W. (1994). Course of multi-impulsive bulimia. *Psychological Medicine*, **24**, 591–604.

Field, A. E., Colditz, G. A., & Peterson, K. E. (1997). Racial/ethnic and gender differences in concern with weight and bulimic behaviours among adolescents. *Obesity Research*, **5**, 447–454.

Finch, J. F., Okun, M. A., Pool, G. J., & Ruehlman, L. S. (1999). A comparison of the influence of conflictual and supportive social interactions on psychological distress. *Journal of Personality*, **67**, 581–621.

First, M. B., Spitzer, R. L., Gibbon, M., & Williams, J. B. W. (1996). *Structured clinical interview for DSM-IV Axis 1 disorders.* New York: Biometrics Research Department, New York State Psychiatric Institute.

First, M. B. & Pincus, H. A. (1999). Classification in psychiatry: ICD-10 v. DSM-IV. *British Journal of Psychiatry*, **175**, 205–209.

Fitzgibbon, M. L. & Blackman, L. R. (2000). Binge eating disorder and bulimia nervosa: differences in the quality and quantity of binge eating episodes. *International Journal of Eating Disorders*, **27**, 238–243.

Folsom, V., Krahn, D., Nairn, K., Gold, L., Demitrak, M. A., & Silk, K. R. (1993). The impact of sexual and physical abuse on eating disordered psychiatric symptoms: A comparison of eating disordered and psychiatric inpatients. *International Journal of Eating Disorders*, **13**, 249–257.

Fombonne, E. (1995). Anorexia nervosa: no evidence of an increase. *British Journal of Psychiatry*, **31**, 451–465.

Forisha, B., Grothaus, K., & Luscombe, R. (1990). Dinner conversation: meal therapy to differentiate eating behaviour from family process. *Journal of Psychosocial Nursing and Mental Health Services*, 28, 12–16.

Fornari, V., Edelman, R., & Katz, J. L. (1990). Medication manipulation in bulimia nervosa: an additional diagnostic criterion? *International Journal of Eating Disorders*, 9, 585–588.

Franko, D. L., Zuroff, D. C., & Rosenthal, F. (1986). Construct validation of the Bulimic Thoughts Questionnaire. Paper presented at the annual meeting of the Society of Behavioural Medicine, March 1986, San Francisco.

Franko, D. L. & Zuroff, D. C. (1992). The bulimic automatic thoughts test: initial reliabilty and validity data. *Journal of Clinical Psychology*, 48, 505–509.

Franko, D. & Walton, B. E. (1993). Pregnancy and eating disorders: a review and clinical implications. *International Journal of Eating Disorders*, 13, 41–48.

Franko, D. L. (1997). Ready or not? Stages of change as predictors of brief group therapy outcome in bulimia nervosa. *Group*, 21, 39–45.

Fransella, F. & Crisp, A. H. (1979). Comparisons of weight concepts in groups of neurotic, normal and anorexic females. *British Journal of Psychiatry*, 134, 79–81.

Fransella, F. & Button, E. (1983). The construing of self and body size in relation to maintenance of weight gain in anorexia nervosa. In *Anorexia Nervosa: Recent Developments in Research* (P. L. Darby, P. E. Garfinkel, D. M. Garner & D. V. Coscina, ed.). New York: Alan R. Liss.

Freeman, R. J., Thomas, C. D., Solyom, L., & Miles, J. E. (1983). Body image disturbances in anorexia nervosa: a reexamination and new technique. In *Anorexia Nervosa: Recent Developments in Research* (P. L. Darby, P. E. Garfinkel, D. M. Garner & D. V. Coscina, ed.). New York: Alan R. Liss.

Freeman, R. J., Beach, B., Davis, R., & Solyom, L. (1985). The prediction of relapse in bulimia nervosa. *Journal of Psychiatric Research*, 19, 349–353.

Freeman, C. P., Barry, F., Dunkeld-Turnbull, J., & Henderson, A. (1988). Controlled trial of psychotherapy for bulimia nervosa. *British Medical Journal*, 296, 521–525.

French, S. A., & Jeffrey, R. W. (1994). Consequences of dieting to lose weight: effects on physical and mental health. *Health Psychology*, 13, 195–212.

French, S. A., Perry, C. L., Leon, G. R., & Fulkerson, J. A. (1995). Changes in psychological variables and health behaviours by dieting status over a three year period in a cohort of adolescent females. *Journal of Adolescent Health*, 16, 438–447.

Freud, A. (1958). Adolescence. *The Psychoanalytic Study of the Child*, 13, 255–278.

Freud, S. (1918/59). From the history of an infantile neurosis. *Collected Papers*, Vol. 3. New York: Basic Books.

Friedman, A. G., Seime, R. J., Roberts, T., & Fremouw, W. J. (1987). Ipecac abuse: a serious complication in bulimia nervosa. *General Hospital Psychiatry*, 9, 225–228.

Friedman, M. A., & Whisman, M. A. (1998). Sociotrophy, autonomy, and bulimic symptomatology. *International Journal of Eating Disorders*, 23, 439–442.

Fullerton, D. T., Wonderlich, S. A., & Gosnell, B. A. (1995). Clinical characteristics of eating disorder patients who report sexual or physical abuse. *International Journal of Eating Disorders*, 17, 243–249.

Furnham, A. & Patel, R. (1994). The eating attitudes and behaviours of Asian and British schoolgirls: a pilot study. *International Journal of Social Psychiatry*, 40, 214–226.

Garfield, S. L. (1994). Eclecticism and integration in psychotherapy: developments and issues. *Clinical Psychology: Science and Practice*, 1, 123–137.

Garfinkel, P. E. & Garner, D. M. (1982). *Anorexia Nervosa: A Multidimensional Perspective*. New York: Brunner/Mazel.

Garfinkel, P. E., Kennedy, S. H., & Kaplan, A. S. (1995a). Views on classification and diagnosis of eating disorders. *Canadian Journal of Psychiatry*, 40, 445–456.

Garfinkel, P. E., Lin, E., Goering, P., Spegg, C., Goldbloom, D. S., Kennedy, S., Kaplan, A. S., & Woodside, D. B. (1995b). Bulimia nervosa in a Canadian community sample: prevalence and comparison of subgroups. *American Journal of Psychiatry*, 152, 1052–1058.

Garner, D. M. & Garfinkel, P. E. (1979). The Eating Attitudes Test: an index of the symptoms of anorexia nervosa. *Psychological Medicine*, 9, 273–279.

Garner, D. M. & Garfinkel, P. E. (1980). Sociocultural factors in the development of anorexia nervosa. *Psychological Medicine*, 10, 647–656.

Garner, D. M., Garfinkel, P. E., Schwartz, D., & Thompson, M. (1980). Cultural expectations of thinness in women. *Psychological Reports*, 47, 483–491.

Garner, D. M. & Bemis, K. M. (1982). A cognitive-behavioural approach to anorexia nervosa. *Cognitive Therapy and Research*, 6, 123–150.

Garner, D. M., Garfinkel, P. E., & Olmsted, M. P. (1983a). An overview of sociocultural factors in the development of anorexia nervosa. In *Anorexia Nervosa: Recent Developments in Research* (P. L. Darby, P. E. Garfinkel, D. M. Garner & D. V. Coscina, ed.). New York: Alan R. Liss.

Garner, D. M., Olmsted, M. P., & Polivy, J. (1983b). Development and validation of a multidimensional Eating Disorder Inventory for anorexia nervosa and bulimia. *International Journal of Eating Disorders*, 2, 15–34.

Garner, D. M., Olmsted, M. P., Polivy, J., & Garfinkel, P. E. (1984a). Comparison between weight preoccupied women and anorexia nervosa. *Psychosomatic Medicine*, 46, 255–266.

Garner, D. M., Rockert, W., Olmsted, M. P., Johnson, C., & Coscina, D. V. (1984b). Psychoeducational principles in the treatment of bulimia and anorexia nervosa. In *A Handbook of Psychotherapy of Anorexia Nervosa and Bulimia Nervosa* (D. M. Garner & P. E. Garfinkel, ed.). New York: Guilford Press.

Garner, D. M. Garfinkel, P. E., & Irvine, M. J. (1986). Integration and sequencing of treatment approaches for eating disorders. *Psychotherapy and Psychosomatics*, 46, 67–75.

Garner, D. M., Garfinkel, P. E., Rockert, W., & Olmsted, M. P. (1987). A prospective study of eating disturbances in the ballet. *Psychotherapy and Psychosomatics*, 48, 170–175.

Garner, D. M., Olmsted, M. P., Davis, R., Rockert, W., Goldbloom, D., & Eagle, M. (1990). The association between bulimic symptoms and reported psychopathology. *International Journal of Eating Disorders*, 9, 1–15.

Garner, D. M. (1991). *Eating Disorders Inventory 2*. Odessa, Florida: Professional Resources Inc.

Garner, D. M., Shafer, C. L., & Rosen, L. W. (1991). Critical appraisal of the DSM-III-R criteria for eating disorders. In *Child Psychopathology: Diagnostic Criteria and Clinical Assessment* (S. R. Hooper & G. W. Hynd, ed.). Hillsdale, NJ: Lawrence Erlbaum Associates, Inc.

Garner, D. M., Rockert, W., Davis, R., Garner, M. V., Olmsted, M. P., & Eagle, M. (1993). Comparison of cognitive behavioural and supportive expressive therapy for bulimia nervosa. *American Journal of Psychiatry*, 150, 37–46.

Garner, D. M. & Needleman, L. D. (1997). Sequencing and integrating of treatments. In *Handbook of Treatment for Eating Disorders* (2nd edn) (D. M. Garner & P. E. Garfinkel, ed.). New York: Guilford Press.

Gartner, A. F., Marcus, R. N., Halmi, K., & Loranger, A. W. (1989). DSM-III-R personality disorders in patients with eating disorders. *American Journal of Psychiatry*, 146, 1585–1591.

Garvin, V., Striegel-Moore, R. H., & Wells, A. M. (1998). Participant reactions to a cognitive behavioural guided self help programme for binge eating: developing criteria for programme evaluation. *Journal of Psychosomatic Research*, 44, 407–412.

Gavish, D., Eisenberg, S., Berry, E. M., Kleinman, Y., Witztum, E., Norman, J., & Leitersdorf, E. (1987). Bulimia-an underlying behavioural disorder in hyperlipidemic pancreatitis: a prospective multidisciplinary approach. *Archives of Internal Medicine*, 147, 705–708.

Geist, R. A. (1989). Self psychological reflections on the origins of eating disorders. *Journal of the American Academy of Psychoanalysis*, 17, 5–27.

Geller, J., Johnston, C., & Madsen, K. (1997). The role of shape and weight in self-concept: the shape and weight based self-esteem inventory. *Cognitive Therapy and Research*, 21, 5–24.

Geller, J., Johnston, C., Madsen, K., Goldner, E. M., Remick, R. A., & Birmingham, C. L. (1998). Shape- and weight-based self-esteem and the eating disorders. *International Journal of Eating Disorders*, 24, 285–298.

Geller, J., Srikameswaran, S., Cockell, S. J., & Zaitsoff S. L. (2000). Assessment of shape and weight based self esteem in adolescents. *International Journal of Eating Disorders*, 28, 339–345.

Gendall, K. A., Sullivan, P. E., Joyce, P. R., Carter, F. A., & Bulik, C. M. (1997). The nutrient intake of women with bulimia nervosa. *International Journal of Eating Disorders*, 21, 115–127.

Gendlin, E. T. (1996). *Focusing Oriented Psychotherapy*. New York: Guilford.

George, M. S., Brewerton, T. D., & Harden, R. N. (1993). Bulimia nervosa in outpatients with migraine: a pilot study. *Journal of Nervous and Mental Disease*, 181, 704–706.

Gilbert, S. & Thompson, J. K. (1996). Feminist explanations of the development of eating disorders: common themes, research findings and methodological issues. *Clinical Psychology: Science and Practice*, 3, 183–202.

Giles, T. R., Young, R. R., & Young, D. E. (1985). Behavioural treatment of severe bulimia. *Behaviour Therapy*, 16, 393–405.

Gimble, A. I., Davison, C., & Smith, P. K. (1948). Studies on the toxicity, distribution and excretion of emetine. *Journal of Pharmacology and Experimental Therapeutics*, 94, 431–438.

Glassman, E. J. (1988). Development of a self-report measure of soothing receptivity. Unpublished Doctoral Dissertation. Toronto: York University.

Glassman, J. N., Rich, C. L., Darko, D., & Clarkin, A. (1991). Menstrual dysfunction in bulimia. *Annals of Clinical Psychiatry*, 3, 161–165.

Gleaves, D. H. & Eberenz, K. P. (1994). Sexual abuse histories among treatment resistant bulimia nervosa patients. *International Journal of Eating Disorders*, 15, 227–231.

Gleaves, D. H. & Eberenz, K. P. (1995). Correlates of dissociative symptoms among women with eating disorders. *Journal of Psychiatric Research*, 29, 417–426.

Gleaves, D. H., Eberenz, K. P., & May, M. C. (1998). Scope and significance of posttraumatic symptomatology among women hospitalised for an eating disorder. *International Journal of Eating Disorders*, 24, 147–156.

Gleaves, D. H, Lowe, M. R., Snow, A. C., Green, B. A., & Murphy-Eberenz, K. P. (2000). Continuity and discontinuity models of bulimia nervosa: a taxometric analysis. *Journal of Abnormal Psychology*, 109, 56–68.

Godart, N. T., Flament, M. F., Lecrubier, Y., & Jeammet, P. (2000). Anxiety disorders in anorexia nervosa and bulimia nervosa: co-morbidity and chronology of appearance. *European Psychiatry*, 15, 38–45.

Goldberg, D. (2000). Plato versus Aristotle: categorical and dimensional models for common mental disorders. *Comprehensive Psychiatry*, 41, Supplement 1, 8–13.

Goldbloom, D. S., Naranjo, C. A., Bremner, K. E., & Hicks, L. K. (1992). Eating disorders and alcohol abuse in women. *British Journal of Addiction*, 87, 913–919.

Goldbloom, D. S., Olmsted, M., Davis, R., Clewes, J., Heinmaa, M., Rockert, W., & Shaw, B. (1997). A randomised controlled trial of fluoxetine and cognitive behavioural therapy for bulimia. *Behaviour Research and Therapy*, 35, 803–811.

Goldfarb, L. A. (1987). Sexual abuse antecedent to anorexia nervosa, bulimia, and compulsive overeating: three case reports. *International Journal of Eating Disorders*, 6, 675–680.

Goldfein, J. A., Walsh, B. T., & Midlarsky, E. (2000). Influence of shape and weight on self-evaluation in bulimia nervosa. *International Journal of Eating Disorders, 27*, 435–445.

Goldfried, M. R. & Davison, G. C. (1976). *Clinical Behaviour Therapy.* New York: Holt, Reinhart & Winston.

Gomez, R., Gomez, A., DeMello, L., & Tallent, R. (2001). Perceived maternal control and support: effects on hostile biased social processing and aggression among clinic referred children with high aggression. *Journal of Child Psychology and Psychiatry, 42*, 513–522.

Goodman, W. K., Price, L. H., Rasmussen, S. A., Mazure, C., Fleischmann, M., Hill, C. L., Heninger, G. R. & Charney, D. S. (1989). The Yale-Brown obsessive compulsive scale: 1. development, use and reliability. *Archives of General Psychiatry, 46*, 1006–1011.

Goodsitt, A. (1985). Self psychology. In *Handbook of Psychotherapy for Anorexia Nervosa and Bulimia* (D. M. Garner & P. E. Garfinkel, ed.). New York: Guilford.

Goodsitt, A. (1997). Eating disorders: a self psychological perpective. In *Handbook of Treatment for Eating Disorders* (D. M. Garner & P. E. Garfinkel, ed.). New York: Guilford.

Gordon, J., Ramsay, R., & Treasure, J. (1997). Use of asprin to facilitate vomiting in a young woman with bulimia nervosa: a case report. *International Journal of Eating Disorders, 21*, 201–203.

Gordon, R. A. (2001). Eating disorders East and West: a culture-bound syndrome unbound. In *Eating Disorders and Cultures in Transition* (M. Nasser, M. A. Katzman, & R. A. Gordon, ed.). Hove, East Sussex: Brunner Routledge.

Gotestam, K. G. & Agras, W. S. (1995). General population-based epidemiological study of eating disorders in Norway. *International Journal of Eating Disorders, 18*, 119–126.

Gralewski, C. & Schneider, M. F. (2000). An Adlerian approach. In *Comparative Treatments of Eating Disorders* (K. Miller & J. S. Mizes, ed.). London: Free Association Books.

Gray, J. J. & Ford, K. (1985). The incidence of bulimia in a college sample. *International Journal of Eating Disorders, 4*, 201–210.

Gray, J. J., Ford, K., & Kelly, L. M. (1987). The prevalence of bulimia in a black college population. *International Journal of Eating Disorders, 6*, 733–740.

Green, M. W., Rogers, P. J., Elliman, N. A., & Gatenby S. J. (1994). Impairment of cognitive performance associated with dieting and high levels of dietary restraint. *Physiology and Behaviour, 55*, 447–452.

Greenberg, L. S. & Safran, J. D. (1987). *Emotion in Psychotherapy.* New York: Guilford.

Greenfield, D., Mickley, D., Quinlan, D. M., & Roloff, P. (1993). Ipecac abuse in a sample of eating disordered outpatients. *International Journal of Eating Disorders, 13*, 411–414.

Griffiths, R. A., Beumont, P. J. V., Giannakopoulos, E., Russell, J., Schotte, D., Thornton, C., Touyz, S. W., & Varano, P. (1999). Measuring self-esteem in dieting disordered patients: the validity of the Rosenberg and Coopersmith contrasted. *International Journal of Eating Disorders, 25*, 227–231.

Grilo, C. M. & Shiffman, S. (1994). Longitudinal investigation of the abstinence violation effect in binge eaters. *Journal of Consulting and Clinical Psychology, 62*, 611–619.

Grinc, G. A. (1982). A cognitive behavioural model for the treatment of chronic vomiting. *Journal of Behavioural Medicine, 5*, 135–141.

Grissett, N. I., & Norvell, N. K. (1992). Perceived social support, social skills, and quality of relationships in bulimic women. *Journal of Consulting and Clinical Psychology, 60*, 293–299.

Grogan, S. (1999). *Body Image.* London: Routledge.

Gross, J. & Rosen, J. C. (1988). Bulimia in adolescents: prevalence and psychosocial correlates. *International Journal of Eating Disorders, 7*, 51–61.

Guertin, T. L. (1999). Eating behaviour of bulimics, self-identified binge eaters, and non-eating-disordered individuals: what differentiates these populations? *Clinical Psychology Review, 19*, 1–23.

Guidano, V. F. & Liotti, G. (1983). *Cognitive Processes and Emotional Disorders: A Structural Approach to Psychotherapy.* New York: Guilford Press.

Guidano, V. F. (1987). *Complexity of the Self.* New York: Guilford Press.

Gupta, M. A., Gupta, A. K., Shork, N. J., & Watteel, G. N. (1995). Perceived touch deprivation and body image: some observations among eating disordered and non-clinical subjects. *Journal of Psychosomatic Research*, 39, 459–464.

Habermas, T. (1989). The psychiatric history of anorexia nervosa and bulimia nervosa: weight concerns and bulimic symptoms in early case reports. *International Journal of Eating Disorders*, 8, 259–273.

Habermas, T. (1992). Further evidence on early case descriptions of anorexia nervosa and bulimia nervosa. *International Journal of Eating Disorders*, 11, 351–359.

Hackmann, A. (1998). Working with images in clinical psychology. In (A. S. Bellack & M. Hersen, ed.). *Comprehensive Clinical Psychology*, Vol. 6. New York: Elsevier.

Hackmann, A., Surawy, C., & Clark, D. M. (1998). Seeing yourself through others' eyes: a study of spontaneously occuring images in social phobia. *Behavioural and Cognitive Psychotherapy*, 26, 3–12.

Hackmann, A., Clark, D. M., & McManus, F. (2000). Recurrent images and early memories in social phobia. *Behaviour Research and Therapy*, 38, 601–610.

Hadigan, C. M., Kissileff, H. R., & Walsh, B. T. (1989). Patterns of food selection during meals in women with bulimia. *American Journal of Clinical Nutrition*, 50, 759–766.

Haiman, C. & Devlin, M. J. (1999). Binge eating before the onset of dieting: a distinct subgroup of bulimia nervosa? *International Journal of Eating Disorders*, 25, 151–157.

Haley, J. (1976). *Problem Solving Therapy.* San Francisco: Jossey Bass.

Hall, R. C. W., Hoffman, R. S., Beresford, T. P., Wooley, B., Tice, L., & Hall, A. K. (1988). Hypomagnesemia in patients with eating disorders. *Psychosomatics*, 29, 264–272.

Halmi, K. A., Falk, J. R., & Schwartz, E. (1981). Binge-eating and vomiting: a survey of a college population. *Psychological Medicine*, 11, 697–706.

Hamilton, K. & Waller, G. (1993). Media influences on body size estimation in anorexia and bulimia: an experimental study. *British Journal of Psychiatry*, 162, 837–840.

Harter, S. (1998). The development of self representations. In *Handbook of Child Psychology: Vol. 3. Social, emotional and personality development* (W. Damon, ed.). New York: Wiley.

Hartmann, A., Herzog, T., & Drinkmann, A. (1992). Psychotherapy of bulimia nervosa: what is effective? A meta analysis. *Journal of Psychosomatic Research*, 36, 159–167.

Hastings, T. & Kern, J. M. (1994). Relationships between bulimia, childhood sexual abuse, and family environment. *International Journal of Eating Disorders*, 15, 103–111.

Haviland, W. A. (1997). *Anthropology.* Fort Worth, Texas: Harcourt Brace & Company.

Hawkins, R. C. & Clement, P. F. (1980). Development and construct validation of a self-report measure of binge eating tendencies. *Addictive Behaviours*, 5, 219–226.

Hay, P. J., Fairburn, C. G., & Doll, H. A. (1996). The classification of bulimic eating disorders: a community based cluster analysis study. *Psychological Medicine*, 26, 801–812.

Hay, P. J. & Fairburn, C. G. (1998). The validity of the DSM-IV scheme for classifying bulimic eating disorders. *International Journal of Eating Disorders*, 23, 7–15.

Hay, P. J. & Bacaltchuk, J. (2000). Psychotherapy for bulimia nervosa and bingeing. *The Cochrane Library*, 4.

Heatherton, T. F. & Baumeister, R. F. (1991) Binge eating as escape from self-awareness. *Psychological Bulletin*, 110, 86–108.

Heatherton, T. F., Polivy, J., & Herman, C. P. (1991). Restraint, weight loss, and variability of body weight. *Journal of Abnormal Psychology*, 100, 78–83.

Heesacker, R. S. & Neimeyer, G. J. (1990). Assessing object relations and social cognitive correlates of eating disorder. *Journal of Counselling Psychology*, 37, 419–426.

Heffernan, K. (1996). Eating disorders and weight concern among lesbians. *International Journal of Eating Disorders*, 19, 127–138.

Hellin, K. & Waller, G. (1992). Mothers' mood and infant feeding: prediction of problems and practices. *Journal of Reproductive and Infant Psychology*, 10, 39–51.

Henderson, S., Byrne, D. G., & Duncan-Jones, P. (1981). *Neurosis and the Social Environment*. Sydney: Academic Press.

Henderson, M. & Freeman, C. P. (1987). A self rating scale for bulimia: the BITE. *British Journal of Psychiatry*, 150, 18–24.

Herman, C. P. & Mack, D. (1975). Restrained and unrestrained eating. *Journal of Personality*, 43, 647–660.

Herman, C. P. & Polivy, J. (1975). Anxiety, restraint and eating behaviour. *Journal of Abnormal Psychology*, 84, 666–672.

Herman, C. P., Polivy, J., Pliner, P., Threlkeld, J., & Munic, D. (1978). Distractibility in dieters and nondieters: an alternative view of 'externality'. *Journal of Personality and Social Psychology*, 36, 536–548.

Herman, C. P. & Polivy, J. (1984). A boundary model for the regulation of eating. In *Eating and its Disorders* (A. J. Stunkard & E. Stellar, ed.). New York: Raven Press.

Herpertz, S., Wagenar, R., Albus, C., Kocnar, M., Wagner, R., Best, F., Scleppinghoff, B. S., Filz, H-P., Forster, K., Thomas, W., Mann, K., Kohle, K., & Senf, W. (1998). Diabetes mellitus and eating disorders: a multicentre study on the comorbidity of the two diseases. *Journal of Psychosomatic Research*, 44, 503–515.

Hersen, M. & Barlow, D. H. (1976). *Single Case Experimental Designs: Strategies for Studying Behaviour Change*. New York: Pergamon Press.

Herzog, D. B. (1982). Bulimia: the secretive syndrome. *Psychosomatics*, 23, 481–487.

Herzog, D. B., Keller, M. B., Lavori, P. W., & Ott, I. L. (1987). Short term prospective study of recovery in bulimia nervosa. *Psychiatry Research*, 23, 45–55.

Herzog, D. B., Keller, M. B., & Lavori, P. W. (1988). Outcome in anorexia nervosa and bulimia nervosa: a review of the literature. *Journal of Nervous and Mental Disease*, 176, 131–143.

Herzog, D. B., Franko, D. L., & Brotman, A. W. (1989). Integrating treatments for bulimia nervosa. *Journal of the American Academy of Psychoanalysis*, 17, 141–150.

Herzog, D. B., Hartmann, A., Sandholz, A., & Stammer, H. (1991a). Prognostic factors in outpatient psychotherapy of bulimia. *Psychotherapy and Psychosomatics*, 56, 48–55.

Herzog, D. B., Keller, M. B., Lavori, P. W., & Sacks, N. R. (1991b). The course and outcome of bulimia nervosa. *Journal of Clinical Psychiatry*, 52, Supplement 4–8.

Herzog, D. B., Keller, M. B., Lavori, P. W., Kenny, G. M., & Sacks, N. R. (1992). The prevalence of personality disorders in 210 women with eating disorders. *Journal of Clinical Psychiatry*, 53, 147–152.

Herzog, D. B. & Sacks, N. R. (1993). Bulimia nervosa: comparison of treatment responders vs. nonresponders. *Psyhcopharmacology Bulletin*, 29, 121–125.

Herzog, D. B., Sacks, N. R., Keller, M. B., Lavori, P. W., von Ranson, K. B., & Gray, H. M. (1993). Patterns and predictors of recovery in anorexia nervosa and bulimia nervosa. *Journal of the American Academy of Child and Adolescent Psychiatry*, 32, 835–842.

Herzog, D. B., Dorer, D. J., Keel, P. K., Selwyn, S. E., Ekeblad, E. R., Flores, A. T., Greenwood, D. N., Burwell, R. A., & Keller, M. B. (1999). Recovery and relapse in anorexia nervosa and bulimia nervosa: a 7. 5 year follow up study. *Journal of the American Academy of Child and Adolescent Psychiatry*, 38, 829–837.

Hetherington, M. M., Spalter, A. R., Bernat, A. S., Nelson, M. L., & Gold, P. W. (1993). Eating pathology in bulimia nervosa. *International Journal of Eating Disorders*, 13, 13–24.

Hetherington, M. M., Altemus, M., Nelson, M. L., Bernat, A. S., & Gold, P. W. (1994). Eating behaviour in bulimia nervosa: multiple meal analysis. *American Journal of Clinical Nutrition*, **60**, 864–873.

Hetherington, M. M., Stoner, S. A., Andersen, A. E., & Rolls, B. J. (2000). Effects of acute food deprivation on eating behaviour in eating disorders. *International Journal of Eating Disorders*, **28**, 272–283.

Hewitt, P. L. & Flett, G. L. (1990). Perfectionism and depression: a multidimensional analysis. *Journal of Social Behaviour and Analysis*, **5**, 423–438.

Hewitt, P. L. & Flett, G. L. (1991). Dimensions of perfectionism in unipolar depression. *Journal of Abnormal Psychology*, **100**, 98–101.

Hill, A. J., Weaver, C., & Blundell, J. E. (1990). Dieting concerns of 10-year-old girls and their mothers. *British Journal of Clinical Psychology*, **29**, 346–348.

Higgins, E. T. (1987). Self-discrepancy: a theory relating self and affect. *Psychological Review*, **94**, 319–340.

Hoek, H. W. (1991). The incidence and prevalence of anorexia nervosa and bulimia nervosa in primary care. *Psychological Medicine*, **21**, 455–460.

Hoek, H. W., Bartelds, A. I. M., Bosveld, J. J. F., van der Graaf, Y., Limpens, V. E. L., Maiwald, M., & Spaaij, C. J. K. (1995). Impact of urbanisation on detection rates of eating disorders. *American Journal of Psychiatry*, **152**, 1272–1278.

Hohlstein, L. A., Smith, G. T., & Atlas, J. G. (1998). An application of expectancy theory to eating disorders: development and validation of measures of eating and dieting expectancies. *Psychological Assessment*, **10**, 49–58.

Holden, N. L. & Robinson, P. H. (1988). Anorexia nervosa and bulimia nervosa in British blacks. *British Journal of Psychiatry*, **152**, 544–549.

Holden, N. L. (1990). Is anorexia nervosa an obsessive-compulsive disorder? *British Journal of Psychiatry*, **157**, 1–5.

Holderness, C. C., Brooks-Gunn J., & Warren, M. P. (1994). Comorbidity of eating disorders and substance abuse: review of the literature. *International Journal of Eating Disorders*, **16**, 1–34.

Hollanders, H. E. (1996). *Eclecticism integration among counsellors in Britain in relation to Kuhn's concept of paradigm formation*. PhD thesis, University of Keele.

Hollanders, H. E. (1999). Eclecticism and integration in counselling; implications for training. *British Journal of Guidance and Counselling*, **27**, 483–500.

Hollanders, H. E. & McLeod, J. (1999). Theoretical orientation and reported practice: a survey of eclecticism among counsellors in Britian. *British Journal of Guidance and Counselling*, **27**, 405–414.

Hollon, S. D. & Kendall, P. C. (1980). Cognitive self statements in depression: development of an Automatic Thoughts Questionnaire. *Cognitive Therapy and Research*, **4**, 109–143.

Hooper, R. (1811). *Quincey's Lexicon—Medicum. A New Medical Dictionary*. London: Hurst, Rees, Orme & Co.

Hooven, C., Gottman, J. M., & Katz, L. F. (1995). Parental metaemotion structure predicts family and child outcomes. *Cognition and Emotion*, **9**, 229–264.

Hoyle, R. H., Kernis, M. H., Leary, M. R., & Baldwin, M. W. (1999). *Selfhood: Identity, Esteem, and Regulation*. Boulder, Colorado: Westview Press.

Hsu, L. K. G. & Holder, D. (1986). Bulimia nervosa: treatment and short term outcome. *Psychological Medicine*, **16**, 65–70.

Hsu, L. K. G. (1990). Experiential aspects of bulimia nervosa. *Behaviour Modification*, **14**, 50–65.

Hsu, L. K. G. (1996). Epidemiology of the eating disorders. *The Psychiatric Clinics of North America*, **19**, 681–700.

Hudson, J. I., Pope, H. G., Jonas, J. M., & Yurgelen-Todd, D. (1983a). Family history of bulimia nervosa. *British Journal of Psychiatry*, **142**, 133–138.

Hudson, J. I., Wentworth, S. M., & Hudson, M. S. (1983b). Bulimia and diabetes. *New England Journal of Medicine*, **309**, 431–432.

Hudson, J. I. & Pope, H. G. (1984). *The Psychobiology of Bulimia*. Washington, DC: American Psychiatric Press.

Hudson, J. I., Wentworth, S. M., Hudson, M. S., & Pope, H. G. (1985). Prevalence of anorexia nervosa and bulimia among young diabetic women. *Journal of Clinical Psychiatry*, **46**, 88–89.

Humphrey, L. L. (1986). Family relations in bulimic-anorexic and nondistressed families. *International Journal of Eating Disorders*, **5**, 223–232.

Humphrey, L. L. & Stern, S. (1988). Object relations and the family system in bulimia: A theoretical integration. *Journal of Marital and Family Therapy*, **14**, 337–350.

Hunt, J. & Cooper, M. J. (2001). Selective memory bias in women with bulimia nervosa and depression. *Behavioural and Cognitive Psychotherapy*, **29**, 93–102.

Huon, G. F. & Brown, L. B. (1985). Evaluating a group treatment for bulimia nervosa. *Journal of Psychiatric Research*, **19**, 479–483.

Huon, G. F., Braganza, C., Brown, L. B., Ritchie, J. E., & Roncolato, W. G. (1998). Reflections on prevention in dieting induced disorders. *International Journal of Eating Disorders*, **23**, 455–458.

Huon, G. & Strong, K. (1998). The initiation and maintenance of dieting: structural models for large-scale longitudinal investigations. *International Journal of Eating Disorders*, **23**, 361–370.

Huon, G., Hayne, A., Guneardene, A., Strong, K., Lunn, N., Piira, T., & Lim, J. (1999). Accounting for differences in dieting status: steps in the refinement of a model. *International Journal of Eating Disorders*, **26**, 420–433.

Iwamasa, G. Y. & Orsillo, S. M. (1997). Individualising treatment manuals as a challenge for the next generation. *Behaviour Therapy*, **28**, 511–515.

Jager, B., Liedkte, R., Kunsebeck, H. W., Lempa, W., Kersting, A., & Seide, L. (1996). Psychotherapy and bulimia nervosa: evaluation and long term follow up of two conflict oriented treatment conditions. *Acta Psychiatrica Scandanivica*, **93**, 268–278.

James, W. (1890/1950). *The Principles of Psychology*. New York: Dover.

Janet, P. (1903). *Les obsessions et la psychasthenie*. Felix Alcan: Paris.

Jansen, A., Klaver, J., Merckelbach, H., & van den Hout, M. (1989a). Restrained eaters are rapidly habituating sensation seekers. *Behaviour Research and Therapy*, **27**, 247–252.

Jansen, A., van den Hout, M. A., De Loof, C., Zandbergen, J., & Griez, E. (1989b). A case of bulimia successfully treated by cue exposure. *Journal of Behaviour Therapy and Experimental Psychiatry*, **20**(4), 327–332.

Jansen, A., van den Hout, M., & Griez, E. (1990). Clinical and non-clinical binges. *Behavioural Research and Therapy*, **28**, 439–444.

Jansen, A., Broekmate, J., & Heymans, M. (1992a). Cue exposure vs self control in the treatment of binge eating: a pilot study. *Behaviour Research and Therapy*, **30**, 235–241.

Jansen, A., van den Berg, J., & Bulten, K. (1992b). No counterregulation after breaking the external restraint of children. *Behaviour Research and Therapy*, **30**, 59–62.

Jarman, M. & Walsh, S. (1999). Evaluating recovery from anorexia nervosa and bulimia nervosa: integrating lessons learned from research and clinical practice. *Clinical Psychology Review*, **19**, 773–788.

Jimerson, D. C., Lesem, M. D., Kaye, W. H., & Brewerton, T. D. (1992). Low serotonin and dopamine metabolite concentrations in cerebrospinal fluid from bulimic patients with frequent binge episodes. *Archives of General Psychiatry*, **49**, 132–138.

Jimerson, D. C., Wolfe, M. E., Franko, D. L., Covino, N. A., & Sifneos, P. E. (1994). Alexithymia ratings in bulimia nervosa: clinical correlates. *Psychosomatic Medicine*, 56, 90–93.

Joergensen, J. (1992). The epidemiology of eating disorders in Fyn County, Denmark, 1977–1986. *Acta Psychiatrica Scandanavica*, 85, 30–34.

Johnson, C. & Berndt, D. J. (1983). Preliminary investigation of bulimia and life adjustment. *American Journal of Psychiatry*, 140, 774–777.

Johnson, C. L., Stuckey, M. K., Lewis, L. D., & Schwartz, D. M. (1983). Bulimia: a descriptive survey of 316 cases. *International Journal of Eating Disorders*, 2, 3–16.

Johnson, C. L., Lewis, C., Love, S., Lewis, L., & Stuckey, M. (1984). Incidence and correlates of bulimic behaviour in a female high school population. *Journal of Youth and Adolescence*, 13, 15–26.

Johnson, C. & Flach, A. (1985). Family characteristics of 105 patients with bulimia. *American Journal of Psychiatry*, 142, 1321–1324.

Johnson, W. G., Schlundt, D. G., & Jarrell, M. P. (1986). Exposure with response prevention, training in energy balance, and problem solving therapy for bulimia nervosa. *International Journal of Eating Disorders*, 5, 35–45.

Johnson, C. L. & Connors, M. (1987). *The Aetiology and Treatment of Bulimia Nervosa: A Biopsychosocial Perspective*. New York: Basic Books.

Johnson, C. L. & Sansone, R. A. (1993). Integrating the twelve step approach with traditional psychotherapy for the treatment of eating disorders. *International Journal of Eating Disorders*, 14, 121–134.

Johnson, C. (1995). Psychodynamic treatment of bulimia nervosa. In *Eating Disorders and Obesity: A Comprehensive Handbook* (K. D. Brownell & C. G. Fairburn, ed.). New York: Guilford.

Johnson, W. G., Carr-Nangle, R. E., Nangle, D. W., Antony, M. M., & Zayfert, C. (1997). What is binge eating? A comparison of binge eater, peer, and professional judgements of eating episodes. *Addictive Behaviours*, 22, 631–635.

Johnson, S. M., Maddeaux, C., & Blouin, J. (1998). Emotionally focussed family therapy for bulimia: changing attachment patterns. *Psychotherapy: Theory, Practice and Training*, 35, 238–247.

Johnson, W. G., Boutelle, K. N., Torgrud, L., Davig, J. P., & Turner, S. (2000). What is a binge? The influence of amount, duration, and loss of control criteria on judgements of binge eating. *International Journal of Eating Disorders*, 27, 471–479.

Johnson-Sabine, E., Wood, K., Patton, G., Mann, A., & Wakeling, A. (1988). Abnormal eating attitudes in London schoolgirls-a prospective epidemiological study: factors associated with abnormal response on screening questionnaires. *Psychological Medicine*, 18, 615–622.

Johnson-Sabine, E., Reiss, D., & Dayson, D. (1992). Bulimia nervosa: a 5 year follow up study. *Psychological Medicine*, 22, 951–959.

Joiner, T. E., Heatherton, T. F., & Keel, P. K. (1997a). Ten-year stability and predictive validity of five bulimia-related indicators. *American Journal of Psychiatry*, 154, 1133–1138.

Joiner, T. E., Heatherton, T. F., Rudd, M. D., & Schmidt, N. B. (1997b). Perfectionism, perceived weight status, and bulimic symptoms: two studies testing a diathesis stress model. *Journal of Abnormal Psychology*, 106, 145–153.

Joiner, T. E., Schmidt, N. B., & Wonderlich, S. A. (1997c). Global self esteem as contingent on body satisfaction among patients with bulimia nervosa: lack of diagnostic specificity? *International Journal of Eating Disorders*, 21, 67–76.

Joiner, T. E. (1999). Self verification and bulimic symptoms: do bulimic women play a role in perpetuating their own dissatisfaction and symptoms? *International Journal of Eating Disorders*, 26, 145–151.

Jones, R., Peveler, R. C., Hope, R. A., & Fairburn, C. G. (1993). Changes during treatment for bulimia nervosa: a comparison of three psychological treatments. *Behaviour Research and Therapy*, 31, 479–485.

Jones, T. M., & Luke, L. C. (1998). Life threatening airway obstruction: a hazard of concealed eating disorders. *Journal of Accident and Emergency Medicine*, 15, 332–336.

Kales, E. F. (1990). Macronutrient analysis of binge eating in bulimia. *Physiology and Behaviour*, 48, 837–840.

Kanakis, D. M. & Thelen, M. H. (1995). Parental variables associated with bulimia nervosa. *Addictive Behaviours*, 20, 4, 491–500.

Kanarek, R. (1997). Psychological effects of snacks and altered meal frequency. *British Journal of Nutrition*, 77, Supplement 1, 105–118.

Kanner, A. D., Coyne, C., Schaefer, C., & Lazarus, R. S. (1981). Comparison of two modes of stress measurement: daily hassles and uplifts versus major life events. *Journal of Behavioural Medicine*, 4, 1–39.

Katzman, M. A., Wolchik, S. A., & Braver, S. L. (1984). The prevalence of frequent binge eating and bulimia in a nonclinical college sample. *International Journal of Eating Disorders*, 3, 51–63.

Kaufman, R. M. & Heiman, M. (1965). *Evolution of Psychosomatic Concepts*. New York: International Universities Press.

Kaye, W. H., Gwirtsman, H. E., George, D. T., Weiss, S. R., & Jimerson, D. C. (1986). Relationship of mood alterations to bingeing behaviour in bulimia. *British Journal of Psychiatry*, 149, 479–485.

Kazdin, A. E. & Mazurick, J. L. (1994). Dropping out of child psychotherapy: distinguishing early and late dropouts over the course of treatment. *Journal of Consulting and Clinical Psychology*, 62, 1069–1074.

Keefe, R. S. E. (1995). The contribution of neuropsychology to psychiatry. *American Journal of Psychiatry*, 152, 6–15.

Keel, P. K. & Mitchell, J. E. (1997). Outcome in bulimia nervosa. *American Journal of Psychiatry*, 154, 313–321.

Keel, P. K., Mitchell, J. E., Miller, K. B., Davis, T. L., & Crow, S. J. (2000a). Predictive validity of bulimia nervosa as a diagnostic category. *American Journal of Psychiatry*, 157, 136–138.

Keel, P. K., Mitchell, J. E., Miller, K. B., Davis, T. L., & Crow, S. J. (2000b). Social adjustment over 10 years following diagnosis with bulimia nervosa. *International Journal of Eating Disorders*, 27, 21–28.

Keel, P. K., Mayer, S. A., & Harnden-Fischer, J. H. (2001). Importance of size in defining binge eating episodes in bulimia nervosa. *International Journal of Eating Disorders*, 29, 294–301.

Keller, M. B., Herzog, D. B., Lavori, P. W., Bradburn, I. S. & Mahoney, E. M. (1992). The naturalistic history of bulimia nervosa: extraordinary high rates of chronicity, relapse, recurrence and psychosocial morbidity. *International Journal of Eating Disorders*, 12, 1–10.

Kelly, G. A. (1955). *The Psychology of Personal Constructs*. New York: Norton.

Kendall, P. C. & Hollon, S. D. (1979). *Cognitive Behavioural Interventions: Theory, Research and Procedures*. New York: Academic Press.

Kendall, P. C. & Korgeski, G. P. (1979). Assessment and cognitive behavioural interventions. *Cognitive Therapy* and Research, 3, 1–21.

Kendall, P. C. (1981). Assessment and cognitive behavioural interventions: Purposes, proposals and problems. In *Assessment Strategies for Cognitive Behavioural Interventions* (P. C. Kendall & S. D. Hollon, ed.). New York: Academic Press.

Kendall, P. C. & Hollon, S. D. (1981). *Assessment Strategies for Cognitive Behavioural Interventions*. New York: Academic Press.

Kendell, R. E. (1988). *The Role of Diagnosis in Psychiatry*. Oxford: Blackwell Scientific Publications.

Kendell, R. E. (1989). Clinical validity. *Psychological Medicine*, 19, 45–55.

Kendler, K., MacLean, C., Neale, M., Kessler, R., Heath, A., & Eaves, L. (1991). The genetic epidemiology of bulimia nervosa. *American Journal of Psychiatry*, 148, 1627–1637.

Kennedy, S. H., McVey, G., & Katz, R. (1990). Personality disorders in anorexia nerovsa and bulimia nervosa. *Journal of Psychiatric Research*, 24, 259–269.

Kennedy, S. H., Kaplan, A. S., Garfinkel, P. E., Rockert, W., Toner, B., & Abbey, S. E. (1994). Depression in anorexia nervosa and bulimia nervosa: discriminating depressive symptoms and episodes. *Journal of Psychosomatic Research*, 7, 773–782.

Kenny, F. T. & Solyom, L. (1971). The treatment of compulsive vomiting through faradic disruption of mental images. *Canadian Medical Association Journal*, 105, 1071–1073.

Kenny, M. E. (1990). College seniors' perceptions of paternal attachment: the value and stability of family ties. *Journal of College Student Development*, 31, 479–486.

Kenny, M. E. & Hart, K. (1992). Relationship between parental attachment and eating disorders in an inpatient and a college sample. *Journal of Counselling Psychology*, 39, 521–526.

Kent, A., Lacey, J. H., & McCluskey, S. E. (1992). Pre-menarchal bulimia nervosa. *Journal of Psychosomatic Research*, 36, 205–210.

Kern, J. M. & Hastings, T. (1995). Differential family environments of bulimics and victims of childhood sexual abuse. *Journal of Clinical Psychology*, 51, 499–506.

Kernberg, O. F. (1994). Aggression, trauma, and hatred in the treatment of borderline patients. *Psychiatric Clinics of North America*, 17, 701–714.

Kettlewell, P. W., Mizes, J. S., & Wasylyshyn, N. A. (1992). A cognitive behavioural group treatment of bulimia. *Behaviour Therapy*, 23, 657–670.

Keys, A., Brozek, J., Henschel, A., Mickelson, O., & Taylor, H. L. (1950). *The Biology of Human Starvation*. Minneapolis, MN: University of Minnesota Press.

King, M. B. (1986). Eating disorders in a general practice population. *British Medical Journal*, 293, 1412–1414.

King, G. A., Polivy, J., & Herman, C. P. (1991). Cognitive aspects of dietary restraint: effects on person memory. *International Journal of Eating Disorders*, 10, 313–321.

Kinzel, J. F., Trauweger, C., Trefalt, E., Mangweth, B., & Bubl, W. (1999). Binge eating disorder in females: a population-based investigation. *International Journal of Eating Disorders*, 25, 287–292.

Kiriike, N., Nagata, T., Matsunaga, H., Tobitan, W., & Nishiura, T. (1998). Single and married patients with eating disorders. *Psychiatry and Clinical Neurosciences*, 52, S306–S308.

Kirkley, B. G., Agras, W. S., & Weiss, J. J. (1985a). Nutritional inadequacy in the diets of treated bulimics. *Behaviour Therapy*, 16, 287–291.

Kirkley, B. G., Schneider, J. A., Agras, W. S., & Bachman, J. A. (1985b). Comparison of two group treatments for bulimia. *Journal of Consulting and Clinical Psychology*, 53, 43–48.

Kirsh, S. J. & Cassidy, J. (1997). Preschoolers' attention to and memory for attachment relevant information. *Child Development*, 68, 1143–1153.

Klerman, G. L., Weissman, M. M., Rounsaville, B. J., & Chevron, E. S. (1984). *Interpersonal Therapy for Depression*. New York: Basic Books.

Kog, E. & Vandereycken, W. (1985). Family characteristics of anorexia nervosa and bulimia: a review of the research literature. *Clinical Psychology Review*, 5, 159–180.

Kog, E., Vandereycken, W., & Vertommen, H. (1985). Towards a verification of the psychosomatic family model: a pilot study of ten families with an anorexia/bulimia nervosa patient. *International Journal of Eating Disorders*, 4, 525–538.

Kohut, H. (1971). *The Analysis of the Self: A Systemic Approach to the Psychoanalytic Treatment of Narcissistic Personality Disorders*. New York: International Universities Press.

Koslow, R. E. (1998). Age-related reasons for expressed interest in exercise and weight control. *Journal of Applied Social Psychology*, **18**, 349–354.

Kotila, L. & Lonnqvist, J. (1987). Adolescent suicide attempts 1973–1982 in the Helsinki area. *Acta Psychiatrica Scandanivica*, **76**, 346–354.

Krahn, D. D., Nairn, K., Gosnell, B. A., & Drewnowski, A. (1991). Stealing in eating disordered patients. *Journal of Clinical Psychiatry*, **52**, 112–115.

Krieg, J-C. (1991). Eating disorders as assessed by cranial computerised tomography. In *Fuel Homeostasis and the Nervous System* (M. Vranic, S. Efendic, & C. H. Hollenberg, ed.). New York: Plenum Press.

Kuczmarski, R. J., Flegal, K. M., Campbell, S. M., & Johnson, C. L. (1994). Increasing prevalence of overweight among US adults. *Journal of the American Medical Association*, **272**, 205–211.

Kulbartz-Klatt, Y. J., Florin, I., & Pook, M. (1999). Bulimia nervosa: mood changes do have an impact on body width estimation. *British Journal of Clinical Psychology*, **38**, 279–287.

Lacey, J. H. (1983). Bulimia nervosa, binge eating, and psychogenic vomiting: a controlled treatment study and long term outcome. *British Medical Journal*, **286**, 1609–1613.

Lacey, J. H. (1984). Moderation of bulimia. *Journal of Psychosomatic Research*, **28**, 397–402.

Lacey, J. H. & Gibson, E. (1985). Does laxative abuse control body weight? A comparative study of purging and vomiting bulimics. *Human Nutrition; Applied Nutrition*, **39A**, 36–42.

Lacey, J. H. & Evans, C. D. H. (1986). The impulsivist: a multi-impulsive personality disorder. *British Journal of Addiction*, **81**, 641–649.

Lacey, J. H. & Smith, G. (1987). Bulimia nervosa: the impact on mother and baby. *British Journal of Psychiatry*, **150**, 777–781.

Lacey, J. H. (1990). Incest, incestuous fantasy and indecency: a clinical catchment area study of normal-weight bulimics. *British Journal of Psychiary*, **157**, 399–403.

Lacey, J. H. (1993). Self-damaging and addictive behaviour in bulimia nervosa: a catchment area study. *British Journal of Psychiatry*, **163**, 190–194.

Lacey, J. H. (1995). In patient treatment of multi impulsive bulimia nervosa. In *Eating Disorders and Obesity: A Comprehensive Handbook* (K. D. Brownell & C. G. Fairburn, ed.). New York: Guilford.

LaChaussee, J. L., Kissileff, H. R., Walsh, B. T., & Hadigan, C. M. (1992). The single item meal as a measure of binge-eating behaviour in patients with bulimia nervosa. *Physiology and Behaviour*, **51**, 593–600.

Laessle, R. G., Waadt, S., & Pirke, K. M. (1987a). A structured behaviourally oriented group treatment for bulimia nervosa. *Psychotherapy and Psychosomatics*, **48**, 141–145.

Laessle, R. G., Zoettl, C., & Pirke, K. M. (1987b). Metaanalysis of treatment studies for bulimia. *International Journal of Eating Disorders*, **6**, 647–653.

Laessle, R. G., Schweiger, U., & Pirke, K. M. (1988). Depression as a correlate of starvation in patients with eating disorders, *Biological Psychiatry*, **23**, 719–725.

Laessle, R. G., Krieg, J. C., Fichter, M. M., & Pirke, K. M. (1989a). Cerebral atrophy and vigilance performance in patients with anorexia nervosa and bulimia nervosa. *Neuropsychiatry*, **21**, 187–191.

Laessle, R. G., Tuschel, R. J., Waadt, S. & Pirke, K. M. (1989b). The specific psychopathology of bulimia nervosa: a comparison with restrained and unrestrained (normal) eaters. *Journal of Consulting and Clinical Psychology*, **57**, 772–775.

Laessle, R. G., Beumont, P. J. V., Butow, P., Lennerts, W., O'Connor, M., Pirke, K. M., Touyz, S. W., & Waadt, S. (1991). A comparison of nutritional management with stress management in the treatment of bulimia nervosa. *British Journal of Psychiatry*, **159**, 250–261.

Laessle, R. G., Platte, P., Schweiger, U., & Pirke, K. M. (1996). Biological and psychological correlates of intermittent dieting behaviour in young women: a model for bulimia nervosa. *Physiology and Behaviour*, **60**, 1–5.

Lakatos, I. (1974). Falsification and the methodology of scientific research programs. In *Criticism and the Growth of Knowledge*. (I. Lakatos & A. Musgrave, eds). London: Cambridge University Press.

Laliberte, M., Boland, F. J., & Leichner, P. (1999). Family climate factors specific to disturbed eating and bulimia nervosa. *Journal of Clinical Psychology*, 55, 1021–1040.

Lancelot, C. & Kaslow, N. J. (1994). Sex role orientation and disordered eating in women: a review. *Clinical Psychology Review*, 14, 139–157.

Lasagna, L. (1988). *Phenylpropanolamine: a Review*. New York: Wiley.

Lattimore, P. J. & Butterworth, M. (1999). A test of the structural model of initiation of dieting among adolescent girls. *Journal of Psychosomatic Research*, 46, 295–299.

Lauder, T. D., Williams, M. V., Campbell, C. S., Davis, G., & Sherman, R. (1999). Abnormal eating behaviours in military women. *Medicine and Science in Sport and Exercise*, 31, 1265–1271.

Lauer, C. J., Gorzewski, B., Gerlinghoff, M., Backmund, H., & Zihl, J. (1999). Neuropsychological assessments before and after treatment in patients with anorexia nervosa and bulimia nervosa. *Journal of Psychiatric Research*, 33, 129–138.

Lawrence, M. (1987). *Fed up and Hungry: Women, Oppression and Food*. London: The Women's Press.

Layden, M. A., Newman, C. F., Freeman, A., & Morse, S. B. (1993). *Cognitive Therapy of Borderline Personality Disorder*. Needham Heights, Massachusetts: Allyn & Bacon.

Lazarus, R. S. (1966). *Psychological Stress and the Coping Process*. New York: Mcgraw-Hill.

Lazarus, R. S. & Folkman, S. (1984). *Stress, appraisal and coping*. New York: Springer.

Lean, M. E., Powrie, J. K., Anderson, A. S., & Garthwaite, P. H. (1990). Obesity, weight loss and prognosis in type 2 diabetes. *Diabetic Medicine*, 7, 228–233.

Lee, N. F. & Rush, A. J. (1986). Cognitive behavioural group therapy for bulimia. *International Journal of Eating Disorders*, 5, 599–615.

Lee, S. (1993). How abnormal is the desire for slimmness? A survey of eating attitudes and behaviours among Chinese undergraduates in Hong Kong. *Psychological Medicine*, 23, 25–36.

Lehoux, P. M., Steiger, H., & Jabalpurlawa, S. (2000). State/trait distinctions in bulimic syndromes. *International Journal of Eating Disorders*, 27, 36–42.

Leitenberg, H., Gross, J., Peterson, J., & Rosen, J. L. (1984). Analysis of an anxiety model and the process of change during exposure plus response prevention treatment of bulimia nervosa. *Behaviour Therapy*, 15, 3–20.

Leitenberg, H. & Rosen, J. C. (1986). A behavioural approach to treatment of bulimia nervosa. *Adolescent Psychiatry*, 133, 33–57.

Leitenberg, H., Rosen, J. C., Gross, J., Nudelman, S., & Vara, L. S. (1988). Exposure plus response prevention treatment of bulimia nervosa. *Journal of Consulting and Clinical Psychology*, 56, 535–541.

Leitenberg, H. & Rosen, J. (1989). Cognitive behavioural therapy with and without exposure plus response prevention in treatment of bulimia nervosa: comment on Agras, Schneider, Arnow, Raeburn and Telch. *Journal of Consulting and Clinical Psychology*, 57, 776–777.

Leitenberg, H., Rosen, J. C., Wolf, J., Vara, L. S., Detzer, M. J., & Srebnik, D. (1994). Comparison of cognitive behaviour therapy and desipramine in the treatment of bulimia nervosa. *Behaviour Research and Therapy*, 32, 37–45.

Leon, G. R., Fulkerson, J. A., Perry, C. L., & Cudeck, R. (1993). Personality and behavioural vulnerabilities associated with risk status for eating disorders in adolescent girls. *Journal of Abnormal Psychology*, 102, 438–444.

Lepore, S. J. (1992). Social conflict, social support, and psychological distress: evidence of cross-domain buffering effects. *Journal of Personality and Social Psychology*, 63, 857–867.

Lerner, H. (1983). Contemporary psychoanalytic perspectives on gorge vomiting: a case illustration. *International Journal of Eating Disorders*, 3, 47–63.

Leung, F., Schwartzman, A., & Steiger, H. (1996). Testing a dual process family model in understanding the development of eating pathology: a structural equation modeling analysis. *International Journal of Eating Disorders*, 20, 367–375.

Leung, N., Waller, G., & Thomas, G. (1999). Core beliefs in anorexic and bulimic women. *Journal of Nervous and Mental Disease*, 187, 736–741.

Leung, N., Thomas, G., & Waller, G. (2000a). The relationship between parental bonding and core beliefs in anorexic and bulimic women. *British Journal of Clinical Psychology*, 39, 205–213.

Leung, N., Waller, G., & Thomas, G. V. (2000b). Outcome of group cognitive behaviour therapy for bulimia nervosa: the role of core beliefs. *Behaviour Research and Therapy*, 38, 145–156.

Levens, M. (1995). The use of concrete metaphors for the body. In *Arts Therapies and Clients with Eating Disorders: Fragile Board* (D. Dokter, ed). London: Jessica Kingsley.

Levin, A. P., Kahan, M., Lamm, J. B., & Spauster, E. (1993). Multiple personality in eating disorder patients. *International Journal of Eating Disorders*, 13, 235–239.

Levy, A. B., Dixon, K. N., & Stern, S. L. (1989). How are depression and bulimia related? *American Journal of Psychiatry*, 146, 162–169.

Lewandowski, L. M., Gebing, T. A., Anthony, J. L., & O'Brien, W. H. (1997). Meta analysis of cognitive behavioural treatment studies for bulimia. *Clinical Psychology Review*, 17, 703–718.

Lewis, G., David, A., Andreasson, S., & Allebeck, P. (1992). Schizophrenia and city life. *The Lancet*, 340, 137–140.

Liedkte, R., Jager, B., Lempa, W., Kunsbebeck, H. W., Grone, M., & Freyberger, H. (1991). Therapy outcome of two treatment models for bulimia nervosa: preliminary results of a controlled study. *Psychotherapy and Psychosomatics*, 56, 56–63.

Linden, W. (1980). Multi-component behaviour therapy in a case of compulsive binge eating followed by vomiting. *Journal of Behaviour Therapy and Experimental Psychiatry*, 11, 297–300.

Lindner, R. M. (1955). *The fifty-minute hour*. New York: Jacob Aronson.

Linehan, M. M. (1993). Cognitive Behavioural Treatment of Borderline Personality Disorder. New York: Guilford.

Linville, P. W. (1987). Self complexity as a cognitive buffer against stress related illness and depression. *Journal of Personality and Social Psychology*, 52, 663–676.

Loeb, K. L., Pike, K. M., Walsh, B. T., & Wilson, G. T. (1994). Assessment of diagnostic features of bulimia nervosa: interview versus self report format. *International Journal of Eating Disorders*, 16, 75–81.

Long, C. G. & Cordle, C. J. (1982). Psychological treatment of binge eating and self induced vomiting. *British Journal of Medical Psychology*, 55, 139–145.

Lowe, M. R., Gleaves, D. H., DiSimone-Weiss, R. T., Furgueson, C., Gayda, C. A., Kolsky, P. A., Neal-Walden, T., Nelson, L. A., & McKinney, S. (1996). Restraint, dieting, and the continuum model of bulimia nervosa. *Journal of Abnormal Psychology*, 105, 508–517.

Lowe, M. R., Gleaves, D. H., & Murphy-Eberenz, K. P. (1998). On the relation of dieting and bingeing in bulimia nervosa. *Journal of Abnormal Psychology*, 107, 263–271.

Luborsky, L. (1984). *Principles of Psychoanalytic Psychotherapy: A Manual for Supportive Expressive Treatment*. New York: Basic Books.

Luce, K. H. & Crowther, J. H. (1999). The reliability of the Eating Disorder Examination Self Report Questionnaire Version (EDE-Q). *International Journal of Eating Disorders*, 25, 349–351.

Luka, L. P., Agras, W. S., & Schneider, J. A. (1986). Thirty month follow up of cognitive behavioural group therapy for bulimia. *British Journal of Psychiatry*, 148, 614–615.

Lyddon, W. J. (1990). First and second order change: implications for rationalist and constructivist cognitive therapies. *Journal of Counselling and Development*, **69**, 122–127.

Maddocks, S. E., Kaplan, A. S., Woodside, D. B., Langdon, L., & Piran, N. (1992). Two year follow up of bulimia nervosa: the importance of abstinence as the criterion of outcome. *International Journal of Eating Disorders*, **12**, 133–141.

Mahon, J., Winston, A. P., Palmer, R. L., & Harvey, P. K. (2001). Do broken relationships in childhood relate to bulimic women breaking off psychotherapy in adulthood? *International Journal of Eating Disorders*, **29**, 139–149.

Mahoney, M. J. & Mahoney, K. (1976). Self control techniques with the mentally retarded. *Exceptional Children*, **42**, 338–339.

Mahoney, M. J. (1993). Introduction to special section: theoretical developments in the cognitive psychotherapies. *Journal of Consulting and Clinical Psychology*, **61**, 187–193.

Mann, T., Nolen-Hoeksema, S., Huang, K., Burgard, D., Wright, A., & Hanson, K. (1997). Are two interventions worse than one? Joint primary and secondary prevention of eating disorders in college females. *Health Psychology*, **16**, 215–225.

Manno, B. R. & Manno, J. E. (1977). Toxicology of ipecac: a review. *Clinical Toxicology*, **10**, 221–242.

Marcus, M. D., Smith, D., Santelli, R., & Kaye, W. (1992). Characterisation of eating disordered behaviour in obese binge eaters. *International Journal of Eating Disorders*, **12**, 249–255.

Margison, F. R., Barkham, M., Evans, C., McGrath, G., Clark, J. M., Audin, K., & Connell, J. (2000). Measurement and psychotherapy: evidence based practice and practice based evidence. *British Journal of Psychiatry*, **177**, 123–130.

Markus, H. (1977). Self-schemata and processing information about the self. *Journal of Personality and Social Psychology*, **35**, 63–78.

Markus, H. & Nurius, P. (1986). Possible selves. *American Psychologist*, **41**, 954–969.

Markus, H., Hamill, R., & Sentis, K. P. (1987). Thinking fat: self-schemas for body weight and the processing of weight relevant information. *Journal of Applied Social Psychology*, **17**, 50–71.

Markus, H. R., Mullaly, P. R., & Kitamaya, S. (1997). Selfways: diversity in modes of cultural participation. In *The Conceptual Self in Context* (U. Neisser & D. A. Jopling, ed.). Cambridge: Cambridge University Press.

Marschark, M., Richman, C. L., Yuille, J. C., & Hunt, R. R. (1987). The role of imagery in memory: on shared and distinctive information. *Psychological Bulletin*, **102**, 28–41.

Masterson, J. F. (1977). Treating the borderline patient in psychotherapy. *Canadian Psychiatric Association Journal*, **22**, 109–116.

Matsunaga, H., Mityata, A., Iwasaki, Y., Matsui, T., Fujimoto, K., & Kiriike, N. (1999). A comparison of clinical features among Japanese eating disordered women with obsessive-compulsive disorder. *Comprehensive Psychiatry*, **40**, 337–342.

Matsunaga, H., Kaye, W. H., McConaha, C., Plotnicov, K., Pollice, C. & Rao, R. (2000). Personality disorders among subjects recovered from eating disorders. *International Journal of Eating Disorders*, **227**, 353–357.

McCallum, K. E., Lock, J., Kulla, M., Rorty, M., & Wetzel, R. D. (1992). Dissociative symptoms and disorders in patients with eating disorders. *Dissociation*, **5**, 227–235.

McCaulay, M., Mintz, L., & Glenn, A. A. (1988). Body image, self-esteem, and depression-proneness: closing the gender gap. *Sex Roles*, **18**, 381–391.

McClelland, L., Mynors-Wallace, L., Fahy, T., & Treasure, J. (1991). Sexual abuse, disordered personality and eating disorders. *British Journal of Psychiatry*, **158**, Supplement 10, 63–68.

McCrae, R. R. & Costa, P. T. (1985). Updating Norman's 'adequate taxonomy': intelligence and personality dimensions in natural language and in questionnaires. *Journal of Personality and Social Psychology*, **49**, 710–721.

McFarlane, T., McCabe, R. E., Jarry, J., Olmsted, M. P., & Polivy, J. (2001). Weight-related and shape-related self-evaluation in eating-disordered and non-eating-disordered women. *International Journal of Eating Disorders*, 29, 328–335.

McKenzie, S. J., Williamson, D. A., & Cubic, B. A. (1993). Stable and reactive body image disturbance in bulimia nervosa. *Behaviour Therapy*, 24, 195–207.

McKisack, C. & Waller, G. (1997). Factors influencing the outcome of group psychotherapy for bulimia nervosa. *International Journal of Eating Disorders*, 22, 1–13.

McManus, F., Waller, G., & Chadwick, P. (1996). Biases in the processing of different forms of threat in bulimic and comparison women. *Journal of Nervous and Mental Disease*, 184, 547–554.

McNamara, K. & Loveman, C. (1990). Differences in family functioning among bulimics, repeat dieters, and nondieters. *Journal of Clinical Psychology*, 46, 518–523.

McNulty, P. A. (1997). Prevalence and contributing factors of eating disorder behaviours in active duty Navy men. *Military Medicine*, 162, 753–758.

Meehl, P. E. (1995). Bootstraps taxometrics: solving the classification problem in psychopathology. *American Psychologist*, 50, 266–275.

Meijboom, A., Jansen, A., Kampman, M., & Schouten, E. (1999). An experimental test of the relationship between self esteem and concern about body shape and weight in restrained eaters. *International Journal of Eating Disorders*, 25, 327–334.

Merluzzi, T. V., Glass, C. R., & Genest, M. (1981). *Assessment in Cognitive Behaviour Modification*. New York: Guilford Press.

Miller, J. G. (1984). Culture and the development of everyday social explanation. *Journal of Personality and Social Psychology*, 46, 961–978.

Miller, D. A. F., McCluskey-Fawcett, K., & Irving, L. M. (1993). The relationship between childhood sexual abuse and subsequent onset of bulimia nervosa. *Child Abuse and Neglect*, 17, 305–314.

Miller, K. & Mizes, J. S. (2000). *Comparative Treatments of Eating Disorders*. London: Free Association Books.

Millon, T., Green, C. J., & Meagher, R. B. (1982). A new psycodiagnostic tool for clients in rehabilitation settings: the MBHI. *Rehabilitation Psychology*, 27, 23–35.

Millon, T. (1983). The DSM-III: an insider's perspective. *American Psychologist*, 38, 804–814.

Milosevic, A. & Slade, P. (1989). The orodental status of anorexics and bulimics. *British Dental Journal*, 157, 16–19.

Minuchin, S. (1974). *Families and Family Therapy*. Cambridge, MA: Harvard University Press.

Minuchin, S., Rosman, B. L., & Baker, L. (1978). *Psychosomatic Families: Anorexia Nervosa in Context*. Cambridge, Massachussetts: Harvard University Press.

Mira, M., Stewart, P. M., & Abraham, J. (1989). Vitamin and trace element status of women with disordered eating. *American Journal of Clinical Nutrition*, 50, 940–944.

Mitchell, J. E. & Pyle, R. L. (1982). The bulimic syndrome in normal weight individuals: a review. *International Journal of Eating Disorders*, 1, 61–73.

Mitchell, J. E., Hatsukami, D., Goff, G., Pyle, R. L., Eckert, E. D., & Davis, L. E. (1983a). Intensive outpatient group treatment for bulimia. In *Handbook of Psychotherapy for Anorexia Nervosa and Bulimia* (D. M. Garner & P. E. Garfinkel, ed.). New York: Guilford Press.

Mitchell, J. E., Pyle, R. L., Eckert, E. D., Hatsukami, D., & Lentz, R. (1983b). Electrolyte and other physiological abnormalities in patients with bulimia. *Psychological Medicine*, 13, 273–278.

Mitchell, J. E., Hatsukami, D., Eckert, E. D., & Pyle, R. L. (1985). Characteristics of 275 patients with bulimia. *American Journal of Psychiatry*, 142, 482–485.

Mitchell, J. E., Boutacoff, L. I., Hatsukami, D., Pyle, R. L., & Eckert, E. D. (1986a). Laxative abuse as a variant of bulimia. *The Journal of Nervous and Mental Disease*, 174, 174–176.

Mitchell, J. E., Hatsukami, D., Pyle, R. L., & Eckert, E. D. (1986b). The bulimia syndrome: course of illness and associated problems. *Comprehensive Psychiatry*, 27, 165–170.

Mitchell, P. (1987). Heroin induced vomiting in bulimia. *American Journal of Psychiatry*, 144, 249–250.

Mitchell, J. E., Hatsukami, D., Pyle, R. L., Eckert, E. D., & Boutacoff, L. I. (1987). Metabolic acidosis as a marker for laxative abuse in patients with bulimia. *International Journal of Eating Disorders*, 6, 557–560.

Mitchell, J. E., Pyle, R. L., & Milner, R. A. (1987b). Gastric dilation as a complication of bulimia. *Psychosomatics*, 23, 96–97.

Mitchell, J. E., Seim, H. C., Colon, E., & Pomeroy, C. (1987c). Medical complications and medical management of bulimia. *Annals of Internal Medicine*, 107, 71–77.

Mitchell, J. E., Pomeroy, C., & Huber, M. (1988). A clinician's guide to the eating disorders medicine cabinet. *International Journal of Eating Disorders*, 7, 211–223.

Mitchell, J. E., Pyle, R. L., Hatsukami, D. K., Goff, G. Glotter, D., & Harper, J. (1989). A 2–5 year follow up study of patients treated for bulimia. *International Journal of Eating Disorders*, 8, 157–165.

Mitchell, J. E., Pyle, R. L., Eckert, E., & Hatsukami, D. (1990a). The influence of prior alcohol and drug abuse problems on bulimia nervosa treatment outcome. *Addictive Behaviours*, 15, 169–173.

Mitchell, J. E., Pyle, R. L., Eckert, E. D., Hatsukami, D., Pomeroy, C., & Zimmerman, R. (1990b). A comparison study of antidepressants and structured intensive groupo psychotherapy in the treatment of bulimia nervosa. *Archives of General Psychiatry*, 47, 149–157.

Mitchell, J. E., Pyle, R. L., & Eckert, E. (1991a). Sauna abuse as a clinical feature of bulimia nervosa. *Psychosomatics*, 32, 417–419.

Mitchell, J. E., Pyle, R. L., & Eckert, E. (1991b). Diet pill usage in patients with bulimia nervosa. *International Journal of Eating Disorders*, 2, 233–237.

Mitchell, J. E., Pyle, R. L., Hatsukami, D., & Eckert, E. (1991c). Enema abuse as a clinical feature of bulimia nervosa. *Psychosomatics*, 32, 102–104.

Mitchell, J. E., Pyle, R. L., Pomeroy, C., Zollman, M., Crosby, R., Seim, H., Eckert, E. D., & Zimmerman, R. (1993). Cognitive-behavioural group psychotherapy of bulimia nervosa: importance of logistical variables. *International Journal of Eating Disorders*, 14, 277–287.

Mitchell, J. E., Maki, D. D., Adson, D. E., Ruskin, B. S., & Crow, S. (1997). The selectivity of inclusion and exclusion criteria in bulimia nervosa treatment studies. *International Journal of Eating Disorders*, 22, 243–252.

Mitchell, J. E., Mussell, M. P., Peterson, C. B., Crow, S., Wonderlich, S. A., Crosby, R. D., Davis, T., & Weller, C. (1999). Hedonics of binge eating in women with bulimia nervosa and binge eating disorder. *International Journal of Eating Disorders*, 26, 165–170.

Mitrany, E., Lubin, F., Chetrit, A., & Modan, B. (1995). Eating disorders among Jewish female adolescents in Israel: a 5 year study. *Journal of Adolescence*, 16, 454–457.

Mizes, J. S. & Lohr, J. M. (1983). The treatment of bulimia (binge-eating and self induced vomiting). *International Journal of Eating Disorders*, 2, 59–65.

Mizes, J. S. & Fleece, E. L. (1986). On the use of progressive relaxation in the treatment of bulimia: a single subject design study. *International Journal of Eating Disorders*, 5, 169–176.

Mizes, J. S. (1988). Personality characteristics of bulimic and non eating disordered female controls: a cognitive behavioural perspective. *International Journal of Eating Disorders*, 7, 541–550.

Mizes, J. S. & Klesges, R. C. (1989). Validity, reliability, and factor structure of the anorectic cognitions questionnaire. *Addictive Behaviours*, 14, 589–594.

Mizes, J. S. (1992). Validity of the Mizes Anorectic Cognitions scale: a comparison between anorectic, bulimic, and psychiatric controls. *Addictive Behaviours*, 17, 283–289.

Morbidity and Mortality Weekly Report (1989). Tobacco use by adults: US 1987. *Centres for Disease Control*, 38, 685–687.

Morgan, C. D., Wiederman, M. W., & Pryor, T. L. (1995). Sexual functioning and attitudes of eating disordered women: a follow up study. *Journal of Sex and Marital Therapy*, 21, 67–77.

Morgan, J. F., Lacey, J. H., & Sedgwick, P. M. (1999). Impact of pregnancy on bulimia nervosa. *British Journal of Psychiatry*, 174, 135–140.

Morris, A., Cooper, T., & Cooper, P. J. (1989). The changing shape of female fashion models. *International Journal of Eating Disorders*, 8, 593–596.

Moskowitz, J. M. (1989). The primary prevention of alcohol problems: A critical review of the research literature. *Journal of Studies on Alcohol*, 50, 54–88.

Mullen, P. E., Martin, J. L., Anderson, J. C., Romans, S. E., Herbison, G. P. (1993). Childhood sexual abuse and mental health in adult life. *British Journal of Psychiatry*, 163, 721–732.

Mumford, D. B. & Whitehouse, A. M. (1988). Increased prevalence of bulimia nervosa among Asian schoolgirls. *British Medical Journal*, 297, 718.

Mumford, D. B., Whitehouse, A. M., & Platts, M. (1991). Socio-cultural correlates of eating disorders among Asian schoolgirls in Bradford. *British Journal of Psychiatry*, 158, 222–228.

Mumford, D. B., Whitehouse, A. M., & Choudry, I. Y. (1992). Survey of eating disorders in English-medium schools in Lahore, Pakistan. *International Journal of Eating Disorders*, 11, 173–184.

Murray, S., Touyz, S., & Beumont, P. (1990). Knowledge about eating disorders in the community. *International Journal of Eating Disorders*, 9, 87–93.

Murray, C., Waller, G., & Legg, C. (2000). Family dysfunction and bulimic psychopathology: the mediating role of shame. *International Journal of Eating Disorders*, 28, 84–89.

Mussell, M. P., Mitchell, J. E., Fenna, C. J., Crosby, R. D., Miller, J. P., & Hoberman, H. M. (1997). A comparison of onset of binge eating versus dieting in the development of bulimia nervosa. *International Journal of Eating Disorders*, 21, 353–360.

Mussell, M. P., Mitchell, J. E., Crosby, R. D., Fulkerson, J. A., Hoberman, H. M., & Romano, J. L. (2000). Commitment to treatment goals in prediction of group cognitive behavioural therapy treatment outcome for women with bulimia nervosa. *Journal of Consulting and Clinical Psychology*, 68, 432–437.

Nadaoka, T., Oiji, A., Takahashi, S., Morioka, Y., Kashiwakura, M., & Totsuka, S. (1996). An epidemiological study of eating disorders in a northern area of Japan. *Acta Psychiatrica Scandanivica*, 93, 305–310.

Nagata, T., Matsuyama, M., Kiriike, N., Iketani, T., & Oshima, J. (2000). Stress coping strategy in Japanese patients with eating disorders. *The Journal of Nervous and Mental Disease*, 188, 280–286.

Nakamura, K., Yamamoto, M., Yamazaki, O., Kawashima, Y., Muto, K., Someya, T., Sakurai, K., & Nozoe, S. (2000). Prevalence of anorexia nervosa and bulimia nervosa in a geographically defined area of Japan. *International Journal of Eating Disorders*, 28, 173–180.

Nasser, M. (1986). Comparative study of the prevalence of abnormal eating attitudes among Arab female students of both London and Cairo universities. *Psychological Medicine*, 16, 621–625.

Nasser, M. (1994). Screening for abnormal eating attitudes in a population of Egyptian secondary school girls. *Social Psychiatry and Psychiatric Epidemiology*, 29, 25–30.

Neimeyer, R. A. (1993). An appraisal of constructivist psychotherapies. *Journal of Consulting and Clinical Psychology*, 61, 221–234.

Neisser, U. (1967). *Cognitive Psychology*. Englewood Cliffs, New Jersey: Prentice Hall.

Nemiah, J. C. (1950). Anorexia nervosa: a clinical psychiatric study. *Medicine*, 29, 225–268.

Neumark-Sztainer, D., Story, M., Resnick, M. D., Garwick, A., & Blum, R. W. (1995). Body dissatisfaction and unhealthy weight control practices among adolescents with and without chronic illness: a population based study. *Archives of Pediatric and Adolescent Medicine*, 149, 1330–1335.

Nevo, S. (1985). Bulimic symptoms: prevalence and ethnic differences among college women. *International Journal of Eating Disorders*, 4, 151–168.

Newton, J. R., Freeman, C. P., Hannan, W. J., & Cowen, S. (1993). Osteoporosis and normal weight bulimia-which patients are at risk? *Journal of Psychosomatic Research*, 37, 239–247.

Niego, S. H., Pratt, E. M., & Agras, W. S. (1997). Subjective or objective binge: is the distinction valid? *International Journal of Eating Disorders*, 22, 291–298.

Nielsen, S., Moller-Madson, S., Isager, T., Jorgensen, J., Pagsberg, K., & Theander, S. (1998). Standardised mortality in eating disorders—a quantitative summary of the previously published and new evidence. *Journal of Psychosomatic Research*, 44, 413–434.

Niems, D. M., McNeill, J., Giles, T. R., & Todd, F. T. (1995). Incidence of laxative abuse in community and bulimic populations: a descriptive review. *International Journal of Eating Disorders*, 17, 211–228.

Nobakht, M. & Dezhkam, M. (2000). An epidemiological study of eating disorders in Iran. *International Journal of Eating Disorders*, 28, 265–271.

Norcros, J. & Goldfried, M. (1992). *Psychotherapy Integration*. New York: Basic Books.

Nowalk, M. P. & Wing, R. R. (1985). Changes in nutrient intake of hypertensives during a behavioural weight control programme. *Addictive Behaviours*, 10, 357–363.

Oatley, K. & Jenkins, J. M. (1996). *Understanding Emotion*. Oxford: Blackwell Publishers Ltd.

O'Kearney, R. (1996). Attachment disruption in anorexia nervosa and bulimia nervosa: a review of theory and empirical research. *International Journal of Eating Disorders*, 20, 115–127.

Olesker, W. (1984). Sex differences in 2 and 3 year olds: mother child relations, peer relations, and peer play. *Psychoanalytic Psychology*, 1, 269–288.

Olmsted, M. P., Davis, R., Rockert, W., Irvine, M. J., Eagle, M., & Garner, D. M. (1991). Efficacy of a brief group psychoeducational intervention in bulimia nervoas. *Behaviour Research and Therapy*, 29, 71–83.

Olmsted, M. P., Kaplan, A. S., & Rockert, W. (1994). Rate and prediction of relapse in bulimia nervosa. *American Journal of Psychiatry*, 151, 738–743.

Olmsted, M. P. & Kaplan, A. S. (1995). Psychoeducation in the treatment of eating disorders. In *Eating Disorders and Obesity: A Comprehensive Handbook* (K. D. Brownell & C. G. Fairburn, ed.). New York: Guilford Press.

Olmsted, M. P., Kaplan, A. S., Rockert, W., & Jacobsen, M. (1996). Rapid responders to intensive treatment of bulimia nervosa. *International Journal of Eating Disorders*, 19, 279–285.

O'Neil, M. K. & White, P. (1987). Psychodynamic group treatment of young adult bulimic women: preliminary positive results. *Canadian Journal of Psychiatry*, 32, 153–155.

Oppenheimer, R., Howells, K., Palmer, R. L., & Chaloner, D. A. (1985). Adverse sexual experiences in childhood and clinical eating disorder: a preliminary description. *Journal of Psychiatric Research*, 19, 357–361.

Oppliger, R. A., Landry, G. L., Foster, S. W., & Lambrecht, A. C. (1993). Bulimic behaviours among interscholastic wrestlers: a statewide survey. *Pediatrics*, 91, 826–831.

Orbach, S. (1983). Food, fatness and femininity. *The Practitioner*, 227, 860–864.

Ordman, A. M. & Kirschenbaum, D. S. (1985). Cogntive behaviour therapy for bulimia: an initial outcome study. *Journal of Consulting and Clinical Psychology*, 53, 305–313.

Osler, W. (1892). *Principles and Practice of Medicine*. New York: Appleton.

Padesky, C. A. & Greenberger, D. (1995). *Clinician's Guide to Mind over Mood*. New York: Guilford.

Paivio, A., Yuille, J. C., & Madigan, S. A. (1968). Concreteness, imagery, and meaningfulness values for 925 nouns. *Journal of Experimental Psychology*, **76**, Supplement, 1–25.

Paivio, A. (1971). *Imagery and Verbal Processes*. New York: Holt, Rinehart & Winston.

Paivio, A. (1986). *Mental Representations: A Dual Coding Approach*. New York: Oxford University Press.

Palmer, R. L. (1979). The dietary chaos syndrome: a useful new term? *British Journal of Medical Psychology*, **52**, 187–190.

Palmer, E. P. & Guay, A. T. (1985). Reversible myopathy secondary to abuseof ipecac in patients with major eating disorders. *New England Journal of Medicine*, **313**, 1457–1459.

Palmer, R. L., Oppenheimer, R., Dignon, A., Chaloner, D. A., & Howells, K. (1990). Childhood sexual experiences with adults reported by women with eating disorders: an extended series. *British Journal of Psychiatry*, **156**, 699–703.

Palmer, R. L. (1993). Weight concern should not be a necessary criterion for the eating disorders: a polemic. *International Journal of Eating Disorders*, **14**, 459–465.

Parker, G., Tupling, H., & Brown, L. B. (1979). A parental bonding instrument. *British Journal of Medical Psychology*, **52**, 1–10.

Parker, G. (1983). Parental 'affectionless control' as an antecedent to adult depression. A risk factor delineated. *Archives of General Psychiatry*, **40**, 956–960.

Parry-Jones, W. L. & Parry-Jones, B. (1994). Implications of historical evidence for the classification of eating disorders. *British Journal of Psychiatry*, **165**, 287–292.

Patton, G. C. (1992). Eating disorders, antecedents, evolution and course. *Annals of Medicine*, **24**, 281–285.

Paxton, S. J., Schutz, H. K., Wertheim, E. H., & Muir, S. L. (1999). Friendship clique and peer influences on body image concerns, dietary restraint, extreme weight loss behaviours, and binge eating in adolescent girls. *Journal of Abnormal Psychology*, **108**, 255–266.

Paykel, E. S. (1979). Reading about depression: clinical aspects. *British Journal of Psychiatry*, **134**, 211–213.

Peeters, F. & Meijboom, A. (2000). Electrolyte and other blood serum abnormalities in normal weight bulimia nervosa: evidence for sampling bias. *International Journal of Eating Disorders*, **27**, 358–362.

Pemberton, A. R., Vernon, S. W., & Lee, E. S. (1996). Prevalence and correlates of bulimia nervosa and bulimic behaviours in a racially diverse sample of undergraduate students in two universities in southeast Texas. *American Journal of Epidemiology*, **144**, 450–455.

Perpina, C., Hemsley, D., Treasure, J., & de Silva, P. (1993). Is selective processing of food and body words specific to patients with eating disorders? *International Journal of Eating Disorders*, **14**, 359–366.

Persons, J. B. (1991). Psychotherapy outcome studies do not accurately represent current models of psychopathology. *American Psychologist*, **46**, 99–106.

Persons, J. B. (1997). Dissemination of effective methods: behaviour therapy's next challenge. *Behaviour Therapy*, **28**, 465–471.

Phelan, P. W. (1987). Cognitive correlates of bulimia: the Bulimic Thoughts Questionnaire. *International Journal of Eating Disorders*, **6**, 593–607.

Phelps, L., Andrea, R., Rizzo, F. G., Johnston, L., & Main, C. M. (1993). Prevalence of self induced vomiting and laxative/medication abuse among female adolescents: a longitudinal study. *International Journal of Eating Disorders*, **14**, 375–378.

Piaget, J. (1932). *The Moral Judgement of the Child*. New York: Macmillan.

Pine, F. (1988). The four psychologies of psychoanalysis and their place in clinical work. *Journal of the American Psychoanalytic Association*, **36**, 571–596.

Pinel, J. P. J. (2000). *Biopsychology*. New York: Allyn & Bacon.

Pirke, K. M., Schweiger, U., Lemmel, W., Kreig, J. C., & Berger, M. (1985). The influence of dieting on the menstrual cycle of healthy young women. *Journal of Clinical Endocrinology and Metabolism*, 60, 1174–1179.

Pliner, P., Herman, C. P., & Polivy, J. (1990). Palatability as a determinant of eating: finickiness as a function of taste, hunger, and the prospect of good food. In *Taste, Experience, and Feeding* (E. D. Capaldi & T. D. Powley, ed.). Washington, DC: American Psychological Association.

Pliner, P. & Haddock, G. (1996). Perfectionism in weight concerned and unconcerned women: an experimental approach. *International Journal of Eating Disorders*, 19, 381–389.

Podar, I., Hannus, A., & Allik, J. (1999). Personality and affectivity characteristics associated with eating disorders: a comparison of eating disordered, weight preoccupied and normal samples. *Journal of Personality Assessment*, 73, 133–147.

Polivy, J. & Herman, C. P. (1985). Dieting and bingeing: a causal analysis. *American Psychologist*, 40, 193–201.

Polivy, J. & Herman, C. P. (1987). Diagnosis and treatment of normal eating. *Journal of Consulting and Clinical Psychology*, 55, 635–644.

Polivy, J., Heatherton, C. P., & Herman, C. P. (1988). Self esteem, restraint, and eating behaviour. *Journal of Abnormal Psychology*, 97, 354–356.

Polivy, J., Zeitlin, S. B., Herman, C. P., & Beal, A. L. (1994). Food restriction and binge eating: a study of former prisoners of war. *Journal of Abnormal Psychoogy*, 103, 409–411.

Polivy, J. (1996). Psychological consequences of food restriction. *Journal of the American Dietetic Association*, 96, 589–592.

Pollitt, E. & Mathews, R. (1998). Breakfast and cognition: an integrative summary. *American Journal of Clinical Nutrition*, 67, 804S–813S.

Pomeroy, C., Mitchell, J. E., Seim, H. C., & Seppala, M. (1988). Prescription diuretic abuse in patients with bulimia nervosa. *Journal of Family Practice*, 27, 493–496.

Pope, H. G., Hudson, J. I., Jonas, J. M., & Yurgelun-Todd, D. (1985a). Antidepressant treatment in bulimia: a two year follow up study. *Journal of Clinical Psychopharmacology*, 5, 320–327.

Pope, H. G., Hudson, J. I., & Mialet, J-P. (1985b). Bulimia in the late nineteenth century: the observations of Pierre Janet. *Psychological Medicine*, 15, 739–743.

Pope, H. G., Hudson, J. I., & Jonas, J. M. (1986a). Bulimia in men: a series of fifteen cases. *Journal of Nervous and Mental Disease*, 174, 117–119.

Pope, H. G., Hudson, J. I., Nixon, R. A., & Heridge, P. (1986b). The epidemiology of ipecac abuse. *New England Journal of Medicine*, 314, 245.

Pope, H. G., Champoux, R. F., & Hudson, J. I. (1987a). Eating disorder and socioeconomic class: anorexia nervosa and bulimia in nine communities. *The Journal of Nervous and Mental Disease*, 175, 620–623.

Pope, H. G., Frankenberg, F. R., Hudson, J. I., Jonas, J. M., & Yurgelen-Todd, D. (1987b). Is bulimia associated with borderline personality disorder? *Journal of Clinical Psychiatry*, 48, 181–184.

Pope, H. G., Hudson, J. I., & Yurgelun-Todd, D. (1989). Depressive symptoms in bulimic, depressed, and non-psychiatric control subjects. *Journal of Affective Disorders*, 16, 93–99.

Pope, H. G. & Hudson, J. I. (1992). Childhood sexual abuse a risk factor for bulimia nervosa? *American Journal of Psychiatry*, 149, 455–463.

Posobiec, K. & Renfrew, J. W. (1988). Successful self management of severe bulimia: a case study. *Journal of Behaviour Therapy and Experimental Psychiatry*, 19, 63–68.

Powers, P. S. & Johnson, C. (1996). Small victories: prevention of eating disorders among athletes. *Eating Disorders: The Journal of Treatment and Prevention*, 4, 364–367.

Prather, R. C. & Williamson, D. A. (1988). Psychopathology associated with bulimia, binge eating, and obesity. *International Journal of Eating Disorders*, 7, 177–184.

Pratt, D., Cooper, M. J., & Hackmann, A. (submitted). Imagery and its' characteristics in people who are anxious about spiders.

Pratt, E. M., Niego, S. H., & Agras, W. S. (1998). Does the size of a binge matter? *International Journal of Eating Disorders*, 24, 307–312.

Prentice, A. M., Goldberg, G. R., Jebb, S. A., Black, A. E., Murgatroyd, P. R., & Diaz, E. O. (1991). Physiological responses to slimming. *Proceedings of the Nutrition Society*, 50, 441–458.

Pribor, E. F. & Dinwiddie, S. H. (1992). Psychiatric correlates of incest in childhood. *American Journal of Psychiatry*, 149, 52–56.

Probst, M., Vandereycken, W., Vanderlinden, J., & Van Coppenolle, H. (1998). The significance of body size estimation in eating disorders: its relationship with clinical and psychological variables. *International Journal of Eating Disorders*, 24, 167–174.

Proudfoot, A. T. & Wright, N. (1970). Acute paracetamol poisoning. *British Medical Journal*, 3, 557–558.

Pryor, T. & Weiderman, M. W. (1996). Measurement of nonclinical personality characteristics of women with anorexia nervosa or bulimia nervosa. *Journal of Personality Assessment*, 67, 414–421.

Pryor, T. & Weiderman, M. W. (1998). Personality features and expressed concerns of adolescents with eating disorders. *Adolescence*, 33, 291–300.

Pumariega, A. J., Pursell, J., Spock, A., & Jones, J. D. (1986). Eating disorders in adolescents with cycstic fibrosis. *Journal of the American Academy of Child Psychiatry*, 25, 269–275.

Pyle, R. L., Mitchell, J. E., & Eckert, E. D. (1981). Bulimia: a report of 34 cases. *Journal of Clinical Psychiatry*, 42, 60–64.

Pyle, R. L., Mitchell, J. E., Eckert, E. D., Halvorsen, P. A., Neuman, P. A., & Goff, G. M. (1983). The incidence of bulimia in freshman college students. *International Journal of Eating Disorders*, 2, 75–85.

Pyle, R. L., Mitchell, J. E., Eckert, E. D., Hatsukami, D. K., & Goff, G. (1984). The interruption of bulimic behaviours: a review of three treatment programmes. *Psychiatric Clinics of North America*, 7, 275–286.

Pyle, R. L., Mitchell, J. E., Eckert, E. D., Hatsukami, D., Pomeroy, C., & Zimmerman, R. (1990). Maintenance treatment and 6 month outcome for bulimic patients who responded to initial treatment. *American Journal of Psychiatry*, 147, 871–875.

Rand, C. S. W. & Kuldau, J. M. (1991). Epidemiology of bulimia and symptoms in a general population: sex, age, race and socioeconomic status. *International Journal of Eating Disorders*, 11, 37–44.

Rathner, G., Tury, F., Szabo, P., Geyer, H., Runpold, G., Forgaces, A., Sollner, W., & Plottner, G. (1995). Prevalence of eating disorders and minor psychiatric morbidity in Central Europe before the political changes in 1989: a cross cultural study. *Psychological Medicine*, 25, 1027–1035.

Rathner, G. (2001). Post-communism and the marketing of the thin ideal. In *Eating Disorders and Cultures in Transition* (M. Nasser, M. A. Katzman, & R. A. Gordon, ed.). Hove, East Sussex: Brunner Routledge.

Raymond, N. C., Mussell, M. P., Mitchell, J. E., de Zwaan, M., & Crosby, R. D. (1995). An age-matched comparison of subjects with binge eating disorder and bulimia nervosa. *International Journal of Eating Disorders*, 18, 135–143.

Reas, D. L., Williamson, D. A., Martin, C. K., & Zucker, N. L. (2000). Duration of illness predicts outcome for bulimia nervosa: a long term follow up study. *International Journal of Eating Disorders*, 27, 428–434.

Rebert, W. M., Stanton, A. L., & Schwartz, R. M. (1991). Influence of personality attributes and daily moods on bulimic behaviour. *Addictive Behaviours*, **16**, 497–505.

Reiss, D. & Johnson-Sabine, E. (1995). Bulimia nervosa: 5 year social outcome and relationship to eating pathology. *International Journal of Eating Disorders*, **18**, 127–133.

Reiss, D. (1996). Abnormal eating attitudes and behaviours in two ethnic groups from a female British urban population. *Psychological Medicine*, **26**, 289–299.

Reitan, R. M. (1958). Validity of the Trail Making Test as an indicator of organic brain damage. *Perceptual and Motor Skills*, **8**, 271–276.

ReynaMcGlone, C. L., Ollendick, T. H., & Hart, K. J. (1986). *Self efficacy and bulimia: development and validation of the self assessment scale.* Poster presented at the meeting of the Association for the Advancement of Behaviour Therapy, Chicago, Ilinois.

Rice, J. P., Rochberg, N., Endicott, J., Lavori, P. W., & Miller, C. (1992). Stability of psychiatric diagnoses: an application to the affective disorders. *Archives of General Psychiatry*, **49**, 824–830.

Riddlesburger, M. M., Cohen, H. L., & Glick, P. L. (1992). The swallowed toothbrush: a radiographic clue of bulimia. *Pediatric Radiology*, **21**, 262–264.

Rieger, E., Schotte, D. E., Touyz, S. W., Beumont, P. J., Griffiths, R., & Russell, J. (1998). Attentional biases in eating disorders: a visual probe detection procedure. *International Journal of Eating Disorders*, **23**, 199–205.

Rigotti, N. A., Nussbaum, S. R., Herzog, D. B., & Neer, R. M. (1984). Osteoporosis in women with anorexia nervosa. *New England Journal of Medicine*, **311**, 1601–1606.

Rimm, D. C. & Masters, J. C. (1979). *Behaviour Therapy: Techniques and Empirical Findings.* New York: Academic Press.

Rizvi, S. L., Peterson, C. B., Crow, S. J., & Agras, W. S. (2000). Test-retest reliability of the Eating Disorder Examination. *International Journal of Eating Disorders*, **28**, 311–316.

Robb, N. D., Smith, B. G. N., & Geidrys-Leeper, E. (1995). The distribution of erosion in the dentitions of patients with eating disorders. *British Dental Journal*, **178**, 171–175.

Robins, E. & Guze, S. B. (1970). Establishment of diagnostic validity in psychiatric illness: its application to schizophrenia. *American Journal of Psychiatry*, **126**, 983–987.

Robins, L. N., Helzer, J. E., Croughan, J., & Ratcliff, K. S. (1981). National Institute of Mental Health Diagnostic Interview Schedule. *Archives of General Psychiatry*, **38**, 381–389.

Robins, L. N., Helzer, J. E., Ratcliff, K. S., & Seyfried, W. (1982). Validity of the diagnostic interview schedule, version II: DSM-III diagnoses. *Psychological Medicine*, **12**, 855–870.

Rogers, C. R. (1951). *Client Centered Therapy.* Boston: Houghton Mifflin.

Rogers, P. J., Edwards, S., Green, M. W., & Jas, P. (1992). Nutritional influences on mood and cognitive performance: the menstrual cycle, caffeine and dieting. *Proceedings of the Nutrition Society*, **51**, 343–351.

Rogers, L., Resnick, M. D., Mitchell, J. E., & Blum, R. W. (1997). The relationship between socioeconomic status and eating disordered behaviours in a community sample of adolescent girls. *International Journal of Eating Disorders*, **22**, 15–23.

Rook, K. S. (1984). The negative side of social interaction: impact on psychological well being. *Journal of Personality and Social Psychology*, **46**, 1097–1108.

Root, M. P. P., Fallon, P., & Friedrich, W. N. (1986). *Bulimia: A Systems Approach to Treatment.* New York: Norton.

Root, M. P. P. & Fallon, P. (1988). The incidence of victimisation experiences in a bulimic sample. *Journal of Interpesonal Violence*, **3**, 161–173.

Rorty, R. M., Yager, J., & Rossotto, E. (1993). Why and how do women recover from bulimia nervosa? The subjective appraisals of forty women recovered for a year or more. *International Journal of Eating Disorders*, **14**, 249–260.

Rorty, R. M., Yager, J., & Rossotto, E. (1994). Childhood sexual, physical, and psychological abuse and their relationship to comorbid psychopathology in bulimia nervosa. *International Journal of Eating Disorders*, **16**, 317–334.

Rorty, R. M. & Yager, J. (1996). Histories of childhood trauma and complex post traumatic sequelae in women with eating disorders. *Psychiatric Clinics of North America*, **19**, 773–791.

Rorty, R. M., Yager, J., Buckwalter, J. G., & Rossotto, E. (1999). Social support, social adjustment, and recovery status in bulimia nervosa. *International Journal of Eating Disorders*, **26**, 1–12.

Rorty, R. M., Yager, J., Buckwalter, J. G., Rossotto, E., & Guthrie, D. (2000a). Development and validation of the Parental Intrusiveness Rating Scale among bulimic and comparison women. *International Journal of Eating Disorders*, **28**, 188–201.

Rorty, R. M., Yager, J., Rossotto, E., & Buckwalter, G. (2000b). Parental intrusiveness in adolescence recalled by women with a history of bulimia nervosa and comparison women. *International Journal of Eating Disorders*, **28**, 202–208.

Rosen, B. (1979). A method of structured brief psychotherapy. *British Journal of Medical Psychology*, **52**, 157–162.

Rosen, J. C. & Leitenberg, H. (1982). Bulimia nervosa: treatment with exposure and response prevention. *Behaviour Therapy*, **13**, 117–124.

Rosen, J. C., Leitenberg, H., Fondarco, K. M., Gross, J., & Willmuth, M. (1985a). Standardised test meals in the assessment of eating behaviours in bulimia nervosa: consumption of feared foods when vomiting is prevented. *International Journal of Eating Disorders*, **4**, 59–70.

Rosen, J. C., Leitenberg, H., Gross, J., & Willmuth, M. (1985b). Standardised test meals in the assessment of bulimia nervosa. *Advances in Behaviour Research and Therapy*, **7**, 181–197.

Rosen, J. C., Gross, J., & Vara, L. (1987). Psycological adjustment of adolescents attempting to lose or gain weight. *Journal of Consulting and Clinical Psychology*, **55**, 742–747.

Rosen, J. C. (1990). Body image disturbance in eating disorders. In *Body Images: Development, Deviance and Change* (T. F. Cash & T. Pruzinsky ed.). New York: Guilford.

Rosen, J. C., Srebnik, D., Salzberg, E., & Wendt, S. (1991). Development of a body image avoidance questionnaire. *Psychological Assessment*, **3**, 32–37.

Rosen, J. C., Reiter, J., & Orosan, P. (1995). Cognitive behavioural body image therapy for body dysmorphic disorder. *Journal of Consulting and Clinical Psychology*, **3**, 263–269.

Rosen, J. C. (1996). Body image assessment and treatment in controlled studies of eating disorders. *International Journal of Eating Disorders*, **20**, 331–343.

Rosen, J. C. & Ramirez, E. (1998). A comparison of eating disorders and body dysmorphic disorder on body image and psychological adjustment. *Journal of Psychosomatic Research*, **44**, 441–449.

Rosenberg, M. (1965). *Society and the Adolescent Self Image*. Princeton, New Jersey: Princeton University Press.

Rossiter, E. M. & Wilson, G. T. (1985). Cognitive restructuring and response prevention in the treatment of bulimia nervosa. *Behaviour Research and Therapy*, **23**, 349–360.

Rossiter, E. M., Wilson, G. T., & Goldstein, L. (1989). Bulimia nervosa and dietary restraint. *Behaviour Research and Therapy*, **4**, 465–468.

Rossiter, E. M., Agras, W. S., Telch, C. F., & Schneider, J. A. (1993). Cluster B in personality disorder characteristics predict outcome in the treatment of bulimia nervosa. *International Journal of Eating Disorders*, **13**, 349–357.

Roth, D. M. & Ross, D. R. (1988). Long term cognitive interpersonal group therapy for eating disorders. *International Journal of Group Psychotherapy*, 38, 4591–4510.

Rowston, W. M. & Lacey, J. H. (1992). Stealing in bulimia nervosa. *The International Journal of Social Psychiatry*, 38, 309–313.

Roy-Byrne, P., Lee-Benner, K., & Yager, J. (1984). Group therapy for bulimia. *International Journal of Eating Disorders*, 3, 97–116.

Royal College of Psychiatrists (1992). *Eating Disorders*. Council Report CR14. London: Royal College of Psychiatrists.

Ruderman, A. J. & Grace, P. S. (1987). Bulimics and restrained eaters: a personality comparison. *Addictive Behaviours*, 13, 359–368.

Ruderman, A. J. & Besbeas, M. (1992). Psychological characteristics of dieters and bulimics. *Journal of Abnormal Psychology*, 101, 383–390.

Ruggiero, G. M., Hannower, W., Mantero, M., & Papa, R. (2000). Body acceptance and culture: a study in northerna and southern Italy. *European Eating Disorders Review*, 8, 40–50.

Russell, G. F. M. (1979). Bulimia nervosa: an ominous variant of anorexia nervosa. *Psychological Medicine*, 9, 429–448.

Russell, G. F. M., Szmuckler, G., Dare, C., & Eisler, I. (1987). An evaluation of family therapy in anorexia nervosa and bulimia nervosa. *Archives of General Psychiatry*, 44, 1047–1056.

Russell, G. F. M., Szmuckler, G. I., Dare, C., & Eisler, I. (1995). An evaluation of family therapy in anorexia nervosa and bulimia nervosa. *Archives of General Psychiatry*, 44, 1047–1056.

Russell, G. F. M. (1997). The history of bulimia nervosa. In *Handbook of Treatment for Eating Disorders* (D. M. Garner & P. E. Garfinkel, ed.). New York: Guilford.

Rust, M-J. (1995). Bringing the 'man' into the room: art therapy group work with women with compulsive eating problems. In *Arts Therapies and Clients with Eating Disorders: Fragile Board* (D. Dokter, ed.). London: Jessica Kingsley.

Rutter, M. (1972). *Maternal Deprivation Reassessed*. London: Penguin Harmondsworth.

Ryle, G. (1949). *The Concept of Mind*. London: Hutchinson.

Sagi, A. & Hoffman, M. L. (1976). Empathic distress in the newborn. *Developmental Psychology*, 12, 175–176.

Sanftner, J. L., Barlow, D. H., Marschall, D. E., & Tangney, J. P. (1995). The relationship of shame and guilt to eating disorder symptomatology. *Journal of Social and Clinical Psychology*, 14, 315–324.

Salako, L. A. (1970a). Effects of emetine on neurotransmitter transmission. *European Journal of Pharmacology*, 11, 342–348.

Salako, L. A. (1970b). Inhibition of neuromuscular transmission in the intact rat by emetine. *Journal of Pharmacay and Pharmacology*, 22, 69–70.

Salkovskis, P. M., Jones, R. Q., & Kucyj, M. (1987). Water intoxication, fluid intake, and non specific symptoms in bulimia nervosa. *International Journal of Eating Disorders*, 6, 525–536.

Sands, S. (1989). Female development and eating disorders: a self psychological perspective. In *Progress in Self Psychology*, Vol. 5 (A. Goldberg, ed). New York: Analytic Press.

Sands, S. (1991). Bulimia, dissociation and empathy: A self psychology view. In *Psychodynamic Treatment of Anorexia Nervosa and Bulimia* (C. Johnson, ed.). New York: Guilford.

Sands, S. H. (2000). Self psychology therapy. In *Comparative Treatments of Eating Disorders* (K. Miller & J. S. Mizes, ed.). London: Free Association Books.

Santonastaso, P., Zanetti, T., Sala, A., Favaretto, G., Vidotto, G., & Favaro, A. (1996). Prevalence of eating disorders in Italy: a survey on a sample of 16 year old students. *Psychotherapy and Psychosomatics*, 65, 158–162.

Saul, S. H., Dekker, A., & Watson, C. G. (1981). Acute gastric dilation with infarction and perforation. *Gut*, 22, 978.

Scanlon, E., Ollendick, T. H., & Bayer, K. (1986). *The role of cognitions in bulimia: an empirical test of basic assumptions.* Paper presented at the Association for the Advancement of Behaviour Therapy, Chicago, Illinois.

Schilder, P. (1950). *The image and appearance of the human body.* New York: International Universities Press.

Schlesier-Carter, B., Hamilton, S. A., O'Neil, P. M., Lydiard, R. B., & Malcolm, R. (1989). Depression and bulimia: the link between depression and bulimic cognitions. *Journal of Abnormal Psychology*, 98, 322–325.

Schmidt, U. & Marks, I. M. (1989). Exposure plus response prevention of bingeing vs exposure plus response prevention of vomiting in bulimia nervosa: a crossover study. *Journal of Nervous and Mental Disease*, 177, 259–266.

Schmidt, U. & O'Donoghue, G. (1992). Bulimia nervosa in thyroid disorder. *International Journal of Eating Disorders*, 12, 93–96.

Schmidt, U. & Treasure, J. (1993). *Getting Better Bit(e) by Bit(e).* Hove: Lawrence Erlbaum Associates.

Schmidt, U., Jiwany, A., & Treasure, J. (1993a). A controlled study of alexithymia in eating disorders. *Comprehensive Psychiatry*, 34, 54–58.

Schmidt, U., Slone, G., Tiller, J., & Treasure, J. (1993b). Childhood adversity and adult defence style in eating disorder patients-a controlled study. *British Journal of Medical Psychology*, 66, 353–362.

Schmidt, U., Tiller, J., & Treasure, J. (1993c). Self treatment of bulimia nervosa: a pilot study. *International Journal of Eating Disorders*, 13, 273–277.

Schmidt, U., Evans, K., Tiller, J., & Treasure, J. (1995). Puberty, sexual milestones and abuse: how are they related in eating disorder patients? *Psychological Medicine*, 25, 413–417.

Schneider, J. A. & Agras, W. S. (1985). A cognitive behavioural group treatment of bulimia. *British Journal of Psychiatry*, 146, 66–69.

Schneider, J. A., O'Leary, A., & Agras, W. S. (1987). The role of perceived self efficacy in recovery from bulimia: a preliminary examination. *Behaviour Research and Therapy*, 25, 429–432.

Schotte, D. E., McNally, R. J., & Turner, M. L. (1990). A dichotic listening analysis of body weight concern in bulimia nervosa. *International Journal of Eating Disorders*, 9, 109–113.

Schulman, R. G., Kinder, B. N., Powers, P. S., Prange, M., & Gleghorn, A. (1986). The development of a scale to measure cognitive distortions in bulimia. *Journal of Personality Assessment*, 50, 630–639.

Schulte, D., Kunzel, R., Pepping, G., & Schulte-Bahrenberg, T. (1992). Tailor made versus standard therapy of phobic patients. *Advances in Behaviour Research and Therapy*, 14, 67–92.

Schumaker, J. F., Groth-Marnat, G., Small, L., & Macaruso, P. A. (1986). Sensation seeking in a female bulimic population. *Psychological Reports*, 59, 1151–1154.

Schupak-Neuberg, E. & Nemeroff, C. (1993). Disturbances in identity and self regulation in bulimia nervosa: implications for a metaphorical perspective of 'body as self'. *International Journal of Eating Disorders*, 13, 335–347.

Schwartz, R. C., Barrett, M. J., & Saba, G. (1983). Family therapy for bulimia nervosa. In *Handbook of Psychotherapy for Anorexia Nervosa and Bulimia* (D. M. Garner & P. E. Garfinkel, ed.). New York: Guilford Press.

Sebastian, S. B., Williamson, D. A., & Blouin, D. C. (1996). Memory for fatness stimuli in the eating disorders. *Cognitive Therapy & Research*, 20, 275–286.

Seim, H. C., Mitchell, J. E., Pomeroy, C., & de Zwaan, M. (1995). Electrocardiographic findings associated with very low calorie dieting. *International Journal of Obesity*, 19, 817–819.

Selvini-Palazzoli, M. (1978). *Self Starvation.* New York: Aronson.

Shaw, B. F. & Dobson, K. S. (1981). Cognitive assessment of depression. In *Cognitive Assessment* (T. V. Merluzzi., C. R. Glass, & M. Genest, ed.). New York: Guilford Press.

Shaw, R. J. & Steiner, H. (1997). Temperament in juvenile eating disorders. *Psychosomatics*, **38**, 126–131.

Shepard, R. N. & Feng, C. (1972). A chronometric study of mental paper folding. *Cognitive Psychology*, **3**, 228–243.

Shisslak, C. M., Crago, M., Neal, M. E., & Swain, B. (1987). Primary prevention of eating disorders. *Journal of Consulting and Clinical Psychology*, **55**, 660–667.

Shweder, R. A. & Bourne, E. J. (1982). Does the concept of the person vary cross-culturally? In *Cultural Conceptions of Mental Health and Therapy* (A. J. Marsella & G. M. White, ed.). Dordrecht, Holland: D. Reidel.

Silverstein, B., Perdue, L., Wolf, C., & Pizzolo, C. (1988). Bingeing, purging, and estimates of parental attitudes regarding female achievement. *Sex Roles*, **19**, 723–733.

Silverstone, P. H. (1992). Is chronic low self-esteem the cause of eating disorders? *Medical Hypotheses*, **39**, 311–315.

Simmons, M. S., Grayden, S. K., & Mitchell, J. E. (1986). The need for psychiatric dental liaison in the treatment of bulimia. *American Journal of Psychiatry*, **143**, 783–784.

Singerman, B. (1981). DSM-III: Historical antecedents and present significance. *Journal of Clinical Psychiatry*, **42**, 409–410.

Silvera, D. H., Bergersen, T. D., Bjorgum, L., Perry, P. A., Rosenvinge, J. H., & Holte, A. (1998). Analysing the relation between self-esteem and eating disorders: differential effects of self-liking and self-competence. *Eating and Weight Disorders*, **3**, 95–99.

Slade, P. D. (1982). Towards a functional analysis of anorexia nervosa and bulimia nervosa. *British Journal of Clinical Psychology*, **21**, 167–169.

Slade, P. D. (1988). Body image in anorexia nervosa. *British Journal of Psychiatry*, Supplement 2, 20–22.

Slade, P. D., Dewey, M. E., Newton, T., Brodie, D. A., & Kiemle, G. (1990). Development and preliminary validation of the Body Satisfaction Scale (BSS). *Psychology and Health*, **4**, 213–222.

Slade (1994). What is body image? *Behaviour Research and Therapy*, **32**, 497–504.

Slobada, A. (1995). Individual music therapy with anorexic and bulimic patients. In *Arts Therapies and Clients with Eating Disorders: Fragile Board* (Dokter, D. ed.). London: Jessica Kingsley.

Smith, A. & Miles, C. (1986). Effects of lunch on selective and sustained attention. *Neuropsychobiology*, **16**, 117–120.

Smith, A. P. & Miles, C. (1987). The combined effects of occupational health hazards: an experimental investigation of the effects of noise, nightwork and meals. *International Archives of Occupational and Environmental Health*, **59**, 83–89.

Smith, A., Leekam, S., Ralph, A., & McNeill, G. (1988). The influence of meal composition on post lunch changes in performance efficiency and mood. *Appetite*, **10**, 195–203.

Smith, D. E. (1995). Binge eating in ethnic minority groups. *Addictive Behaviours*, **20**, 695–703.

Smoller, J. W., Wadden, T. A., & Stunkard, A. J. (1987). Dieting and depression: a critical review. *Journal of Psychosomatic Research*, **31**, 429–440.

Smucker, M. R. & Niederee, J. (1995). Treating incest related PTSD and pathogenic schemas through imaginal exposure and rescripting. *Cognitive and Behavioural Practice*, **2**, 63–92.

Sohlberg, S. & Norring, C. (1989). Ego functioning strongly predicts status after one year in adult patients with anorexia nervosa and bulimia nervosa. *Acta Psychiatrica Scandanivica*, **80**, 325–333.

Sohlberg, S., Norring, C., Holmgren, S., & Rosmark, B. (1989). Impulsivity and long term prognosis of psychiatric patients with anorexia nervosa/bulimia nervosa. *Journal of Nervous and Mental Disease*, **177**, 249–258.

Sohlberg, S. (1990). Personality, life stress and the course of eating disorders. *Acta Psychiatrica Scandanivica, Supplement,* **361,** 29–33.

Sohlberg, S. (1991). Impulse regulation in anorexia nervosa and bulimia nervosa: some formulations. *Behavioural Neurology,* **4,** 189–202.

Sohlberg, S. & Norring, C. (1992). A three year prospective study of life events and course for adults with anorexia nervosa/bulimia nervosa. *Psychosomatic Medicine,* **54,** 59–70.

Sohlberg, S. & Norring, C. (1995). Co-occurrence of ego function change and symptomatic change in bulimia nervosa: a six year interview study. *International Journal of Eating Disorders,* **18,** 13–26.

Sordelli, A., Fossati, A., Devoti, R-M., LaViola, S., & Maffei, C. (1996). Perceived parental bonding in anorectic and bulimic patients. *Psychopathology,* **29,** 64–70.

Soukup, V. M., Beiler, M. E., & Terrell, F. (1990). Stress, coping style and problem solving ability among eating disordered inpatients. *Journal of Clinical Psychology,* **46,** 592–599.

Soundy, T. J., Lucas, A. R., Suman, V. J., & Melton, L. J. (1995). Bulimia nervosa in Rochester, Minnesota from 1980 to 1990. *Psychological Medicine,* **25,** 1065–1071.

Sours, J. A. (1980). *Starving to Death in a Sea of Objects.* New York: Jason Aronson.

Spranger, S. C., Waller, G., & Bryant-Waugh, R. (2001). Schema avoidance in bulimic and non eating disordered women. *International Journal of Eating Disorders,* **29,** 302–306.

Staffieri, J. R. (1967). A study of social stereotype of body image in children. *Journal of Personality and Social Psychology,* **7,** 101–104.

Steel, J. M., Young, R. J., Lloyd, G. G., & Clarke, B. F. (1987). Clinically apparent eating disorders in young diabetic women: associations with painful neuropathy and other complications. *British Medical Journal,* **294,** 859–862.

Steel, Z. P., Farag, P. A., & Blaszczynski, A. P. (1995). Interrupting the binge purge cycle in bulimia: the use of planned binges. *International Journal of Eating Disorders,* **18,** 199–208.

Steel, Z., Jones, J., Adcock, S., Clancy, R., Bridgford-West, L., & Austin, J. (2000). Why the high rate of drop out from individualised cognitive behaviour therapy for bulimia nervosa? *International Journal of Eating Disorders,* **28,** 209–214.

Steere, J., Butler, G., & Cooper, P. J. (1990). The anxiety symptoms of bulimia nervosa: a comparative study. *International Journal of Eating Disorders,* **9,** 293–301.

Steiger, H. (1989). An integrated psychotherapy for eating disorder patients. *American Journal of Psychotherapy,* **43,** 229–237.

Steiger, H., van der Feen, J., Goldstein, C., & Leichner, P. (1989). Defence styles and parental bonding in eating disordered women. *International Journal of Eating Disorders,* **8,** 131–140.

Steiger, H., Goldstein, C., Mongrain, M., & van der Feen, J. (1990). Description of eating disordered, psychiatric, and normal women along cognitive and psychodynamic dimensions. *International Journal of Eating Disorders,* **9,** 129–140.

Steiger, H. & Zanko, M. (1990). Sexual traumata in eating disordered, psychiatric and normal female groups: comparison of prevalences and defence styles. *Journal of Interpersonal Violence,* **5,** 74–86.

Steiger, H., Leung, F., Thibaudeau, J., & Houle, L. (1993). Prognositc utility of subcomponents of the borderline personality construct in bulimia nervosa. *British Journal of Clinical Psychology,* **32,** 187–197.

Steiger, H., Stotland, S., Ghadirian, A. M., & Whitehead, V. (1995). Controlled study of eating concerns and psychopathological traits in relatives of eating disordered probands: do familial traits exist? *International Journal of Eating Disorders,* **18,** 107–118.

Steiger, H., Jabalpurwala, S., & Champagne, J. (1996). Axis II comorbidity and developmental adversity in bulimia nervosa. *The Journal of Nervous and Mental Disease,* **184,** 555–560.

Steiger, H. & Stotland, S. (1996). Prospective study of outcome in bulimics as a function of Axis II comorbidity: long term responses on eating and psychiatric symptoms. *International Journal of Eating Disorders*, 20, 149–161.

Steiger, H., Gauvin, L., Jabalpurwala, S., Seguin, J. R., & Stotland, S. (1999a). Hypersensitivity to social interactions in bulimic syndromes: relationship to binge eating. *Journal of Consulting and Clinical Psychology*, 67, 765–775.

Steiger, H., Lehoux, P. M., & Gauvin, L. (1999b). Impulsivity, dietary control and the urge to binge in bulimic syndromes. *International Journal of Eating Disorders*, 26, 261–274.

Stein, A. & Fairburn, C. G. (1989). Children of mothers with bulimia nervosa. *British Medical Journal*, 299, 777–778.

Stein, A., Woolley, H., Cooper, S. D., & Fairburn, C. G. (1994). An observational study of mothers with eating disorders and their infants. *Journal of Child Psychology and Psychiatry*, 35, 733–748.

Stein, A., Murray, L., Cooper, P. J., & Fairburn, C. G. (1996). Infant growth in the context of maternal eating disorders and maternal depression: a comparative study. *Psychological Medicine*, 26, 569–574.

Stein, S., Chalhoub, N., & Hodes, M. (1998). Very early onset bulimia nervosa: report of two cases. *International Journal of Eating Disorders*, 24, 323–327.

Stein, A., Woolley, H., & McPherson, K. (1999). Conflict between mothers with eating disorders and their infants during mealtimes. *British Journal of Psychiatry*, 175, 455–461.

Steinberg, B. F. & Shaw, R. J. (1997). Bulimia as a disturbance of narcissism: self esteem and the capacity to self soothe. *Addictive Behaviours*, 22, 699–710.

Steiner-Adair, C. (1986). The body politic: normal female adolescent development and the development of eating disorders. *Journal of the American Academy of Psychoanalysis*, 14, 95–114.

Steiner-Adair, C. (1989). Developing the voice of the wise woman: college students and bulimia. *Journal of College Student Psychotherapy*, 3, 151–163.

Steinhausen, H-C. (1997). Clinical guidelines for anorexia nervosa and bulimia nervosa. *European Child and Adolescent Psychiatry*, 6, 121–128.

Steinhausen, H-C., Winkler, C., & Meier, M. (1997). Eating disorders in adolescence in a Swiss epidemiological study. *International Journal of Eating Disorders*, 22, 147–151.

Stern, D. (1985). *The Interpersonal World of the Infant*. New York: Basic Books.

Stevens, E. V. & Salisbury, J. D. (1984). Group therapy for bulimic adults. *American Journal of Orthopsychiatry*, 54, 156–161.

Stice, E. (1994). A review of the evidence for a sociocultural model of bulimia nervosa and an exploration of the mechanisms of action. *Clinical Psychology Review*, 14, 633–661.

Stice, E., Nemeroff, C., & Shaw, H. E. (1996a). A test of the dual pathway model of bulimia nervosa: evidence for restrained-eating and affect-regulation mechanisms. *Journal of Social and Clinical Psychology*, 15, 340–363.

Stice, E., Ziemba, C., Margolis, J., & Flick, P. (1996b). The dual pathway model differentiates bulimics, subclinical bulimics, and controls: testing the continuity hypothesis. *Behaviour Therapy*, 27, 531–549.

Stice, E. (1998). Modelling of eating pathology and social reinforcement of the thin-ideal predict onset of bulimic symptoms. *Behaviour Research and Therapy*, 36, 931–944.

Stice, E. & Agras, W. S. (1998). Predicting onset and cessation of bulimic behaviours during adolescence: a longitudinal grouping analysis. *Behaviour Therapy*, 29, 257–276.

Stice, E., Killen, J. D., Hayward, C., & Taylor, C. B. (1998). Age of onset for binge eating and purging during adolescence: a four year survival analysis. *Journal of Abnormal Psychology*, 107, 671–675.

Stice, E. (1999). Clinical implications of psychosocial research on bulimia nervosa and binge eating disorder. *Psychotherapy in Practice*, 55, 675–683.

Stice, E., Mazotti, L., Weibel, D., & Agras, W. S. (2000). Dissonance prevention program decreases thin ideal internalisation, body dissatisfaction, dieting, negative affect, and bulimic symptoms: a preliminary experiment. *International Journal of Eating Disorders*, **27**, 206–217.

Stice, E., Chase, A., Stormer, S., & Appel, A. (2001). A randomised trial of a dissonance based eating disorder prevention programme. *International Journal of Eating Disorders*, **29**, 247–262.

Striegel-Moore, R. H., Silberstein, L. R., & Rodin, J. (1986). Toward an understanding of risk factors for bulimia. *American Psychologist*, **41**, 246–263.

Striegel-Moore, R. H., Silberstein, L. R., Frensch, P., & Rodin, J. (1989). A prospective study of disordered eating among college students. *International Journal of Eating Disorders*, **8**, 499–509.

Striegel-Moore, R. H., Nicholson, T. J., & Tamorlane, W. V. (1992). Prevalence of eating disorder symptoms in preadolescent and adolescent girls with IDDM. *Diabetes Care*, **15**, 1361–1368.

Striegel-Moore, R. H., Silberstein, L. R., & Rodin, J. (1993). The social self in bulimia nervosa: public self-consciousness, social anxiety, and perceived fraudulence. *Journal of Abnormal Psychology*, **102**, 297–303.

Striegel-Moore, R. H., Garvin, V., Dohm, F-A., Rosenheck, R. A. (1999). Eating disorders in a national sample of hospitalised female and male veterans: detection rates and psychiatric comorbidity. *International Journal of Eating Disorders*, **25**, 405–414.

Strober, M. & Humphrey, L. L. (1987). Familial contributions to the aetiology and course of anorexia and bulimia. *Journal of Consulting and Clinical Psychology*, **55**, 654–657.

Strong, K. G. & Huon, G. F. (1998). An evaluation of a structural model for studies of the initiation of dieting among adolescent girls. *Journal of Psychosomatic Research*, **44**, 315–326.

Stroop, J. (1935). Studies of interference in serial verbal reactions. *Experimental Psychology*, **18**, 643–661.

Stuart, R. & Davis, B. (1972). *Slim Chance in a Fat World*. Champaign, IL: Research Press.

Stuart, G. W., Laraia, M. T., Ballenger, J. C., & Lydiard, R. B. (1990). Early family experiences of women with bulimia and depression. *Archives of Psychiatric Nursing*, **4**, 43–52.

Stunkard, A. J. (1976). *The Pain of Obesity*. Palo Alto, California: Bull.

Stunkard, A. (1980). Psychoanalysis and psychotherapy. In *Obesity* (A. Stunkard, ed.). Philadelphia, PA: Saunders.

Stunkard, A. (1990). A description of eating disorders in 1932. *American Journal of Psychiatry*, **147**, 263–268.

Stunkard, A. (1997). Eating disorders: the last 25 years. *Appetite*, **29**, 181–190.

Sugarman, A. & Kurash, C. (1982). The body as a transitional object in bulimia. *International Journal of Eating Disorders*, **1**, 57–67.

Sugarman, A., Quinlan, D. M., & Devenis, L. (1982). Ego boundary disturbance in anorexia nervosa: preliminary findings. *Journal of Personality Assessment*, **46**, 455–461.

Sullivan, H. S. (1953). *The interpersonal theory of psychiatry*. New York: W. W. Norton & Co.

Sullivan, P. F., Bulik, C. M., Carter, F. A., & Joyce, P. R. (1995). The significance of a history of childhood sexual abuse in bulimia nervosa. *British Journal of Psychiatry*, **167**, 679–682.

Sullivan, P. F., Bulik, C. M., Carter, F. A., Gendall, K. A., & Joyce, P. R. (1996a). The significance of a prior history of anorexia in bulimia nervosa. *International Journal of Eating Disorders*, **20**, 253–261.

Sullivan, P. F., Bulik, C. M., Carter, F. A., & Joyce, P. R. (1996b). Correlates of severity in bulimia nervosa. *International Journal of Eating Disorders*, **20**, 239–251.

Sullivan, P. F., Bulik, C. M., & Kendler, K. S. (1998). The epidemiology and classification of bulimia nervosa. *Psychological Medicine*, **28**, 599–610.

Sullivan, P. F., Gendall, K. A., Bulik, C. M., Carter, F. A., & Joyce, P. R. (1998). Elevated total cholesterol in bulimia nervosa. *International Journal of Eating Disorders*, 23, 425–432.

Sundgot-Borgen, J. (1994). Risk and trigger factors for the development of eating disorders in female elite athletes. *Medicine and Science in Sports and Exercise*, 26, 414–419.

Swann, W. B., Stein-Seroussi, A., & Giesler, R. B. (1992). Why people self verify. *Journal of Personality and Social Psychology*, 62, 393–401.

Swift, W. J. & Letven, R. (1984). Bulimia and the basic fault: a psychoanalytic interpretation of the bingeing vomiting syndrome. *Journal of the American Academy of Child Psychiatry*, 23, 489–497.

Swift, W. J., Ritholz, M., Kalin, N. H., & Kaslow, N. (1987). A follow up study of thirty hospitalised bulimics. *Psychosomatic Medicine*, 49, 45–55.

Szabo, P. & Tury, F. (1991). The prevalence of bulimia nervosa in a Hungarian college and secondary school population. *Psychotherapy and Psychosomatics*, 56, 43–47.

Szmuckler, G. I. (1984). Anorexia nervosa and bulimia in diabetes. *Journal of Psychosomatic Research*, 28, 365–369.

Szrynski, V. (1973). Anorexia nervosa and psychotherapy. *American Journal of Psychotherapy*, 27, 492–505.

Szymanski, L. A. & Seime, R. J. (1997). A re-examination of body image distortion: evidence against a sensory explanation. *International Journal of Eating Disorders*, 21, 175–180.

Tajfel, H. & Turner, J. C. (1979). An integrative theory of intergroup conflict. In *The Social Psychology of Intergroup Relations* (W. G. Austin & S. Worchel, ed.). Monterey, CA: Brooks/Cole.

Tantillo, M. (1998). A relational approach to group therapy for women with bulimia nervosa: moving from understanding to action. *International Journal of Group Psychotherapy*, 48, 477–498.

Taylor, G. J., Ryan, D., & Bagby, R. M. (1985). Toward the development of a new self-report alexithymia scale. *Psychotherapy and Psychosomatics*, 44, 191–199.

Taylor, G. J., Bagby, R. M., & Parker, J. D. A. (1997). *Disorders of Affect Regulation: Alexithymia in Medical and Psychiatric Illness*. Cambridge: Cambridge University Press.

Teasdale, J. D. & Barnard, P. J. (1993). *Affect, Cognition and Change: Remodelling Depressive Thought*. Hillsdale, New Jersey: Lawrence Erlbaum.

Telch, C. F. & Agras, W. S. (1993). The effects of a very low calorie diet on binge eating. *Behaviour Therapy*, 24, 177–193.

Tellegen, A. (1982). *Brief Manual for the Differential Personality Questionnaire*. Unpublished manuscript, University of Minnesota.

Tellegen, A. (1985). Structures of mood and personality and their relevance to assessing anxiety, with an emphasis on self report. In *Anxiety and the Anxiety Disorders* (A. H. Tuma & J. D. Maser, ed.). Hillsdale, New Jersey: Lawrence Erlbaum.

Thackwray, D. E., Smith, M. C., Bodfish, J. W., & Meyers, A. W. (1993). A comparison of behavioural and cognitive behavioural interventions for bulimia nervosa. *Journal of Consulting and Clinical Psychology*, 61, 639–645.

Then, D. (1992). *Women's magazines: messages they convey about looks, men and careers*. Paper presented at the Annual Convention of the American Psychological Association, Washington, DC.

Thiels, C., Schmidt, U., Treasure, J., Garthe, R., & Troop, N. (1998a). Guided self change for bulimia nervosa incorporating use of a self care manual. *American Journal of Psychiatry*, 155, 947–953.

Thiels, A., Zuger, M., Jacoby, G. E., & Schussler, G. (1998b). Thirty-month outcome in patients with anorexia or bulimia nervosa and concomitant obsessive-compulsive disorder. *American Journal of Psychiatry*, 155, 244–249.

Thienemann, M. & Steiner, H. (1993). Family environment of eating disordered and depressed adolescents. *International Journal of Eating Disorders*, 14, 43–48.

Thompson, D. A., Berg, K. M., & Shatford, L. A. (1987). The heterogeneity of bulimic sympotatology: cognitive and behavioural dimensions. *International Journal of Eating Disorders*, 6, 215–234.

Thompson, R. A. (1994). Emotion regulation: a theme in search of definition. *Monographs of the Society for Research in Child Development*, 59, *(2–3)*, 25–52.

Thornton, C. & Russell, J. (1997). Obsessive compulsive comorbidity in the dieting disorders. *International Journal of Eating Disorders*, 21, 83–87.

Tice, L., Hall, R. C., Beresford, T. P., Quinones, J., & Hall, A. K. (1989). Sexual abuse in patients with eating disorders. *Psychiatric Medicine*, 7, 257–267.

Tiggemann, M. & Stevens, C. (1999). Weight concern across the life-span: relationship to self-esteem and feminist identity. *International Journal of Eating Disorders*, 26, 103–106.

Tiller, J. & Treasure, J. (1992). Purging with paracetamol: report of four cases. *British Medical Journal*, 305, 618.

Tiller, J., Macrae, A., Schmidt, U., Bloom, S., & Treasure, J. (1994). The prevalence of eating disorders in thyroid disease: a pilot study. *Journal of Psychosomatic Research*, 38, 609–616.

Tiller, J. M., Sloane, G., Schmidt, U., Troop, N., Power, M., & Treasure, J. L. (1997). Social support in patients with anorexia nervosa and bulimia nervosa. *International Journal of Eating Disorders*, 21, 31–38.

Tobe, B. A. & Wolinsky, J. (1986). From exhaustion, exposure, and hunger to extreme voraciousness: bulimia. *British Medical Journal*, 293, 1647–1648.

Tobin, D. L. & Griffing, A. S. (1995). Coping and depression in bulimia nervosa. *International Journal of Eating Disorders*, 18, 359–363.

Tobin, D. L. & Griffing, A. S. (1996). Coping, sexual abuse, and compensatory behaviour. *International Journal of Eating Disorders*, 20, 143–148.

Tobin, D. L. & Griffing, A. S. (1997). An examination of subtype criteria for bulimia nervosa. *International Journal of Eating Disorders*, 22, 179–186.

Tordjman, S., Zittoun, C., Anderson, G. M., Flament, M., & Jeammet, P. (1994). Preliminary study of eating disorders among French adolescents and young adults. *International Journal of Eating Disorders*, 16, 301–305.

Torem, M. S. (1990). Multiple personality underlying eating disorders. *American Journal of Psycotherapy*, 44, 357–368.

Touyz, S. W., Liew, V. P., Tseng, P., Frisken, K., Williams, H., & Beumont, P. J. V. (1993). Oral and dental complications in dieting disorders. *International Journal of Eating Disorders*, 14, 341–348.

Treasure, J. (1988). The ultrasonographic features in anorexia nervosa and bulimia nervosa: a simplified method of monitoring hormonal status during weight gain. *Journal of Psychosomatic Research*, 32, 623–634.

Treasure, J., Schmidt, U., Tiller, J., Todd, G., Keilen, M., & Dodge, E. (1994). First step in managing bulimia nervosa: a controlled trial of a therapeutic manual. *British Medical Journal*, 308, 686–689.

Treasure, J., Schmidt, U., Troop, N., Tiller, J., Todd, G., & Turnbull, S. (1996). Sequential treatment for bulimia nervosa incorporating a self care manual. *British Journal of Psychiatry*, 168, 94–98.

Treasure, J. L., Katzman, M., Schmidt, U., Troop, N., Todd, G., & de Silva, P. (1999). Engagement and outcome in the treatment of bulimia nervosa: first phase of a sequential design comparing motivation enhancement therapy and cognitive behavioural therapy. *Behaviour Research and Therapy*, 37, 405–418.

Troop, N. A., Holbrey, A., Trowler, R., & Treasure, J. L. (1994). Ways of coping in women with eating disorders. *The Journal of Nervous and Mental Disease*, 182, 535–540.

Troop, N. A., Schmidt, U. H., & Treasure, J. (1995). Feelings and fantasy in eating disorders: a factor analysis of the Toronto Alexithymia Scale. *International Journal of Eating Disorders*, 18, 151–157.

Troop, N., Schmidt, U., Tiller, J., Todd, G., Keilen, M., & Treasure, J. (1996). Compliance with a self care manual for bulimia nervosa: predictors and outcome. *British Journal of Clinical Psychology*, 35, 435–438.

Troop, N. A. & Treasure, J. L. (1997). Psychosocial factors in the onset of eating disorders: responses to life-events and difficulties. *British Journal of Medical Psychology*, 70, 373–385.

Troop, N. A., Holbrey, A., & Treasure, J. L. (1998). Stress, coping, and crisis support in eating disorders. *International Journal of Eating Disorders*, 24, 157–166.

Turnbull, S. J., Schmidt, U., Troop, N. A., Tiller, J., Todd, G., & Treasure, J. L. (1997). Predictors of outcome for two treatments for bulimia nervosa: short and long term. *International Journal of Eating Disorders*, 21, 17–22.

Turner, H. & Bryant-Waugh, R. (submitted). Eating Disorder Not Otherwise Specified (EDNOS): profile of clients presenting at a community eating disorder service.

Turner, H. & Cooper, M. J. (2002). Cognitions and their origins in women with anorexia nervosa, normal dieters and female controls. *Clinical Psychology and Psychotherapy*, 9, 242–252.

Tuschen, B. & Bents, H. (1995). Intensive brief inpatient treatment of bulimia nervosa. In *Eating Disorders and Obesity: A Comprehensive Handbook* (K. D. Brownell & C. G. Fairburn, ed.). New York: Guilford.

Van den Broucke, S. & Vandereycken, W. (1988). Anorexia nervosa and bulimia in married patients: a review. *Comprehensive Psychiatry*, 29, 165–173.

Van den Broucke, S., Vandereycken, W., & Vertommen, H. (1994). Psychological distress in husbands of eating disorder patients. *American Journal of Orthopsychiatry*, 64, 270–279.

Van den Broucke, S., Vandereycken, W., & Vertommen, H. (1995). Marital intimacy in patients with an eating disorder: a controlled self-report study. *British Journal of Clinical Psychology*, 34, 67–78.

Vandereycken, W. & Meermann, R. (1984). Anorexia nervosa: is prevention possible? *Journal of Psychiatry in Medicine*, 14, 191–205.

Vandereycken, W. (1987). The constructive family approach to eating disorders: critical remarks on the use of family therapy in anorexia nervosa and bulimia. *International Journal of Eating Disorders*, 6, 455–467.

van der Kolk, B. A. (1987). *Psychological Trauma.* Washington, DC: American Psychiatric Press.

van der Ster Wallin, G., Norring, C., & Holmgren, S. (1994). Binge eating versus nonpurged eating in bulimics: is there a carbohydrate craving after all? *Acta Psychiatrica Scandinavica*, 89, 376–381.

Van Strien, T., Cleven, A., & Schippers, G. (2000). Restraint, tendency toward overeating and ice cream consumption. *International Journal of Eating Disorders*, 28, 333–338.

Vitousek, K. B. & Hollon, S. D. (1990). The investigation of schematic content and processing in the eating disorders. *Cognitive Therapy & Research*, 14, 191–214.

Vitousek, K. & Manke, F. (1994). Personality variables and disorders in anorexia nervosa and bulimia nervosa. *Journal of Abnormal Psychology*, 103, 137–147.

Vize, C. M. & Coker, S. (1994). Hypercholesterolemia in bulimia nervosa. *International Journal of Eating Disorders*, 15, 293–295.

Vize, C. M. & Cooper, P. J. (1995). Sexual abuse in patients with eating disorder, patients with depression, and normal controls: a comparative study. *British Journal of Psychiatry*, 167, 80–85.

Vohs, K. D., Bardone, A. M., Joiner, T. E., Abramson, L. Y., & Heatherton, T. F. (1999). Perfectionism, perceived weight status, and self-esteem interact to predict bulimic symptoms: a model of bulimic symptom development. *Journal of Abnormal Psychiatry*, 108, 695–700.

Von Ranson, K. M., Kaye, W. H., Weltzin, T. E., Rao, R., & Matasunaga, H. (1999). Obsessive-compulsive disorder symptoms before and after recovery from bulimia nervosa. *American Journal of Psychiatry*, 156, 1703–1708.

Wade, T., Tiggemann, M., Martin, N., & Heath, A. (1997). A comparison of the Eating Disorder Examination and a general psychiatric schedule. *Australian and New Zealand Journal of Psychiatry*, 31, 852–857.

Waller, D. A., Newton, P. A., Hardy, B. W., & Svetlik, D. (1990). Correlates of laxative abuse in bulimia. *Hospital and Community Psychiatry*, 41, 797–799.

Waller, G. (1991). Sexual abuse as a risk factor in the eating disorders. *British Journal of Psychiatry*, 159, 664–667.

Waller, G. (1992). Sexual abuse and the severity of bulimic symptomatology. *British Journal of Psychiatry*, 161, 771–775.

Waller, G., Hamilton, K., & Shaw, J. (1992). Media influences on body size estimation in eating disordered and comparison subjects. *British Review of Bulimia and Anorexia Nervosa*, 6, 81–87.

Waller, G., Hamilton, K., Rose, N., Sumra, J., & Baldwin, G. (1993). Sexual abuse and body image distortion in the eating disorders. *British Journal of Clinical Psychology*, 32, 350–352.

Waller, G. & Ruddock, A. (1993). Experiences of disclosure of child sexual abuse and psychopathology. *Child Abuse Review*, 2, 185–195.

Waller, G. (1994). Childhood sexual abuse and borderline personality disorder in the eating disorders. *Child Abuse and Neglect*, 18, 97–101.

Waller, G. & Calam, R. (1994). Parenting and family factors in eating problems. In *Understanding Eating Disorders: Anorexia Nervosa* (L. Alexander-Mott & B. Lumsden ed.). *Bulimia Nervosa, and Obesity*. Philadelphia, Pennsylvania: Taylor & Francis.

Waller, G., Shaw, J., Hamilton, K., Baldwin, G., Harding, T., & Summer, A. (1994). Beauty is in the eye of the beholder: media influences on the psychopathology of eating problems. *Appetite*, 23, 287.

Waller, G. & Hodgson, S. (1996). Body image distortion in anorexia and bulimia nervosa: the role of perceived and actual control. *Journal of Nervous and Mental Disease*, 184, 213–219.

Waller, G. (1997). Drop out and failure to engage in individual outpatient cognitive behaviour therapy for bulimic disorders. *International Journal of Eating Disorders*, 22, 35–41.

Waller, G. & Meyer, C. (1997). Cognitive avoidance of threat cues: association with Eating Disorder Inventory scores among a non eating disordered population. *International Journal of Eating Disorders*, 22, 299–308.

Waller, G., Ohanion, V., Meyer, C., & Osman, S. (2000). Cognitive content among bulimic women: the role of core beliefs. *International Journal of Eating Disorders*, 28, 235–241.

Waller, G., Shah, R., Ohanion, V., & Elliott, P. (2001). Core beliefs in bulimia nervosa and depression: the discriminant validity of Young's schema questionnaire. *Behaviour Therapy*, 32, 139–153.

Walsh, B. T., Kissileff, H. R., Cassidy, S. M., & Dantzic, S. (1989). Eating behaviour of women with bulimia. *Archives of General Psychiatry*, 46, 54–58.

Walsh, B. T., Hadigan, C. M., Kissileff, H. R., & LaChaussee, J. L. (1992). Bulimia nervosa: a syndrome of feast and famine. In *The Biology of Feast and Famine* (G. H. Anderson & S. H. Kennedy, ed.). New York: Academic Press.

Walsh, B. T., Wilson, G. T., Loeb, K. L., Devlin, M. J., Pike, K., Roose, S. P., Fleiss, J., & Waternaux, C. (1997). Medication and psychotherapy in the treatment of bulimia nervosa. *American Journal of Psychiatry*, 154, 523–531.

Walsh, B. T., Agras, W. S., Devlin, M. J., Fairburn, C. G., Wilson, G. T., Kahn, C., & Chally, M. K. (2000). Fluoxetine for bulimia nervosa following poor response to psychotherapy. *American Journal of Psychiatry*, 157, 1332–1334.

Wardle, J. (1990). Overeating: a regulatory behaviour in restrained eaters. *Appetite*, 14, 133–136.

Warheit, G. J., Langer, L. M., Zimmerman, R. S., & Biafora, F. A. (1993). Prevalence of bulimic behaviours and bulimia among a sample of the general population. *American Journal of Epidemiology*, **137**, 569–576.

Warren, C. & Cooper, P. J. (1988). Psychological effects of dieting. *British Journal of Clinical Psychology*, **27**, 269–270.

Watts, F. N., Trezise, L., & Sharrock, R. (1986). Processing of phobic stimuli. *British Journal of Clinical Psychology*, **25**, 253–259.

Waugh, E. & Bulik, C. M. (1999). Offspring of women with eating disorders. *International Journal of Eating Disorders*, **25**, 123–133.

Weiderman, M. W. & Pryor, T. L. (1997). MCMI-II personality scale scores among women with anorexia nervosa or bulimia nervosa. *Journal of Personality Assessment*, **69**, 508–516.

Weingarten, H. P. (1983). Conditioned cues elicit feeding in sated rats: a role for learning in meal initiation. *Science*, **220**, 431–433.

Weiss, L., Katzman, M., & Wolchik, S. (1985). *Treating Bulimia: A Psychoedcational Approach*. New York: Pergamon.

Weissman, M. W., Prusoff, B. A., Thompson, W. D., Harding, P. S., & Myers, J. K. (1978). Social adjustment by self report in a community sample and in psychiatric outpatients. *The Journal of Nervous and Mental Disease*, **166**, 317–326.

Welch, G. J. (1979). The treatment of compulsive vomiting and obsessive thoughts through graduated response delay, response prevention and cognitive correction. *Journal of Behaviour Therapy and Experimental Psychiatry*, **10**, 72–82.

Welch, S. L. & Fairburn, C. G. (1994). Sexual abuse and bulimia nervosa: three integrated case-control comparisons. *American Journal of Psychiatry*, **151**, 402–406.

Welch, S. L. & Fairburn, C. G. (1996). Impulsivity or comorbidity in bulimia nervosa: a controlled study of deliberate self-harm and alcohol and drug misuse in a community sample. *British Journal of Psychiatry*, **169**, 451–458.

Welch, S. L., Doll, H. A., & Fairburn, C. G. (1997). Life events and the onset of bulimia nervosa: a controlled study. *Psychological Medicine*, **27**, 515–522.

Welch, S. L. & Fairburn, C. G. (1998). Smoking and bulimia nervosa. *International Journal of Eating Disorders*, **23**, 433–437.

Wells, A. & Matthews, G. (1994). *Attention and Emotion: A Clinical Perspective*. Hove, UK: Erlbaum.

Wells, A. (1997). *Cognitive Therapy of Anxiety Disorders*. Chichester, UK: John Wiley & Sons.

Wells, A., Clark, D. M., & Ahmad, S. (1998). How do I look with my mind's eye: perspective taking in social phobic imagery. *Behaviour Research and Therapy*, **36**, 631–634.

Wells, A. & Papageorgiou, C. (1999). The observer perspective: biased imagery in social phobia, agoraphobia, and blood/injury phobia. *Behaviour Research and Therapy*, **37**, 653–658.

Wells, A. (2000). *Emotional Disorders and Metacognition*. Chichester, UK: John Wiley & Sons.

Weltzin, T. E., Hsu, L. K. G., Pollice, C., & Kaye, W. H. (1991). Feeding patterns in bulimia nervosa. *Biological Psychiatry*, **30**, 1093–1110.

Weltzin, T. E., Bulik, C. M., McConaha, C. W., & Kaye, W. H. (1995). Laxative withdrawal and anxiety in bulimia nervosa. *International Journal of Eating Disorders*, **17**, 141–146.

Whelan, E. & Cooper, P. J. (2000). The association between childhood feeding problems and maternal eating disorder: a community study. *Psychological Medicine*, **30**, 69–77.

Whitaker, A., Davies, M., Shaffer, D., Johnson, J., Abrams, S., Walsh, B. T., & Kalikow, K. (1989). The struggle to be thin: a survey of anorexic and bulimic symptoms in a non-referred adolescent population. *Psychological Medicine*, **19**, 143–163.

Whitaker, A., Johnson, J., Shaffer, D., Rapoport, J. L., Kalikow, K., Walsh, B. T., Davies, M., Braiman, S., & Dolinsky, A. (1990). Uncommon troubles in young people: prevalence estimates of selected psychiatric disorders in a nonreferred adolescent population. *Archives of General Psychiatry*, 47, 487–496.

Whitehouse, A. M. & Button, E. J. (1988). The prevalence of eating disorders in a UK college population: a reclassification of an earlier study. *International Journal of Eating Disorders*, 7, 393–397.

Whitehouse, A. M., Cooper, P. J., Vize, C. V., & Vogel, L. (1992). Prevalence of eating disorders in three Cambridge general practices: hidden and conspicuous morbidity. *British Journal of General Practice*, 42, 57–60.

Whittal, M. L., Agras, W. S., & Gould, R. A. (1999). Bulimia nervosa: a meta analysis of psychosocial and pharmacological treatments. *Behaviour Therapy*, 30, 117–135.

Wicker, F. W., Payne, G. C., & Morgan, R. D. (1983). Participant descriptions of guilt and shame. *Motivation and Emotion*, 7, 25–39.

Wiederman, M. W. & Pryor, T. (1996). Multi-impulsivity among women with bulimia nervosa. *International Journal of Eating Disorders*, 20, 359–365.

Wiederman, M. W., Pryor, T., & Morgan, C. D. (1996). The sexual experience of women diagnosed with anorexia nervosa or bulimia nervosa. *International Journal of Eating Disorders*, 19, 109–118.

Wiederman, M. W. & Pryor, T. (1997a). Body dissatisfaction and sexuality among women with bulimia nervosa. *International Journal of Eating Disorders*, 21, 361–365.

Wiederman, M. W. & Pryor, T. (1997b). A comparison of ever-married and never-married women with anorexia nervosa or bulimia nervosa. *International Journal of Eating Disorders*, 22, 395–401.

Wilcox, D. T., Karamanoukian, H. L., & Glick, P. L. (1994). Toothbrush ingestion by bulimics may require laparotomy. *Journal of Pediatric Surgery*, 29, 1596.

Wilfley, D. E., Agras, W. S., Telch, C. F., Rossiter, E. M., Schneider, J. A., Cole, A., Sifford, L., & Raeburn, S. D. (1993). Group cognitive behavioural therapy and group interpersonal psychotherapy for the nonpurging bulimic individual: a controlled comparison. *Journal of Consulting and Clinical Psychology*, 61, 296–305.

Wilfley, D. E., Schreiber, G. B., Pike, K. M., Striegel-Moore, R. H., Wright, & Rodin, (1996). Eating disturbance and body image: A comparison of a community sample of adult Black and White women. *International Journal of Eating Disorders*, 20, 377–387.

Wilkins, J. A., Boland, F. J., & Albinson, J. (1991). A comparison of male and female university athletes and non athletes on eating disorder indices: are athletes protected? *Journal of Sport and Behaviour*, 14, 129–143.

Willard, S. G., McDermott, B. E., & Woodhouse, L. M. (1996). Lipoplasty in the bulimic patient. *Plastic and Reconstructive Surgery*, 98, 276–278.

Williams, P., Hand, D., & Tarnopolsy, A. (1982). The problem of screening for uncommon disorders— a comment on the Eating Attitudes Test. *Psychological Medicine*, 12, 431–434.

Williams, H. & Beumont, P. J. V. (1993). Oral and dental complications in dieting disorders. *International Journal of Eating Disorders*, 14, 341–348.

Williams, J. M. G. (1994). Interacting cognitive subsystems and unvoiced murmurs. A review of "Affect, Cognition and Change" by John Teasdale and Philip Barnard. *Cognition and Emotion*, 8, 571–579.

Williams, J. M. G., Watts, F. N., MacLeod, C., & Mathews, A. (1997). *Cognitive Psychology and Emotional Disorders* (2nd edn). Chichester, UK: John Wiley.

Williamson, D. A., Prather, R. C., Bennett, S. M., Davis, C. J., Watkins, P. C., & Grenier, C. E. (1989). An uncontrolled evaluation of inpatient and outpatient therapy for bulimia nervosa. *Behaviour Modification*, 13, 340–360.

Williamson, D. A. (1990). *Assessment of Eating Disorders: Obesity, Anorexia, and Bulimia Nervosa*. New York: Pergamon.

Williamson, D. A., Cubic, B. A., & Gleaves, D. H. (1993a). Equivalence of body image disturbance in anorexia and bulimia nervosa. *Journal of Abnormal Psychology*, 102, 177–180.

Williamson, D. A., Gleaves, D. H., Watkins, P. C., & Schlundt, D. G. (1993b). Validation of self ideal body size discrepancy as a measure of body dissatisfaction. *Journal of Psychopathology and Behavioural Assessment*, 15, 57–68.

Willmuth, M. E., Leitenberg, H., Rosen, J. C., Fondacaro, K. M., & Gross, J. (1985). Body size distortion in bulimia nervosa. *International Journal of Eating Disorders*, 4, 71–78.

Willmuth, M. E., Leitenberg, H., Rosen, J. C., & Cado, S. (1988). A comparison of purging and non-purging normal weight bulimics. *International Journal of Eating Disorders*, 7, 825–835.

Wilsnack, R. W., Wilsnack, S. C., & Klassen, A. D. (1984). Women's drinking and drinking problems: patterns from a 1981 national survey. *American Journal of Public Health*, 74, 1231–1238.

Wilson, G. T., Rossiter, E., Kleifield, E. I., & Lindholm, L. (1986). Cognitive behavioural treatment of bulimia nervosa: a controlled evaluation. *Behaviour Research and Therapy*, 24, 277–288.

Wilson, G. T. & Smith, D. (1989). Assessment of bulimia nervosa: an evaluation of the Eating Disorder Examination. *International Journal of Eating Disorders*, 8, 173–179.

Wilson, G. T. & Eldredge, K. L. (1991). Frequency of binge eating in bulimic patients: diagnostic validity. *International Journal of Eating Disorders*, 10, 557–561.

Wilson, G. T., Eldredge, K. L., Smith, D., & Niles, B. (1991). Cognitive behavioural treatment with and without response prevention for bulimia. *Behaviour Research and Therapy*, 29, 575–583.

Wilson, G. T. & Fairburn, C. G. (1993). Cognitive treatments for eating disorders. *Journal of Consulting and Clinical Psychology*, 61, 261–269.

Wilson, G. T. (1996). Treatment of bulimia nervosa: when CBT fails. *Behaviour Research and Therapy*, 34, 197–212.

Wilson, G. T. (1997). Treatment manuals in clinical practice. *Behaviour Research and Therapy*, 35, 205–210.

Wilson, G. T. (1998). The clinical utility of randomised controlled trials. *International Journal of Eating Disorders*, 24, 13–29.

Wilson, G. T. & Fairburn, C. G. (1998). Treatments for eating disorders. In *A Guide to Treatments that Work* (P. E. Nathan & J. M. Gorman eds.). New York: Oxford University Press.

Wilson, G. T. (1999). Cognitive behaviour therapy for eating disorders: progress and problems. *Behaviour Research and Therapy*, 37, Supplement 1S79–95.

Wilson, G. T., Loeb, K. L., Walsh, B. T., Labouvie, E., Petkova, E., Liu, X., & Waternaux, C. (1999). Psychological versus pharmacological treatments of bulimia nervosa: predictors and processes of change. *Journal of Consulting and Clinical Psychology*, 67, 451–459.

Wilson, G. T., Vitousek, K. M., & Loeb, K. L. (2000). Stepped care treatment for eating disorders. *Journal of Consulting and Clinical Psychology*, 68, 564–572.

Windle, M. (1992). A longitudinal study of stress buffering for adolescent problem behaviour. *Developmental Psychology*, 28, 522–530.

Wing, J. K. (1975). Epidemiological methods and the clinical psychiatrist. In *Methods of Psychiatric Research* (P. Sainsbury & N. Kreitman, ed.). Oxford: Oxford University Press.

Wing, R. R. (1992). Weight cycling in humans: a review of the literature. *Annals of Behavioural Medicine*, 14, 113–119.

Winnicott, D. W. (1953). Transitional objects and transitional phenomena. *International Journal of Psychoanalysis*, 34 (reprinted in *Collected Papers*, 1958, London: Tavistock).

Winnicott, D. W. (1965). *The Maturational Process and the Facilitating Environment*. New York: International University Press.

Winzelberg, A. J., Eppstein, D., Eldredge, K. L., Wilfly, D., Dasmahapatra, R., Dev, P., & Taylor, C. B. (2000). Effectiveness of an Internet based programme for reducing risk factors for eating disorders. *Journal of Consulting and Clinical Psychology*, **68**, 346–350.

Wiseman, C. V., Gray, J. J., Mosimann, J. E., & Ahrens, A. H. (1992). Cultural expectations of thinness in women: an update. *International Journal of Eating Disorders*, **11**, 85–89.

Wiseman, C. V., Turco, R. M., Sunday, S. R., & Halmi, K. A. (1998). Smoking and body image concerns in adolescent girls. *International Journal of Eating Disorders*, **24**, 429–433.

Wlodarczyk-Bisaga, K. & Dolan, B. (1996). A two stage epidemiological study of abnormal eating attitudes and their prospective risk factors in Polish schoolgirls. *Psychological Medicine*, **26**, 1021–1032.

Wolchik, S. A., Weiss, L., & Katzman, M. A. (1986). An empirically validated short term psychoeducational group treatment programme for bulimia. *International Journal of Eating Disorders*, **5**, 21–34.

Wolf, E. M. & Crowther, J. H. (1992). An evaluation of behavioural and cognitive behavioural group interventions for the treatment of bulimia nervosa in women. *International Journal of Eating Disorders*, **11**, 3–15.

Wonderlich, S. A., Fullerton, D., Swift, W. J., & Klein, M. H. (1994a). Five year outcome from eating disorders: relevance of personality disorders. *International Journal of Eating Disorders*, **15**, 233–243.

Wonderlich, S., Ukestad, L., & Perzacki, R. (1994b). Perceptions of nonshared childhood environment in bulimia nervosa. *Journal of the American Academy of Child and Adolescent Psychiatry*, **33**, 740–747.

Wonderlich, S., Klein, M. H., & Council, J. R. (1996a). Relationship of social perceptions and self concept in bulimia nervosa. *Journal of Consulting and Clinical Psychology*, **64**, 1231–1237.

Wonderlich, S. A., Wilsnack, R. W., Wilsnack, S. C., & Harris, T. R. (1996b). The relationship of childhood secual abuse and bulimic behaviour: results of a US national survey. *American Journal of Public Health*, **86**, 1082–1086.

Wonderlich, S. A., Brewerton, T. D., Jocic, Z., Dansky, B. S., & Abbott, D. W. (1997). Relationship of childhood sexual abuse and eating disorders. *Journal of the American Academy of Child and Adolescent Psychiatry*, **36**, 1107–1115.

Woodman, M. (1980). *The Owl was a Baker's Daughter: Obesity, Anorexia Nervosa and the Repressed Feminine*. Toronto: Inner City Books.

Woods, S. C. (1991). The eating paradox: how we tolerate food. *Psychological Review*, **98**, 488–505.

Woods, S. C. & Strubbe, J. H. (1994). The psychology of meals. *Psychonomic Bulletin and Review*, **1**, 141–155.

Woodside, D. B., Shekter-Wolfson, L. F., Garfinkel, P. E., Olmsted, M. P. (1995a). Family interactions in bulimia nervosa II: complex intrafamily comparisons and clinical significance. *International Journal of Eating Disorders*, **17**, 117–126.

Woodside, D. B., Shekter-Wolfson, L., Garfinkel, P. E., Olmsted, M. P., Kaplan, A. S., & Maddocks, S. E. (1995b). Family interactions in bulimia nervosa 1. Study design, comparisons to established population norms, and changes over the course of an intensive day hospital treatment for bulimia nervosa. *International Journal of Eating Disorders*, **17**, 105–115.

Woodside, D. B., Lackstrom, J., Shekter-Wolfson, L., & Heinmaa, M. (1996). Long term follow up of patient reported family functioning in eating disorders after intensive day hospital treatment. *Journal of Psychosomatic Research*, **41**, 269–277.

Wooley, O. W. & Wooley, S. (1980). The Beverly Hills eating disorder: the mass marketing of anorexia nervosa. *International Journal of Eating Disorders*, **1**, 57–69.

Wooley, S. C. & Wooley, O. W. (1984). Intensive residential and outpatient treatment of bulimia. In *Handbook of Psychotherapy for Anorexia Nervosa and Bulimia Nervosa* (D. M. Garner & P. E. Garfinkel, ed.). New York: Guilford Press.

World Health Organisation (1977). *Manual of the International Statistical Classification of Diseases, Injuries and Causes of Deaths* (9th revision), Vol. 1. World Health Organisation, Geneva.

World Health Organisation. (1992). The ICD-10 classification of mental and behavioural disorders. World Health Organisation, Geneva.

Wyatt, G. (1985). The sexual abuse of Afro-American and white American women in childhood. *Child Abuse and Neglect*, 9, 507–519.

Yates, A. J. & Sambrailo, F. (1984). Bulimia nervosa: a descriptive and therapeutic study. *Behaviour Research and Therapy*, 22, 503–517.

Yates, A., Shisslak, C. M., Allender, J. R., & Wolman, W. (1988). Plastic surgery and the bulimic patient. *International Journal of Eating Disorders*, 7, 557–560.

Yates, W. R., Sieleni, B., Reich, J., & Brass, C. (1989). Comorbidity of bulimia nervosa and personality disorder. *Journal of Clinical Psychiatry*, 50, 57–59.

Young, J. E. (1990). *Cognitive Therapy for Personality Disorders: A schema focussed approach*. Sarasota, Florida: Professional Resource Exchange.

Young, J. E. & Rygh, J. (1994). *Young-Rygh Avoidance Inventory*. New York: Cognitive Therapy Centre, New York. (Available at http://www.schematherapy.com.)

Zanarini, M. C., Frankenburg, F. R., Pope, H. G., Yurgelen-Todd, D., & Cicchetti, C. J. (1990). Axis II comorbidity of normal weight bulimia. *Comprehensive Psychiatry*, 31, 20–24.

Zerbe, K. J. (1995). Integrating feminist and psychodynamic principles in the treatment of an eating disorder patient: implications for using countertransference responses. *Bulletin of the Menninger Clinic*, 59, 160–176.

Zilber, N., Schufman, N., & Lerner, Y. (1989). Mortality among psychiatric patients: the groups at risk. *Acta Psychiatrica Scandanivica*, 79, 249–256.

Ziolko, H-U. (1996). Bulimia: a historical outline. *International Journal of Eating Disorders*, 20, 345–358.

Zotter, D. L. & Crowther, J. H. (1991). The role of cognitions in bulimia nervosa. *Cognitive Therapy and Research*, 15, 413–426.

Zuckerman, M. (1971). Dimensions of sensation seeking. *Journal of Counselling and Psychology*, 36, 45–52.

Zuckerman, M. (1977). *Preliminary manual with scoring keys and norms for Form V of the Sensation Seeking Scale*. Newark, NJ: University of Delaware Press.

Zumpf, C. L. & Harter, S. (1989). *Mirror, mirror on the wall: the relationship between appearance and self worth in adolescent males and females*. Paper presented at the Annual Meeting of the Society for Research in Child Development, Kansas City, Missouri.

Index